SECOND EDITION

Edited by Jill Stackhouse
Bemidji State University

SPATIAL CONNECTIONS:
World Regional Geography

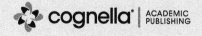

cognella® | ACADEMIC PUBLISHING

Bassim Hamadeh, CEO and Publisher
Kassie Graves, Director of Acquisitions
Jamie Giganti, Senior Managing Editor
Miguel Macias, Senior Graphic Designer
Mark Combes, Senior Field Acquisitions Editor
Natalie Lakosil, Senior Licensing Manager
Kaela Martin and Rachel Singer, Associate Editors
Kat Ragudos, Interior Designer

Cover image copyright © 2013 iStockphoto LP/RomoloTavani.
copyright © 2014 iStockphoto LP/Pogonici.

Printed in the United States of America

ISBN: 978-1-63487-171-6 (pbk) / 978-1-63487-172-3 (br)

 | ACADEMIC PUBLISHING

CONTENTS

MAPS

World Regions: One Perspective

Map 1. The World at a Glance

The World at a Glance

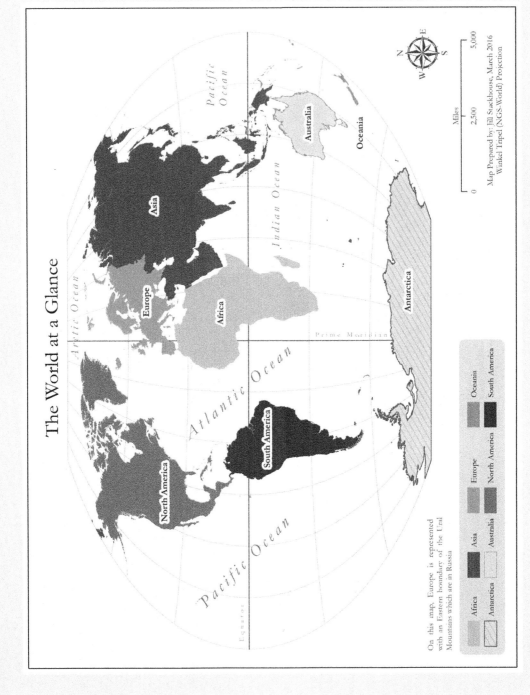

On this map, Europe is represented with an Eastern boundary of the Ural Mountains which are in Russia

| Africa | Asia | Europe | Oceania |
| Antarctica | Australia | North America | South America |

Map Prepared by: Jill Stackhouse, March 2016
Winkel Tripel (NGS-World) Projection

"World Regions: One Perspective." Copyright © 2016 by Jill Stackhouse.

Map 2. World Regions: One Perspective

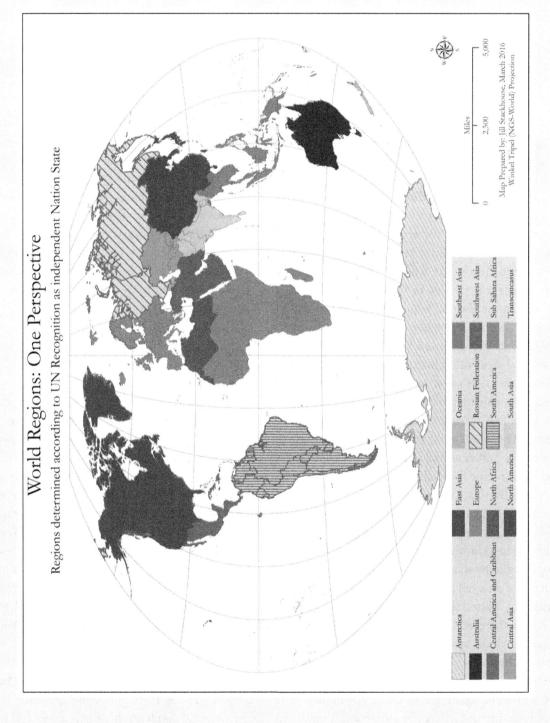

World Regions: One Perspective

Regions determined according to UN Recognition as independent Nation State

Antarctica
Australia
Central America and Caribbean
Central Asia

East Asia
Europe
North Africa
North America

Oceania
Russian Federation
South America
South Asia

Southeast Asia
Southwest Asia
Sub Sahara Africa
Transcaucasus

Miles
0   2,500   5,000

Map Prepared by: Jill Stackhouse, March 2016
Winkel Tripel (NGS-World) Projection

Jill Stackhouse, "World Regions: One Perspective" Copyright © 2016 by Jill Stackhouse.

Preface
A Conversation about Studying Geography

You may not believe it, but all of you are geographers. Even if you might say "I'm not good at geography" you're really better at it than you think. You already know a great deal about your neighborhood or town. This means you're observing the world around you in spatial terms. If you notice differences in the area you live and around you and ask "why" you're building on a geographic foundation. You might wonder why certain things happen the way they do or wonder if what is going on in Asia or Europe really truly makes a difference in your own neighborhood. We hear a great deal about "globalization this" and "globalization that"; and more often than not we hear it is a "small world." We know of, or might have a suspicion that there is a considerable interconnectedness across the globe but we're not really sure how we fit into that picture. This course is about seeing where we fit in as global citizens and it is a course about taking your geographic foundation and building on it.

Consider this. When you walked to class, to the library, to the gym or to the store geography was part of your life; when you logged on to check your email, catch the news, a weather update or an entertainment blog, geography was part of your life; when you talked to a friend on a cell phone, listened to music, grabbed lunch, got dressed this morning, or simply had a cup of coffee, there was an aspect of geography to all of those activities, whether directly or indirectly, you were connected at a global level. Really!

Maybe you never took a geography course, but every now and again you watch the end of the movie credits to find out where the movie was filmed; this is a geographer in the making. Perhaps your only introduction to Geography was in middle school when you were asked to memorize all the capitals and states in the United States. You may have been asked to write a brief essay about a foreign country's imports, exports and natural resources. Maybe you were asked to learn the specific geography of your country or state such as its mountains, rivers, cities or provinces. You're already ahead! This is great! Every little bit you learn lays a foundation for more information; like anything you begin, you have to start somewhere. It is certainly okay if "you don't know everything." This is the very reason you've decided to enroll in this class!

THE STUDY OF GEOGRAPHY

Some professions are generally easier to describe; certainly accounting, medicine or engineering are more recognizable even without knowing the complexities of the profession. It tends to take a bit more explanation to describe what a geographer does but you will soon discover that like most professions the intricacies of studying geography can be examined and easily understood. You will also discover that much of the information you learn in this class may help you in other classes and vice versa. Geography is a rich, diverse and integrative subject that connects the physical world with the human dimensions of the world. The beauty of this course of study is at a college level you can take single course in geography, such as the World Regional Geography course you're enrolled in or as you will see throughout the semester, much of the material you learn here will nicely complement other courses you will pursue.

In the most literal sense Geography is writing about the earth (*geo* – the earth and *graphy* – writing).

This very broad definition doesn't really narrow it down much, does it? Then again, this is very much what geographers do; they write about the earth. Individually, however, geographers don't typically seek to write about the entire globe at one time, instead, geographers write about specific locations with a specific focus. Just as an historian might specialize in an era or a biologist might specialize in a particular species, so too does a geographer specialize, meaning, just like other professionals, they observe and study the world through different lenses such as a culture, physical, economic, political, or historical lens.

Geography goes to great lengths to answer the question **"why what is where?"** Geographers don't stop at the "where"; they study the "whys" of where things are, and the "whats" are not only mountains, rivers and lakes, but cities, dams, military bases, dumps sites, nuclear power plants, earthquake epicenters, schools, political borders (physical or otherwise), voter turnout, oil refineries, shipping lanes... well, you get the picture.

Let's go back to those state capitals you learned for a minute. Why is Washington D.C. located where it is? Why isn't the capital of the United States New York City? What politics were at play to move it to its present location? Take that another step and ask why is the capital of New York, Albany and not New York City? Geographers ask "why" frequently. This includes the human "whys" and the physical "whys." Geographers seek to answer the "why what is where" in such a way as to lend understanding to all the intricate interconnections, those behind-the-scenes elements that explain why your coffee comes from Kenya, your sugar for your cereal comes from Brazil, and the T-Shirt you're wearing today was made in Vietnam.

"Geography is a discipline of diversity under whose spatial umbrella we study, analyze processes, systems, behaviors and countless other phenomena that have spatial expression. It is this tie that binds geographers, this interest in patterns, distributions, diffusions, circulations, interactions, juxtapositions – the way in which physical and human worlds are laid out, interconnect and interact." [1]

Some describe "the power of geography" in terms of the contributions the discipline makes to broaden our understanding of the world's complexity and patterns of development.[2] Geographers look at global and local networks (human and hi-tech) and global and local landscapes (natural and built). Geographers may start from the ground up looking at how nature influences human activities and then examine how human activities influence natural events. These two-way influences are the spatial connections the articles in this anthology seek to reveal. With an expanded awareness of the world around us, we are in a better position to manage its complexities and the dynamic pace at which we experience change. For the beginner, the study of geography can help us understand where we fit in, giving us that foundation to begin asking the "whys" and the tools to begin answering them.

THINKING GEOGRAPHICALLY: THE SPATIAL COMPONENT

Space and understanding spatial dynamics may be more complex than you first might have imagined. The first thing that makes this a bit confusing is the concept of spatial analysis; you quite likely examine or questions events or outcomes in this way, but maybe don't know that this is what you're doing. The idea of "spatial" can lend itself to a bit of confusion for beginning geographers.

When students first come to a geography course, there is a general expectation that the world will be divided along recognizable political boundaries such as national borders, city limits, or county lines,

1   de Blij, Harm. 2005. Why Geography Matters: Three Challenges Facing America. Oxford University Press: New York. 8.

2   Marston, Sallie; Knox, Paul; Liverman, Diana: 2008. World Regions in a Global Context: Peoples, Places, and Environments, Third Edition. Pearson-Prentice Hall: New Jersey. 2.

In part this is true, but geography is multi-scalar, which means geographers may look at the world from a broad global level to a neighborhood level. Spatial analysis is done at an infinite number of scales.

What it means is that when geographers examine space they are looking at geographical phenomena from four key perspectives: Location, Scale, Territory and Sense of Place.

Location: This perspective is likely the most familiar to you as you've been asked in the past to label places on a map. The most fundamental way we think about location is through a grid points, our latitude and longitude. This absolute space is explained through mathematics and geometry. We can also examine location of people and things in terms of their positions and their relation to each other. This allows us to begin thinking about the patterns across space.

Location may be defined three different ways: **Absolute, Relative** and **Nominal**. When you label a city on a map, for instance Chicago, you are providing a **nominal** or descriptive name of a place. The dot you may be labeling on the map is identified with a specific latitude and longitude location on this earth, which is its **absolute location**. **Nominal locations** may vary in terms of how they are spelled or there may be many descriptive names of places that are useful to certain groups, Chicago, "The Windy City", Chi-town, or The Second City. Absolute location doesn't really change although how it is represented can vary depending on who is making the maps. **Relative location** describes a location in relation to another place. Chicago is on Lake Michigan, Chicago is a Mid-West city or Chicago is a little over 700 miles west of New York City. While these are simple examples, it is these relationships of places to other places that give rise to spatial analysis.

Scale: Before online mapping, most first experiences with geographic scale have been the scale bar graphic at the bottom of a map, telling us the ratio of map units there are to earth units. One inch = 63,360 inches (1 inch = 1 mile) is one example. This means there are infinite scales we can examine on maps; you experience this every time you zoom in or zoom out on an interactive map. We also represent scale when describing activity. For example, we might represent activity on a global scale (telecommunication networks, airline traffic, disease vectors), a national scale (Education levels in a country, voter turnout and patterns), a regional scale which might be represented at a sub-national scale such as the Midwest or New England or at a macro-regional scale, such as a trade organization like the European Union or NAFTA. We might look at spatial events at an urban scale, county scale, neighborhood scale (how many banks are operating in a town) and some geographers will take scale to the body level, looking at our coding (ethnicity, gender and various other factors that play into out interpretation of spatial events). Scale shapes how we interpret spatial dynamics both in how much area we might cover or how much detail we might delve into.

Territory: This particular element of space can be challenge because we're not necessarily just talking about area, but about governance and power structures within that area. An important attribute of space is power to control it; this power carries certain implications. National governments certainly have the power to enforce, guard and police their territories by controlling who crosses the boundaries. It also speaks to the power that controls what happens inside these boundaries: education, training, legal statutes, taxation, voting privileges and so on.

Geographers investigate types of governance and power structures that control the activities that might take place inside an area and in cooperation (or antagonism) with other areas. For example, land set aside for public recreation comes under pressure from how many people use it to those who want to use the land for private enterprise. Territory doesn't simply mean how many square miles which is often how it is initially understood.

Place: This component of space is a distinctive amalgamation of human and physical features on the earth's surface including environmental conditions, landscapes (both physical and human), cultural practices and social and economic activities. The characteristics of place are profoundly shaped by human activity such as forms of government, religious and linguistic traditions, norms attributed to gender roles, levels of wealth and inequality, types of work done and things people sell. This particular list is endless because it is also framed by how we, as individuals see the place.

Understanding the uniqueness of a place calls on you to consider the historical and contemporary processes at play. How have these processes shaped a place and how have the characteristic of the historical place shaped what it would become? Geographers also need to examine the role a place plays in a larger context (a different scale) and to comprehend that divers factors are indeed interrelated such as cultural practices, economic activities, and the natural environment.

WHAT YOU CAN GET OUT OF THIS COURSE

You may be asking why this should matter to you. For one thing, you are a part of this dynamic and introductory courses to geography give our lives a global context, reveal our role or what our role might be in this global dynamic. Even though you might not see a direct connection of your life to events across the globe today, the study of geography brings some of those direct and indirect connections into relief. So, while knowing where the oceans, countries, cities and mountains are is an important beginning, it is just a beginning. There is so much more geography that unfolds on these landscapes; maps help show these relationships in a spatial context and encourage more inquiry.

That T-Shirt you put on this morning, where was it made? Why was it made there and not somewhere else, perhaps closer? Those bananas you bought at the grocery store, where did they grow, who harvested them, and how did they get to your grocery store so far from a tropical climate? How did the emergency vehicle that passed you know the fastest route? Where was the microchip in your phone manufactured? Where was the phone itself assembled? Why would civil protests in North Africa and the Middle East contribute to price

fluctuations for gasoline? Why is water rationed in some states and not others? Why have irrigation programs destroyed ecosystems and how has civil tumult resulted in the migrations of millions? How can China's coal burning influence air quality in the state of Washington? Why are intensely biodiverse areas such as rainforests vulnerable? Why are certain populations more vulnerable to natural disasters? While you may not know the answers today it is important to know that these questions are examples of spatial connections and geographic landscapes.

This introductory course and this book ask you to pause momentarily and consider all the levels of spatial connections that are implied in each of the examples. It asks you to reflect on dynamics that have invoked changes on the global, regional and local landscapes. When you do this you set yourself on a course of inquiry that can be most rewarding. Geography is one of those wonderful subjects, even if it isn't your major that helps you understand where you fit in. Yes, you will learn lots of details and facts and figures, but keep in mind, it is how you use this information to explain geographic or spatial connections and further, to explain why they are important. Ask yourself how, in even the smallest of ways are your activities and actions a part of the global picture.

And then ask yourself how maps can help you understand these landscapes and these connections. You can find maps on just about any phenomenon you might want to examine. There are maps of medieval black death, cancer, Ebola or AIDS cases, fire damage, deforestation rates, birth rates, death rates, health expenditures, hospital services, fast-food chains, consumer purchases, radio stations, cell phone towers, internet users, computer owners, burglary rates, homicide rates, car thefts, park admittance numbers, high traffic days, low traffic days, highway safety, you name it and you can probably find a map. And on the off chance you can't find a map you need, you could certainly make one, and geographers do!

ABOUT THE BOOK

This book is designed to give you a feel for how big the world is. Oh yes, we are always hearing about how "small" the world is, how closely connected we are via the internet, trade, politics, economics and history. However, learning about the globe is not done quickly or is it done in a single broad sweep. The world is vast; there is breadth and depth to the study of Geography. We have to peel away layer after layer, examine all the interconnections from below the earth's surface to the stratosphere and everything in between including national and international politics, national and international population dynamics, and national, international historic, cultural and economic processes, to name a few. The articles in this book ask you to draw on what you know and to look up what you don't know. Always ask yourself how understanding these connections will help you in developing spatial connections of your own.

The articles in this book have been selected to satisfy three primary objectives. (1) They will give you an introduction to some of these interconnections, to the process of assessing complicated relationships across the globe, and to the landscapes upon which everything plays out. (2) They seek to open the path of your inquiry into where you fit in to this interconnected and dynamic world of ours. (3) They will supplement the class lecture by offering specific and different examples to help you put the concepts discussed in class together. This book does not serve as a replacement for an atlas or a text used for studying world geography; instead it offers an alternative approach, one that introduces various perspectives through more specific examples. The articles included in this book are only a few of the thousands of examples of spatial connections and geographic landscapes.

No introduction to Geography can hope to cover all the relationships that exist nor can it provide all perspectives. As such, parts of the world may not be represented, not because they are unimportant but because it is impossible to provide a comprehensive text that represents the world's complexity. Changes are taking place as you read the articles, new connections are forged, and others disappear. The intent of this anthology then is to provide you with a snapshot of global landscapes.

GEOGRAPHIC LANDSCAPES

Landscape? What do we mean by this term? In the more than a decade I have been teaching an introduction to World Geography course, I have heard a number of responses to the question "What do geographers map?" Most of the answers are physical characteristics: rivers, mountains, lakes, oceans and an occasional country or capital city. Most students come to geography with their focus on the physical or environmental characteristics of geography which is perfectly acceptable, but the landscapes described in this text go well beyond the physical features of the earth.

Geographers use the term landscape to describe the canvas upon which certain activities will unfold; it may be a broad sweeping canvas or one narrowly defined. We use landscapes to describe cities, political, economic or social processes; within these sub-disciplines of geography other landscapes are revealed. It is the relationship between events, activities and development across these landscapes that broaden our understanding of global change. Geographers thus explore the many connections that can define a landscape. For example, how is Mumbai, India's urban landscape similar to and different from Lagos, Nigeria? Can one reasonably expect to draw a comparison between these two cities in a manner that might be used to broaden our understanding of urban dynamics? Geographers ask why what processes occurred where and continue in this vein to explore comparative processes elsewhere around the world. We may ask why Russia's or Japan's population is declining in the midst of a population growth rate that predicts population numbers between the 9 and 11 billion mark by 2050. Or we may question how and why India's population is still regarded as a rural population when there are so many cities like Mumbai and Delhi that are megacities, cities exceeding 10 million people. We may ask why some countries in Latin America are experiencing longer life spans while Botswana's life expectancy has declined measurably in the last decade. Geographers explore these phenomena and the specific landscapes by examining intervening factors that contribute to change and examine the ramifications for the future. Physical, economic, social, political – none of these processes are circumscribed; decisions or events in one part of the world can influence other people, countries and environments.

Landscapes are frameworks for inquiry; asking the "who", "what", "how" and "why" and then setting about to answer these same questions is what geographers seek to do. The landscape is the spatial context upon which we focus our study and like all the geographic landscapes we discuss in this course, you experience and are a part of them every day. This book, then introduces articles that are devoted to one or two or all five landscapes. You will notice, however, that the articles represent common themes across a particular world region, but the material and ideas definitely overlap onto other landscapes.

Human landscapes describe the spatial organization of human activity and their relationship to the earth and to one another. Human landscapes may be formed, for example by cultural legacies, patterns of migrations, diversity, language, and religion or population dynamics. You will discover that discussion of human or cultural geography truly overlaps into many other disciplines and vice versa. Think about some of the things you see every day that could represent these human and cultural connections.

- Neighborhoods, houses, school campuses, libraries
- Monuments, museums, community parks, sports fields
- Foreign films, home made films on the Internet
- Churches, synagogues, mosques, temples
- Advertising on billboards, T-Shirts, Internet, baseball caps

- Bi-lingual or multi-lingual advertising, languages spoken, languages heard, learning a new language
- Various styles of dress from traditional national costumes to peer-inspired clothing, color or style
- Restaurants with international cuisine
- Friends from different towns, counties, states or countries

You probably see these things all the time and don't give it much thought because they are... well, part of the landscape. There are countless perspectives by which to study a human landscape, and although the examples above may seem basic at first glance, our objective is to unpack a complex chain of events that resulted in the landscapes we examine. Our objective in this course is to see, and look at these things differently; when we examine these human landscapes we will study the influences on the landscapes and corresponded reactions to the outcomes. We will look at history, politics, economic, culture and natural environments as having a bearing on the human landscapes.

Urban Landscapes place human activity, its spatial organization within an urban context. We have spent centuries migrating towards urban centers, at times it has been a slow and steady pace and at times a rapid one. The results of rapid movement into urban centers produce distinctive landscapes. The emergence of cities and landscapes within cities is often explained by other aspects of geography including human, economic, physical and environmental and political influences.

When you go "downtown" in the area you live, what do you see? Where is "downtown" from where you live? Is there an "uptown?" Do you consider this the center of the city or are you going to a suburban downtown? Is the "downtown" an obvious location or is it less geographically clear?

Where are the government buildings? Where does the primary business activity take place? Do you see a robust downtown business center complete with customers walking around from store to store? Or do you see vacant storefronts? Is there a shopping mall or are there several shopping centers nearby? Is the activity in the downtown busy at night too, or just during the day? Do you sometimes joke about your town "rolling up the sidewalks at 8:00 PM? Or do you describe your downtown as a place that never sleeps?

Do you see signs of community organizations and their efforts to "revitalize downtown", an historic preservation group maintaining certain houses and buildings in a specific way or are there individual efforts at gentrification? Do you find that certain business activities are grouped together? Who works there: blue collar, white collar, service, or high-tech, professional? How do the buildings look; are all they similar in style or height or are they old, new, or in a state of disrepair?

How do people get to "downtown?" Do they walk, drive, or ride the bus or train? Does a highway divide your town or does one bypass it? What have been the changes in your town since the highway was built?

Is the air clean and fresh or do you sometimes detect nearby manufacturing processes?

Are there community parks that people can go to in your town? Is there a public library, grocery store, hospital in or near the downtown? Are there residents who live in the city center in apartments or condominiums or lofts? Who are they and what factors play into their ability to live in these locations?

Do you describe some areas of your city as "better" than others? What are the reasons you draw this comparison? How do you define "better?"

Has your home town grown quickly over the past decade or are people leaving to live other places? What reasons can you give that explain these changes?

If you have asked yourself any of these questions you've started asking some of the "whys" of urban landscapes. These are the types of questions that are used to answer "what has influenced the development of an urban area?" Answers to these questions add to your understanding of the connection between urban environments and economic, human, political, historical or environmental influences.

Economic Landscapes represent economic geography. This is a highly diverse field that examines regional development, corporations and labor, corporate cultures, trade and industrialization, consumption and production and issues of uneven development and globalization. The spatial context and scale of economic landscapes, as with others can be global, continental, national, urban, neighborhood and community.

Economic landscapes, without a doubt are interconnected with other geographic landscapes we discuss in this class. The movement of money, the system of trade, the inclusion or exclusion of nations in international trade, the investment made at national and local levels can explain why and how landscapes are shaped. It isn't just a matter of walking into a store and purchasing an electronic component made in South Korea but economic geography explains why the component was made there, why you were able to purchase it locally, labor laws and trade laws that help explain why it was priced the way it was, government economic policies that encourage the production of such products, basic factors like supply, demand, elasticity and inelasticity and the list goes on. Economic geographers examine such aspects as regional development, industrialization, or consumption at global, regional, national, and local levels. Just as you play a role in all geographic landscapes, your purchases or wage earning is a direct part of the local landscape.

We often hear the term "globalization" in relation to economic patterns and trends, but not to the exclusion of other geographic landscapes. What is your definition of globalization? Why does this term come up so often and in what context? How would you use your definition of globalization to describe globalizing effects in your home town? Economic geography looks at the factors of technology, industrialization and labor processes in relation to a globalizing, or sometimes referred to as a shrinking world.

In just the past few years we've seen some significant global changes, in particular from East and South Asia. Major economic changes in India and China have had, and will continue to have a significant impact on global economies. Let's not overlook however, growth and economic change in Mexico, Brazil and of course newly emerging economies. Emerging economies and developing nations are establishing trading partners with large and small economies around the world. We are seeing China's reach expand internationally and expand quickly. At the same time, we are seeing some national economies decline, contract or suffer extended periods of recession. Another significant dynamic evident on the economic landscape is rising affluence and changes in consumption patterns.

Another pattern of economic change geographers examine is the social change and influence of economic policies on the standard of living in countries. Often, not all people benefit from the economic growth and rising affluence equally; geographers look at these trends and factors that might contribute to such an uneven development. Geographers also consider country economies on the threshold of major change. In a location, such as the Caspian Sea which has considerable access to important natural resources, such as oil and natural gas, is also an area that is emerging from a command economy into a free market economy. Orchestrating major economic change concurrent with major political restructuring weighs heavy on emerging nations.

Environmental Landscapes reveal the earth's physical processes and human interaction. Aspects of physical geography are natural in origin: rocks and minerals, soil, flora and fauna, landforms, weather and climate to name a few. These landscapes are typically what newcomers to geography associate with maps. Mountains, rivers, oceans are places we learn to locate on maps quite early on. There are branches of geography that study geologic or biological processes in a spatial context.

Our objective in this anthology is to consider an environment-human connection. We will mull over how landscapes could be, and have been influenced by human interaction. Geographers examine the distribution or spatial context of these components. Environmental landscapes may be natural in origin, but the landscapes can be, and have been influenced by human interaction.

Have you ever asked yourself how much a gallon of gas really costs? You know what you pay or you've seen or heard about gas prices fluctuating but have you wondered why or what's behind the change. Many environmental geographers look not only at the physical environment but also at human interaction and many times, as is the case of fossil fuels, timber, natural gas, water, and other precious minerals, the extraction of natural resources. Physical and environmental geographers examine physical conditions such as climate change or desertification as both a physical change and a human change. Both these examples are representative of an environment-human connection.

We hear of earthquakes, hurricanes or cyclones, tornadoes or flooding. All of these natural processes have direct physical and human consequences. Geographers examine the spatial context of these events from many perspectives, certainly from a physical perspective but also from a human, economic and often times a political perspective. Changes in human landscapes are linked to changes in the physical landscape.

While oil, fossil fuel extraction and gas prices are often in the news, water is equally, and many argue more crucial a resource in its use and availability. Many of us take for granted that the water will flow from the tap, this is not true for many. Access to potable water is a critical challenge for well over 1 billion people on this earth.[3] Fossil fuel shortages and fresh water shortages are key challenges this world faces today.

When you read the articles consider questions of natural resource sustainability, how they are used and how and why some individuals have access to resources and others do not. Don't stop at water and fossil fuels, but consider how use of renewable resources has been developed and whether you've observed with changes in physical, economic, social and political landscapes. These types of questions are the beginning to a deeper understanding of the human-environment spatial connection.

Historical and Political Landscapes are often combined although they are distinct sub-fields of the discipline. Remember, these landscapes do not stand alone nor are there any discrete boundaries

XV

---

3   United Nations Water for Life Decade 2005-2015 Factsheet, www.un.org/waterforlifedecade/factsheet.html

between areas of study. While these spatial connections overlap it is often the predominant focus in a study that defines which branch of geography the study falls under.

Political Geography focuses on the complexity of politics and both human and physical geography, with the understanding that this is a two-way dynamic. As with other landscapes, political landscapes are at all scales from the global scale to the individual. From a historical perspective we will examine events, issues, or policies framed historically but generate consequences or conditions today. We will look at both historical and political foundations to territory and space.

An historical view describes events within a specific time and space. Examination of them allows for analysis of similar or consequent events at a later time. Historical events may be driven by social, economic or cultural conditions that generate significant change even decades later. A revolution, be it social or industrial creates change across a landscape and most certainly at various scales.[4]

Political geography considers the dynamics of politics, policies, or social system within a spatial context: national territories are often used to frame political discussions but more and more we see consequences with a broader and global reach. Political geography also examines the challenges of government systems within a global and local context. How one government influences change over a broader group of nations may also be a focus. Issues of dominance and national hegemony also can foment political tension creating strained relationships between countries. The global war on terrorism represents a global conflict that not only has political and historical roots, but also ideological, cultural and economic roots. Issues of global political influence are news stories today, reinforcing the notion that what may be happening on the other side of the globe can, indeed influence your life at home.

We sometimes think the study of history is just a long list of memorizing dates and events, but it is much more complex than that. Historical and political references together go a long way toward answering questions about current local and global dynamics. For example, the "Cold War" ended in 1989 when the Soviet Union started to break apart and the Berlin Wall started to come down. When it ended, the era of two major superpowers, the United States and the United Soviet Socialist Republic also ended. What emerged were several new nations onto the global stage. Issues of transition, issues of inclusion into global economics and politics are extremely important for these new nations just as the legacy of the long-standing political contention between these two superpowers is distinct. The emergence of several newly independent nations in the early 1990s produced an entirely different world map and in many cases, regional descriptions. The nations of Central Asia, once republics in the Soviet Union gained independence during the time. What challenges did they face early on and what challenges do they contend with today? The many challenges of introducing democratic governance must take into account culture, political, historical, economic and social considerations.

The legacy of the Cold War is seen in political, environmental, social, economic and urban landscapes today. Differences in development programs and economic systems help explain some of difficulties countries once under the influence of the two superpowers experience today. Why would this be important when discussing today's global political situation? How does this history bear out on today's landscapes?

Political and ideological contention between nations did not end with the Cold War. On today's global stage we find many examples of conflict, international tension, military action and social unrest. We heard about civil protests in North Africa and the Middle East and we hear of military action in Iraq and Afghanistan and an ongoing, unresolved multi-decade conflict in the Democratic Republic of Congo. We hear of new countries emerging. South Sudan in July 2011 after a long legacy of civil war and internal conflict

---

4 Remember, geographic study takes place at many different scales: local, city, county, province, state, nation, continent, and global.

emerges as an independent nation complete with the challenges of building social and political stability. We also hear of, in the same region Darfur and extreme human rights violations. In the same region we hear of famine and struggles with food insecurity.

The articles in this anthology do not cover all the challenges mentioned above. The objective of these articles is to introduce a wide variety of issues from places where change is met with challenge. Ask yourself, when reading these articles why and how some countries are better off economically than others? Ask yourself how you define "better off." How do economic systems play a role in the political and historical landscapes? How do issues of democracy and democratic governance play a role in the global political scene today? Consider what is taking place in the news on the days you read the articles and examine the changes, hurdles and problem solving that has already taken place.

This is a particularly complex set of issues, ones not easily solved; consider alternative paths which these countries may follow in the next decade and what influences might be strongest in securing their future.

WHAT DOES A GEOGRAPHER DO, ANYWAY?

Throughout the course you will be learning a new vocabulary, a series of terms often used by geographers to describe events, dynamics or interconnections. You will also be introduced to information about these events, when they happened, why and how it changed the landscape. You will look at a number of maps to help put these events into spatial context. New maps, new vocabulary and new information are all part and parcel of learning about the world. When you begin reading the articles in the anthology, take what you've learned in the lecture and apply it to the articles. The articles represent examples of similar conditions or circumstances, so it is up to you to begin applying the material for the course to your at-home reading, in order to better understand the concepts.

When you read each article ask yourself: (1) Do I know where this place is on the map? (2) Who are its neighbors? (3) Have I heard of this place before? (4) In what context have I heard about this place: news, lecture, another class, television show, movie or friend? (5) Was I able to apply any previous knowledge about the place to understanding this article? (6) What other landscapes are represented in the article and why does this overlap exist? (7) How could this information help me understand how I fit in to the global picture? And some basics: (8) did you look up the location represented if you didn't know where it was? (9) Did you look up any words you didn't understand? (10) Did you understand the main message of the article? If you didn't, did you write down some questions that you could ask in class that will help clarify it for you?

Remember, learning about the whole world may feel a bit daunting, but the best thing about a World Regional Geography course is that world is divided up into easier to understand regions. Remember too, you've started from scratch on other subjects or skills you've learned, Mathematics, History, Riding a Bike, Learning to Drive. Studying geography just like any other discipline means you have to start learning the language, whether it is new terminology or the language of maps. All of us geographers started at the same point you are today, building that foundation. And all it took was curiosity and the desire to learn more. Once we began building the foundation we simply added to it through reading, travel and experience. Once you set yourself on the path to answer "why", your journey has begun!

You will have to look a few things up along the way, but this practice never stops, we're always looking things up! It most definitely means asking questions, so don't be afraid to jump right in and get started. It is a wonderfully exciting world to learn about and the more we know, the better our understanding of all those with whom we share this globe will be, and the better global citizens we will be.

1

Tourism in Cuba

Barriers to Economic Growth and Development

By Hilary Becker

The Cuban economy, once the envy of the Caribbean and Latin America, has struggled and languished behind many of its counterparts. In the past, economic and political decisions have tended toward quick fixes rather than sustainable, long-term, integrated growth strategies in the development of the economy. Cuba's traditional way of thinking has focused on identifying "the one" industry or "ally" that would drive the future of Cuba—from sugar exports to Russia, to tourism, to medical services, to Venezuela, to small business. Today, Cuba is moving away from a mindset of monoculture toward an integrated, multipronged approach to economic development and sustainability based on tourism, small business, services, mining, fisheries, and oil.

Cuba currently has a population of just over 11 million with a declining growth rate of −0.1 percent. Cuba's GDP is estimated at US$114.1 billion in 2010 with a growth rate of 1.5 percent in 2010, up from 1.1 percent in 2002. In 2010, GDP was comprised of 72.9 percent services, 22.7 percent industry, and 4.2 percent agriculture. These shares have remained relatively unchanged since 2008 but are significantly different from 2002 when the percentages were 57.9, 34.5, and 7.6 respectively. The inflation rate of 0.7 percent in 2010 was down from 4.2 percent in 2008 and 7.1 percent in 2002. Meanwhile, the country has a well-educated workforce of 5.1 million people, with a 97 percent literacy rate (CIA website, 2010).

Cuba has recently announced a new development approach—the single biggest change in economic policy since the revolution. Under the leadership of Raúl Castro, the government has attempted to improve efficiency through restructuring the economy, layoffs, small business growth, property reform, and environmental reform as a response to economic problems. The Cuban government has a history of making rash moves in response to economic difficulties, opening markets only for brief periods of time. GDP contracted after 2008 due to a variety of factors including hurricane damage, rising costs of oil and food imports, low world nickel prices, and declines in tourism, sugar production, and medical exports.

Structural reforms proposed during the Sixth Congress of the Communist Party of Cuba (PCC) in April 2011 have established a comprehensive framework for economic reform as a response to the abovementioned strains on GDP. The *Lineamientos de la política económica y social del partido y la revolución* ("Guidelines to the Economic and Social Policy of the Party and Revolution") provide an overview manifesto of the changes sought by the Cuban government. This chapter focuses mainly on the impact of the decision to develop sustainable tourism within the Cuban market.

IMPORTANCE OF TOURISM TO THE CUBAN MARKET

For many countries in the Caribbean, tourism has become the primary source of economic activity. For example, tourism represents over 80 percent of the GDP in Antigua and Barbuda, over 50 percent in the Bahamas and Barbados, and just under 50 percent in St. Lucia.[1]

Throughout the past thirty years, the growth of tourism worldwide has been driven in large part by increased global wealth and a more active aging population. Due to advances in health care there is a growing population of retired individuals with large accumulated wealth and a greater ability to afford luxury travel. In addition, technology and communication advances have allowed corporations to expand their business operations to other countries, requiring executives to travel more frequently and creating a market for upscale business accommodation. Lastly, workers worldwide are demanding more free time for family vacations in family-oriented hotels and attractions.

Cuba's initial growth in the tourism industry occurred in the 1940s when the US Congress sought to shut down the influence of organized crime in Las Vegas, which created opportunities for Havana in particular as a suitable alternative, fueling Cuban tourism growth until 1959.

In the 1970s tourism began to rapidly develop once again, largely as a response to slowed economic growth. The resort area of Varadero expanded its hotels at a particularly rapid pace. However, growth took place without proper environmental planning, causing severe damage to the once virgin beach of Varadero. The construction of hotel complexes too close to the ocean and the removal of natural protective vegetation along the beach eliminated the natural barrier that impeded the sand from blowing off the beach and thus stopped the natural cycle of regeneration (Becker, 2009).

Following the collapse of the Soviet Union in 1988, Cuba faced a loss of more than US$6 billion of aid and credits. In response, the Foreign Investment Act (Law 77) allowed foreign ownership in the form of joint ventures, international associations, economic contracts, or 100 percent foreign ownership as a response to Cuba's need to access hard currency. As of 2000, 392 economic associations and joint ventures had been registered in the areas of basic industry (92), tourism (70), construction (33), and to lesser extents in other areas, with the major principals being Spain (97), Canada (75), and Italy (55) (Pérez Villanueva, 2001). During the same growth period, the government allowed the establishment of the home tourism market known as *casas particulares* (similar to bed and breakfasts) in 1993. Just prior to the collapse of the Soviet Union, a small group of eight individuals working in the Cuban Ministry of Tourism (MINTUR) began working on a twenty-year economic development plan to expand the role of tourism through the 1990s and 2000s. For the first time, Cuban policymakers began to consider the environmental impact of the tourism industry and develop criterion of sustainability.

Cuba has officially identified eight main regional poles for tourism: Varadero, Cayo Coco, Cayo Largo, Holguín/Guardalavaca, Santiago de Cuba, Havana, Jardines del Rey, and Pinar del Río; however, currently 70 percent of the tourism revenue is generated between Havana and Varadero (Gutiérrez and Gancedo, 2002).

Economic policy shifts in 1997 called for an increase in hard currency and created a fundamental shift in the Cuban economy from sugar and tobacco to tourism, biotechnology, mining, and other areas, following a decline in world sugar prices and the economic collapse of the stock markets. In the tourism sector, the shift resulted in government investments of as much as 25 percent of total investments increasing in the balance of payments from 6 percent in 1990 to 43 percent in 2000 and to 69.3 percent in 2007 (Becker, 2009).[2]

During the 1990s, tourism revenue increased by eightfold and arrivals fivefold. As a result, the number of hotel rooms tripled, direct employment doubled to an estimated 100,000 employees in the tourism industry (21,000 with university degrees), and production of supplies yielded domestically for the tourism market increased thirty-five- to fortyfold, which now account for 67 percent of total supplies to the tourist market. Cuba thus improved its tourist

3

visits ranking from twenty-third of twenty-five to ninth of twenty-five in North and South America and the Caribbean (Figueras, 2003).

In 2001, prior to September 11, tourism was up 8.7 percent. Immediately following the 2001 terrorist attacks on the United States, travel to Cuba declined, although the impact was not as severe as in other parts of the world. Tourism declined by 10 percent in the September to December period and 21 percent during the January to February period. An increase of 6.3 percent was noted in the following March to October period in 2002; however, estimates of a 10 percent growth during this period had been expected prior to the September 11 attacks (Figueras, 2003). In an economic response to the decline in tourism, the Cuban government closed about twenty hotels altogether and floors or sections of several others, rather than performing repairs and upgrades (Coyula, 2002).

THE WORLD TRADE ORGANIZATION (WTO) CHALLENGES

The WTO expects unprecedented growth in worldwide tourism in the next twenty years. Estimates suggest that travel will grow from 560 million tourists with US$400 billion in revenues in 1995 to more than 1.6 billion tourists and US$2 trillion by 2020. The WTO and the Canadian government have indicated the following major challenges facing the tourism industry:

- Attracting new personnel
- Introducing technological innovations to improve efficiency and service levels
- Increasing visitations during off-peak periods
- More cohesive marketing and promotional plans
- Investment in tourism infrastructure
- Broadening sustainable tourism and best practices (ic.gc.ca, 2011; UNWTO, 2011)

In addition to these challenges, Cuba faces additional difficulties resulting from its political ideology and the impact of the US embargo.

However, these challenges are being met in Cuba. For example, Cuba has circumvented difficulties in attracting new tourism personnel through tourism-focused education programs and wage incentives. In many countries, the level of pay offered to frontline workers in the tourism industry is often minimum wage, making it difficult to attract qualified individuals. Cuba's system allows for any worker to enter the field of tourism, and with gratuities, workers can supplement their income in the same manner that employees in other countries do, such as waiters, waitresses, and maids. Further, Cuba has FORMATUR, a fully funded tourism school, which turns out approximately 16,000 qualified students into the tourism sector (Gutiérrez and Gancedo, 2002). The University of Havana has also introduced a bachelor's degree in tourism studies.

Additionally, while the problem of low visitation during off-peak periods is one faced by every country, Cuba is uniquely situated to counteract this issue. Cuba, along with the Dominican Republic and Mexico, attracts tourists from other Spanish-speaking countries. Due to its geographic proximity to both North and South America, visitors from North America visit principally from December to April, while those countries in the Southern Hemisphere visit from May to September.

Other issues identified by the WTO are also being addressed. MINTUR has adopted a twenty-year tourism growth plan of integrated and coordinated marketing plans with tourism partners. The Cuban government has increased infrastructure funding for tourism, implementing a head tax in Havana to help fund the reconstruction of Old Havana and the Malecón waterfront. Cuba has also engaged in the development of sustainable tourism practices under the guidance of CITMA, the Cuban Ministry of Science, Technology, and the Environment.

THE FUTURE OF CUBAN TOURISM

The tourism industry in Cuba is poised for substantial growth in the next ten years. A lift of the US embargo would present the greatest opportunity for growth. Despite that, other opportunities exist for Cuba to expand tourism, which were addressed as fundamental objectives at the Sixth Congress of the PCC in 2011.

Cuba is currently working within their twenty-year tourism development plan, which includes sustainable growth and environmental protection. The plan includes an expansion to a total maximum of 207,200 rooms, up from the current 70,000 rooms (Becker, 2009).

Varadero, as an example, has just over 17,000 rooms and will expand to 27,000 with a planned growth of about 2,000 rooms per year over the next ten years. The plan also determines the maximum estimate of 130,000 visitors daily, up from 47,000 daily in 2000 in the seven zones of Varadero, leading to determinations of power and water consumption needs to accommodate this growth. The establishment of two new power plants, a planned road system, and modifications to the entrance of Varadero, along with expansion of hotels toward the airport are all part of the projections. Development of a new marina with 500 new berths and expansion of the existing marina to 1,200 berths are also part of the plan to accommodate a growing number of tourists. The Varahicacos caves area, however, is being limited to 2,000 guests per day and is under the guidance of the Blue Flag Certification process (Becker 2009).

Opportunities for growth in tourism exist. The areas listed below have not been fully explored within the Cuban market by MINTUR.

Cruises

Cruise ships are a virtually untapped resource in the Cuban tourism sector. Of the 2.2 million tourists visiting Cuba in 2007, only 200,000 arrived via cruise ships, mostly operated by European cruise lines into Havana (ONE, 2010a). Comparatively, Puerto Rico had approximately 1.2 million of its 4.2 million visitors arriving via cruise ships, of which 80 percent were American, while the Bahamas received 2.5 million of their 4.1 million tourists via cruise ships (Barberia, 2002). The Florida Caribbean Cruise Association (FCCA) estimates that the Caribbean was the destination

of 37.02 percent of the 14.4 million cruise passengers in 2009 (FCCA, 2011). It is estimated that each tourist visiting via cruise ships will spend approximately US$150 while visiting the island, a total of US$285,000 in a single port of call for an average-size cruise ship. Cuba has, in response, invested in infrastructure expansion to upgrade the port facilities in Havana in conjunction with Costa Crociere, the fifth-largest cruise line in the world.

Should these expansions in cruise ship tourism occur, it would be expected that the current container shipments of resources coming into the Havana harbor would be moved to Mariel, to the west of Havana, while cruise ships and tourism development would take over the Havana Bay area, with refineries being moved to Cienfuegos and the electrical generation plant to Matanzas (Ritter, 2011a).

Fishing

The shores surrounding Cuba and its mainland offer opportunities for sports fishery tourism development. There is largemouth bass in Lakes Zaza and Rodondo, excellent bone fishing in Ciénaga de Zapata and Isla de la Juventud, and Sailfish and Marlin off the northern coast. Fishing represents a multibillion dollar industry in Florida and the Bahamas, which has similar geography to Cuba in terms of flats and lakes.

Scuba Diving

Scuba diving could potentially draw large numbers of tourists, with excellent diving opportunities off the coast of Cayo Largo, Isla de la Juventud, and Ciénaga de Zapata, and a Blue Hole, similar to the one in Belize, which attracts many divers. To a lesser extent, diving is already available in Varadero, Holguín/Guardalavaca, and other resort areas as well as in the many keys off the coast of Cuba (Becker, 2009).

Ecotourism

Ecotourism, which is still in its infancy in Cuba, represents an important opportunity primarily in the Viñales region with the Mogotes and Ciénaga de Zapata, which has an area similar in scope to the Florida Everglades. Ciénaga, a UNESCO Biosphere Reserve, has over thirty species of reptiles, 175 species of birds—some endemic to Cuba—and fishing opportunities (UNESCO, 2010). In the east, Baracoa offers great opportunities for development of ecotourism, as do the many keys that surround the island.

Las Terrazas, located in the Sierra del Rosario Mountains, is a unique tourism complex designed and developed in 1968 as a leader in the integration of ecotourism and the local community that lives and works within the complex. Additional growth is expected to nearly double the size currently devoted to ecotourism. The region, originally settled by the French settlers from Haiti, saw its forests destroyed to establish housing and farming. In 1967, the government created a reforestation program, planting nearly 10 million trees over 5,000 hectares to re-establish the forests in the region. Las Terrazas also benefited from the unique policy allowing workers to retain 100 percent of profits, as opposed to remitting it back to the government. Profits were then reinvested to expand and grow the complex, offering a model for further growth in tourism in other areas of Cuba. Today, Las Terrazas still keeps 30 percent of their profits for expansion.

Health Tourism

Health tourism and exchanges can offer another avenue for future growth. Cuba is a leader in biotechnology and, as such, has successfully developed cures and treatments for many ailments. Currently, the market is fairly small with just over 9,000 foreigners officially being treated by Cuba's health tourism company, representing over US$40 million in revenues of which US$25 million were re-invested into hospitals.

American Tourism

The tourism industry in Cuba has been dominated by tourists from Canada, Germany, Italy, and Spain. However estimates indicate that a lift of the US embargo could result in as many as 3 million additional US tourists with a combined impact of US$5 billion to the Cuban economy. During the 1990s, the number of American tourist visits grew from 10,000 to over 77,000 by 2002, falling back to 36,800 in 2006. ONE indicated the number of American tourists to Cuba as 52,455 tourists in 2010; however, both *The Economist* ("The Worm that Turned," 2011) and *The New York Times* list the actual number to be in excess of 400,000. This would make the United States the second-largest tourist group in Cuba, following Canada, which should reach 1 million tourists in 2011.

American tourists may be motivated to visit Cuba for a variety of reasons, including curiosity about America's history with Cuba, snow-bird watching, conventions, jazz and salsa festivals, fishing tournaments, religion, as well as academic interests. University students could make Cuba the destination of choice for spring break, detracting from typical party spots in Florida, Mexico, Texas, and Lake Havasu.

Cubans Living Abroad

Psychological tourism presents the single largest potential growth in tourism, represented by the estimated 400,000 American trips to Cuba in 2010, with many Cuban-Americans visiting family. For young Cuban Americans, tourism is an opportunity to get to know their heritage. In 2011, the Obama administration eased travel restrictions for Cubans with family in Cuba and for religious and educational travel and also allowed increases in remittances to family members on the island. Cuban American visitors represent a large but different type of tourism client; typical Cuban American travelers are not looking for the typical fun-and-sun vacation but are rather there to visit family. They are more likely to use *casas particulares* and *paladares* rather than hotels and government-owned restaurants. Cuban Americans currently represent the largest

6

segment of tourists renting automobiles in Cuba for vacations and travel.

Golf

Major expansions have been approved by the Cuban government to take advantage of this potential growth. Leisure Canada, Inc., is planning a multiproperty oceanfront complex on 5.5 square kilometers in Jibacoa, with plans for 2,000 rooms, bungalows, and two championship golf courses, as well as a five-star property managed by Sol Melia to be constructed in Cayo Lago. Leisure Canada, Inc., entered into a joint venture with Gran Caribe, S.A., and will use state owned land through ninety-nine-year leases, as well as a 737-room all-suites hotel in Miramar, Havana, with a convention and entertainment complex.[3]

Standing Feather International is in the final stages of negotiating construction of a US$515 million golf and property destination in Guardalavaca. Other developments include the potential of upward of forty golf courses. The initial four projects approved amount to total investments of more than US$1.5 billion and include plans for villas that could be sold to foreign investors in Guardalavaca and Varadero (Ritter, 2011b).

Sustainable Tourism

In 1999, the Sustainable Tourism Zone of the Caribbean established the following definition of sustainable tourism:

> Sustainable tourism constitutes an adequate response to the challenges of increasing rates of growth in employment and foreign exchange earnings, protecting and preserving the environment and natural resources, protecting cultural patrimony and values. We support community participation, as well as the involvement of local interests in aspects of the tourism development process, such as policy making, planning, management, ownership and the sharing of

benefits generated by this activity. (STZC, 1999)

Later in 2003, the Association of Caribbean States (ACS) identified four regions within Cuba that were suitable for sustainable tourism development: Viñales, Las Terrazas, Ciénaga de Zapata, and Varadero.

In 2006, the author was contacted by the World Wildlife Fund to be the lead researcher on a project in sustainable tourism development in Cuba in association with the Fundación Antonio Núñez, MINTUR, and Air Transat. The work was performed in the four regions identified by the ACS, identifying four principal areas of sustainability including economic, social, environmental, and, for Cuba, political. The methodology followed that of the ACS process.

A series of workshops with local principals established the development of sustainable tourism measures and utilized "blue ocean strategy" to recommend new ecotourism products, as well as plans for future expansion, working in partnership with airlines, hotels, restaurants, nightclubs, and tourist venues (Kim and Mauborgne, 2005). With Cuba currently redesigning its image and product offerings, now is the perfect time for the Cuban government to engage in blue ocean strategic thinking.

CHALLENGES

Among the many challenges facing the growth and success of tourism in Cuba is the current economic crisis in Europe and the United States. The global recession has negatively impacted discretionary travel income, most likely reducing the number of tourists visiting Cuba.

Another major threat for tourism also involves the offshore oil drilling off the coast of Cuba. Recently, Cuba has entered into joint ventures with such firms as Russian Zarubezhneft, Spain's Repsol-YPF, Venezuela's PDVSA, and Vietnam's PetroVietnam ("Cuban Russian Firms," 2011). The 2010 BP oil spill in the Gulf of Mexico caused billions of dollars of damage, and a similar spill near Cuba would devastate the tourism sector and the already fragile Cuban economy.

One of the growth areas discussed earlier pertained to ecotourism; however, Cuba must first understand the limitations posed by the economic nature of ecotourism. Precisely for its sustainability function, ecotourism offers only a limited number of rentable rooms, thus requiring a different type of evaluation from other forms of tourism, due to its inability to gain economies of scale. In environmentally delicate areas, the necessary limitation on the number of tourists also limits profits.

Golf is a highly sought-after tourism activity and can be very profitable. Indeed, Cuba has tremendous opportunities for growth in this regard; however, the environmental cost of a golf course—ranging from the need for water to deforestation and damage to the ecosystem—is also high. There has been a recent move toward more environmentally sustainable golf course developments that will limit the negative impact on the environment for the proposed golf courses in Cuba.

Any effort toward sustainable tourism must involve CITMA. Its work in developing standards and guidelines for tourism has been decisive in turning around the environmental destruction that the tourism industry wreaked in Varadero and Havana Bay. Sustainable indicators and development limits have been imposed on all new efforts to ensure that the pursuit of foreign direct investment (FDI) leads to Cuba's sustainable long-term development.

RECENT CHANGES BY THE CUBAN GOVERNMENT

The new policies will focus on small business growth, property and real estate ownership reform, and environmental reforms, all of which impact the tourism industry.

In 2010, Cuba announced a downsizing of approximately 500,000 state workers in the short term with estimates ranging as high as 1.8 million, or 25 percent of the workforce, in the long run. This represents a major ideological shift from the 1992 Cuban Constitution, Article 45, which states "work in a socialist society is a right and duty and a source

of pride for every citizen." To accommodate these changes, the Cuban government has expanded small business ownership by issuing up to 250,000 additional licenses in specific areas (178 types of small business) including the tourism industry through taxis, *casas particulares,* and *paladares* (CTC, 2010).

For over a decade, these changes have been argued as necessary for Cuba's growth and development, as well as a stimulant for economic and personal growth (Becker, 2003, 2009). If the US economic embargo is lifted, the estimated influx of 3 million visitors from the United States (Becker 2003) will exceed the current total tourist visits of 2.4 million, which already account for hotel occupancy of over 60 percent (ONE, 2010). The licensing of *casas particulares* offers a potential solution to accommodate some of the overflow of tourists until the infrastructure in hotel accommodation can catch up to demand. New reforms in housing allow Cubans to not only buy and sell property but also own up to two properties, one in the city and one in the country. These additional houses could offer an opportunity for tourism revenues to be earned by Cubans renting the second property to tourists.

Along with the small business reforms, there is a need for tax reform, better integration of small business with government programs, training, and financing. In a forthcoming paper, the author argues that a Ministry of Small Business Enterprise needs to be established. The current taxation system requires small businesses to be taxed at approximately 40–45 percent with an additional tax of approximately 20 percent to accommodate pension plans of employees, essentially taxing small businesses in the 60–65 percent range. Revenues of *casas particulares* are received in CUCs (Cuban convertible pesos), but taxes to the government are to be paid in Cuban pesos, requiring an additional conversion tax.

The government does not have an adequate system for training potential entrepreneurs or financing entrepreneurial endeavors. These are two of the principal reasons why small businesses fail in Cuba. The government needs to establish

8

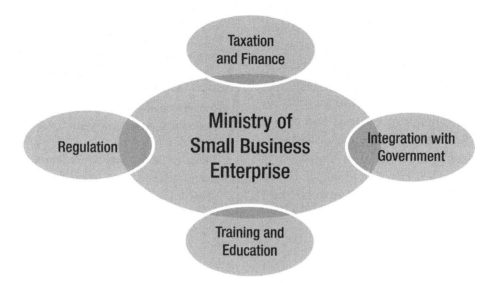

Figure 1.1 Proposal for New Ministry of Small Business Enterprise.

limitations on the number of small businesses in a particular area, as current regulations could potentially allow for more than two hundred *casas particulares* and fifty *paladares* to open within the same neighborhood (numbers are presented as an example to indicate that no restrictions or research has been performed on sustainable business enterprises in any given neighborhood). These problems are further compounded by a lack of liquidity in banks and insufficient financing provided to small businesses. Many of these new businesses will suffer from insufficient demand for products and services as typical Cubans do not have the financial ability to support these enterprises.

The currently authorized 178 business ventures are not sufficient in scope, as they do not include adequate intellectual business opportunities, which could entice professionals engaged in consulting, engineering, and training and information services. These forms of business opportunities could aid government efficiency by supporting government operations and preventing a potential "brain drain," with young students following higher income opportunities in entrepreneurial activities instead of professions such as engineering, medicine, and information systems.

The above proposal for the development of a new Ministry of Small Business Enterprise will need to coordinate taxation and financing, provide adequate training and education programs for entrepreneurs, integrate small businesses with the government, and promote and enforce regulations that will focus on reducing possible corruption and the development of the black market.

These changes were expected to be completed by March of 2011, but hesitation within the Cuban government has prolonged the implementation of the layoffs, allowing the opportunity for more studies to be performed and a smoother implementation of changes to be provided.

The Cuban government should also take note of business models in countries that have undergone similar changes. In addition to China and Russia, Vietnam, which has a similar history to Cuba, should be considered. Vietnam used a modified blended economy that they refer to as the "Doi Moi" or multifaceted integrated economy. At one point in 1989, Vietnam had as little as US$20 million in their central reserve, but their economy has recovered through liberalized prices, subsidy cuts, and opening of the economy, similar to the proposed changes in Cuba (Vo Tri Thanh, 2011).

9

Since 2002, Vietnam has opened between 30,000 and 40,000 new businesses, established free trade areas, joined regional markets, and normalized relations with the United States (in 2005). Vietnam also suffered problems during the transition; inflation ran nearly 20 percent during the transition period and over 95 percent of businesses established were small. The biggest problem faced by Vietnam was the ideological problem of trying to decide "What is a market economy in a socialist environment?" This is a question Cubans must face themselves (Vo Tri Thanh, 2011).

Similar to Vietnam, Cuba offers a large, low-cost, yet educated labor pool, as well as natural resources such as oil, seafood, and agricultural land. The lessons of Vietnam's struggles for Cuba is to ensure that FDI promotes quality instead of just quantity, with proper choices in partners focusing on technology transfer, sustainability, and environmental protection. Ultimately, Cuba will look to move up the value chain, as Vietnam has, from being a manufacturer to distributor and ultimately to consumer.

Cuba has engaged in a positive path of growth that could allow them to once again become a leader among Caribbean and Latin America countries. At a minimum, Cuba should move forward economically given the changes made. The transformations employed by the Cuban government are irreversible but will require prudent monitoring and vision to see it through to fruition.

1. See ec.europa.eu/trade.
2. The 2007 figure includes "remittances paid" for the more than 5,000 doctors working abroad in Venezuela and elsewhere as the tourism sector was combined with these services sector.
3. Leisure Canada website: www.leisurecanada.com/cuba.htm. The website has since been closed.

2

From Pits of Despair to Altars of Love

Kenema, Sierra Leone

By Greg Campbell

Crouched by the mine's edge, I tried to ignore the grilling persistence of the equatorial sun overhead and concentrate on the dirt under my feet. Like everyone around me, I was looking for diamonds.

Unlike the others, though, I squatted and flicked through the gravel on the edge of the water with a stick, trying without much luck to tell the difference between a diamond and a chip of quartz. The others knew what they were doing. I was there to watch.

We were somewhere in the jungle near a town called Bomboma in eastern Sierra Leone, at an open pit mine that had once been culled for diamonds by the Revolutionary United Front. The mine we were in, however, was in a region that had been reclaimed by the government and the men working there were all licensed to find wealth under the jungle floor. No one was really sure of the demarcation, though. The RUF was still nearby and its area of influence and control seemed to change daily, even though UN peacekeepers were also deployed nearby, actively pursuing a disarmament and demobilization agreement intended to end the savagery and displacement of this decade-long war once and for all.

But the war was never more than an economic endeavor, a ten-year-long jewelry heist that continued despite the UN's efforts and the RUF's promises to stop mining. The only difference between an RUF mine and the one we were in is that there were no rifles in sight at ours.

Visiting a diamond mine in Sierra Leone is not easy. Even the operators of those legitimately licensed by the government in Free-town are understandably very nervous about their portrayal in the international media. Therefore, American photojournalist Chris Hondros and I had to pose as government contractors preparing a report on working conditions at government mines, something we weren't aware we had to do until we met our clandestine guide to the Bomboma mine.

Our original plan was to simply wander around the diamond mining and trading town of Kenema until we ran into a miner who, we naively assumed, would be pleased to have two American journalists witness his daily toil in the countryside. But by unfortunate coincidence, the first man we discussed our plans with happened to be an African named Mr. Beh, who was, unbeknown to us at the time, an official with the Sierra Leone Ministry of Mines and Natural Resources, an organization that likes to know who's looking at the mines and why. He seemed jovial and more than willing to take us where we wanted to go, and we had no reason to be suspicious until we left the building where we'd met him after making plans to rendezvous in the morning.

Out on the street, one of our local contacts, a reporter for the state-run radio station, caught up to us and told us to forget our plans with Mr. Beh. The Ministry of Mines and Natural Resources was notoriously paranoid, she said, and it could mean weeks worth of paperwork and intense interrogation before we would be allowed to visit a mine. And even if we were granted permission, it would be to visit a mine vetted entirely of diggers who may be inclined to complain about their working conditions. In fact, she said, if anyone were to ask from that point forward, we should simply say that we were researchers or employees with a nongovernmental organization, anything but journalists. Kenema is a small town and two white reporters stood out noticeably from the rest of the crowd. Being uncooperative with the diamond authorities, even though we were registered with the UN, could lead to arrest, she warned. It was our first introduction to the opaque and clandestine nature of the diamond business. Even legitimate mining operations played it close to the vest.

"My mother was killed here," said our guide, a man who represented a mostly ineffective union for those who toiled in the mines. He pointed to an intersection of two footpaths marked by a knee-high boulder. "Every time I come through here, I think of her."

His mother had been killed while walking from one village to another when the RUF controlled the region. After harassing her, someone stuck a rifle in her gut and blew her into the witchgrass, where she lay until he and other relatives sneaked back to retrieve her body for burial.

We were deep in the jungle, moving along footpaths that seemed to wind along the bottom of a green ocean. Overhead, a cathedral of interlocking branches and an umbrella of dancing leaves 50 feet up hid us from passing helicopters. Dusty shafts of golden sunlight reached like impossibly long crystals through the branches to the ground. Down here, it was easy to imagine how incredibly difficult it must be to fight in the bush. The vegetation was so thick that a regiment of RUF could have been standing two feet off the path and I never would have seen them. Automatic weapons and grenades are good only for a short distance in the jungle; the woody jigsaw of branches and trunks form a natural shield that absorbs and deflects bullets and shrapnel. The RUF perfected fighting in this sort of environment, using the jungle to sneak up close to their enemies and lay ambushes for government troops. They would strike without warning, spewing fire and rockets from the dense forest, then melt back into the trees.

Our journey that morning had started at our guide's hut on the side of a dirt road just outside Kenema, about five miles from the Bomboma mine. He was still rubbing the sleep from his eyes when we nudged into his dark bedroom. "This is going to be slightly dangerous," he said, reaching for a cigarette on the nightstand. "No one can know you're reporters. I want you to see the mines like they really are. And when we come back, don't tell anyone that I took you. I could get arrested."

And we couldn't drive to the mine, either; cars were rare enough in the bush, but a car carrying two white men was bound to draw attention. Therefore, we were going to hike, he said.

We began in Tissor, a small collection of mud huts with thatched roofs assembled in a neat clearing of hard-packed dirt that had been swept clean of leaves and debris. Chickens squawked underfoot and men and women who were so old they seemed to have been carved from wood stared impassively from porches and stools. The village was unremarkable except for its one facet of civic pride: It was here that the first Kamajor militia was formed to fight against the RUF.

In one step, we went from the open clearing into the jungle, like walking from one room into another and having the door slam shut behind you. In the forest, the air was cool and dark and the path ahead of us looked like a giant green tunnel. We walked for miles, emerging from time to time into clearings where men and women burned fields for rice farms. We sidestepped snakes, jumped thick columns of venomous black ants that were more dangerous than snakes, and kicked through the husks of hundreds of mangos, discarded by local diamond-diggers who ate their breakfast during the walk to the mines. And of course, our eyes scanned the ground for milky crystals amid the well-packed gravel. Only a year before some lucky person had found a 25-carat diamond in the middle of Hangha Road in Kenema, a discovery that led

13

to what was probably the town's first-ever civic beautification project as everyone dredged the sewers and sifted mounds of garbage looking for more. "Diamonds," we'd been told the previous evening, "are everywhere."

A few hours later, we emerged from the bush into Bomboma, a village occupied entirely by diamond-diggers and their families. The requisite flock of chickens scattered before us and cook-smoke plumed out from under A-shaped thatch huts. Naked toddlers played with machetes longer than their bodies and, at one house, a group of women dressed in bright scarves attended to a sick woman, covering her skin in a fine white powder.

The first order of business was to convince the village chief that we were from some invented agency of the government, here to independently analyze working conditions at the mine. Any visit to an African village requires the blessing of the local chief, an affair that can involve up to two dozen people and take minutes or days depending on the leader's disposition. We found the old man sitting on the floor, propped up against a wall in an inner courtyard of his house, a simple two-room structure made of packed mud and palm fronds, just like every other building. His face was grizzled with white beard-stubble and he wore a black Adidas T-shirt and soccer shorts. He spoke only the Mende language, so we couldn't follow the specifics of the fabricated story our guide was relating to him, but could see that the chief seemed pleased that someone cared to send two representatives into the bush to check on them. White men in the African outback tend to draw a crowd, and Bomboma was no different. Workers preparing to go to the digging site were happy to be distracted by the sight of two unusual strangers, one of whom carried what looked like a shiny cannon over his shoulder. They stared at Hondros's Nikon and regarded us with friendly curiosity, as if we'd just beamed down from outer space.

After another walk through the forest we soon stepped out onto the banks of the massive Bomboma mine. I immediately understood the paranoia of the Ministry of Mines and Natural Resources. The pit looked more like a slave colony than the first step on the journey of a diamond that would end up in one of the world's largest and most profitable international luxury-commodities markets. On all sides, rib-skinny men stripped to their shorts were covered with mud and slime, the inevitable result of their jobs digging for diamonds. Even though it was barely 10 A.M., they all looked exhausted.

And for good reason: It's hard to imagine a job more difficult or demanding. The workday starts at sunrise and ends at sunset. There are no lunch breaks and no days off. For their efforts at recovering diamonds from the soil, the diggers each receive two cups of rice and the equivalent of 50 cents per day. Bonuses based on the value of their personal production are dependent almost entirely on the trustworthiness of the miner they work for.

The mine was roughly circular and about 300 yards in diameter. Here and there, earthen ledges connected one bank to another across muddy knee-deep pools of groundwater. High up on the banks, surrounding the pit like the jagged teeth of a colossal jungle monster, stood conical mounds of gravel that had been dug from the hole by hand. In such nonindustrialized mines, the process of looking for diamonds is almost exactly the same as it was half a century ago, except that gas-powered water pumps have replaced the bucket brigades of the old days. Essentially, a gigantic hole is dug into the ground until the prospectors hit groundwater, at a depth of usually 30 feet or so. The diamond-iferous soil is carefully piled around the edge and covered with palm fronds. Attacking one pile at a time, diggers shovel the dirt into a wooden trough with a mesh sieve at the bottom. Water is pumped through the trough to separate big rocks from the small ones and a boy at the bottom of the trough shovels out the fine gravel, making another pile. In turn, that pile is dumped by the bucketload into circular sieves called "shake-shakes" and shirtless men and boys twirl the muck around and around at the surface of the water, forcing the heavier pebbles—including any diamonds—into the center and the clay and silt slurry to the outer edge.

Teams of about six washers toil under the tropical sun, carefully watched over by one of the miner's foremen, whose job is to keep an eye out for theft. Even

14

the least muscular man washing gravel is rippled with perfectly defined muscles, sculpted from years of prospecting. Their motions are fluid and robotic: twirl, twirl, twirl, scoop, sift, dump, over and over and over. Watching them work, it astounded me how they ever found a single diamond, but their eyes were so attuned to picking out the stones—and there was a never-ending supply of gravel to be washed—that there was no hesitation or concern that diamonds were being overlooked.

When a diamond is actually discovered, there's hardly the celebration one might expect. Instead, one of the washers simply stops all motion, peering intently into his sieve, brushing rocks out of the way. He then plucks a tiny stone from the center of the mesh and gives a low whistle to the foreman, who ambles over to assess the discovery. There in his palm rests the source of all the country's unrest, a puny diamond barely a quarter carat in weight, standing out from his brown hand like an improbably large grain of salt.

It had been formed eons ago, crystallized under extreme pressure and temperature dozens of miles below the surface and carried up through a kimberlite pipe, subsequently shaken loose and eroded out, and then sent on a desultory, waterborne journey that took centuries to carry it here, near the village of Bomboma, where it was embedded in red dirt and gravel under the floor of a wild jungle. People have lost their hands, their lives, and their families for little stones like this one, which looked quite insignificant there on the bank of the pit. The diamond was then wrapped in paper and disappeared into the foreman's shirt pocket. Eventually, after passing from African hands to Lebanese dealers, it will wind up in London and then probably Antwerp, Belgium, or Bombay, India, or New York City, where it will be cut and polished if the quality justifies it. On its own, the little rock that was discovered as I crouched by the mine's edge is too small to make a very impressive engagement ring, but it might end up as part of a $1,000 necklace or bracelet. Our guide guessed that if the quality was decent, the miner might get $5 for it from one of the diamond merchants in Kenema.

The digger who found it gets another bucket filled with gravel to wash.

About 50 miles north of the pit in Bomboma, a British geologist named J. D. Pollett made a discovery in 1930 similar to ours. He found diamonds on the bank of the Gbobora River, not realizing at the time that he had stumbled onto one of West Africa's most valuable diamond deposits that would, over the next 40 years, produce more than 50 million carats of diamonds, half of which were of astounding gem quality.[1] Pollett estimated that the diamond field he discovered extended over an area of perhaps 3,000 square miles, bounded on the west by the Sewa River and extending east into Liberia. Towns within that area—Kenema, Yengema, Koidu, Tongo Field, and Bo—would be transformed within two decades from sleepy bush villages in the middle of a rain forest that few people would ever care to visit to centers of violent intrigue and international commerce, both legal and illegal. On that day in 1930, Sierra Leone officially became diamondiferous, a designation that has always been both a blessing and a curse for any nation with a similar geology; the promise of vast wealth invariably invites chaos. The discovery of those diamonds—which, until then, had been deemed to be just another worthless piece of gravel by the locals—placed Sierra Leone on a course that would effectively destroy the entire country by the end of the century.

At the time of the discovery, Sierra Leone had been a British colony for 50 years. Founded by former North American slaves freed for fighting on behalf of England in the Revolutionary War, the country was still 80 percent unexplored when Pollett and other teams of geologists forged into the bush to survey its lands and resources. The vast majority of trade, commerce, and political activity took place in Freetown, home to former slaves and captives from across West Africa and the Americas. Freetown's population was composed of people who became known collectively as Krios, and since very few, if any, originally came from Sierra Leone, they didn't stray far from the capital and enjoyed the modernity that flowed from their British rulers.

The Africans who lived in the bush had no idea of the wealth that they trampled and ignored daily. To them, diamonds held no value whatsoever. It's easy to imagine that the people of the Temne, Mende, and Kru tribes—who lived agrarian lives based on animist beliefs and rituals, much like their ancient ancestors had—were probably amused by the sight of white men digging excitedly for stones that they considered utterly worthless. That attitude was destined to be short-lived.

As far back as the sixteenth century, some societies had viewed diamonds as talismans of strength, fortitude, and courage, attributes undoubtedly derived from the stones' hardness, transparency, and purity. Since diamonds were even more rare then than they are now, it's not surprising that they quickly were ascribed magical qualities. Diamonds were said to reveal the guilt or innocence of accused criminals and adulterers by the colors they reflected. They were said to reanimate the dead and render the virtuous invisible. The stones were also believed to bring the wearer all forms of good fortune, unless it had a blood-red flaw in the middle, in which case it meant certain death.[2]

Theories about the origins of diamonds were no less fantastical. Fourteenth-century alchemists revealed the shortcomings of mineral sciences of the day by suggesting that male and female diamonds reproduce "and bring forth small children that multiply and grow all the year," in the words of the author Sir John Mandeville: "I have oftentimes tried the experiment that if a man keep with them a little of the rock and water them with May dew often, they shall grow every year and the small will grow great," he once wrote.

Several cultures passed along the story of the great Valley of Diamonds, supposedly located on the island of Ceylon. In one version of the tale, Sindbad the Sailor is accidentally deposited there after piggybacking on a huge raptor in an attempt to escape one of the many life-threatening situations he frequently found himself in. But instead of being whisked to freedom, he was dropped in a high-walled gorge, the floor of which was covered in gorgeous diamonds. The trouble was that there was no way out and the diamonds were guarded by gigantic serpents whose gaze caused instant death. Fortunately for Sindbad, ingenuity was an early quality of diamond merchants and the men of Ceylon had invented a crafty system to get the goods. Traders would skin the carcass of a sheep and hurl it into the valley. When it hit bottom, the gemstones would adhere to the flesh and prove to be a tantalizing treat for the oversized eagles that nested on the valley's edge. An eagle would retrieve the sheep—and the diamonds attached to it—and return to its nest, where the traders would converge to scare it into flight and collect the bounty. Sindbad tied himself to a sheep carcass with his unwound turban and was thus lifted to freedom on the talons of an eagle, but not before stuffing his pockets with all the diamonds he could carry.

Diamonds are, in fact, the products of heat and pressure. About 120 miles below the earth's surface, carbon atoms are superheated at 3,600 degrees and compressed under incredible pressures in what's called the diamond-stability field, the level within the earth that possesses the right pressure and temperature to turn carbon into diamonds. Geologists surmise that this superhard carbon material was then driven toward the surface at speeds of up to 25 miles per hour during an explosive geological event, carried along with magma and gas to a much cooler depth that prevented the diamonds from being reheated into a more common carbon form such as graphite. These volcanic eruptions originated far below the diamond-stability field, punching through layer after layer of earth, picking up anything and everything that they intersected, resulting in a bubbling stew of geological debris that, when hardened, is known as kimberlite. Many kimberlites didn't make it to the surface, but for those that got close, the lessening pressure of overhead rock allowed the eruption to pick up speed. Gaseous explosions probably blew through the jungle canopy as the pipes surfaced, showering diamonds and everything else for miles around like so much birdshot.

Kimberlite pipes are found all over the world, but not all of them contain diamonds, as many a would-be millionaire has discovered in places like Pittsburgh, Pennsylvania, and Ithaca, New York,

16

both home to kimberlites that have yielded no diamonds. But the kimberlites that blasted into what would eventually become Sierra Leone—two small chimneys that are about a billion years old and likely stood more than 1,500 feet above the plains—bore beautiful, innumerable diamonds. Millennia of erosion and lavish summer rains on the tropical forests that grip Africa from The Gambia to Somalia have hidden the diamonds under the region's red and yellow dirt like so many undiscovered Easter eggs.[3]

All who have ever coveted this wealth—government regimes, smugglers, lovers, merchants—have historically never cared where they were found or under what conditions they were extracted so long as they could turn a profit or showcase one, or several, on a golden band or necklace. Although diamonds are no longer believed to cure disease or act as crystal balls, they still symbolize wealth, power, love, and honor.

Only in the past two years—as public knowledge has increased about the bloodbaths being waged over the control of Sierra Leone's vast wealth—have people begun to learn that diamonds found in their local jewelry stores may have begun their journey in the hands of those who have tortured and killed to gain them.

"For eight months last year, I sat in this office and I didn't buy a single diamond," complained Fawaz S. Fawaz, a heavyset beer-barrel of a man, as he lit a fresh Marlboro off the smoldering butt of his last one. "There are no good diamonds coming in."

He balanced the smoke on top of a pile of crushed filters burying an ashtray on the countertop and continued his clumsy surgery on a tropical bird bought from a little boy on the street. The colorful, scared creature was a gift for Fawaz's young son and once he'd clipped the wings, he untied the twine on its legs and handed it off to a servant, who scurried away to deliver it.

Fawaz is a Lebanese diamond merchant, one of scores whose signs clog the main pothole-ridden road through Kenema, the smoking, popping, wheezing hub of diamond commerce in the heart of the Sierra Leone jungle.

Given its reputation as a diamond capital, it was no surprise when Kenema was attacked by the RUF and its mines captured in 1993. The town was then on the front lines of the diamond war and it was briefly recaptured by government forces in 1994, only to have the RUF win it back a few months later. Kenema stayed under RUF control until 1998, when ECOMOG forces reclaimed it for good. Three years later, in the summer of 2001, it was difficult to imagine that full-scale diamond production had ever been interrupted. Indeed it really hadn't: It was simply conducted by the rebels and many Lebanese endured the threat of dying in a gun battle or artillery barrage to remain behind to deal with them for their diamonds. Unlike other liberated towns that are characterized by the sleepy drudgery of rural life, Kenema is a hectic, overcrowded anthill of nonstop commercial activity. Guarded by a battalion of Zambian soldiers serving with the United Nations Mission in Sierra Leone (UNAMSIL) and a remote base to what seems like every nongovernmental organization ever incorporated, Kenema is proof that properly motivated and controlled greed can overcome the threats of warfare.

The main thoroughfare, Hangha Road, is littered with Lebanese storefronts with large signs announcing "Diamond Merchant" in hand-painted letters. Every merchant's logo is a jumbo-sized brilliant-cut diamond, but the images add little luster to the garbage-strewn streets filled with beggars and refugees who still hang onto the old gambler's notion that they are just one lucky find away from eternal wealth. In the early days, that was certainly the case. Diamonds turned up in garden patches, latrines, and the middle of the streets. Like most other places in Sierra Leone, Kenema hid its dollar-value well: The town smelled like stagnant water and untreated wounds and clouds of disease-bearing mosquitoes hung in the air like a cartoon's crowded thought balloons.

Still, Kenema was more pleasant than most places emerging from the war. On a road parallel to Hangha, a mile-long marketplace seemed to explode with wares: Everything from doorknobs to underwear was on sale. On the other side of town, a food market was hip-to-elbow with colorfully dressed women selling mounds of cassava powder by the cupful and endless rows of tables assembled helter-skelter offering fish meat that had been sitting in the sun all day, attracting battalions of huge black flies. A stroll through the food market certainly took care of your appetite; the reeking fish alone were enough to make most visitors swear off eating for the foreseeable future. In an alley, a group of men assembled shake-shakes from freshly cut pine, imported wire mesh, and ten-penny nails, banging them together much as their grandfathers had in the 1930s and 1940s. The finished products were stacked like oversized poker chips next to a towering pile of used shovels and picks for sale. And it wouldn't have been Africa if every other square foot of roadway wasn't occupied by salesmen hawking rare parrots, fish heads, tablecloths, camouflage T-shirts, and black-market cigarettes.

All the Lebanese shops were nearly identical: Each offered racks and racks of cheap Japanese boom boxes for sale, along with shortwave radios, Sony Walkmans, and various other electronic products. But that was just window dressing and giveaways, throwbacks to the time when Lebanese families made their living selling consumer goods in Freetown; the real business happened in the back rooms, usually past a phalanx of slender young men in Tupac Shakur T-shirts guarding the doorway. In these rooms, whose decorations didn't extend beyond the proprietor's state diamond license and maybe a grainy photo of an olive-skinned family on a rare visit to Lebanon, was where the real wheeling and dealing transpired. There was always a desk with a white velvet pad in the center, a low-hanging lamp directly overhead, a full ashtray, seven or eight magnifying lenses of different powers, and an array of jeweler's loupes. From the despairing tone of some of the Lebanese traders we visited, it seemed as though there was probably a thick film of dust on most of those lenses.

"All of the good diamonds are in Kono," Fawaz said, waving his hand to indicate the area 50 miles to the north where the RUF still reigned. He'd invited me and Hondros into his storefront for a cup of Lebanese coffee, which he ordered by simply shouting into the throng on the street, seemingly

to no one. Dressed in gray polyester slacks and a tissue-thin 1950s-era button-down short-sleeved shirt—left unbuttoned near the neck to reveal a jet-black carpet of chest hair and a thick gold chain—the 50-plus-year-old Fawaz looked more like a counterman in a Philadelphia deli during the 1960s than a wealthy merchant in the jungles of Sierra Leone, through whose hands countless valuable gemstones have flowed. The Fawaz name was emblazoned on billboards up and down Hangha Road, but he insisted that the network of Fawaz cousins and brothers that operated in Kenema and other diamond villages was small compared to other merchants in town. But at the time of our visit, they were all pretty much muttering the same complaint: No good diamonds have been coming in from the fields.

Whether that was true or whether Fawaz simply didn't want to show us any goods is beside the point. One of Sierra Leone's most important diamond areas—Tongo Field—was a mere 30 miles away from where we sat and under complete control of the RUF. It was universally assumed that rebel couriers sold diamonds in Kenema. We'd seen diamonds everywhere there—including a large, eight-sided rough stone that an old man wandering in the market had popped out of his mouth—and it's likely that many of the stones skirted the legitimate channels. While the official currency is the leone (worth 2,000 to the U.S. dollar), in places like Kenema the currency of choice for anything beyond food and clothing was diamonds. If you needed a new car or motorcycle, you paid in diamonds because they were often easier to come by— and easier to carry—than a mountain of leones. If you owed your friend a favor for watching out for your family during the war, you gave him a nice piece of rough. Even a school for children orphaned by the war, in Freetown's Aberdeen district, sells RUF-mined diamonds to reporters and personnel from nongovernmental organizations and the UN so that they can buy food and books for the students.

Fawaz and those like him are important middlemen in the legitimate diamond trade. Licensed by the Sierra Leone government, they're the first purchasers along a lengthy chain of buyers that ends with consumers in developed countries shopping for tennis bracelets. Out here, amid the sweltering heat and the potential of renewed RUF gunfire, he buys and sells diamonds that will be cherished as keepsakes forever by people whose only experience with such treacherous environments is gleaned from rare three-minute reports on CNN.

Like Fawaz, the majority of such dealers are Lebanese whose parents and grandparents moved to West Africa by the thousands in the wake of World War II to sell consumer goods and general merchandise. Some 120,000 Lebanese are estimated to live throughout West Africa, most of them in the import–export business.[4] When diamonds were discovered in Sierra Leone they were well positioned to enter the gem business, because soon after the war the country was thrown into its first significant bout of internal turmoil over the precious stones.

Until The Early 1950S, diamond production in Sierra Leone was dominated by one company, Sierra Leone Selection Trust (SLST), a branch of the London-based exploration company West African Selection Trust. The company had holdings in gold mines in Ghana and was owned by the South African diamond powerhouse, De Beers Consolidated Mines, Ltd. SLST was founded in Freetown in 1934, after De Beers's vanguard of miners had plucked more than 32,000 carats of stones from the Sierra Leone jungle by hand. The company convinced the government—which was still administered by England—to grant it an exclusive mining concession, meaning that all the diamonds found in the rain forest went to one company.

That was the theory at least. In truth, Sierra Leone provided a horrible mining environment. The deposits were located in the heart of an unexplored jungle, scattered among chieftaincies and villages that weren't used to the sight of white men digging for rocks. The tropical vegetation in the bush grows as thick as anywhere on earth, communications with Freetown were almost nonexistent, and travel into the provinces—often with heavy equipment and supplies—was a days-long endeavor from origin to destination. This harsh reality of jungle mining immediately raised concerns about security.

The diamond-bearing region was so extensive and dense with vegetation, wild animals, and villages that few SLST officers were optimistic about being able to control one of diamond mining's inherent costs of business: theft through illicit mining.

In fact, the problem was worse than anyone anticipated. At first, mining went smoothly and SLST built a then-modern processing facility in Yengema, a town in the Kono District. Labor was abundant as the locals took advantage of endless opportunities to mine rivers and wash gravel.

Things changed drastically in the wake of World War II, when Sierra Leoneans serving the British in the Royal West African Frontier Force returned from the battlefields of Burma, having learned the value of the innocuous stones that were being mined out from beneath the feet of villagers. It's not surprising what happened after tales of limitless fortunes began circulating through the bush:

Miners abandoned their jobs and became independent operators. They were also illegal operators, since only SLST had the right to mine for diamonds in Sierra Leone.

But that hardly mattered. In the postwar years, Sierra Leone saw a massive diamond rush as thousands of locals and an equal number of neighboring Liberian and Guinean hopefuls struck out into SLST's private reserve of diamond mines. The boom very nearly sank the country in the mid-1950s as farmers ignored their fields and instead washed gravel day in and day out, usually under the cover of night when they were less likely to be discovered. A food shortage struck the interior and, for the first time, Sierra Leone had to import staples like rice, a grain that was usually so abundant that the country normally exported it. More than an estimated 30,000 illegal miners were operating in 1954, a human tide that was almost impossible to stem.[5] Many of these miners were supported by wealthy Lebanese financiers, most of whom had moved to Free-town in the wake of the war to sell general merchandise. Their business clout and expertise, their possession of import/export licenses, and their ties to supplies in Freetown made them natural partners for the men toiling in the bush.

19

The Sierra Leone Army, a 1,300-strong force of soldiers whose general duties consisted of little more than guarding their own barracks in Freetown, was dispatched to the Kono District to provide security for SLST, which began to form its own militias, often from the ranks of the local police forces. Violent clashes between miners and these militias became regular events, but even the threat of gun battles didn't slow the illicit trade; the returns provided by illegal mining far outweighed the risks.

The majority of stones were smuggled out of the country. By 1955, it became obvious that there was no way SLST—even with the help of the army and a growing paramilitary police force— could control the smuggling situation. SLST and the government eventually dissolved the single-concession agreement and implemented an aggressive licensing program for indigenous diggers. But even with the dissolution of SLST's private concession and new laws allowing independent operators to sell their goods in Sierra Leone, most miners had already developed contacts outside the country, which also allowed them to avoid export taxes.

With the help of Saika Stevens, the minister of mines for Sierra Leone's government-elect, De Beers instituted the Diamond Corporation of Sierra Leone (DCSL), a company that would buy diamonds from those who were at the time "stealing" them from SLST and selling them in Monrovia, the nearby capital of neigh-boring Liberia. In turn, DCSL would transport the diamonds to the Diamond Trading Company (DTC) in London, another De Beers concern, which was part of the Central Selling Organization (CSO), the global diamond funnel established by De Beers in the 1930s. At the time, the CSO sold 80 percent of the world's diamonds to the retail marketplace.

For the scheme to work, however, De Beers had to buy the diamonds in the bush in order to compete directly with the illicit traffickers. In real terms, what this meant was that some brave soul— who would have to be an expert in evaluating diamonds—would have to leave the comfort and safety of a downtown office and set off into the heart of an unmapped jungle with a backpack crammed with cash. At the diamond mines and in countless villages he would then compete with savvy local middlemen and smugglers who likely wouldn't be too inclined to share their lucrative turf with the legitimate diamond cartel.

In the beginning, things didn't work out too well. The handful of London buyers who agreed to this risky assignment were up against hundreds of traffickers who outbid them for the diamonds in order to keep a loyal customer base among the diggers. The DCSL buyers were also constrained by rates dictated from London. It took five years and the creation of a new government office before the diamond buyers were able to offer rates similar to those offered in Monrovia. Although illicit sales of diamonds were never halted, by 1960 the estimated loss to the illicit market fell to its lowest point since the diamond rush began.

The job of buying diamonds in the bush fell almost exclusively to the Lebanese traders once the system worked through all of its initial kinks. They were revered in diamond offices in Freetown. "After all, they accomplished the most dangerous part of the buyer's mission, for the idea of walking through the forest carrying large sums of cash appealed to no one," writes Jacques Legrand in *Diamonds: Myth, Magic, and Reality.* "All things considered, the profits made by the Lebanese were commensurate with the work they performed and an equilibrium was established to everyone's satisfaction."[6]

Diamonds only added to the increasing political tension of pre-independence Sierra Leone. Those who would be charged with assuming the mantle of government from the British in 1961 faced both an economic windfall as well as a witch's brew of serious political and economic issues that would challenge any well-seasoned government. Sierra Leoneans, with the oversight of a British administration, had experienced no success in harnessing the country's most valuable natural resource, as the diamond boom of the 1950s had shown. More diamonds were smuggled away than were exported, robbing the country of taxes and contracts that could have been used to build roads, utilities, and medical and educational facilities. Control of the diamond fields would require an incredibly delicate and astute, yet forceful and uncompromising government. The head of state would have to adopt strict border policies with Liberia, modernize export laws, and establish creative trade and labor agreements with diamond exploration companies. The entire monetary system should probably have been overhauled prior to independence. One of the reasons smugglers went to Monrovia was because Liberia's dollar was fixed to the value of the U.S. dollar until 1997, making it the equivalent of hard currency. The much softer currency of Sierra Leone was good only in Sierra Leone.

None of these measures was taken, however, and the smuggling did not stop once Sierra Leone was granted independence on April 27, 1961. Maintaining the diamond infrastructure was left to the Lebanese traders in towns like Kenema and Bo, and they had organized it in the first place to address the needs of smugglers.

The system employed by people like Fawaz is simple and dates back to the early diamond-rush days of the 1950s. Individual miners obtain a license from the government to dig on a certain plot of land or riverbank. Since the license is extremely expensive to the average would-be miner—who also needs to pay off the inevitable series of bribes—he often needs to find a sponsor, usually a Lebanese merchant. The merchant provides shovels, gasoline-powered water pumps, sieves, food, and pay for the miner's hired diggers. In exchange, the diamonds are sold to the merchant, minus the overhead. Fawaz himself, though he works in one of Africa's most valuable diamondiferous regions

and is a conduit for what is eventually hundreds of thousands of dollars worth of gemstones, has never even visited a mine.

When war broke out in 1991, the system was so well established—and the profits so lucrative—that many Lebanese abandoned their businesses only under the most threatening circumstances. Even at the height of the RUF conflict, with the sounds of rocket blasts echoing off Kenema's high hills, many merchants continued to man their offices and buy stones from the rebels. Official diamond exports from Sierra Leone practically ceased in the mid-1990s—whereas 2 million carats per year were exported in the 1960s, a paltry 9,000 carats were exported in 1999—but the old smuggling routes to Monrovia were still open for business.

And there was certainly no lack of buyers. Everyone from legitimate brokers employed by Belgian cutting houses to agents of the Iranian-backed Lebanese terrorist organization Hezbollah crowded the streets and hotels of Monrovia, eager for the chance to buy diamonds from the RUF. Monrovia was a no-man's-land of freewheeling dealing in diamonds that had been soaked in the blood of innocent Sierra Leoneans. For the legitimate brokers, it meant cheap goods and high profits; for the terrorists, it presented a picture-perfect opportunity to launder vast amounts of money undetected, an important development in the role diamonds would come to play in international terrorism in the beginning of the new century.

Midwestern Rivers and the Population Center of the United States

By David Carle and Janet Carle

→ in medias res...

Coal was not yet done with us as we entered eastern Kentucky. One of the worst coal industry disasters occurred on October 11, 2000, when a dam storing toxic slurry (on an MTR site operated by Massey Energy) gave way and sent 300 million gallons (twenty-five times the volume of the Exxon Valdez oil spill) of black goo downstream through the community of Inez (37°52′N). The sludge moved down Coldwater and Wolf Creeks to the Tug Fork, and some material reached the Ohio River. No human lives were lost, but the EPA called it "the largest environmental catastrophe in the history of the southeastern United States."

In Inez, residents were preparing for a Harvest Festival when we arrived. A young woman selling popcorn had been a high school cheerleader when the flood of coal waste came. "It was thick, black, and gooey," she remembered, "so solid that thrown rocks bounced off of it. They brought in big vacuum machines to clean it up. Things are clean now, and they widened the creek in case it ever happens again." She finished that thought with a giggle. The idea of it happening again must be unnerving, yet the townsfolk remain.

Through West Virginia and across Kentucky and parts of Indiana and Illinois, we explored a slice of the vast Ohio River watershed: the New and Gauley Rivers, the Kentucky River, and the main course of the Ohio River en route to the Mississippi. Settlers, settlements, transport, pollution, and the rivers' inclinations to flood are all elements in this part of the story.

The look of the forested land changed as we moved westward through Kentucky to Fort Boonesborough State Park (37°56′N). There, beside the Kentucky River, a party of settlers led by Daniel Boone arrived on April 1, 1775. Seeing the advantages the river offered, they established Kentucky's second pioneer settlement. The riverside setting has changed since Boone's day thanks in part to locks built early in the century to facilitate barge travel.

Near Port Royal, Kentucky, we had lunch with author and poet Wendell Berry; his wife, Tanya; and their grown son, Dave, at their farm. The Kentucky River, visible from their house, is part of the special character of the property. "It lies within a hundred steps of my door," Wendell wrote in an essay titled "A Native Hill" (Berry, 2002, 3). Small streams on his property feed the river—which merges with the Ohio River just a few miles downstream—and water figures in many of Wendell's poems and essays. "The creation is musical," he wrote, "and this is part of its music, as birdsong is, or the words of poets. The music of the streams is the music of the shaping of the earth, by which the rocks are pushed and shifted downward toward the level of the sea" (2002, 19).

Wendell is tall and lanky with penetrating blue eyes. Tanya was warmly welcoming and is an excellent cook; she grew up in Mill Valley, California, another 38th-parallel location, and speculated that the similar angle of light might be something agreeably familiar about Port Royal. Wendell became

22

most animated as he drove us around the farm and through his "biscuit woods," containing a mix of black walnut, butternut, ash, and tulip poplar trees that provide good fuel for baking. It was wonderful to spend time with someone whose books and poems so eloquently explore the importance of place and home and sustainable farming.

Lexington bills itself as the "Horse Capital of the World" and, besides its famous horse stables and racetracks, houses the International Museum of the Horse (38°08′N). Although our primary interests along the 38th parallel ~~were~~ *Where* water and the environment, an intriguing horse theme had become evident. In China, there were the ancestors of the modern horse, the Przewalski's breed. Turkmenistan's Akhal-Teke horses are ancestors of the Arabian breed. Spain's Andalusian horses originated along our chosen latitude, and the Atlantic Coast of the United States had the island-dwelling Chincoteague ponies. Spanish mustangs run wild just east of our Mono Lake Basin home.

Certainly, different breeds of horses are associated with other latitudes, but a connection between 38°N and grazing animals of all types, including the cattle, yaks, sheep, and goats we encountered in parts of Asia and Europe, is more than coincidence. An article in the *Stockman Grass Farmer* advised ranchers who want to produce grass-fed beef to move close to the 38th parallel: "Almost all of the year-around grass finishing in the world occurs within 100 miles north and south of this degree of latitude. It is far enough North to grow cool-season perennials but far enough South to avoid long periods of deep snow" (Nation, 2010, 24). Latitude also affects temperature; cattle eat less in extreme heat. Holstein females, important as dairy cattle, weigh more when born and when mature above latitude 38°N in the United States. Daily maximum temperatures become limiting in warmer climates, so "at latitudes of less than 34°N in the United States and Caribbean, Holstein females weigh 6 to 10 percent less at birth … and average approximately 16 percent lower in weight at maturity … than in the northern latitudes" (National Research Council, 1981, 80).

At Louisville, the state's largest city (38°15′N), an interstate highway passes between the city and its Ohio River waterfront, blocking views and access. The freeway remains, but now a lush park, with sculptures and architecture that celebrate water, draws people under the freeway to reach the river's edge to view the bustling river traffic. The city of San Francisco went through a similar recovery of its bayshore waterfront after an earthquake made it feasible to move a badly located freeway.

Industrialization and urbanization along the Ohio River in each of the eight states drained by its 200,000-square-mile watershed have made it the most toxic river in the nation. As we saw at Chesapeake Bay, storm runoff from diverse sources is today's major challenge. Pollution from point sources such as factories was more successfully managed after the national Clean Water Act was passed in 1972, yet the Ohio River Foundation has become frustrated with lax enforcement in the past decade and has begun independent monitoring investigations to identify polluters and force compliance. That program is similar to the efforts of the NGO Green Camel Bell we saw in China. We were startled to realize that an independent organization was needed to audit and aid government enforcement in the United States, where "the political will to enforce water pollution laws has waned and is now further stressed by economic recession and shrinking government budgets," according to the foundation (Ohio River Foundation, 2012).

Out in the river, opposite Louisville, are the Falls of the Ohio, the only point between Pennsylvania and the Mississippi where boats once encountered dangerous rapids, until the Louisville and Portland Canal Company built locks and canals in 1830. The U.S. Army Corps of Engineers took over the operation in 1874 and enlarged the canals, then added a new dam in 1962. On the Indiana side of the river, one family has run Schimpff's Candy Store in Jeffersonville since the 1850s. Red marks painted on the outside of the storefront mark where the flood of 1937 reached, when the Ohio and Mississippi Rivers left their banks for more than a thousand miles. It was the worst natural disaster in the United States before Hurricane Katrina. Over eight hundred thousand people were displaced from flooded homes, and hundreds died.

A chilly morning brought our first view of the grand Mississippi River when we arrived at Grand Tower, Illinois (37°37'N). Looking for a place to warm up, we found the Mississippi River Museum, being used as an office by County Clerk Charles Burdick, who had navigated 12,350 miles of inland waterways as a riverboat pilot and captain. The Mississippi River runs from Minnesota to New Orleans, and its watershed extends across 41 percent of the continental United States. The big river is fed through major tributaries, like the Ohio and Missouri Rivers, and smaller ones that reach into thirty-one states, with connections to the Great Lakes and, via the Gulf Intracoastal Waterway, Texas.

Kaskaskia Island was visible on the far side of the Mississippi from Fort Kaskaskia, the only piece of Illinois *west* of the river (37°58'N). The land ended up on the wrong side after the Mississippi River changed course in an 1881 flood. "Kaskaskia, where the West began, Mother of 1,000 Cities, Paris of the West," was the first capital of the Illinois Territory and the capital of the state until 1820, but the flood washed away its physical connection to the rest of Illinois. Our visit to Kaskaskia found only quiet farm fields.

A highway bridge at Chester, Illinois, led us to the beautiful little French-flavored town of St. Genevieve, the oldest town in Missouri. A car ferry also crosses the river there, at *exactly* 38°. Of course, a ride over and back as walk-on passengers was irresistible. The Mississippi was a mile wide at that point and looked exceptionally swift and powerful from a small ferryboat chugging across its surface.

"I'm out planting a forest. Please leave your name and number, and I'll try to get back to you before it matures." That is the answering machine message heard in the opening scene of a video produced by the Pioneer Forest about its founder, Leo Drey.

Wendell Berry had suggested we visit the forest to learn about its half-century-long experiment in sustainable forestry near Salem, Missouri (37°34'N). Forest manager Terry Cunningham and two other foresters told us about the unique program. The vision started with Drey, who began purchasing land in 1954; the total eventually reached 150,000 acres, most from a distillery company that had used the oak wood for barrels. It became the largest private landholding in Missouri and remains open for public use. Drey aimed to demonstrate methods of sustainable logging, without going broke in the process.

The Pioneer Forest follows a long-term cycle of single-tree harvesting that minimizes erosion and runoff on the watershed, makes for an aesthetically pleasing forest with trees of different ages, and improves reproduction and overall health of the trees. The best trees are left in place, instead of the worst, and the forest ecosystem remains relatively undisturbed. This approach contrasts with clear-cutting, favored by the Forest Service in such mixed hardwood forests despite the increased risk of erosion and of regrowth that creates thickets that must be aggressively thinned. An aerial photograph of part of the Pioneer Forest revealed widely spaced stumps within an otherwise untouched canopy of large trees.

Reducing the soil disturbance caused by clearcutting minimizes watershed impact, and that is one of the Pioneer Forest's chief contributions. The forest staff share their system with other private forest landowners, and also hope to influence policies along the Current River in the Ozark National Riverways Park, which borders the Pioneer Forest. Part of the National Park System, Ozark National Riverways controls only a narrow quarter-mile strip of shoreline along the riverbank. All-terrain vehicles driven into the river and across its banks create erosion. The Pioneer Forest staff would prefer management more in line with standard National Park Service resource protection, which bans destructive activities.

In nearby Edgar Springs, Missouri, we located an intriguing geographic landmark. Each national census identifies the nation's "mean center of population," a rather strange statistic that calculates the point at which an imaginary rigid, flat map would balance if all residents of the nation were of identical weight. When Alaska and Hawaii became states in 1960, the center point moved about two miles farther south and ten miles farther west. For the past several decades, the point has hovered around

24

the 38th parallel, gradually shifting westward and southward. The 2000 Census placed it 2.8 miles east of Edgar Springs, a tiny town in central Missouri (37°41′N; 91°48′W). The town's distinction was noted on a highway sign, but we went into town to see what else might be found.

The lady at the general store said she thought there was a stone marker at the north end of town with information about the designation, but added, "I never go that way." We found the marker outside the gates of a cemetery, where other stones told another local population story. (The 2010 Census has since documented a continued southwest drift: new "population center" markers will be needed near Plato, Missouri, at 37°30′N.)

More than 80 years ago, during the first years of the Great Depression, a dam was built on Missouri's Osage River by the Union Electric Company to create the Lake of the Ozarks (38°12′N). Once the reservoir was completed in 1931, water extended 180 miles upstream from the dam, with 1,100 miles of coastline, making it the largest man-made lake in the nation. That intricate shoreline reflects the complexity of the Ozark Mountains in Missouri, where the Osage River meanders across the western half of the state. Another major dam was later added upriver, backing water into Harry S. Truman Reservoir. Before all of this dam building, the Osage River had been followed by traders and settlers coming west from St. Louis to Independence, Missouri, to begin traveling the Santa Fe Trail.

Much of that historic route also coincided with the 38th parallel, and with our path westward after the oak woodlands of the Ozarks gave way to prairie on the plains of eastern Kansas.

4

Disappearing Forests
Actions to Save the World's Trees

By Rick Docksai

Halting deforestation will require the cooperation and coordination of the world's governments, businesses, and civil society. Networks of activists are now slowing the destruction of forest areas, promoting sustainable farming and ranching practices, and restoring forest cover wherever possible. These efforts will not only benefit both human and forest well-being, but also help mitigate climate change.

As the effects of climate change are felt across the globe, Earth-conscious innovators pursue a list of technological wonders to offset our species' carbon footprint: geoengineering, alternative energy, hybrid vehicles, etc. Each techno-fix shows some potential for success, and each might have a role to play in years to come.

But let's not forget one design feat that is fully within our means to deploy here and now: more trees.

The efforts of governments, businesses, and nonprofit organizations everywhere have begun to curb deforestation and bring some hitherto-destroyed forest areas back to life. As their efforts gain ground—and they can, with more support from citizens and communities worldwide—those trees will naturally reduce atmospheric carbon and boost both the planet's health and ours.

GLOBAL FOREST HEALTH TODAY

Brazil hit a milestone in 2012: Forest loss that year, at 4,500 square kilometers, was the lowest since 1988—and a steep drop-off from the 27,000 square kilometers of forest cover that the country lost in 2004.

Depletion of the Amazon's forest cover had been widespread in the twentieth century as Brazil developed economically: The cleared forests made way for logging, cattle ranching, and farming of cash crops such as soybeans. Then, starting in the late 1980s, the government initiated measures to halt deforestation; more recently, it committed to bringing deforestation down to less than a fifth of the 2004 level by 2020. As of 2013, it is almost 80% there.

Conservationists keep pushing for the forests' viability over the long term. Deforestation continues, even if it is drastically reduced and no longer has the tacit acceptance of government and business leaders.

"The situation is not stable yet. We have to consider we have a lot of achievements and good

Figure 4.1. Swaths of rain forest in Brazil's Panatanal region have been cut for farmland.

results, but we still have high rates of deforestation," says Luis Fernando Guedes Pinto, certification manager for IMA-FLORA, a Brazilian environmental conservation nonprofit that partners with the Rainforest Alliance. "We still need many interventions that can lead to improvements in farming and forest management."

Concerns over Brazil's Amazon rain forests, which shrank by about 18% in the last century due to deforestation, have been growing steadily in Brazil and worldwide: The Amazon is home to between one-third and one-half of the world's remaining tropical forest land.

Another large share of world rain-forest cover lies in Africa. Unfortunately it is in even more trouble. Impoverished African families and communities struggle to scratch out livelihoods from the land, as they have for generations, by foraging for wood to use as fuel and by clearing forests to make way for small-scale farming.

While Africans' efforts to survive are indisputably justified, the toll on the continent's natural resources is steep: Forests in Africa are being cleared nearly three times faster than the global average, according to the Forest Philanthropy Action Network (FPAN). Ghana and Nigeria each have only around 5% of the forest cover that they

Figure 4.2. Forests that disappear can sometimes be brought back, through community tree plantings, or "reforestation" efforts. This Thai villager has just planted a new mangrove tree in a forest in Satun, Thailand.

had 75 years ago. Particularly severe deforestation is also taking place in Liberia, Kenya, Uganda, and areas of Cameroon, Sudan, and Ethiopia.

FPAN names small-scale agriculture as a principal contributing cause. Fuel needs are another cause, since communities comb their neighboring forests for wood chips and branches that they can feed to their wood-burning stoves. According to the UN's Food and Agriculture Organization, fuel accounts for about 80% of the wood that African consumers use every year.

Worldwide, 32 million acres of forests—an area almost the size of Nicaragua—are cleared each year. This is an improvement over the rates of two decades ago: The net rate for global deforestation totaled 0.14% from 2005 to 2010, versus 0.20% from 1990 to 2000. Moreover, domestic forest acreage either held steady or grew during the 2005-2010 time frame in 80 countries, including China, Costa Rica, India, the Philippines, Russia, the United States, and Uruguay.

Nevertheless, reduced global deforestation is *still* deforestation. While the world's forests are shrinking more slowly, they are shrinking. And as they do, the Earth's capacity for capturing and storing planet-warming carbon dioxide shrinks along with it. At the present rates, deforestation accounts for 10%–15% of global greenhouse gas emissions, according to FPAN, since every tree, when chopped, releases its store of carbon dioxide.

As a comparison, guess how much carbon-dioxide generation traceable to human activity comes just from automobile traffic. According to the World Resources Institute, it's around 15%.

CERTIFYING FOREST-FRIENDLY FARM PRACTICES

Examples of remediation efforts are all around us. Governments, businesses, and nonprofit groups are teaming up to stop the human activities that are contributing to forest destruction and to bring back lost forest cover wherever possible. It is doable, but it takes a concerted effort, constant commitment by all to keep improving the methods and results.

27

"If we just stop here and make everything 'sustainable at today's levels,' that's not really sustainable. We need to think differently. Simply just being a bit more sustainable than we are now, I don't think is going to cut it," said Ian Cheshire, director of Kingfisher, a home- improvement retail company. Cheshire spoke during the May 15, 2013, workshop "Greenovation: How the Certification and Sustainability Sectors Are Reinventing the Future of Their Industries," which was convened in New York City by the nonprofit Rainforest Alliance. Kingfisher is one of the millions of companies, farms, and ranches to whom the Rainforest Alliance has been administering training, certification, and continuing oversight and support in making their business practices as environmentally friendly as possible.

The Rainforest Alliance formed in the late 1980s, when global awareness of the plight of tropical forests was on the rise. Bucking the stereotype of environmental activism locked in a war of wills against business interests, the organization was an early proponent of "smart wood"—i.e., procuring timber at moderate rates and with due concern for the forests' health—and market-driven forestry certification, by which businesses could choose to learn environmentally healthy prac-tices and receive recognition when they make those practices standard throughout their operations.

The Rainforest Alliance works with the Sustainability Action Network (SAN), an organization whose activities include the development of standards of sustainable farming and ranching. The Alliance teaches these standards to participating farmers and ranchers and then follows up with them to make sure that they are making progress on their farms and ranches toward meeting the standards. Those who do meet the standards are officially "certified" and get to post a Rainforest Alliance seal of approval on their products' packaging.

"The whole point of certification is to give people directions or goals and to ensure that they're moving in those directions, and to use the certifications to communicate to the world that they're continuing to improve," says Karen Lewotsky, manager of sustainable agriculture at the Rainforest Alliance.

The Alliance has worked with more than 11 million producers since its founding. As of March 2013, it has certified 174 million acres worldwide—added up, a land mass almost the size of Chile. Rainforest Alliance–certified farms now produce 10.2% of the world's cocoa, 11.2% of its tea, and 15% of its bananas. Its share of the world's coffee is smaller, at 4.6%, but the potential for growth is certainly there, given growing publicity. Kenco, Kraft, and McDonald's all served Rainforest Alliance—certified coffee at the 2012 Olympic Games in London.

The standards include dozens of individual rules that cover the full range of environmental and human health, including requiring crop rotation, restrictive pesticide and fertilizer usage, the maintenance of minimum distances between crops, and the construction of protective barriers along neighboring rivers and other waterways. There are also guidelines for humane treatment of the farm animals and adequate pay, benefits, and labor conditions for all farm workers.

The standards additionally include a stipulation that the farmers and ranchers set aside portions of their land as protected reserves on which no development will take place. As of 2013, certified farms and ranches across the globe have designated 28 million acres of land as protected reserves.

Certification also requires certain quantities of crops to be grown under the shade of trees. The bar is higher for coffee and cocoa farmers, who must keep at least 40% of their crops under the shade of forest cover. This rule isn't in place just so that there will be more trees. Shade-grown coffee and cocoa plants require less water and fertilizer, in addition to producing more stable yields year-to-year. Also, the trees' roots act as a buffer protecting waterways from harmful runoff and land erosion. The soil and any accompanying manure and agrochemicals cling to the roots instead of washing into nearby lakes and streams. The water ecosystems and, of course, the forests that feed off of them are all healthier as a result.

HOW HEALTHIER FORESTS IMPROVE AGRICULTURE

These forest-cover stipulations make economic as well as environmental sense. The coffee and cocoa farmers attest that the shade cover improves the flavor of their coffee crops. Since enough consumers seem to agree, the certified farmers earn a premium for their shaded coffee once it sells.

The certification standards raise productivity, too: In Côte d'Ivoire, home to 40% of the world's cocoa supply, certified cocoa farms grow 508 pounds of cocoa per acre, compared with an average of 294 on the noncertified farms. Financial gains from certification extend to numerous other crops, as well. Overall, Ivoirians whose farms are certified are earning $161 per acre, compared with $45 per acre for noncertified farms.

In March 2012, the Fazendas São Marcelo Ltda. chain of ranches in Brazil became the first-ever beef producers to gain Rainforest Alliance certification. The chain's four ranches, located in the Mato Grosso state of western Brazil and holding 60,000 cattle on 79,000 acres of farmland, has 32,000 acres of rainforest land set aside as a buffer zone between the pastures and the forests. As a bonus to the environment, that reserve is also a popular shelter area for migrating birds and other wildlife.

The cows get a natural feed that reduces methane emissions—no small perk, given that livestock are the source of 18% of the world's greenhouse-gas emissions, according to the Rainforest Alliance. And their pastures are dotted with groves of trees, which give the cows shade cover from heat, wind, and rain. The green cover compensates for some of the forest land that the ranchers initially had to clear. It also makes the cows happier and healthier. Cows enjoy shade on hot days just as people do, explains Lewotsky. That makes a difference in overall cattle growth and the quality of the beef.

Building embankments along the waterways is yet another sustainable practice that the ranches have put in place. The ranchers plant trees near the shores to hold off erosion, and they build rock paths near the water along which the cows may walk. As Lewotsky points out, the rock paths prevent the cows from plodding around in the mud and inadvertently dislodging more of its dirt (and their own manure) into the adjacent water.

In the year since the Fazendas group attained its certification, the Rainforest Alliance and partner nonprofits have been disseminating these same sustainable ranching methods to other cattle growers far and wide. Thus, more ranches elsewhere have also attained certification. And in March 2013,

Figure 4.3. A coffee farmer on a Rainforest Alliance– certified farm in Vietnam's Central Highlands region weeds by hand instead of using potentially harmful herbicides, and then uses the organic material he gathers for a compost pile.

Figure 4.4. Cattle graze amid overhead trees, whose shade cover makes the cows more comfortable and benefits the surrounding ecosystem.

Gucci unveiled a new line of bags, all made using leather from Rainforest Alliance–certified ranches.

SUSTAINABILITY SELLS

That McDonald's, Kraft, and Gucci would all go through the trouble of adding certified-sustainable products to their inventories really isn't a surprise. Demand for environmentally friendly products is growing among the world's consumers. If a product is verifiably green, then a large number of potential buyers will choose it over a competitor product that isn't, all other factors being equal.

A 2012 poll from Harris Interactive found that 79% of Americans actively search for green products, and 31% say they would pay extra for products that were more environmentally sustainable than other products (versus 28% who said so in 2010). The number is higher, 45%, among 18- to 24-year-olds. A full quarter of U.S. adults in the survey identified environmental issues as "extremely" important.

"Ultimately there is a certain level of profitability, and you've got buyers all over the world who are concerned about this," says Lewotsky. "Buyers want that reassurance. They're going into the store and saying 'What am I willing to pay for?'"

This same environmental awareness is likewise gaining traction among companies' shareholders, who are becoming more likely to expect business operations to live up to standards of sustainability. Thus, the producers feel an incentive from above to replace environmentally harmful practices with more benign ones, and the retailers come under pressure to line their store shelves with green products.

"There is an expectation. You look at almost any large organization these days you're going to come across some sort of sustainability manager. They're looking at how to increase sustainability in the company," Lewotsky says. "That's something people will seek out and will talk about. And you can do it at a lot of different places in the supply chain."

The process requires multiple levels of buy-in, however.

"Certification is a great vehicle for bringing some of the messages across. But unless all of the stakeholders, particularly the government and industry, get together and get this done, we will only make a small dent on the issue of sustainability, unfortunately," according to Daudi Lelijveld, vice president of sustainability at the Alliance-certified cocoa grower Barry Callebaut, which runs numerous sustainable cocoa farms in Côte d'Ivoire.

Brazil is arguably a great test case in what can happen when stakeholders from many sectors work together. Starting in the 1980s, Brazil-ian government leaders were well aware of the slow death that the Amazon was suffering from human activity. The officials went to work cordoning off swaths of rain forest as national parks and enacting new legal curbs on forest destruction.

In the last few years, the government has utilized satellite technology to step up these protective measures. Brazil's space agency deployed satellites to gather data on forest cover all across the country, and the national environmental agency studied the satellite photos to spot signs of troubled areas and or-ganize teams of on-the-ground monitors to visit the sites.

"Brazil has had an outstanding space program for three decades, and so they're using that technology to better monitor deforestation throughout the region," says Gary Hartshorn, president and CEO of the World Forestry Center.

Government officials have seized 2,000 square meters of illegally cut timber in the past year alone. The confiscated wood gets sold at auctions, with the proceeds directed to environmental conservation programs. Meanwhile, IMAFLORA and other nonprofit groups have been teaching communities about the benefits of forest conservation and methods that the communities can employ to farm the land more sustainably.

In meeting the nation's goal of slowing deforestation, Brazilian leaders credit the combined efforts of public—private monitoring and corrective action with making a big difference in a relatively short time frame.

Businesses Helping Businesses Be More Sustainable

The tea company Tetley latched onto sustainable growing and manufacturing in the early 1990s, and by the middle of the decade it had instituted resource-saving and ecosystem-preserving measures within every step of its supply chain. Its leadership then decided to help other businesses to do the same. So it reached out to the multinational Unilever with a proposal that the two companies collaborate to monitor each other's supply chains. Unilever agreed and, in 1997, co-founded with Tetley the Ethical Tea Partnership.

The initiative now has 50 tea makers under its umbrella. Each one commits to having teams of monitors regularly visit its tea plantations to ensure that the la-borers work under fair labor conditions and that standards for water use, energy consumption, chemical usage, waste management, ecosystem conservation, and other environmental indicators are all adequate.

It's not often that one hears of a business helping another business to improve its production methods, especially when both businesses are competitors—Unilever's product line includes tea and other beverages. But Tetley's leadership was willing to think beyond sheer competitive advantage, and the whole industry is arguably better for it.

Tetley merged with Tata in 2000, and so its operations are now within the Rainforest Alliance network of certified businesses. Plenty of other businesses within this network share the Tetley executives' belief in the value of helping other businesses, even rival businesses, on sustainability. Kingfisher, for example, is leading open-source dialogues with other companies on developing performance indicators and recommendations for businesses to improve their impacts on the environment. It will disseminate the finalized methods over the next few years.

"We cannot rely on the consumer to lead the change. It's up to us to try and make a difference. It's up to us to learn from each other," said Chris Coates, director of sales for IndoTeak Design, a Rainforest Alliance-certified maker of teak wood products, during the May 2013 Greenovation workshop.

—Rick Docksai

MEETING AFRICA'S WOOD DEMANDS

Communities throughout Africa value their forests, but they also need to survive. Lack of infrastructure and lack of money leave too many Africans having to choose between either chopping down trees and overhunting, or not having food and fuel. If they and the rest of the world community want to save Afri-ca's forests, then economic improvement will have to take place, Harts-horn says.

"Not knowing where the next meal is coming from, it's understandable they might be running snares or hunting for bush meat," he says. "It's pretty fundamental that you have socioeconomic develop-ment that allows people to think about tomorrow and not just about today."

Africa's forests face continued assaults from log-ging and the collection of wood for fuel. But FPAN sees great potential for relief from another form of sustainable industry: wood plantations. The plant-ers maintain set plots of trees that they replenish with new seedlings continuously, ensuring steady incomes for themselves and consistent supplies of wood for the local markets.

Plantations produce substantially more wood per acre than do natural forests. Domestic timber plantations are a sizable industry in certain parts of the tropics, though there are relatively few in Africa. FPAN projects that Africa could establish enough domestic timber plantations to supply wood fuels to all Africans who needed them, and that the amount of required land would be a mere

Figure 4.5. At this tree plantation, young saplings are raised in rows within protective netting. Once they mature, they will replace the trees that loggers have previously cut.

20% of the total square mileage of forests that are now being exploited.

Helping African households obtain fuel-efficient stoves would be another huge improvement, according to FPAN. The organization estimates that, if Kenya's 6 million rural households were out-fitted with fuel-efficient stoves, the country's annual fuel wood consumption would be reduced by 50%. This would translate to 8.4 million fewer tons of carbon dioxide being released into the atmosphere per year.

Here, too, government cooperation with nonprofits can help, in this case for guiding the placement of new plantations and enacting incentives to spur consumer demand. Bernard Mercer, co-founder of FPAN, favors more plantations established close to urban centers and govern-mental subsidies to incentivize buying wood from plantations.

Most of Africa's governments are considerably weaker and more cash-poor than their counter-parts in other parts of the globe, he notes. So private donors should consider offering financial support to help cover such subsidies, expand the distribu-tion systems for fuels, and, in addition, help shore up individual republics' struggling environmental protection agencies.

World government leaders who want to help, meanwhile, might consider Reducing Emissions from Deforestation and Forest Degradation (REDD) agreements: i.e., paying developing countries not to clear their threatened forests. The receiving coun-tries use the money for creating forest reserves, pro-moting land conservation within the communities that live on forested land, enacting and enforcing limits on logging, and restoring forest cover.

The World Bank oversees several REDD pro-grams, while the UN's REDD Programme, founded in 2008, now provides funds to the forest-conservation programs of 16 partner countries, including Bolivia, the Democratic Republic of the Congo, Indonesia, the Philippines, Tanzania, and Zambia. UN del-egates from rain forest nations had been arguing for including REDD in climate-change-reduction initiatives precisely because of deforestation's role in raising greenhouse-gas emissions. FPAN agrees and hopes to see REDD put in place in every country throughout Africa.

But REDD programs are far from perfect. First, solid data on the partner countries' present defor-estation and their conservation efforts are sparse. It is an open debate as to how much good REDD programs have achieved for the targeted forest regions so far.

Additionally, many African countries that are not yet REDD program partners might have great difficulty qualifying, due to inadequate governance, underdeveloped infrastructure, and poor public-sector and private-sector transparency. Also, there is too little data on forest degradation—i.e., forest environments not necessarily cleared in full, but critically damaged from being stripped of wood for fuel or due to wildlife populations being depleted by poachers, for instance.

According to Mercer, a REDD program will be more effective when there are private-sector initiatives developing profitable REDD projects. Cap-and-trade mechanisms that would let busi-nesses purchase and sell "forest-carbon credits" is one solution that Mercer strongly supports. In a 2011 interview with environmental news service

MongaBay.com, he said that the enactment of an international forest-carbon-credit law would be "the best news for African governments." He pointed out that a number of philanthropists and foundations are encouraging the admission of forest-carbon credits into the European Union's Emissions Trading Scheme.

ECONOMIC GROWTH VERSUS FOREST GROWTH

The lands that constitute present-day Costa Rica were solid forest when Columbus and his men set foot in the region in the 1490s. By 1987, slash-and-burn farming and ranching had left forests covering a mere 23% of the country, but forest cover rebounded to 57% of Costa Rica by 2007.

What happened in that short 20-year span to bring so much forest acreage back so quickly? World Forestry Center's Hartshorn credits many factors, including aggressive conservation measures and the imposition of gasoline taxes to pay for land restoration. But he gives one factor ultimate importance: a growing economy.

New jobs opened up in industries such as software, as multinationals like Intel set up new facilities in the country. Ecotourism also offered young people satisfying new careers that promoted the forests to the outside world instead of draining it of its resources. As a result, progressively more Costa Ricans found livelihoods in occupations other than farming, and consequently there were declining numbers of farmers seeking land for crops and herds in the first place.

"There has been a lot of abandonment of pasture lands," Hartshorn says.

Industrial growth is typically not a trend that environmental activists presume to be a boon for the environment. That is understandable, since any industry can harm ecosystems if its operators go about it in the wrong way. But consider the ecological situation of Europe, North America, and other comparatively affluent parts of the world with the beleaguered forests of Africa. Those countries that are wealthier have cleaner air and water, healthier forests, and much larger swaths of protected land than their less-affluent counterparts, for the simple reason that with greater economic wealth comes more funding that can go toward conservation. Additionally, there are many more job opportunities in sectors

---

FOR MORE INFORMATION

Organizations:

World Forestry Center, www.worldforestry.org
Rainforest Alliance, www.rainforest-alliance.org
World Resources Institute, www.wri.org
Forests Philanthropy Action Network, www.forest-snetwork.org/

Publications:

"State of the World's Forests 2012." Food and Agriculture Organization of the United Nations. 2012.
"About the UN-REDD Programme." UN-REDD Programme. 2009 Moukkadem, Karimeh. "How Do We Save Africa's Forests?"
MongaBay.com. June 19, 2011.

that do not require felling trees to make way for subsistence-level farming.

FOREST CONSERVATION IN A HUNGRY GROWING WORLD

The world community now understands the unique value of forests more than ever, and it is doing more than ever to make sure that healthy forests will stay with us forever. But the room for improvement is still vast, while the window of time for achieving it is drawing to a close.

Today, 387.5 million acres of the planet's forests are now safely under sustainable management. If the world community committed itself to it, we could restore another 3.7 billion acres of hitherto-destroyed or degraded forest land, according to the International Union for the Conservation of Nature. But the planet continues to lose 35.8 million acres of forests each year.

Human activity still encroaches on forests, and the near future bears troubling trends: Demand for beef is soaring, especially in China, India, and other emerging economies, adding to the pressure to clear more forest land for cattle.

Add to this the compound problem of climate change, which not only threatens forests directly, but also compromises farmers' crop yields, inducing them to possibly destroy more forest land to make way for more crops. The end result is more climate change: Trees sequester huge volumes of carbon dioxide when alive and release it when cut. So a vicious cycle will likely persist, progressively lowering both human and environmental health as it continues.

Forest cover is one of our surest defenses against further global warming, and one of the simplest ones to deploy. There is no technological innovating required to plant an acre of trees. The means have been with us for millennia, and the costs and risks are immensely less than constructing new arrays of solar panels or wind turbines or pursuing geoengineering schemes.

Alternative-energy systems will indisputably form a critical component in humanity's long-term progression toward sustainable living. It's possible that some geoengineering ventures will also play a role. But the consensus among sustainability-minded activists, entrepreneurs, scholars, and public officials is increasingly clear: No long-term solution will be complete unless it includes protecting and expanding our forests.

34

5

The Dying Bear

Russia's Demographic Disaster

By Nicholas Eberstadt

December marks the 20th anniversary of the end of the Soviet dictatorship and the beginning of Russia's postcommunist transition. For Russians, the intervening years have been full of elation and promise but also unexpected trouble and disappointment. Perhaps of all the painful developments in Russian society since the Soviet collapse, the most surprising—and dismaying—is the country's demographic decline. Over the past two decades, Russia has been caught in the grip of a devastating and highly anomalous peacetime population crisis. The country's population has been shrinking, its mortality levels are nothing short of catastrophic, and its human resources appear to be dangerously eroding.

Indeed, the troubles caused by Russia's population trends—in health, education, family formation, and other spheres—represent a previously unprecedented phenomenon for an urbanized, literate society not at war. Such demographic problems are far outside the norm for both developed and less developed countries today; what is more, their causes are not entirely understood. There is also little evidence that Russia's political leadership has been able to enact policies that have any long-term hope of correcting this slide. This peacetime population crisis threatens Russia's economic outlook, its ambitions to modernize and develop, and quite possibly its security. In other words, Russia's demographic travails have terrible and outsized implications, both for those inside the country's borders and for those beyond. The humanitarian toll has already been immense, and the continuing economic cost threatens to be huge; no less important, Russia's demographic decline portends ominously for the external behavior of the Kremlin, which will have to confront a far less favorable power balance than it had been banking on.

TOO MUCH MORTALITY

Even in the Soviet years, Russia was less than a paragon of a healthy society. The syndrome of long-term stagnation and then decline in public health, never before seen in an industrialized country, first emerged during the Brezhnev era and continued to dog Russia until the downfall of the communist system. Still, in the late 1980s, the days of Mikhail Gorbachev's perestroika, Russian births exceeded deaths by an average of more than 800,000 per year. But the collapse of communism in Eastern Europe and then of the Soviet Union itself sent a series of demographic shocks reverberating across the Eastern bloc: virtually every former Warsaw Pact country experienced a sharp drop in births and a spike in deaths, as if beset by a sudden famine, epidemic, or war. Most of these perturbations were temporary—but not in Russia, where they proved to be more extreme and more enduring than in virtually any other former communist state.

Post-Soviet Russia has become a net mortality society, steadily registering more deaths than births. Since 1992, according to Rosstat, Russia's federal statistics agency (also known as Goskomstat since Soviet times), about 12.5 million more Russians have been buried than born—or nearly three funerals for every two live deliveries for the past 20 years. Globally, in the years since World War II, there has been only one more horrific surfeit of deaths over births: in China in 1959–61, as a result of Mao Zedong's catastrophic Great Leap Forward.

As a result of this imbalance, Russia has entered into a process of depopulation. Immigration, mainly from neighboring former Soviet states, has cushioned the fall somewhat but has not been able to prevent it. Since 1992, according to official Russian figures, Russia's population has fallen nearly every year (1993 and 2010 are the exceptions, with the latter experiencing an increase of just 10,000 people). According to these figures, between 1993 and 2010, Russia's population shrank from 148.6 million to 141.9 million people, a drop of nearly five percent. (Russia's 2010 census will eventually adjust the latter total upward by around one million people due to the undercounting of immigrants, but this does not change the overall picture.)

Russia is not alone in its population decline; this is a phenomenon that is increasingly common among modern societies, including affluent democratic ones. Three of the world's G7 states—Germany, Japan, and Italy—are at the cusp of sustained population decline or have already entered into it. Yet there is a fundamental difference between those countries and Russia: Germany, Japan, and Italy are confronting the prospect of population decline at a time of robust and steadily improving levels of public health. Russia, however, is suffering an extraordinary and seemingly unending mortality crisis, in which health conditions are deteriorating and are further fueling high death rates.

The overall magnitude of Russia's downward health spiral is catastrophic. According to estimates from the Human Mortality Database, a research consortium, overall life expectancy at birth in Russia was slightly lower in 2009 (the latest year for which figures are available) than in 1961, almost half a century earlier. The situation is even worse for Russia's adult population: in 2009, life expectancy at age 15

for all Russian adults was more than two years below its level in 1959; life expectancy for young men sank by almost four years over those two generations. Put another way, post-Soviet Russia has suffered a cumulative "excess mortality" of more than seven million deaths, meaning that if the country could have simply held on to its Gorbachev-era survival rates over the last two decades, seven million deaths could have been averted. This figure is more than three times the death toll World War I inflicted on imperial Russia.

By various measures, Russia's demographic indicators resemble those in many of the world's poorest and least developed societies. In 2009, overall life expectancy at age 15 was estimated to be lower in Russia than in Bangladesh, East Timor, Eritrea, Madagascar, Niger, and Yemen; even worse, Russia's adult male life expectancy was estimated to be lower than Sudan's, Rwanda's, and even aids-ravaged Botswana's. Although Russian women fare relatively better than Russian men, the mortality rate for Russian women of working age in 2009 was slightly higher than for working-age women in Bolivia, South America's poorest country; 20 years earlier, Russia's death rate for working-age women was 45 percent lower than Bolivia's.

IN SICKNESS AND IN POOR HEALTH

What explains Russia's gruesome deterioration? Although the country's problems with infectious diseases—most alarming, HIV/AIDS and drug-resistant tuberculosis—are well known, they account for only a small fraction of the awful gap between Western and Russian survival rates. Most immediately, the country's fateful leap backward in health and survival prospects is due to an explosion in deaths from cardiovascular disease and what epidemiologists call "external causes," such as poisoning, injury, suicide, homicide, traffic fatalities, and other violent accidents. Deaths from cardiovascular disease and injuries account for the overwhelming majority of Russia's spike in mortality levels and for nearly the entire gap separating Russia's mortality levels from those of Western countries. At the moment, death rates from cardiovascular disease are more than three times as high in Russia as in western Europe, and Russian death rates from injury and violence have been stratospheric, on par with those in African postconflict societies, such as Liberia and Sierra Leone.

Understanding why such death rates are so high in an urbanized and literate society during peacetime, however, is another question altogether. Russia's deadly romance with the vodka bottle certainly has something to do with it; smoking, diet, and poor preventive and curative health care surely exact their toll as well. According to the World Health Organization, as of 2004, daily smokers accounted for a higher fraction of the adult population in Russia—36 percent—than in any other country in Europe. Yet even given all these factors, Russia's health levels are worse and its death levels are higher than Western public health models would predict. The brute fact is that no one understands why Russians are as unhealthy as they are: it could very well be related

to attitudes, viewpoints, and attendant patterns of behavior that fall under the rubric of "mental health." Without delving into cultural or psychosocial speculation, however, suffice it to say that Russian lifestyles are extremely hazardous to one's health—and result in far higher mortality levels than would be expected of a country at such a relatively high income level.

Another cause of Russians' ill health may lie in education, and Russia's educational woes represent a human resource problem as well. On its face, education should be the saving grace of Russian social policy: after all, as many Russians, if not more, attain higher education as do citizens in many affluent Western countries. According to the Organization for Economic Cooperation and Development, the proportion of Russia's adult population with postsecondary training or degrees is higher than in almost any oecd country. And in the Soviet era, Russian scientists and inventors were renowned for their acumen (albeit mainly in fields with military applications).

38

Figure 5.1.

But today, Russia's educational system appears to be broken, or at least the country seems unable to derive the expected benefits from it. All around the world, high levels of education generally correspond with better public health, yet Russia bucks this trend: despite boasting a proportion of adults with a postsecondary education that is 30 percentage points higher than the OECD average, Russia nevertheless manages to achieve an overall adult life expectancy that is barely higher than Senegal's. Part of the problem is that although many Russians go to school, college, and university, that schooling is terribly subpar. Standardized international test results reveal that Russian primary and secondary schooling today is at best mediocre. In a 2009 OECD test to measure scholastic performance, Russian students' reading scores were lower than Turkish students', and Turkey itself is near the bottom of the OECD rankings.

Russia's university and higher education system looks even worse. Although Russia today accounts for about six percent of the world's population with a postsecondary education, barely 0.1 percent of the worldwide patents granted by the U.S. Patent and Trademark Office over the last decade and a half were awarded to Russians. This is not some U.S. conspiracy against Russian inventors: the records of the UN's World Intellectual Property Organization show that Russia's share of out-of-country patent applications over that same period was less than 0.2 percent of the global total. The picture is hardly better when it comes to the output of scientific papers: the number of articles by Russians in peer-reviewed journals was no higher in 2008 than it had been in 1990, whereas output almost everywhere else in the world rose over those same years. By 2008, Russian authors were publishing far fewer scientific papers than the authors of Russia's bric peers: Brazil, China, and India. In effect, Russia stands as a new and disturbing wonder in today's globalized world: a society characterized by high levels of schooling but low levels of health, knowledge, and education.

Family formation trends are a further cause for concern. Between 1987 and 1993, the number of births in Russia dropped precipitously, from 2.5 million to 1.4 million, and it ultimately fell to 1.2 million in 1999, before commencing a turnaround of sorts. In 2010, Russia celebrated 1.79 million births, the highest national total in 20 years. Even so, this total was 25 percent lower than a quarter century earlier and represented a pattern that, if continued, would average out to a long-term fertility level of just over 1.5 births per woman, which is 27 percent below the level required for long-term population stability. Unsurprisingly, there is much variation from this average among Russia's many ethnic groups and territories. Ethnic Russians have one of the country's lowest fertility rates, whereas Chechens appear to have the highest, with Chechnya reporting an average of 3.3 births per woman. (Chechnya is an anomaly even among Russia's Muslim-majority regions: most of them, including Chechnya's neighbors, Dagestan and Ingushetia, report sub-replacement fertility levels.)

Beyond birthrates, the way Russians form families and raise children has also undergone tremendous change over the past two decades, which raises questions about the human and economic potential of the country's rising generation. Marriages in today's Russia, for example, are less stable than marriages even in the Soviet era, when the country's divorce rates were already notoriously high. Russia has 56 divorces for every 100 marriages, an imperfect but telling indicator of long-term marriage prospects. Increasing family instability, of course, is a pervasive trend the world over, taking hold in nearly all of Europe and in many other affluent societies. But Russia's single parents must raise their children on far lower income levels than their counterparts in western Europe and North America. Unlike Europeans or Americans, they can count on little support from social welfare programs. Although Western economic theory would suggest that having fewer children means that parents can invest more in each child, the opposite seems to be happening in Russia: despite its steep drop in births, the country has seen small but ominous decreases in primary school enrollment ratios and alarming increases in child abandonment. According to official statistics, more than 400,000 Russian children below 18 years of age lived in residential care as of 2004, meaning that almost one child in 70 was

39

in a children's home, an orphanage, or a state-run boarding school. Russia is also home to a large and growing contingent of homeless children, which, according to some nongovernmental and charitable organizations, could very well exceed the number of youth under institutional care.

TOO LITTLE, TOO LATE

The Kremlin understands that Russia's adverse demographic patterns are so abnormal and dangerous that they require strong public policies to counteract them. Over the last several years, Moscow has introduced new and ambitious programs aimed at reversing the country's downward demographic spiral. In 2006, then President Vladimir Putin unveiled a program that promised up to $10,000 in credits and subsidies for mothers who had a second or third child. He also issued a decree endorsing a "Concept for Demographic Policy of the Russian Federation up to 2025," which called for Russia's population to stabilize at about 145 million people by 2025, with overall life expectancy at birth at 75 years (versus 67 then) and total fertility rates at 1.95, up 50 percent from the years before the plan was enacted. After 2015, according to the plan, births would exceed deaths in Russia. At the same time that the Kremlin is trying to increase births, it is also implementing new public health measures to drive death rates down, including measures that make alcohol more expensive and harder to purchase.

To judge by its public pronouncements, the Kremlin appears optimistic about its new measures. And indeed, since they have gone into effect, births have risen and death totals have come down; in fact, overall life expectancy in Russia in 2009 was almost 69 years, higher than for any year since the Soviet collapse. Yet such a seemingly positive prognosis flies in the face of some obvious and irreversible demographic realities. For starters, Russia's birth slump over the past two decades has left the country with many fewer potential mothers for the years ahead than the country has today. Women between 20 and 29 years of age bear nearly two-thirds of

Russia's babies. In 2025, Russia is projected to have just 6.4 million women in their 20s, 45 percent fewer than today—and there is relatively little mystery in these projections, given that all women who will be between 20 and 29 years in 2025 are already alive. Under such circumstances, simply maintaining current national birth totals would require heroic upsurges in maternity.

At the same time, Russia's population will be rapidly graying. Between 2011 and 2025, according to U.S. Census Bureau projections, the median age in Russia will rise by almost two days every week, from 38.7 years to 42.4 years. The Census Bureau also anticipates that Russians 65 and older, a cohort that now makes up 13 percent of the country's population, will compose almost 19 percent in 2025. As a result of aging alone, per capita mortality in Russia would rise by more than 20 percent if nothing else changed. And given the immense negative momentum in public health among the Russian population today, attaining any long-term improvements in life expectancy promises to be a formidable task. In order to return even to the working-age death rates of 1964, overall mortality levels for Russian men and women would have to drop by more than 25 percent. Such a reversal would be an impressive achievement to attain by 2025, but even if Russia managed this feat, its working-age mortality levels would be higher than those of Honduras today.

Given these realities, Russia is likely to remain a net mortality society for the foreseeable future. Official Russian statistics anticipate a continuing—and widening—gap separating deaths and births between now and 2030. Rosstat envisions a surfeit of 205,000 deaths over births for 2011, rising to more than 725,000 in 2030, with a cumulative total of 9.5 million more deaths than births between 2011 and 2030. Even in Rosstat's most optimistic scenario, the agency projects a mortality surfeit of 2.7 million between 2011 and 2025, reaching 4.7 million by 2030. In these official Russian forecasts, further depopulation can be forestalled only by massive immigration from abroad.

Russia has certainly benefited over the past two decades from a net influx of millions of workers, most of whom hail from former Soviet states in the Caucasus and Central Asia. (The Russian economy has also been helped by its own flow of émigrés overseas, who send billions of dollars of remittances home each year.) But the outlook for future immigration to Russia is clouded: changes in education policy throughout the former Soviet Union mean that today's immigrants from the Caucasus and Central Asia speak less Russian than their parents and thus have more difficulty integrating into Russian society. Meanwhile, the Russian public's attitude toward newcomers from those regions has grown less welcoming.

No less important is domestic migration, especially in terms of the vast expanse of Russia's Far East, a region of over two million square miles and barely six million inhabitants. One-sixth of the population of this harsh and forbidding territory has moved out since 1989, and the exodus continues. Many Russian analysts and policymakers are worried about what will become of this resource-rich area that adjoins a rising and densely populated China. Some Western scholars, such as Maria Repnikova of the University of Oxford and Harley Balzer of Georgetown University, see great and as yet unexploited opportunities for economic integration between the Russian Far East and its neighbors, especially China. Yet leading Russian demographers have a more dramatic vision: they fear that the region could cease to be part of Russia sometime in the current century, an outcome they see as carrying great geopolitical portent.

THE BEAR LASHES OUT?

Above all, Russia's current demographic patterns will have dreadful consequences for Russians' quality of life. Beyond the effect on individual well-being, the country's demographic decline will have grave implications for economic performance. Although Russia may be blessed with vast natural resources, human resources are what ultimately account for national wealth in today's global economy. Natural resources can augment affluence in societies already relatively rich in human capital, as Canada, the Netherlands, and Norway can attest, but they are no substitute for human capital. In modern times, there is not one example of a raw-materials superpower. And for all its energy riches, Russia earns less in export revenues each year than does Belgium. Although President Dmitry Medvedev warns that Russia must not remain a raw-materials economy and champions his modernization campaign, his administration has done little to position Russia as a knowledge-based economy.

Although the Russian government has acknowledged the country's poor demographic trends, it appears to have both grossly underestimated the severity of the crisis and overestimated the ability of current Kremlin policies to counteract whatever negative effects it thinks may be on the horizon. In 2008, just before the onset of the global economic crisis, the Kremlin unfurled an ambitious economic plan known as Russia 2020. It envisions Russia ascending into the ranks of the top five global economies by 2020 and sets as a goal an average annual economic growth rate of 6.6 percent between 2007 and 2020. Even though Russia's per capita output in 2010 was barely higher than it was in 2007, the Kremlin still embraces the Russia 2020 targets as feasible. But attaining those goals would now require an average growth in labor productivity of more than nine percent per year between 2010 and 2020. Such a tempo of long-term growth in labor productivity was not even reached by China between 1978 and the present day, the greatest period of long-term economic growth ever registered by any country in history.

Rather than focusing on catapulting the Russian economy into the top echelon of global performers, Russian policymakers would be wise to ask what it would take to prevent the Russian economy from shrinking as a share of total global output in the decades ahead. Between 2005 and 2025, according to U.S. Census Bureau projections, Russia's share of the global working-age population is projected to drop from 2.4 percent to 1.6 percent. This implies that Russia's long-term improvements in labor productivity must average two percent more per year than in the rest of the world. Such prospective accomplishments can hardly be taken for granted

> Moscow might become more prone to miscalculation when it comes to relations with both allies and rivals.

given Russia's health and educational problems, not to mention the looming pressures of an aging population. If these accomplishments are not met, Russia's share of world economic output, and the country's global economic influence, will diminish in the years ahead. (This is not to say that Russia will grow poorer, but in a progressively richer, healthier, and more educated world, Russia's human resource constraints may mean that the country should expect a smaller share of the future global economic pie.)

Russia's demographic crisis also has implications for its military capabilities and, by extension, for international security. In 2007, former Russian Prime Minister Sergei Stepashin warned that the "reduction in the size of the population and the reduction of population density … will create the danger of weakening Russia's political, economic, and military influence in the world." As he recognized, Russia's demographic crisis places inexorable limits on the country's defense potential, especially in terms of military manpower. Maintaining the country's current force structure—a military of more than a million soldiers, mainly comprising conscripts obliged to serve one-year terms of service—will not be feasible in the years immediately ahead. Despite plans to transform Russia's armed forces into an all-volunteer service, the Russian military continues to be manned mainly by 18-year-old men. In 1990, slightly more than one million boys were born in Russia; by 1999, however, this number had dropped by 39 percent, to 626,000. Roughly speaking, this means that Russia's pool of prospective recruits is set to fall by almost two-fifths between 2008 and 2017. If Moscow is to prevent this dramatic drop-off in military manpower, it has only two choices: induct fewer qualified conscripts or extend the term of service under the draft beyond the current 12 months. The former is unpalatable because of the need for healthy and educated troops for modern militaries; the latter is politically impossible because of the immense

unpopularity of the draft and the penurious wages paid to Russian soldiers.

Russia's brief war with Georgia in August 2008 was taken by many, including some in the Kremlin, as a sign that Russia was once again militarily resurgent after a decade of post-Soviet weakness. But the military contest with Georgia, a tiny neighbor with barely 20,000 soldiers, hardly qualified as a test of great-power capabilities, much less a test of Russia's global reach. Beyond the question of military manpower, Russia's defense potential today is compromised by the country's crisis in higher education and technical training. The same poor performance in knowledge creation reflected in the number of Russia's international patent awards can also be seen in the defense sector's research and development efforts. Russia's armaments industries have not been knowledge-driven innovators; instead, the defense sector appears largely to be living off the intellectual capital of the Soviet era. Unlike Beijing, which is committed to military modernization in the coming decades, Moscow is in effect preparing to fight this century's wars with last century's technology. In fact, as the Russia analysts Anders Aslund and Andrew Kuchins noted in 2009, as China's military capabilities have improved, Beijing has "reduced its imports of Russian military technology and even exports its own versions to traditional Russian clients such as Angola, Ethiopia and Syria." Russia's dwindling conventional military is on track to become the Polish cavalry of coming generations.

Throughout the Putin and Medvedev eras, the potential security risks to Russia from the ongoing demographic crisis have weighed heavily on the minds of the country's leaders. In his first State of the Nation address, in July 2000, Putin declared that "year by year, we, the citizens of Russia, are getting fewer and fewer.… We face the threat of becoming a senile nation." In his 2006 address, he identified demographics as "the most acute problem facing our country today." In Medvedev's May 2009 National Security Strategy, the country's demographic situation was noted as one of the "new security challenges" that Russia must confront in the years ahead. In other words, the potential ramifications of Russia's population trends are not entirely lost on the Kremlin—and they are hardly just a domestic concern. But how will Russia's bunkered and undemocratic leaders cope with the demographic pressures and unfavorable human resource trends that are undermining their goals? For the international community, this may be the single most disturbing aspect of Russia's peacetime population crisis: it is possible that Russia's demographic decline could prompt Moscow to become a more unpredictable, even menacing, actor on the world stage.

Most immediately and dramatically, the decline could lead Russia's military leaders, aware of their deficiencies in both manpower and advanced technology, to lower the threshold at which they might consider using nuclear weapons in moments of crisis. Indeed, such thinking was first outlined in Putin's 2000 National Security Concept and was reaffirmed in Medvedev's 2009 National Security Strategy. The official Russian thinking is that nuclear weapons are Russia's trump card: the more threatening the international environment, the more readily Moscow will resort to nuclear diplomacy.

For the moment, the Kremlin evidently still believes that its ambitious long-term socioeconomic plans will not only remedy the country's demographic woes but also propel Russia into the select ranks of the world's economic superpowers. But if Russia's demographic decline and relative economic decline continue over the next few decades, as they most likely will, Moscow's leaders will be unable to sustain that illusion.

Indeed, once the Kremlin finally confronts the true depths of the country's ugly demographic truths, Russia's political leaders could very well become more alarmist, mercurial, and confrontational in their international posture. And in the process, Moscow might become more prone to miscalculation when it comes to relations with both allies and rivals. Meanwhile, Russia is surrounded by countries whose stability and comity in the decades ahead are anything but given: for example, Afghanistan, Iran, North Korea, Pakistan, and the Central Asian republics. If Russia's periphery becomes more unstable and threatening at the same time that Russia's rulers realize their relative power is waning, the Kremlin's behavior may well become less confident—and more risky.

Russia's monumental demographic and human resource crisis cannot be remedied without a commensurately monumental nationwide effort by the Russians themselves. Such an effort will require a historic change in Russian mentality, both in the halls of power and among the general population. On the bright side, with hundreds of billions of dollars of foreign exchange in its vaults, Russia probably has the means to finance the education and public health campaigns needed for such a transformation.

Foreign governments and other outside actors can also play a role. To start, the international community should promote technical exchanges and training, joint projects on developing best practices in health and education, and civil-society dialogues to build a domestic Russian constituency for stanching the ongoing hemorrhage of Russian life and talent. And when necessary, foreign policymakers, businesspeople, and officials from nongovernmental organizations should be ready to publicly shame the Russian government for its patent neglect of its people's well-being. After all, a healthy, robust Russia is not just in the interest of the Russian people; it is in the interest of the rest of the world, too.

From Dubai to Cairo

Competing Global Cities, Models, and Shifting Centers of Influence?

By Yasser Elsheshtawy

For decades it was the big, central Arab powers that set the tone for the Arab world and led innovation. But today the region is being led from the outer edges. It's the little guys that are doing the most interesting stuff, and it's the big guys that will be left behind if they don't wake up.

Thomas Friedman, "The Fast Eat the Slow"
(*New York Times*, 2 February 2001)

A prominent *New York Times* journalist recently argued that the direction of influence in the Arab world has shifted from the traditional centers of Cairo, Baghdad, and Damascus to states in the periphery. According to the author these states—those in the Arab Gulf among them—are the most innovative and forward looking. A variety of events and projects are cited as evidence. While the political motives behind such proclamations are questionable it nevertheless raises interesting questions: do these new 'post-traditional' environments exert an influence on the traditional centers of the Middle East? What are the urban and spatial manifestations of such an influence (if they exist)? Should this influence be construed as one-sided or is it part of a larger global network in which influences occur on multiple levels and display numerous directions (rather than the naïve one-sided direction emphasized by the journalist)?

Using this argument as a starting point, this chapter sets out to investigate the influence of the glittering United Arab Emirates city of Dubai, an emerging global player, on Cairo. Traditionally, Cairo had a strong cultural, social, and architectural influence on the Arab world, yet this influence is now diminishing. A series of projects have emerged that respond to Dubai's new prominence. They include: the Smart Village Project (a copy of Dubai Internet City); Ma'adi City Center (a replica of Dubai City Center, a retail chain); and the various gated communities emerging in New Cairo, which are an echo of similar ventures in Dubai. These parallels do exist and in many instances references are made directly to Dubai.

While these projects and events do 'work' in places like Dubai that are not restrained or restricted—in essence a *tabula rasa* allowing for experimentation and a response to global conditions—their appropriateness in a 'traditional' city such as Cairo is questionable. These new projects are created at the periphery and seem to be detached and disconnected from any surrounding reality. While characteristic of all global cities, they are acquiring acute (and some might say amusing) dimensions in Cairo. It is interesting to observe however, that Cairo in its drive to become a global city is apparently drawing inspiration and precedents from a post-traditional center such as Dubai, which in turn is responding to, and is influenced by, larger global conditions and other global cities. This raises the issue of identity. This chapter hopes to tackle this by arguing that in a post-global world the concept of identity has been challenged; it is a changing, fluid, and ambiguous construct. Examining these projects would throw some light on changing notions of Egyptian identity in which its own heritage (in its Muslim and pharaonic incarnations) as well as those of others (Dubai's, for example) are used as 'branding' devices to attract multinationals and in turn 'globalize.' It is assumed that this will be followed by prosperity and happiness (questionable as that may be). In discussing these influences, this chapter will first explore the construct of the global city and the emergence of a network of cities. This will then be followed by an analysis of the case studies noted above, as an example of a perceived reversal of influence which will entail an inquiry into their compatibility (or lack thereof) within an Egyptian context. The relevance of such comparative studies in the context of the post-global/ tradition discourse, using the framework outlined in this abstract, will conclude the chapter.

THEORETICAL FRAMEWORK: GLOBAL CITIES AND NETWORKS

As a result of globalizing processes many scholars have coined the term "global city" to indicate the emergence of a new type of city with certain distinctive characteristics that can be found throughout the world. In particular the relevancy of the nation-state is questioned—in that respect city governments are emerging as the centers of the new global economy. Transactions occur between multinational corporations, financial centers, and cities. However, it is noted that the nation-state still has a role to play, albeit through a restructuring process involving a move into supranational levels (the European Union or the Gulf Cooperative Council, for example). But cities are assuming a powerful role, and as a result of such processes they are increasingly being viewed as a product that needs to be marketed. These marketing efforts involve attracting headquarters or regional branches of international companies and the staging of 'mega-events.' Other projects include luxury housing, dining establishments, and entertainment amenities to attract the professional personnel

required to operate these global activities. Urban projects, such as trade centers, conference centers, and hotels, provide a catalyst for further encouraging investment and tourism. Architecture in many instances is used to create eye-catching impressions—the Guggenheim museum in Bilbao is an example (UN-Habitat 2001). Such projects are the means to revitalize an otherwise stagnant city—a process sometimes called "the Bilbao effect."

As a result of all this some have noted that a dual city is emerging in which social polarization is becoming a dominant feature. The work of Saskia Sassen, is perhaps representative of such a viewpoint (2001). Due to the presence of these high-profile projects there is an influx of a highly skilled, and highly paid, workforce. To maintain and service such activities, however, low-wage employees are needed who form the backbone of corporate and financial activities. Thus, a geographical/spatial division occurs in which there are areas with a high concentration of the poor in contrast to enclaves housing the very rich. Furthermore, whether or not there is a rub-off effect on local industries has been questioned by research. Needless to say such disparities provoke "resentment, social instability and conflict" (UN-Habitat 2001, 30). In other words these megaprojects do not necessarily benefit most of the cities' residents since they are geared to a certain class (for further analysis of these debates, see Vignal and Denis in this volume).

One of the most visible aspects of globalizing cities is what has been sometimes described as the "quartering of urban space" due to a sharper division between rich and poor. This quartering manifests itself in the presence of residential cities—the most distinctive of these is the enclave or 'citadel.' These are "areas that can be considered as protected enclaves of the rich, the representatives of an extremely mobile top, operating at a more global level than ever before … [they] generally consist of expensive apartments in favorable locations" (Marcuse and van Kempen 2000). Examples of these citadels are gated communities and private, high-rise condominiums with heavy security. In simple terms it is an effort to "wall some in and keep others out" (Marcuse and van Kempen 2000, 30).

45

These developments have prompted some such as Castells to note that there is a new spatial logic in these global cities called "space of flows" contrasted with traditional forms of urbanism termed "space of places" (1997). Concentration of high-level services occurs in a few nodal centers. He notes that "it is a process that connects advanced services, producer centers, and markets in a global network with different intensity … depending upon the relative importance of the activities located in each area vis-à-vis the global network" (Castells 1997, 380). Furthermore, "territories surrounding these nodes play an increasingly subordinate function sometimes becoming irrelevant" (Castells 1997, 380). A major characteristic of these metropolitan centers is that services disperse and decentralize to the periphery (e.g., La Défense in Paris, or Canary Wharf in London). Thus, Castells argues that the global city is primarily a "process by which centers of production and consumption of advanced services, and their ancillary local societies, are connected in a global network, while simultaneously downplaying the linkages with their hinterlands, on the basis of information flows" (Castells 1997, 386). What characterizes these mega- or global cities? Again, Castells (and others) suggests that a distinctive feature is that they are "globally connected and locally disconnected, physically and socially" (Castells 1997, 404). They are "discontinuous constellations of spatial fragments, functional pieces, and social segments" (Castells 1997, 407). He then goes on to list some of the common characteristics of these global centers: secluded communities, airport VIP lounges, etc., which all cater to an "international culture" whose identity is linked to multinational corporations. Sassen, in an edited collection, examines what she terms the emergence of a "network of cities" whereby cities in regions begin to form networks, creating a global city web whose constituent cities become global through the networks they participate in. Emphasis is placed on emerging global cities such as São Paulo, Shanghai, Hong Kong, Mexico City, Beirut, and Dubai. Of interest is how these globalizing zones are replicating many features of global cities (Sassen 2002).

What emerges from these readings is that if one were to examine the construct of 'influence' it is far too simplistic to talk of one 'center' or city influencing another. If one conceptualizes these centers as lying on a network their influence becomes multidimensional, exerted in multiple directions. Thus, using the notion of 'flows,' images and ideas move from one part of the world to another instantaneously, and from particular cities to this wider network. The question then is not so much who influenced whom, but to what extent do local conditions allow for the unfolding of global processes? Examining both Dubai and Cairo is particularly illuminating since both are attempting to become global cities—but the results have been quite different.

In looking at the directionality of influence in Cairo there are two possible areas of investigation: state-sponsored projects which more or less adopt an idea without directly copying its form (such projects are modeled on similar ventures throughout the world); direct investment from Dubai-based companies, directly installing a successful Dubai formula. Thus influence can be connected to either idea (lending itself to multiple sources) or form. The first category in Cairo includes the Smart Village project; the second category includes the Ma'adi City Center shopping mall, based on a concept introduced by Dubai's Al-Futtaim group. Both of these are apparently distinctive Dubai-influenced ideas. But they are not unique to the city and occur in other centers throughout the world in different forms. Internet City, for example, is modeled after California's Silicon Valley and technology parks in Southeast Asia. The concept of the hypermarket is not a Dubai invention but one that occurs throughout the developed world. However, the singularity of these projects within an Egyptian context—occurring after their success in Dubai—does of course suggest a strong influence, particularly with regard to the Ma'adi City Center project. The following two sections will explore the extent to which these two projects deviate from, and approximate, the Dubai model.

46

In 1999 Dubai's de facto ruler Shaykh Muhammad bin Rashid announced the creation of an IT (information technology) center called Dubai Internet City (DIC). One year later the center was complete, in landscaping elements and the presence of office buildings, and has since then become an unqualified success. Occupied by big names in the IT industry it has made Dubai the IT hub of the region. Comprised of a series of buildings overlooking an artificial lake and lush gardens, the

Figure 6.1. Dubai Internet City (photograph by Yasser Elsheshtawy).

city is located adjacent to Shaykh Zayed Highway, a newly formed corridor along which the city is currently expanding. Entry is through a gate designed in the form of a traditional wind tower with a series of screens containing a set of 'Islamic' motifs. This gate leads to a series of glass buildings such as one may find in any high-tech park in Malaysia or Silicon Valley.

The entire project is protected by a fence although entry is free to anyone (provided they have a car). Located nearby is Media City, a similar arrangement to Internet City, although in this case related to the media industry. This city is also comprised of office blocks within an artificial landscape. It houses studios and newsrooms and has become a regional center for many media companies such as Reuters, CNN, MBC, and others. The anonymity of the office blocks in either of these two cities, distinguished only by their tenants' logos, highlights the fact that they operate primarily on a global level, in some way disconnected from the surrounding reality.

The Smart Village Project in Cairo is Egypt's attempt to claim the title of the region's IT hub and also to integrate with the burgeoning global economy, with its emphasis on IT and communication-related services. The project is a technology park designed to cater to the IT industry, and represents an attempt by Egypt to enter this market as a service-driven economy. Officials claim that it is modeled after Ireland and India, who have successfully integrated into the global IT service sector. Located along the Cairo—Alexandria desert highway the three-hundred-acre park will eventually house more than fifty office buildings accommodating between twenty thousand and thirty thousand employees. Plots of land are offered to companies, which can then build their own office space. As of now, only three companies have signed up for the project: Microsoft, Vodafone, and Alcatel. A recent visit to the project showed the Microsoft building, in an isolated area, and a call center to be the only buildings actually operating according to plan. A building was being constructed for the Ministry of Communications. The entire park, however, with its various futuristic buildings, had not yet been built. These buildings are to include a pyramid-shaped think-tank café, as well as a main conference and meeting center with a shape reminiscent of communication

47

Figure 6.2. Smart Village project, Cairo–Alexandria highway (photograph by Yasser Elsheshtawy).

satellites. An architectural competition in Egypt was the source of these forms.

The project has its skeptics, of course. Many question its relevance in an Egyptian context. A business publication notes, "The Pyramids Smart Village, Egypt's new technology oasis, is everything that isn't associated with Cairo: spacious, pristine, ultramodern and green" (Hassan 2004). It is always compared to Dubai's, and here the responses vary. On the one hand officials like to argue that the relationship is symbiotic: both projects complement each other—Dubai offers marketing whereas Cairo's focus is on development. Also, great emphasis is placed here on the notion that Cairo is more suitable for an Arab market (Mostafa 2003). Another view suggests that Cairo has more to offer culturally and that Dubai's "antiseptic" living is not suitable for the "taste of the restless adventurers of the new economy" (Thornton 2003). Both of these views are of course misguided, and do in fact play into a few cultural stereotypes: Cairo has the human resources and the brains, but lacks Dubai's money; and the notion that Dubai is located in the middle of the desert ruled by fundamentalists (some sort of Saudi Arabia).

The differences between these two ventures are striking. With regard to location, DIC is located outside the traditional city on a highway leading to Abu Dhabi. Nevertheless, it is located on a growth corridor and will eventually become the center of a new Dubai which is currently being constructed (nearby projects include luxury resorts, the ruler's palace, various gated communities, and of course the Palm Islands [Palm Jumayra and Palm Jebel 'Ali, two reclaimed palm-shaped islands housing a mixed-use development]). Driving to DIC one does not have the feeling of 'leaving' Dubai. Yet this is not the feeling in Cairo. Smart Village is located along the Cairo—Alexandria highway, next to a toll station. The sense of leaving Cairo and embarking on a long journey is strong. Also the architecture of the park is insightful. In Dubai, the office blocks are generic buildings that can be found anywhere in the world. In Cairo, however, an attempt was made to make a compelling architectural statement by proposing buildings with a strong symbolic content (a pyramid-shaped café suspended in the middle of a lake, supposedly to encourage creativity) or a building whose shape is suggestive of communication satellites (expressed by a series of curves). While DIC has added a few vernacular elements (wind towers and ornaments), the Cairo village has a more neutral look—although the main mosque has for some reason been designed with pharaonic imagery. Running the risk of being interpreted as cheap gimmicks, none of these structures have actually been built—but their designs are nevertheless displayed prominently in the local media as a sign of Egypt's entry into the twenty-first century as an IT center.

Another difference relates to accessibility. In Dubai anyone with a car can enter and walk into the project without interference from anyone. The food court is a common meeting place containing a variety of shops and restaurants. It thus integrates strongly with the city. The situation in Cairo is quite different. Here entry is through a guarded gate and subsequent movement within the grounds is closely observed. In both cities photography is only allowed after securing permission from the authorities.

THE CITY CENTER IDEA

The retail sector is one segment where the 'Dubai idea' is directly transplanted into an Egyptian context, as evidenced in the Ma'adi City Center. In mid-November 2001 the Majid Al-Futtaim (MAF) Group of Dubai broke ground in the desert outside Cairo for a 22,500-square-meter shopping mall to be anchored by the French food retailer Carrefour. (See Abaza in this volume for further discussion of this and other luxury malls in Cairo.) The project, Egypt's first hypermarket, is one of three developments planned in the country in the next two to three years by the MAF Group and Carrefour. Long-term plans suggest that twenty centers will be constructed throughout Egypt, according to an interview with the regional director of Carrefour Egypt (al-Saddiq 2005). The Ma'adi City Center is modeled after similar MAF Group and Carrefour projects in the United Arab Emirates, Oman, and Qatar. The partners started the concept in Dubai in

1995 with the Deira City Center, which now gets fifty thousand visitors per day and includes such retailers as U.S. department-store chain J.C. Penney, Swedish furniture maker Ikea, and British chains Woolworth's and Marks & Spencer (Postlewaite 2001). In addition to the French hypermarket the mall includes more than forty shops, several restaurants, and a family-entertainment center.

Official accounts suggest the positive impact on Egypt by pointing out that the market will "feature a large range of top quality Egyptian products and international brands targeted to meet the increasing demands of Egyptian consumers" (Majid Al-Futaim 2001). In addition officials view such a development as a way to modernize Egyptian shopping behavior, as argued by the minister of internal trade: "A new and civilised (sic) marketing approach … will be introduced to peripheral areas outside of the capital, supplying commodities to small traders seven days a week, 365 days a year. It will supplant the traditional weekly *suq* (market) held in villages throughout the countryside" (Sami 2001a). Such efforts are, however, greeted with skepticism in the local media, particularly in light of the failure of a similar venture by the British conglomerate Sainsbury. This particular case is interesting since it prompted many to call for a radical reorganization

49

Figure 6.3. Ma'adi City Center, constructed by the Majid Al-Futtaim Group of Dubai, where Carrefour is located (photograph by Yasser Elsheshtawy).

of the Egyptian retail sector, after it was described by Sainsbury's chairman as "hostile" (Sami 2001b). One retail consultant suggests the possibility of a negative impact on Cairo's small grocery stores: "They've been the staple and the backbone of society for so long they'll never totally disappear, but I think you'll see a lot of them downsizing ... if you can downsize from 75 square meters" (Hinde 2003).

Aside from these economic arguments one particular area of concern is the cultural acceptance of such a project within an Egyptian context. While the concept of hypermarkets has been successful outside Egypt in terms of social approval, some would argue that the Egyptian culture may take time to follow the trend (Rashdan 2003). Essential to society's acceptance of Carrefour is an appreciation for its concept, and what it has to offer. For Egyptians, this means making an effort to spend their free time shopping at Carrefour rather than at smaller, perhaps more conveniently located, neighborhood supermarkets. In a culture that highly values a family-oriented and neighborhood-friendly environment, it is not clear whether Egypt

is a place conducive to hypermarket success. While the market caters to the nearby upper-middle-class suburb of Ma'adi, it is aimed at Greater Cairo as well; however large distances and endemic traffic jams may preclude such an orientation. The center's management, however, argues that the mall caters to middle income families: "People coming to us must have a car, so we only cater to a very small percentage of the population. We are here to complement, not compete" (Hinde 2003). At present, the center is successfully attracting a large number of visitors. It should be noted however that for the most part these visitors represent a certain segment of Egyptian society which has the necessary purchasing power, i.e., Egyptians residing in the Gulf, or expatriates. A common denominator is mobility since the center is only accessible by car. Ordinary Egyptians are thus excluded from this setting.

This raises the issue of location. The center is located in an area of Cairo known as Qattamiya at the foot of the Muqattam mountain, near the suburb of Ma'adi. It is located along a highway leading to a new development appropriately styled New Cairo. The site is surrounded by empty tracts of land,

Figure 6.4. Surroundings of Carrefour/Ma'adi City Center (photograph by Yasser Elsheshtawy).

50

undeveloped areas, and a large public-housing project. The location was chosen specifically to "develop new residential zones" according to the developer (Rashdan 2003). An "example of the type of undeveloped area targeted by the group's development scheme," it thus ties in with what is termed "Carrefour's vision" for Egypt (Rashdan 2003). "France-based Carrefour's vision for Egypt entails a series of 'city centers,' large shopping complexes located on the outskirts of the city that serve not only as places to buy food, but as entertainment and retail destinations, often complete with countless stores, cinemas, restaurants and other activities, with Carrefour as the anchor" (Hinde 2003).

This vision entails, in addition to location, a provision of land large enough to accommodate such a complex; the presence of extensive areas for parking. Thus the Maʿadi City Center stands on a 69,000-square-meter parcel of land, of which 3,500 square meters is taken up by Carrefour (Hinde 2003).

It is interesting to observe that the Egyptian local press largely downplays the Dubai connection and the fact that the entire center is based on a Dubai model. In fact, more emphasis is placed on the French connection, in a sense suggesting that Egypt will become Western by constructing centers such as these. It is suggested that this is a universal or global setting, not tied to a particular culture or region. According to one consultant, "From a shopper's point of view, the shopping center in Qattamia is perfect. Once you walk inside, you could be anywhere in the world" (Hinde 2003). This of course stands in contrast to accounts in the local Gulf press which note with constrained glee that Dubai-based businesses are making inroads into Cairo (and other cities as well).[1]

The similarities between them are quite striking. For one thing, the logo is prominently displayed in Cairo on the mall's entrance but also in advertisements throughout the city. Entering the mall one is struck by the neat detailing of the parking lot with traffic signs pointing out that traffic rules "still" apply in the area (see image, page 243). The atmosphere stands in strong contrast to the stark, and somewhat shabby, surroundings.[2]

The same applies to the interior, which is well decorated to a high standard and enjoys a level of cleanliness not found in other Egyptian malls. The Dubai connection becomes even more apparent due to the presence of a UAE-based bank branch. There are some differences but the most obvious of them is size. Deira City Center is a large center comprised of multiple levels and several buildings. It occupies a space equivalent to several city blocks. In Cairo, however, the City Center is spread out on one level and is dominated by Carrefour. Another difference pertains to location. In Cairo the center is located at the edge of the city making it difficult to reach, unlike Dubai where it is located in the heart of Deira and is a major hangout and meeting place for city residents. The place is notorious for always being crowded, catering to a cash-rich clientele comprised of Arab and Western expatriates in addition to locals from Dubai and other emirates

51

Figure 6.5. The Jumayra Mosque in Bur Dubai (photograph by Yasser Elsheshtawy).

FROM DUBAI TO CAIRO

as well. In Egypt the targeted population seems to be the nearby Ma'adi suburb but other segments are also targeted. Its location however precludes the center from becoming a major meeting place—it has more the feel of a curiosity. While this still holds at the time of writing (2005) the center is viewed as a catalyst spurring urban growth. It remains to be seen if this will actually happen. While it is part of New Cairo which is currently being built, and which may (or may not) become a new center of Cairo, it nevertheless remains an isolated structure along a highway.

DUBAI PARALLELS: CONSTRUCTING AN IDENTITY

The previous section showed that Dubai does indeed exert a strong influence in Egypt. The remainder of this chapter is devoted to examining the influence of Cairo on Dubai—and if in fact such an influence does exist in the first place. In examining these influences it must first be noted that multiple influences operate in Dubai. For example, the DIC concept is based on various models from around the world, as has already been described. Hardly a revolutionary idea, Dubai simply adopted this model. Here the attempt by Dubai to become a global city is apparent—its adoption of Western models and symbols should be understood in that context. Yet it also is looking toward the Middle East's traditional cities in its effort to become the new center of the Arab world. Here the influence is primarily at the level of historical imagery.

This manifests itself at a number of levels. For example, in advertising for the Palm Islands the image of Egypt's pyramids is prominently displayed, suggesting that a new landmark is in the making. Advertisements for the opening of stores in the new extension to the Burjuman Shopping Mall includes images relating to old Arab souks, traditional elements such as *mashrabiya* (latticed wooden windows), etc. Again, the use of historical imagery indicates that officials are trying to ascertain the emergence of Dubai as the new center, replacing the traditional cities of the Middle East. At another level,

the Jumayra Mosque in Bur Dubai is built according to a Cairene Mamluk style.

The mosque seems to have been transported from Cairo to Dubai. The significance behind this is that the mosque represents an itinerary on the tourist trail—shown by Dubai officials as an example of its 'Arab-Islamic' architecture. It is a common sight to see tourists having their pictures taken alongside the mosque—usually in a hurry while the bus is waiting. Aware of the perceived absence of history and cultural roots in Dubai, such adaptations become ways to ascertain rootedness.

This whole notion of appropriating cultural elements, in a sense positioning itself as the region's cultural hub, has been the source of a recent newspaper article in the English language *Al-Ahram Weekly*. Here the writer argues that while Beirut is the "cultural capital" of the Arab world and Cairo its "political and historical" center, Dubai is attempting to take that title away. Noting that Dubai has a "newfound image" the writer argues (with a certain sense of alarm) that Dubai is "emerging as the region's Mecca of business, culture and the arts" (Howeida 2002). This occurs at a number of levels as noted above: establishing international linkages and also making connections to regional and historical elements. The name of its major landmark—the Burj Al-Arab Hotel—suggests that the city is indeed the center of the Arab world. New developments such as Madinat Jumayra are designed to reflect 'traditional' Arabian souks—their audience in both cases are primarily Western tourists and multinationals. But in adapting these elements they show that if one wants to seek an Arabian experience it is sufficient to visit Dubai (Elsheshtawy 2004).

CONCLUSION

The flight from Cairo or Beirut to the Gulf states takes only a couple of hours, and in that time the traveler is transported to what might as well be a different planet. He leaves behind a world of decay and dulled tones and steps into one of glitter and dazzle. Lamb 2002, 34.

Has Dubai been successful in positioning itself as the region's center? A number of events suggest a positive answer. For example, the relocation of businesses from Cairo to Dubai, visits by Egyptian delegations to learn from Dubai, and articles in international business publications heralding the arrival of an Arabian tiger, a place of "new Pharaohs," are all supportive of this viewpoint.[3] Other cities are influenced as well. In the case of Beirut some observers have noted that Dubai has in effect become a "gateway to the East." "The legend of the Lebanese gateway to the Middle East, if it were ever based on anything solid, has now attained the status of myth. Economically, at least, the gateway is lying in ruins" (Champion 2004). Qatar is at the present constructing an island named the Pearl, modeled after the Palm Islands in Dubai. Dubai thus has become, for better or worse, a model for cities throughout the Arab world. Its traditional centers have tried to catch up with these developments but have been unable to do so, and in fact some indications seem to suggest that they have failed. A failed infrastructure and dilapidated housing, some quite near to the new luxury malls, are just some of the urgent issues in Cairo that need to be resolved first.

The whole notion of a global world in which its cities are linked in a network and where images circulate freely challenging traditional notions of identity, place, and heritage does seem to be supported by examining cities such as Dubai. Here the city has been successful in appropriating imagery from the region's traditional centers, in effect replacing them. It is aided by a cash-rich economy (partially relying on oil, even though Dubai is not a major oil producer) and a centralized government facilitating various decision-making processes. Its various 'cities' are indicative of a new form of urbanism in which fragmentation figures highly, and where the built environment is geared to, and becomes supportive of, the new global economy. The impact of such developments on the cities' social structure—the "quartering effect" discussed earlier—has to be further examined and studied. Otherwise, as is the case in Cairo which has explosive sociopolitical issues, such developments could be counteractive and may in fact contribute to the persistent state of underdevelopment present in the region.

REFERENCES

"Allahs blutiges Land—Politik und Kultur." 2003. *Spiegel Special. Das Gold der neuen Pharaonen* (February): 126–29.

Castells, Manuel. 1997. *The Rise of the Network Society.* Oxford: Blackwell.

Champion, Daryl. 2004. "Does the Gateway to the Middle East lie in Ruins?
Golden Days Seem Far Away." *The Daily Star Online,* 10 February, *<http://www.dailystar.com.lb/article.asp?edition_ID=1&article_ID=4238&categ_id=13>* (21 September 2005).

"Dubai: Arabia's Field of Dreams." 2004. *The Economist,* 29 May, 61–62.

"Egyptian Delegation Visits Dubai." 2004. *Gulf News,* 4 January.

Elsheshtawy, Yasser. 2004. "Redrawing Boundaries: Dubai, the Emergence of a Global City." In *Planning the Middle East City: An Urban Kaleidoscope in a Globalizing World,* ed. Yasser Elsheshtawy, 169–99. New York: Routledge.

"GM Relocates Regional Office from Cairo to Dubai." 2004. *Gulf News,* 2 April.

Hassan, Abdalla. 2004. "It Takes a Village." *Arabies Trends,* January, 10.

Hinde, Tim. 2003. "Interview." *Business Today Online,* February, *<http://www.businesstodayegypt.com/default.aspx?issueID=116>* (July 2003).

Howeida, Amira. 2002. "Metamorphoses on the Gulf." *Al-Ahram Weekly Online,* 9–15 May, *<http://weekly.ahram.org.eg/2002/585/fe3.htm>* (23 September 2005).

Lamb, David. 2002. *The Arabs: Journeys Beyond the Mirage.* New York: Vintage Books.

"Majid Al-Futaim Starts Egypt Project." 2001. *Gulf News Online Edition,* 30 November, *<http://www.gulf-news.com/articles/news.asp?ArticleID=34053>* (21 September 2005).

53

Marcuse, Peter, and Robert van Kempen. 2000. *Globalizing Cities: A New Spatial Order?* Oxford: Blackwell.

Mostafa, Hadia. 2003. "Towering Technology." *Business Today Online*, <*http://www.businesstodayegypt.com/default.aspx?issueID=116*> (July 2003).

Nair, Manoj. 2004. "Retail Giant MAF Plans New Egypt Mall." *Gulf News*, 28 January.

Postlewaite, Susan. 2001. "FDI Still Apparent: Gulf Investors Stay Despite Capital Flight." *Business Monthly Online*, November, <*http://www.amcham. org.eg/Publications/BusinessMonthly/December%20 01/Followup(InvestmentGoesOn).asp*> (23 September 2005).

Rashdan, Hannah. 2003. "Egypt Gets Hyper." *Al-Ahram Weekly Online*, 30 January–5 February, <*http://weekly.ahram.org.eg/2003/623/li1.htm*> (23 September 2005).

al-Saddiq, Muhammad. 2005. "Rasadat milyaray dolar li-khitattha al-istismariya fi Masr khilal ashr sanawat." *Al-Ahram*, 15 May.

Sami, Aziza. 2001a. "Supermarketing Hysterics." *Al-Ahram Weekly Online*, 19–25 April, <*http://weekly.ahram.org.eg/2001/530/ec1.htm*> (23 September 2005).

_____. 2001b. "A New Saga." *Al-Ahram Weekly Online*, 18–24 January, <*http://weekly.ahram.org.eg/2001/517/ec1.htm*> (23 September 2005).

Sassen, Saskia. 2001. *The Global City*. Princeton, N.J.: Princeton University Press.

_____, ed. 2002. *Global Networks, Linked Cities*. New York: Routledge.

Thornton, Jasper. 2003. "Utopia in a Village." *Al-Ahram Weekly Online*, 4–10 October, <*http://weekly.ahram.org.eg/2001/554/it2.htm*> (23 September 2005). UN-Habitat. 2001. *Cities in a Globalizing World: Global Report on Human Settlements*. London: Earthscan Publications Ltd.

Watson, Geoffrey. 2004. "Dubai is the Best Place for Regional Business." *Gulf News*, 4 April.

NOTES

1. Countless articles and news items make this observation, for example Nair 2004.
2. As one interesting account noted: "Some other City Centre visitors find the mall's crowd to be overwhelming; but they seem to acknowledge some of its perks. Among these is a very large car park providing free parking directly at the mall's entrance, and the convenience of a variety of stores and products. And while free parking may seem to be a plus for some, Sherif Salama, 39, complained, 'The lagna (traffic inspection) as you enter Carrefour's parking lot is terribly misplaced. How can anyone walk into Carrefour and spend money after receiving a mokhalfa (ticket)?'" (Rashdan 2003).
3. See, for example, "Dubai …" 2004; "GM Relocates …" 2004; "Egyptian Delegation …" 2004; Watson 2004. In addition the last few years have witnessed a plethora of newspaper articles, attempting to describe and analyze this newly emerging city. For example, a recent edition of Der Spiegel on political Islam included an article titled "The Gold of the New Pharaohs." In that article the new developments were being described and it was noted—with alarm—that Dubai would like to become the most modern city in the world, a metropolis which will merge East with West—Dubai as a mixture of Singapore, Seattle, and Saint Tropez ("Allah blutiges Land" 2003, 126–29).

7

AIDS in the Caribbean: The "West Atlantic Pandemic"

By Paul Farmer

The history of the Haitian AIDS epidemic is a brief and devastating one. Less than two decades ago, HIV may not have been present in the country. Now, complications of HIV infection are among the leading causes of death in urban Haiti. How are other Caribbean islands affected? Is Haiti, as some believe it to be, an AIDS- ridden pocket in an otherwise low-prevalence region?[1] Answering these questions is no mean task, as Pape and Johnson (1988a:32) suggest:

> First, in many countries there is no registry system for AIDS and it was only in 1984 that most nations started reporting cases to [the Pan American Health Organization], Secondly, the widely used CDC case definition for AIDS is inappropriate for defining tropical AIDS and requires sophisticated laboratory support that is not readily available in most countries. In our experience in Haiti, the new CDC case definition for AIDS (CDC 1987), which relies more on HIV testing and clinical presentation, should increase the actual number of reported cases by at least 30 percent.

Ironically, given the extreme poverty of Haiti, Haitians with AIDS stand a better chance of an adequate workup than do the citizens of several other Caribbean nations. Although Haiti has the weakest health infrastructure in the region, it has had the largest number of cases, the greatest amount of international scrutiny as "the source of AIDS," and has sustained the most substantial economic blows relative to GNP. Perhaps in part as a result of these negative forces, many Haitian physicians and researchers have been involved in the professional response to the epidemic. Haitians publish more HIV-related studies than do researchers in other Caribbean countries, and the GHESKIO-run national laboratories are experienced in diagnosing AIDS and other forms of HIV infection.

Given these limitations, what do we know about the chief characteristics of the Caribbean pandemic? All of what are termed "the Caribbean basin countries" have reported AIDS cases to the Pan American Health Organization (PAHO). Among the islands, Haiti, the Dominican Republic, Trinidad and Tobago, and the Bahamas account for 82 percent of all cases reported to PAHO between the recognized onset of the epidemic and September 1987. Haiti had reported the largest number of cases in the Caribbean region, which appears to lend credence to the widely shared belief that citizens of that nation are somehow uniquely susceptible to AIDS. When the number of cases is standardized to reflect per capita caseload, however, the uniqueness of Haiti disappears: the attack rate in Haiti is actually lower than that in several other countries in the region (Lange and Jaffe 1987:1410).

During the twelve months preceding September 1987, the number of reported Caribbean cases doubled, with the largest rates of increase in Barbados, Jamaica, Martinique, Guadeloupe, French Guiana, the U.S. Virgin Islands, and Grenada. The epidemic in the Dominican Republic continues to grow: although no cases were reported in 1983, a total of 62 were reported in the subsequent two years. During 1986, the number of Dominican cases more than doubled, and as of the end of 1989, 856 cases had been reported to PAHO.

What is the nature of HIV transmission in these countries? As noted, many public health specialists speak of the entire Caribbean basin as demonstrating "Pattern II," which differs from Pattern I "in that heterosexual intercourse has been the dominant mode of HIV transmission *from the start*.... Homosexuality generally plays a minor role in this pattern" (Osborn 1989:126; emphasis added). The above review of the data from Haiti suggests that the WHO terminology obscures an accurate understanding of the Haitian AIDS epidemic. First, although "the start" was never accurately documented, it seems clear that same-sex relations between men played a crucial role in the Haitian epidemic; second, the WHO scheme highlights similarities between Haiti and Africa, which would be acceptable if such comparisons did not tend to draw attention away from the history of the Caribbean pandemic, which is in fact, causally speaking, much more intimately related to the North American epidemic. Third, the WHO scheme is static, whereas the Haitian epidemic is rapidly changing. Data from other Caribbean countries suggest that the WHO terminology is equally inappropriate there, and that the patterns

seen in Haiti are suggestive of what has occurred in other countries in the region.

Table 7.1 also presents figures suggesting that homosexual contact has played an important role in other Caribbean islands. But even here finer distinctions may be drawn. "For these homosexuals," note Pape and Johnson (1988a: 36) in reference to gay men in Jamaica, the Dominican Republic, and Trinidad, "sexual contact with American homosexuals rather than promiscuity per se appeared to be associated with increased risk of infection." What studies allow such a conclusion? The first case of AIDS in the West Indies was reported on Trinidad in February 1983. Since then, the number of cases has risen steadily, leaving Trinidad with one of the highest attack rates in the Americas. In an important study, Bartholemew and coworkers (1987) compare the epidemiological correlates of infection with two retroviruses: HTLV and HIV. Infection with the former virus, thought to be long endemic in the Caribbean, was significantly associated with age, African descent, number of lifetime sexual partners, and "duration of homosexuality," that is, length of time as a sexually active gay man. In sharp contrast, "age and race were not associated with HIV seropositivity. The major risk factor for HIV seropositivity was homosexual contact with a partner from a foreign country, primarily the United States. Duration of homosexuality and number of lifetime partners were not significandy associated with HIV seropositivity" (Bartholemew et al. 1987:2606). The same risk factors were documented in Colombia, also a Caribbean- basin country. In Bogota, Merino et al. (1990:333—334) observe that "significant behavioral risk factors for HIV—1 seropositivity among this sample of

Table 7.1 *HIV Seroprevalence in Carribbean Homosexual or Bisexuals*

	Jamaica			Dominican Republic			Trinidad		
	Year	N	HIV (%)	Year	N	HIV (%)	Year	N	HIV (%)
Homo/Bisex	'86	125	10	'85	46	17	'83–84	106	40
Controls	'86	4,000	0	'85	306	2.6	'82	983	0.2

SOURCE: Pape and Johnson (1988a)

Colombian homosexual men included receptive anal intercourse and, for the subgroup reporting receptive roles, contact with foreign visitors."[2] The Haitian experience would suggest that Trinidad and Colombia can expect the relative significance of sexual contact with a North American gay man to decrease, as other risk factors—most notably, high numbers of partners—become preeminent.

A similar risk factor was also hypothesized for the Dominican Republic, where Haitians, long despised in the neighboring country, have come under even heavier fire as "AIDS carriers." And yet studies revealed high seroprevalence among homosexual/bisexual male prostitutes living in the tourist areas of the country—10 percent in Santiago and 19 percent in Puerto Plata. "Tourists, and not Haitians, were the most likely source of virus transmission to Dominicans, because contact occurs frequently between tourists (for example, male homosexuals) and Dominicans but rarely between Haitians and Dominicans" (Koenig et al. 1987:634). Further, it seems that the epidemiology of HIV in the Dominican Republic may resemble that in Haiti to an even greater extent than did the Trinidadian epidemiology. Koenig and coworkers underline the role of economically driven prostitution among young Dominican men who consider themselves heterosexual: "Persons who engage in homosexual acts only to earn money usually consider themselves heterosexual. This situation, public health workers have indicated, is particularly prevalent in the tourist areas with young adolescents. It could explain our finding of three positive serum samples in schoolchildren from Santo Domingo" (Koenig et al. 1987:634).[3]

More recent research in the Puerta Plata area suggests that, although homosexual prostitution has diminished, another form of sexual exchange fostered by economic inequity continues to flourish. Garcia and coworkers have studied the "beach boys" who work the area's tourist hotels:

> Beach boys are charming, friendly young heterosexual males who provide escort service to women tourists, most of whom are 30 years old or more. The beach boys are known locally as "Sanky Panky"—a corruption of the term "hanky panky." Because these men have contact with tourists from different countries and continents, they are often skilled, if not fluent, in English, French, German, and Italian. (Garcia 1991:2)

Although termed "brief holiday romances," the escort service typically involves "monetary compensation," and qualitative research allows Garcia (1991:2) to conclude that "beach boys have multiple sexual partners and ply their trade in an area where the prevalence of AIDS is among the highest in the country."

Epidemiologic reports from other parts of the Caribbean suggest a similar history for other growing island epidemics. Composite data from Surinam and what has been termed the "English-speaking Caribbean," which includes twenty island nations, show that while 100 percent of those diagnosed with AIDS in 1983 were homosexual or bisexual, the relative significance of same-sex contact as a risk factor for AIDS plunged to 30 percent over the next five years. Blood-transfusion—related AIDS remained low, at less than 5 percent, and pediatric AIDS continued to account for less than 10 percent of diagnosed cases. Cases among those claiming to be exclusively heterosexual and without history of transfusion or intravenous drug use have soared, from less than 10 percent before 1985 to 60 percent in 1988. The male- to-female ratio has declined each year, as more and more women fall ill with AIDS. These trends necessarily imply that the proportion of pediatric cases will also climb (Hospedales 1989).

Caribbean-wide data suggest that many of the factors that have helped to shape the Haitian epidemic have been important throughout the region. Of these factors, the most important have been economically driven and historically given: sufficient data now exist to support the assertion that economically driven male prostitution, catering to a North American clientele, played a major role in the introduction of HIV to Haiti. Why might Haiti have been particularly vulnerable to such commodification of sexuality? In a country as poor as

Haiti—"the poorest country in the hemisphere"—AIDS might be thought of as an occupational hazard for workers in the tourist industry. A similar observation may be made about several other Caribbean nations.

Throughout the earlier half of this century, tourists' attitudes toward Haiti are nicely summarized by Carpenter (1930:326), whose Anglo-American guide book to the Caribbean qualifies Haiti as "a deplorable and almost unbelievable mixture of barbaric customs and African traditions." Later, in a slightly different era, Haiti's "exoticism" could be peddled as an attraction.[4] Tourism truly began in 1949, when Port-au-Prince celebrated the two hundredth anniversary of its founding with the inauguration of the "Cité de l'Exposition," a long stretch of modern buildings built on the reclaimed swampy waterfront of the capital. The country counted some 20,000 visitors that year, and slightly fewer in 1950 and 1951. During the next few years, however, approximately tourists would spend an average of three days and $105 in Haiti—bringing in approximately 25 percent of Haiti's foreign currency (Francisque 1986:139).

There was every sign that the gains in tourism would be steady, but political instability in 1957, followed by the tyrannical rule of François Duvalier, led North American tourists to avoid Haiti for several years.[5] This was the case even though a number of casinos located in Cuba relocated to Haiti after the overthrow of the Batista dictatorship. After he had silenced domestic opposition, Duvalier attempted to court tourists and their dollars later in the decade. In the same speech in which he welcomed U.S. Vice President Nelson Rockefeller to Haiti and promoted the country as an ideal site for U.S. assembly plants, François Duvalier suggested that "Haiti could be a great land of relaxation for the American middle class—it is close, beautiful, and politically stable" (Trouillot 1990:200).

By 1970, the annual number of visitors was close to 100,000; not counting brief layovers and "afternoon dockings," the annual tally had risen to 143,538 by 1979. Club Méditerranée opened its doors the following year (Barros 1984:750). It seemed as if tourism had arrived. Indeed, the industry, it was predicted, would soon supplant coffee and the offshore assembly plants as the capital's chief source of foreign exchange. But the effects of the "AIDS scare" were dramatic and prompt: the Haitian Bureau of Tourism estimated that tourism declined from visitors in the winter of 1981-82 to under 10,000 the following year. In 1983–84, during the season following the risk-grouping and spate of articles in the popular press, even fewer tourists came to Haiti. Six hotels folded, and as many more declared themselves on the edge of bankruptcy. Several hotel owners were rumored to be planning a lawsuit against the CDC.[6]

Of course fluctuations in tourism and trade may be attributed to many factors, but there was little doubt in Haiti about the cause of the collapse: Haiti had been accused of "starting the AIDS epidemic." To cite Abbott (1988:255) once again: "AIDS stamped Haiti's international image as political repression and intense poverty never had." "Already suffering from an image problem, Haiti has been made an international pariah by AIDS," concluded one 1983 report. "Boycotted by tourists and investors, it has lost millions of dollars and hundreds of jobs at a time when half the work force is jobless. Even exports are being shunned by some" (Chaze 1983:41).

Tourism and poverty did bring something of lasting significance, however: institutionalized prostitution. As one physician-author put it, "This country had—as far as promiscuity was concerned—replaced Cuba" (Météllus 1987:90). And as Haiti became poorer, both men's and women's bodies became cheaper. Although there have been no quantitative studies of Haitian urban prostitution, it was clear that a substantial sector of the trade catered to tourists, and especially North Americans. Some portion of the tourist industry catered specifically to a gay clientele:

> During the past five years Haiti, especially Port-au-Prince, has become a very popular holiday resort for Americans who are homosexual. There are also Haitians who are homosexual, and homosexual prostitution is becoming increasingly common.

59

... For the young Haitian male between the ages of fifteen and thirty there is no likelihood of escaping the despair that abounds in Port- au-Prince. As elsewhere, those with money can purchase whatever they want. (Greco 1983:516)

Although not all gay sex was prostitution, the deepening poverty of Haiti helped to ensure that money played an inordinant role in even "voluntary" same-sex relations: "With the help of money," writes d'Adesky, "what existed as gay life in Haiti in the '60s and '70s flowed like a dream." In a report recently filed in *The Advocate,* d'Adesky writes of "hotels that catered to a gay clientele," of "discreet fucking rooms" in tourist hotels, and of slum houses that "would be emptied for a price and arrangements made." She continues by citing a North American participant in Haiti's "once-flourishing gay subculture."

> "There was a gay life that was very gala and that involved various sectors of society," said AIDS activist Stephen Machón, a former resident of Haiti who saw the tail end of what some call Haiti's gay golden period. "There would be the gay guys and the working boys and the tourists, of course, and the parties would be just fabulous. Some of it took place in the streets, but a lot went on behind the courtyard walls. You could lead a very flamboyant life-style within certain limitations, and it was wonderful." (d'Adesky 1991:31)

During the AMH-sponsored conference in 1983, one Haitian-American researcher read aloud from the pages of the 1983 *Spartacus International Gay Guide,* in which Haiti was enthusiastically recommended to the gay tourist: handsome men with "a great ability to satisfy" are readily available, but "there is no free sex in Haiti, except with other gay tourists you may come across. Your partners will expect to be paid for their services but the charges are nominal." Another advertisement, which ran in

The Advocate, assured the prospective tourist that Haiti is "a place where all your fantasies come true" (Moore and LeBaron 1986:82).

It was not long before interviews with Haitians with AIDS revealed their sexual contact with gay men from North America. In a key paper published in 1984, Guérin and coworkers from Haiti, North America, and Canada stated that "17 percent of our patients had sexual contact with [North] American tourists" (Guérin et al. 1984:256). Murray and Payne (1988:25-26) question the relevance of gay tourism in the Haitian AIDS epidemic: "Insofar as gay travel can be estimated from gay guidebooks, Haiti was one of the least-favored destinations in the Caribbean for gay travelers during the 1970s and the less-favored half of the island of Hispaniola."[7] His assessment is based only on "frequency of listing in gay guidebooks," surely a less significant indicator of the relevance of such tourism than the cluster studies which revealed direct sexual contact between Haitian men and North American gay tourists. It is important to note that the introduction of an epidemic of sexually transmitted disease need not involve some critical mass of sexual contact, but requires only that the infectious agent be introduced into a sexually active population (in this case, Haitian men). The Guérin et al. (1984) study makes this clear. Interestingly, Murray and Payne cite an American journalist's interview with Guérin and not the research published in the *Annals of the New York Academy of Science'.* "At the Haitian end of the hypothesized transmission vector, Dr. Jean- Michel Guérin of GHESKIO told [journalist Anne-Christine] d'Adesky that 'all his patients—without exception—had denied having sex with tourists.'" Yet the *Annals* article, which brought together the research of ten physicians representing research centers in Haiti, the United States, and Canada, clearly specifies which patients acknowledge sexual relations with gay tourists from North America.[8]

The existence of tourism, some of it gay, does not of course prove that such commerce was "the cause" of the Haitian AIDS epidemic, nor is it my intention to argue that it does. Such commerce does, however, throw into relief the ties between Haiti and nearby North America, ties not mentioned in early discussions of AIDS among Haitians, which often posited "isolated Haiti" as the *source* of the pandemic. In fact, a review of even the scholarly literature on Haiti would leave the impression that the country is the most "isolated" or "insular" of Caribbean countries. In an assessment resonant with the U.S. medical community's AIDS-related speculations, the author of one standard text remarks that "Haiti in 1950 was in general what it had been in 1900: a preindustrial society inhabited by ignorant, diseased peasants oblivious to the outside world" (Langley 1989:175). A more attentive study of Haiti's economy reveals that the nation has long been closely tied to the United States. In fact, Haiti plays an interesting role in what Orlando Patterson has termed the "West Atlantic system," an economic network encompassing much of the Caribbean basin and centered in the United States:

> Originally a region of diverse cultures and economies operating within the framework of several imperial systems, the West Atlantic region has emerged over the centuries as a single environment in which the dualistic United States center is asymmetrically linked to dualistic peripheral units. Unlike other peripheral systems of states—those of the Pacific, for example—the West Atlantic periphery has become more and more uniform, under the direct and immediate influence of the all-powerful center, in cultural, political and economic terms. Further, unlike other peripheral states in their relation to their centers, the West Atlantic system has a physical nexus in the metropolis at the tip of Florida. (Patterson 1987:258)

The Caribbean nations with high attack rates of AIDS are all part of the West Atlantic system.

A relation between the degree of "insertion" in this network and prevalence of AIDS is suggested by the following exercise. Excluding Puerto Rico, which is not an independent country, the five Caribbean basin nations with the largest number of cases by 1986 were as follows: the Dominican Republic, the Bahamas, Trinidad/Tobago, Mexico, and Haiti. In terms of trade, which are the five countries most dependent upon the United States? Export indices offer a convenient marker of involvement in the West Atlantic system. In both 1983 and 1977, the years for which such data are available, the same five countries were' most linked to the United States economically—and they are precisely those countries with the largest number of AIDS cases.[9] And the country with the most cases, Haiti, was also the country most fully dependent on U.S. exports. In all the Caribbean basin, only Puerto Rico is more economically dependent on the United States. And only Puerto Rico has reported more cases of AIDS to the Pan American Health Organization.

To understand the West Atlantic AIDS pandemic, a historical understanding of the worldwide spread of HIV is crucial. The thesis that evolving economic forces run parallel to the lineaments of the American epidemics is confirmed by comparing Haiti with a neighboring island, Cuba, the sole country in the region not enmeshed in the West Atlantic system. In Haiti, as we have seen, several epidemiological studies of asymptomatic city dwellers reveal HIV seroprevalence rates of approximately 9 percent. In 1986 in Cuba, only 0.01 percent of 1,000,000 persons tested were found to have antibodies to HIV (Liautaud, Pape, and Pamphile 1988:690). Had the pandemic begun a few decades earlier, the epidemiology of HIV infection in the Caribbean might well have been different. Havana, once the "tropical playground of the Americas," might have been as much an epicenter of the pandemic as Carrefour.

ENDNOTES

1. Studies of U.S. press coverage of AIDS suggest some of the reasons for public perceptions of Caribbean AIDS as a largely Haitian problem. When on July 25, 1985, CBS news ran a story about HIV transmission in Australia, "it was the network's first mention of AIDS outside the United States, Africa, or Haiti" (Kinsella 1989:144).

2. Such has also been the case in Denmark, where sexual contact with a North American gay man, rather than "promiscuity" per se, was an important risk factor in the first cases of AIDS (Gerstoft et al. 1985).

3. When questioned by Payne (1987) regarding the ethnographic validity of their observations of homosexuality in the Dominican Republic, Koenig and coworkers replied that their "information on the Dominican Republic does come from on-site visits to hotels that cater to the gay tourist trade. These places are frequented often by visitors from the United States and Caribbean countries" (Koenig, Brache, and Levy 1987:47). In a retrospective assessment seeming to support Koenig's argument, Garcia (1991:2) writes that "in the

4. 1970s, [Puerta Plata] was favored by gay tourists and is considered to be one of the initial ports of entry for HIV in the Dominican Republic. During the 1970s, tourists were predominantly gay, over-sixty males who engaged in sex with local teenaged male prostitutes:"

5. Haitians, notes Met:raux (1972:359), are "irritated-understandably by the label 'Voodoo-land' which travel agencies have stuck on their home.'"

6. The protagonist of Graham Greene's The Comedians is a Port-au-Prince hotelier who in 1961 remembers fondly the days when tourists flocked to his bar and made love in the pool. "The drummer's fled to New York, and all the bikini girls stay in Miami now," he explains to two prospective clients. "You'll probably be the only guests I have" (Greene 1966:11).

7. Although the lawsuit seemed ridiculous to most non-Haitian commentators, the effects of the CDC classification were probably apparent to some of the agency's operatives before the March 1983 announcement of the risk grouping. Requesting anonymity, one public-health officer made the following observations, cited in a front-page story in the New York Times of July 31, 1983: "It's a working definition. If there turned out to be a large national or ethnic 280. NOTES TO PAGES 148-154 group, you would single that group out. But when you translate a working definition to a small, poverty-struck country like Haiti, it is devastating. It destroys one of their main cash industries-tourism."

8. Payne (1987:47) had previously observed that "several gay travel guides, such as the Bob Damron Guidebook for 1982, contain as many as ten entries for the Bahamas, but only four for the Dominican Republic and one for Haiti."It is important to note, as did Lange and Jaffe (1987), that the AIDS attack rate in the Bahamas was then even higher than that in Haiti.

9. It is not clear how such a misreading might have occurred. Ostensibly, however, d'Adesky has abandoned this tack, as her more recent essay, Derlines the sex-for-money exchanges that took place between tourists and poor Haitian men (see d'Adesky 1991:31).

10. See the International Monetary Fund's summaries of "Directions of Trade Statistics" in that organization's Yearbook 1984.

8

From Ground Zero to the War in Afghanistan

By Rick Fawn

The attacks of September 11 may almost have been predictable. While the name al-Qaeda was not used publicly by its members before 9/11, its adherents had bombed the World Trade Center eight years before, in an attack that, if fully successful, would have killed an estimated 200,000.[1] The group had planned to bomb multiple aircraft over the Pacific in Project Bojinka and to crash a jet into an American government building. The same group succeeded in the simultaneous bombing of US embassies in Dar-es-Salaam and Nairobi in 1998. A related group hijacked an Air France airbus from Algeria in December 1994 with the intention of crashing it into Paris. The operative group, the type of target, and the means had all been in evidence before.

Before 9/11 Osama bin Laden was also identified as the leading terrorist threat to the USA—the CIA revealed after the 9/11 attacks that it had offered a bounty three years earlier for bin Laden dead or alive. This should perhaps not be surprising as bin Laden's 1998 declaration of war on the USA could have been taken seriously in light of tangible attacks rather than rhetoric. Bill Clinton admitted in late September 2001 that as President 'we did everything' to apprehend him: 'I authorized the arrest and, if necessary, the killing of Osama bin Laden, and we actually made contact with a group in Afghanistan to do it.'[2] Not apprehending bin Laden was, Clinton said, the greatest regret of his presidency. Preparations by US intelligence agencies before 9/11 for mass terrorism against mainland America were among the fastest expanding federal programs and also unprecedented among countries.[3]

US intelligence reports in summer 2001 are now known to have warned of attacks against the American mainland. The specific operatives behind the attacks took exploratory or preparatory measures that caused suspicion, but tragically not enough for a rights-based, liberal society to conduct a full-scale investigation or arrest.[4] Zacarias Moussaoui, believed to have been the twentieth hijacker, was arrested a month before 9/11, but his computer was not searched because the FBI could not secure a warrant.

By mid-2002, allegations—some perhaps politically motivated, others probably neutral—bounded about how much intelligence services and even the White House knew about some sort of terrorist attack on the USA. In May 2002 Democrat Senator and Senate Majority Leader Tom Daschle charged that the Bush administration had warnings in August 2001 of a major attack by al-Qaeda that included a hijacking. Two weeks later CIA Director George Tenet was 'in denial' about the CIA's receipt of information on two 9/11 hijackers connected to al-Qaeda two years before the attacks, but accounts by September 2002 suggested that in July 2001 leading US officials already expected a 'spectacular attack' by bin Laden within weeks.[5]

This chapter traces the major events made in response to the September attacks. Its focus is on: coalition building—both diplomatic and military; the decision to wage both war and undertake peacekeeping in Afghanistan; and the measures taken to stabilize that war-ravaged country.

FROM GROUND ZERO TO AFGHANISTAN

By mid-morning on 9/11 the world knew that the impact from two 767s had collapsed the two 110-story towers of the World Trade Center, ignited neighboring buildings, and also completely destroying adjacent several buildings. This devastated area of Manhattan promptly gained the mournful nickname of 'ground zero,' a term previously used by Pentagon staff for the center of their building as a euphemism for the Cold War nuclear strike that never came. But this hub of American military coordination was also in disarray, a third aircraft having slammed into a side of the Pentagon. Buildings throughout the capital, including key government facilities like the White House and Congress, were evacuated amid fears of additional attacks. Speculation grew over the intended target of a fourth hijacked plane—most likely a political target like the White House or Camp David or possibly an east coast nuclear power plant; but this plane was heroically downed by its passengers over Pennsylvania, foiling further malevolence.

Through the attacks, bin Laden achieved more than he expected. In a videotape released in November 2001 bin Laden explained that he had hoped that three or four floors of each tower would burn and that the towers' steel structure would melt from the heat of the detonating fuel, causing only the floors above to collapse. Even he, in self-professed, if diabolic 'optimism,' appeared not to expect each tower to disintegrate completely.

While US forces were caught unaware and were arrayed against a seemingly invisible enemy, retaliatory planning began immediately. Unlike right after the 1995 Oklahoma bombing, in which blame turned quickly to foreign Muslim terrorists rather than home-grown American fundamentalists, forthright statements of culpability were few on the day.

In circumstances of uncertainty and expectations of additional attacks, President Bush was hurried to the safety of a nuclear-bomb-proof bunker briefly while the US government sought not only to operate but also to respond. Bush warned on 9/11 that retaliation was imminent. Planning began that morning for a war in Afghanistan. Bilateral and multilateral diplomacy were used for almost a month before they were complemented by military measures.

On 12 September the essence of the American response was already outlined. Bush labeled the attacks as 'acts of war' and declared that no distinction would be made between those who conducted them and those who shelter the perpetrators. His slogan 'Either you are with us or with the terrorists' defined allegiances. International support was immediately forthcoming from traditional American allies. Unprecedented in its half-century existence, NATO invoked Article 5, offering immediate assistance from all members to the USA, although the Bush administration would pursue its war effort outside NATO structures. The UN Security Council also passed Resolution 1368 that day, which recognized 'the inherent right of individual or collective self-defence' of Article 51 of the UN Charter and which also declared the body's 'readiness to take the necessary steps to respond to the terrorist attacks of September 11 2001 and to combat all forms of terrorism, in accordance with the Charter of the UN.'

A day later US Secretary of State Colin Powell pronounced bin Laden the chief suspect. Bush reiterated this on 15 September when he also declared the USA to be at war. Vice President Dick Cheney followed with warnings of a protracted war. But before applying military might, US authorities approached the Taliban for the release of bin Laden and top associates. The Taliban asked the USA for its proof and offered to try bin Laden in its own courts.

The nature of the attack was assessed on numerous fronts. The New York Stock Exchange was closed for four days; when it reopened on 17 September it suffered its largest single-day loss. The airline industry was perhaps the first economic-sector casualty. Swissair was the first of many Western airlines to declare bankruptcy, citing September 11 as a cause, while others blamed the event for

65

thousands of redundancies, some of which may have occurred regardless. Lost American output in the first week after the attack was estimated at US $40 billion; Chairman of the Federal Reserve Alan Greenspan said the US economy had 'ground to a halt.'[6] The International Monetary Fund (IMF) warned on 26 September of the first global recession in a decade. While the economic impact may have been overstated, the costs of providing additional security have diverted public funds in the USA and elsewhere. Expectations of recession pushed down the price of oil; and Gulf states, as well as Russia, assisted the industrial West by pledging nevertheless to increase petroleum production. And the world remained jittery—New York's Dow Jones Industrial Average lost 163 points when the crash of a light plane into Milan's Pirelli tower was initially feared as terrorism; with prompt news of an accident or the pilot's suicide, the Dow Jones regained 110 points by early afternoon. But this was a mild indication of the effects which further terrorism would have on markets. Initial economic fears were so grave, and the deviousness of the attacks so unprecedented, that al-Qaeda was believed to have placed 'put options' on US airlines before the attacks, allowing it to sell the shares at the pre-attack price but to pay only the depressed post-attack prices. If true, al-Qaeda would have netted billions for its own use and inflicted further insolence to the US economy. While the economic damage could thus have been greater, the saying remained 'Never have so few cost so many so much.'

The emerging American response combined diplomacy with assurances of righting the wrongs of 9/11. At a joint session of Congress on 20 September Bush pledged justice would be done, and demanded that the Taliban surrender al-Qaeda leaders and all terrorists to US authorities, close permanently terrorist camps and allow American verification. The importance of Britain was evident, with Blair attending a White House dinner beforehand (despite being late due to new airport security) and then seated prominently in Congress for Bush's speech in which the President said his country 'had no truer friend than Great Britain.'[7]

Despite being bolstered by the support of Britain and other Western countries, any US-led military operations in landlocked Afghanistan hinged on the support of Pakistan. The Pakistani government, particularly its Inter-Services Intelligence (ISI) agency had nurtured the Taliban, had vested interests in its continued domination of Afghanistan, and was one of only three states to recognize the Taliban as the official regime. Sacrificing bin Laden for the continuation of the Taliban thus seemed a major Pakistani strategic interest. But on 18 September, and again on 28 September, Pakistani representatives were unable to convince the Taliban to surrender bin Laden, and the Taliban signaled the expectation of an attack by closing its air space and putting its defences on alert. However, in a possible bow to American pressure, a Council of 1,000 clerics agreed to turn over bin Laden to the USA and asked him to leave Afghanistan. The Taliban took the extraordinary measure of overturning that, and downgrading it to a 'suggestion.' The Taliban's ambassador to Pakistan, Mullah Abdul Salam Zaeef, rejected Bush's demand of the same day for extradiction of bin Laden as 'an insult of Islam' and proclaimed 'We will never surrender to evil and might.' What diplomatic standing the Taliban had was beginning to erode: while still recognizing the regime, Pakistani diplomats were withdrawn from Kabul. The United Arab Emirates ended its recognition on 22 September; Saudi Arabia followed three days later, declaring that the Taliban harbored, armed and encouraged terrorists.

Apart from the Taliban's increased isolation, the Bush administration now engaged in changing Pakistani policy towards Afghanistan. American sanctions imposed on Pakistan for its 1998 nuclear testing were lifted (as were the corresponding ones on India). On 7 October Musharraf removed Lieutenant-General Mahmood Ahmed as head of the ISI, and other military figures believed to be supportive of the Taliban were 'sidelined.'

In the USA, Bush issued an Executive Order on 24 September to disrupt terrorist finances, with several accounts believed connected to bin Laden or al-Qaeda frozen immediately. His administration made clear that the 'war on terrorism' would have phases,

66

the first of which would be against Afghanistan, a policy underlined by the continuing assembly of American military power in the country's vicinity. Russian President Putin not only said he would increase Russian military supplies to anti-Taliban forces but also would provide intelligence to the USA. Moscow acquiesced as American aircraft arrived in Uzbekistan within days of 9/11 and personnel began arriving in other former Soviet Central Asian republics by early October.[8] Recognizing the need for international, multi-ethnic and multi-faith support, the US government altered the name of its preparation from 'Operation Infinite Justice' to 'Operation Enduring Freedom.' The UN Security Council passed an American-drafted resolution on 28 September imposing extensive requirements on member states to counteract terrorism on their territory.[9]

On 30 September, the Taliban admitted that bin Laden was at an undisclosed location in Afghanistan 'for his safety and security.' The Taliban's ambassador to Pakistan, Mullah Abdul Salam Zaeef, announced that bin Laden was 'under the control of the Islamic Emirate of Afghanistan,' although he added that only those responsible for his security knew his whereabouts, and that 'He's in a place which cannot be located by anyone.'[10] In these circumstances, Pakistani President Musharraf announced on 1 October that his government had done everything possible to achieve a diplomatic solution and that war was not inevitable. At the same time, hundreds of Pakistanis were reported crossing into Afghanistan to prepare for jihad against the United States.[11]

The start of October suggested that strategic shifts might occur within Afghanistan. The Northern Alliance declared that it had made an agreement with exiled Afghan King Zahir Shah to overthrow the Taliban. But the fate of Afghanistan did not hang only on internal machinations. On 6 October Bush told the Taliban its time was short and rejected its suggestion of considering the release of Western aid workers held on charges of proselytizing Christianity as an implied compromise on surrendering bin Laden. What diplomacy had existed between the USA and the Taliban was finished.

On 7 October US attacks began, with British participation, using cruise missiles and aircraft. After repeating demands that bin Laden be surrendered, Bush announced on television that 'None of these demands were met. And now the Taliban will pay the price.' The President said the decision was made 'only after the greatest care and a lot of prayer' and 'We did not ask for this mission, but we will fulfill it.' In terms of the emerging fight Bush concluded that 'The battle is now joined on many fronts' and warned 'We will not falter. And we will not fail.'[12]

The first strikes by tomahawk missiles and about forty aircraft hit targets in Kabul including a presidential palace, a media center and anti-aircraft weapons, and Kandahar's airport, but mostly outlying areas where terrorist training camps were suspected. Bin Laden was believed to have survived. In a videotape released on 7 October, bin Laden took credit for the 9/11 attacks, thereby changing his organization's previous practice of not claiming responsibility for its terrorism. He also called on Muslims to engage in a jihad against the USA and its supporters.

The first indication that the strikes would not necessarily be precise was the accidental bombing of a UN facility that killed four mine-clearance personnel. With augmented Anglo-American bombing underway, the strength of the international coalition was questioned when Blair, on a Middle Eastern diplomatic tour, was refused reception by Saudi officials.

Blair's Middle Eastern visits may have been in Bush's stead for fear of hostile popular receptions and diplomatic rebuffs. Israel's adoption of American rhetoric of fighting a war on terrorism to justify its forceful measures against continuing Palestinian protests and suicide attacks, further inflamed wider Arab opinion. But even if the USA risked not having support for its Afghanistan campaign across the Middle East, Bush was undeterred. On 10 October Bush declared the elimination of global terrorism as 'our calling' and proclaimed 'Now is the time to draw the line in the sand against the evil ones.' The American war took on a more

67

tangible form when, on the same day, the FBI published the names and photographs of its twenty-two 'most wanted' terrorists.

Despite this apparent offensive, major alerts of imminent terrorist attack against the USA were declared, first by the FBI on 11 October, with several others following, including Attorney-General John Ashcroft's of 29 October. When such attacks did not occur, US officials said it was impossible to know whether extra vigilance might have prevented renewed attacks. Tom Ridge, freshly installed to the new post of Director of Homeland Security, said the anthrax attacks and 9/11 were likely connected. With four apparently unrelated people dead from anthrax, speculation over its origins turned to Iraq; but tests of the substance indicated that it was an American strain, and suspicions eventually turned to a US government laboratory outside Washington. Even though Bush would come to declare the anthrax outbreak as 'a second wave of terrorist attacks upon our country,'[13] a year later, blame remained undetermined.

Returning to Asia, although many Muslims throughout the region protested the American actions, and a widespread strike was attempted in Pakistan to undermine the government's support for the US war, the Pakistani government moved to full backing of the USA following Powell's mid-October visit when Musharraf was known bluntly to have requested debt relief. Apart from the lifting of the 1998 sanctions, speculation suggested that Pakistan would receive considerable financial benefits from the USA for changing its policy. By 10 November Bush had publicly pledged over US $1 billion aid to Pakistan.

The war entered a further stage when, on 20 October, the Pentagon acknowledged the first deployment of some 200 ground troops, which were operating near the Taliban's spiritual center of Kandahar in southern Afghanistan. The first American personnel were killed when a helicopter crashed in Pakistan; the American military rejected the Taliban's claim of downing it. The next day American attacks refocused on Taliban positions near the northern city Mazar-e Sharif, where the Northern Alliance had made some advances.

Rumsfeld indicated that the Northern Alliance could also advance towards Kabul as US air targeting of the Taliban had improved because of intelligence supplied by American special forces on the ground.

On 27 October thousands of Pakistani fighters gathered to fight a jihad against the USA. The transnational composition of the Taliban/al-Qaeda forces was further revealed when five of their members killed by an American attack on Kabul turned out to be British citizens. In Pakistan a day later, six masked attackers, thought to be Islamic supporters of al-Qaeda, shot dead fifteen Christian worshipers and a policeman at St. Dominic's Church in Bahawalpur, central Pakistan.

By the end of October US troops were known to be operating in support of the Northern Alliance in northern Afghanistan, while early November saw intensified US bombings, including the use of B-52s to assist a major Northern Alliance advance. Al-Jazeera broadcast another declaration by bin Laden in which he called on Pakistanis to oppose their government and support the Taliban against the USA. The American war effort seemed to be succeeding as Rumsfeld declared on 4 November that while it still retained local power, the Taliban no longer functioned as a government. The next day the US military said it was exploring the use of airbases in post-Soviet Central Asia for its bombing missions, while more Northern Alliance forces amassed north of Kabul.

The construction of a multinational force continued. In a remarkable development, considering its constitutional limitations on the geographical deployment of its soldiers and the Green Party's ideological opposition to military operations, the German government agreed on 6 November to an American request for almost 4,000 German soldiers. A day later the Italian parliament accepted a similar request, assigning 2,700 troops, and on 8 November Jordan's King Abdullah gave verbal backing to the war. Musharraf, however, stated that the war needed to be short and that bombing should cease during the approaching Muslim holy month of Ramadan, which the USA did not do, but it increased humanitarian air drops. Musharraf's government also requested that the Taliban withdraw its diplomats from Karachi, although the final Taliban representation would only be asked to leave Pakistan on 22 November. In broader diplomacy, the UN's special envoy indicated plans for a provisional Afghan government that would contain various representations from the population, including potentially parts of the Taliban, and that would be assisted by an international peacekeeping force.

Despite some successes for the USA in international diplomacy, the war looked less successful than desired in late October and early November. As the bombing continued, Chairman of the US Joint Chiefs of Staff Richard Myers said that targets included air defence and command and control facilities, early warning radar, airfields and other infrastructure. But even Rumsfeld conceded that key targets were few. As B-52s were introduced into the campaign at the end of October to pound Taliban positions, the Taliban Foreign Minister mockingly proposed that Bush and Blair duel with Mullah Mohammed Omar using Kalashnikovs.

At the beginning of November reports declared the bombing was 'way behind schedule,' that coming snow would complicate the war and give the Taliban advantage, and that people were beginning to starve in some provinces.[14] The *New York Times* wrote that the Bush administration had 'underestimated the Taliban's resistance' and that Afghanistan was 'an especially difficult battlefield.'[15]

In a major military breakthrough in Afghanistan the Northern Alliance captured Mazar-i-Sharif on 9 November; two days later it claimed half the country, and approached Kabul. On 13 November Northern Alliance troops entered the capital. Military historian John Keegan suggested the fall of the north and Kabul was 'one of the most remarkable reversals of military fortune since Kitchener's victory at Omdurman in the Sudan in 1898.'[16] This may have been a remarkable military achievement, but its timing was unanticipated. Indeed, Bush had requested the Northern Alliance not to enter Kabul until a provisional government was established, and the UN's representative for Afghanistan, former Algerian Foreign Minister Lakhdar Brahimi, rushed to assemble Afghan leaders for discussions.

In the USA fears surged concerning a new terrorist attack following the crash in Brooklyn on 12 November of American Airlines flight 587. Among the dead were two WTC employees who had survived 9/11. The crash was deemed accidental only after national security alerts were imposed and international financial markets plummeted. The spectre of domestic attack did not diminish, however, as by mid-November the US Department of Justice had accumulated 5,000 names of people living in the USA to be questioned about 9/11.[17]

In Kabul, joy at the end of Taliban rule was evident, with music being played publicly for the first time since the Taliban consolidated its power by seizing Kabul in 1996, men's beards being trimmed or shaven off and women able to bare their faces; but victory was not bloodless, with the International Red Cross reporting that hundreds were killed in the earlier taking of Mazar-i-Sharif.

With the north largely secured, save for the area around Konduz in the northeast, near the Tajik border, Western attention turned to other parts of Afghanistan. Taliban control was eroding elsewhere as Jalalabad fell and the Taliban faced revolt in Kandahar. On 15 November an advance group of 100 British Royal Marines was deployed at Bagram airbase. Arriving without prior knowledge of the Northern Alliance, it was nearly fired on. Thereafter British Foreign Secretary Jack Straw told his Northern Alliance counterpart Abdullah Abdullah that he would personally inform the Northern Alliance of future British arrivals. These unannounced British personnel became the first conventional forces, after the small number of American, to be used in Afghanistan. French forces were meanwhile being prepared for deployment to Mazar-i-Sharif to assist with the distribution of humanitarian aid.

US forces also claimed that bombings of Kandahar and Kabul in mid-November had killed enemy leaders, including Muhammed Atef, a leading al-Qaeda military commander, and one of those named on the American 'most wanted' list. US troops were also blocking south-running roads to capture others. As auspicious as these measures may have appeared, Mullah Omar broadcast on the BBC's Pashtun service his intended aim of the 'destruction of America.'[18] If anti-American sentiment could be stoked by such rhetoric, it did not deter the arrival of soldiers from other countries.

With the military dynamic clearly shifting in favor of anti-Taliban forces by the middle of November, postwar jockeying for power began. Former Afghan President Burhanudi Rabbani, forced from office by the Taliban, returned to Kabul. The Northern Alliance consented to send delegates to a UN-sponsored conference in Bonn to discuss the postwar government with other Afghan groups. A large Russian delegation also arrived in Kabul.

Having yet to sight bin Laden, the US military made radio announcements of rewards of up to US $25 million for information on his location or that of his senior associates. Military officials later admitted that many Afghans would not appreciate this value and that offers, such as a flock of sheep, might have been more relevant. Military efforts now concentrated on southern Afghanistan, where the Taliban continued to hold Kandahar, and on the Taliban's last northern bastion of Konduz. There, a peaceful end to the siege was obstructed by the presence of foreign fighters, including Arabs, Pakistanis and Chechens, who were thought to want to fight to the end rather than surrender. Konduz fell on 26 November after intensive fighting over several days during which a Northern Alliance attack was supported by American air attacks. Simultaneously in southern Afghanistan, US air power focused on caves and tunnels around Kandahar.

The brutality of the war was brought home to the West with the uprising of Taliban prisoners held in the Qala-i-Janghi fortress outside Mazar-i-Sharif, in which CIA agent Johnny 'Mike' Spann was killed. The Northern Alliance retook the facility only after three days and repeated bombings of it by US aircraft. The deaths of hundreds of enemy forces prompted international human rights groups to demand investigations and raised questions of the observance of rules of war and of general human rights by the Northern Alliance. If such questions could be avoided because Taliban/al-Qaeda forces were considered non-Western, then the discovery of American John Walker Lindh among them suggested otherwise.

The first conventional US forces—some hundreds of Marines—were deployed on 25 November outside Kandahar, and then took over an airfield. This measure prompted Bush to prepare Americans for the possibility of combat deaths. One US military official described the rules of engagement as 'unrestricted hunting license'; Special Forces were being used, and hundreds of enemy forces were reported killed without any US casualties.[19]

While fighting continued in Afghanistan, the UN conference to determine Afghanistan's postwar order began in Bonn on 27 November. While UN officials were optimistic about the outcome, several obstacles unsurprisingly arose. Among them were that former Afghan President Rabbani first refused to attend the conference in person, staying in his 'presidential palace' in Kabul, and then objected to a large international peacekeeping deployment. The lesser-known Pashtun Hamid Karzai was able to address the conference by a video link and called for unity among the assembled representatives. Rabbani's personal representative at the conference conveyed that Rabbani was under strong international pressure to change his stand, a situation intensified when Russian diplomats, previous supporters of Rabbani, made clear to other members of the faction Moscow's expectation of their conformity to the desired international outcome. Rabbani may even have been facing an insurrection among his ranks, and in these circumstances, modified his position.

By 2 December a draft agreement was circulated which indicated that former King Zahir Shah, who had already returned to Kabul with a triumphant parade, also would not stand as an interim president, and thereafter Rabbani publicly consented to other candidates to head the provisional government. On 5 December the peace agreement was signed. Karzai, fresh from fighting with US forces against the Taliban in the south, where he was also injured by a mistargeted 2,000-pound American bomb, was named President of the interim body. But just after its signing the agreement seemed weakened when ethnic Uzbek Abdul Rashid Dostum objected to what he called the underrepresentation of his people.

A new dimension in the war emerged as the US Defence Department started on 30 November to formulate the procedures to bring Afghan prisoners before military tribunals. Ashcroft stated that not only would human rights be maintained but also that practices applied to non-American detainees would be in keeping with the American Constitution. These declarations laid the groundwork for one of the most contentious measures by the US government in the war: the establishment of the Camp X-Ray detention center at the American military base at Guantanamo Bay, Cuba. Eventually hundreds of foreign nationals captured in Afghanistan were held there, restrained in small chain-link cages and without an agreed legal status conferring protection to them.

In Afghanistan, by 6 December Kandahar seemed set to fall, with Taliban forces in the city agreeing to surrender to Karzai's new government. But the Taliban then promptly reversed its commitment, while Mullah Omar apparently disappeared. US forces intensified ground and air operations to close suspected Taliban escape routes.

At the end of the first week of December, Kandahar collapsed into anarchy as Afghan factions fought against each other. US Marines engaged in their first combat on the ground on 7 December in southern Afghanistan as they fought enemy forces while following information from Afghan warlords that bin Laden and Mullah Mohammed Omar were cornered in caves along the Pakistani border. US bombers pounded the area. Rumsfeld confessed 'I see, literally, dozens and dozens and dozens of pieces of intelligence every day … and they don't agree.' As to confirmation of bin Laden in the Tora Bora caves, Rumsfeld said 'One can't know with precision until the chase around the yard is over.' Even though talk was at this point of the Taliban having been defeated, Rumsfeld again signaled caution: 'It would be premature to suggest that once Kandahar surrenders that, therefore, we kind of relax and say "well, that takes care of that," because it doesn't.'[20]

Rumsfeld was right. The fall of Kandahar signaled the formal end of Taliban rule, but the fight against its members and al-Qaeda and the search for their chief leaders remained. The story of international presence in Afghanistan after the fall of Kandahar is one of three parts: the continuing American-led war; the implementation of an international stabilization force; and efforts to build political and social stability in this war-torn country. The latter issues are revisited in the book's conclusion.

Fears of terrorism outside Afghanistan did not subside with the fall of Kandahar. Most notably, British-born Richard Reid attempted on 22 December to ignite a 'shoe bomb' on American Airlines flight 63 from Paris to Miami. Through the purchase of a computer by American journalists in Kabul, Reid's previous travel across Europe, the Middle East and Asia, were matched to those of an al-Qaeda operative's nickname. Meanwhile, enemy resistance was much greater than expected, particularly in early December around Kandahar and Spin Boldak, along the Pakistani border. By January 2002, the Pentagon acknowledged 'non-trivial pockets' of resistance; some foreign reports said these included a renegade Taliban/al-Qaeda army of 5,000 soldiers with 450 pieces of armor.[21] US Joint Chiefs of Staff Chairman General Richard Myers said that even if military sweeps did not capture al-Qaeda leaders they collected important intelligence. Efforts to apprehend enemy figures resulted in Musharraf consenting on 8 January 2002 to US soldiers operating in Pakistan to pursue al-Qaeda. Chief of Staff Myers said, however, that US forces would not act unilaterally inside Pakistan.

The American-led fighting was no longer conducted as consistently as before, becoming several different types of operations, with specific objectives. The Pentagon invited allied forces to participate in these difficult operations. Thus, 1,700 Royal Marines were deployed to aid Americans. Previously, British forces were involved in missions such as securing Bagram airbase or contributing in a non-combat role to the international peacekeeping force. Likewise, Canadian troops, with a history

71

of peacekeeping, were deployed in combat missions for the first time since the Korean War. The largest such anti-terrorist maneuver in Afghanistan, Operation Anaconda, ended on 18 March, although many enemy forces were believed to have escaped to Pakistan.

The British began combat operations with US and allied Afghan forces on 16 April 2002 in Operation Ptarmigan, named for the northern bird known for camouflage. Operation Snipe, a two-week operation in the first half of May, was declared a success for having eliminated infrastructure and a 'vast arsenal of weapons' and for depriving the opposition of strategic assets that could be used later. While no enemies were killed or captured, British commander Brigadier Roger Lane said 'We have delivered a significant blow to the ability of al-Qaeda to plan, mount and sustain terrorist operations in Afghanistan and beyond.'[22] Even the size of the arsenal seized was later disputed. Operation Condor began on 16 May 2002 with over 1,000 US and foreign personnel and a similar number of Afghans attacking cave complexes along the Pakistani border. This maneuver demonstrated the need to deploy ground forces rather than to rely solely on US air power and indigenous ground troops. Throughout, however, British forces never engaged enemy forces directly. Operation Ptarmigan unfortunately seemed a euphemism not for the international forces but for the enemy.

With such an atypical conflict, the tactics on both sides necessarily diversified. Remnant Taliban and al-Qaeda forces apparently distributed leaflets in early April 2002 offering up to US $50,000 for a captured Westerner and US $100,000 for a dead one. US commanders admitted that this tactic, similar to an American one, had won over Afghan fighters. And while the US paid its Afghan fighters US $200 per month, vastly more than they could otherwise earn, the practice fuelled inter-Afghan rivalries.[23]

American initiatives continued outside Afghanistan. Yet another new geographic and strategic dimension to the war was added with American use of military bases in Central Asia as coalition aircraft flew military missions from the former Soviet republic of Kyrgyzstan from early March. The Manas base at Bishkek airport would house about 3,000 troops, approximately two-thirds of whom were American who arrived in April. The others were drawn from some dozen additional states.

Even with the sustained international support for the war, and unprecedented American diplomatic and military presence in central and south Asia, many military mistakes and accidents inevitably occurred. In a training exercise near Kandahar an American reservist pilot bombed Canadian troops, killing four and wounding eight. US gunships mistakenly fired on Afghan wedding celebrations in eastern Afghanistan in May—killing as many as a dozen civilians—when they came to support Australian forces under enemy fire.[24] The Afghan government concluded that US bombings had killed forty-six civilians, including twenty-five in the wedding.

Some of these unintended casualties were perhaps an indication of the difficulties of waging the war against an elusive enemy. American and allied Afghan forces encountered heavy resistance in early March 2002 at Shar-i-kot in eastern Afghanistan, where al-Qaeda was believed to be recruiting more local support. On 4 March eight Americans were killed, and forty wounded, in the highest single incident of American combat fatalities. Most were killed when an American Chinook helicopter was shot down, the first time a US aircraft was so destroyed. This suggested that substantial resistance was being mounted in the east of Afghanistan, in what US Central Command described as a 'fight to the death' and in which at least 500 enemy forces were believed killed. At the same time, the Pakistani government announced that it would assign additional troops to its 1,500-mile border with Afghanistan, having already deployed some 60,000.

The continued fighting, its unconventional format and the allied casualties (unlike in Kosovo) may have led US Commander Tommy Franks mistakenly to say: 'First let me say that our thoughts and prayers go to the families and the friends of the service members who have lost their lives in our ongoing operations in Vietnam.'[25]

Searches throughout 2002 of suspected al-Qaeda operational centers in Afghanistan by foreign troops gave indications of the movement's broader terrorist intentions. Among them were videotapes instructing on the use of various weapons, including anti-aircraft, and showing what appeared to be tests of crude chemical weapons on dogs, suggesting that al-Qaeda was developing weapons of mass destruction. The ongoing and expanding nature of the 'war on terrorism' was underscored by Bush's 29 January State of the Union Address in which he labeled Iraq, Iran and North Korea 'an axis of evil.'

Terrorist attacks believed related to al-Qaeda nevertheless continued. Apart from lethal attacks on Christians and on French engineers in Pakistan, the French oiltanker Limburg was damaged off Yemen on 6 October 2002 after being rammed by an explosive-laden dingy in an operation similar to that against USS *Cole*. American Marines stationed in Kuwait were repeatedly shot at in early October 2002, while one was killed and another wounded on 8 October. The extent of al-Qaeda's activities may not be known, but large inter-religious attacks have also occurred. In predominantly Christian Zamboanga, Philippines, for example, 5 people were killed and some 150 injured from the bombing of a shopping center on 17 October. A Christmas Eve bombing in the Philippines that killed 13 and injured 12 was specifically blamed on 'Islamic militants.'[26]

On 12 November 2002 al-Jazeera's broadcast of an undated audiotape of bin Laden, which US authorities generally accepted as genuine, gave credence to those and other attacks as being part of coordinated operations by al-Qaeda. Instead of being dead, bin Laden condemned Bush as a 'modern-day Pharaoh' and Cheney and Powell as 'Hulega of the Mongols.' He threatened Westerners with 'You will be killed as you bomb. And expect more that will further distress you.' He also commended several of the recent attacks on Western targets, including the tourist-frequented Sari Club bombing in Bali that killed over 200 on 12 October, the three-day Moscow hostage siege and the fatal shooting of an American USAID staffer in Amman,

Jordan later that month. Bin Laden's tape also specifically threatened attacks against Australia, Britain, Canada, France, Germany and Italy.

These apparent global dangers make the outcome of Afghanistan more vital. Its future is likely to be punctuated by further enemy resistance and violence. Karzai and key ministers have faced assassination attempts, and Afghan Aviation Minister Abdul Rahman was killed. 'Kamikaze camels,' the ubiquitous beasts strapped with explosives, have been sent wandering towards facilities of the interim government and foreign forces. Even so, a strong recognition, and a smaller tangible commitment, existed among Western governments to secure Afghanistan and begin its wholesale reconstruction. This goal cannot be neglected because as terrorism continues to be a key policy issue, Afghanistan's future will stand in judgment as part of the wider, more permanent goals of the 'war on terrorism.'

NOTES

1. Mark Juergensmeyer, *Terror in the Mind of God: The Global Rise of Religious Violence* (Berkeley, CA: University of California Press, 2000), p. 62; and James Dwyer, David Kocieniewski, Deirdre Murphy and Peg Tyre, *Two Seconds under the World: Terror comes to America—The Conspiracy behind the World Trade Center Bombing* (New York: Crown, 1994).

2. Details of the CIA plan were first published in the *New York Times*, 30 Sept. 2001. An investigation by British-based Financial Times found the Clinton administration declined offers of intelligence sharing from Sudan two months before the 1998 East Africa embassy bombings that would have included 300 pages of detailed information on al-Qaeda. Mark Huband, 'US Rejected Sudanese Files on Al-Qaeda,' *Financial Times*, 30 Nov. 2001.

3. Richard A. Falkenrath, 'Problems of Preparedness: U.S. Readiness for a Domestic Terrorist Attack,' *International Security*, Vol. 25, No. 4 (Spring 2001), pp. 147–8.

4. A leading example was the application by Mohammed Atta, a key instigator of the attacks, to a Florida bank for a loan to finance

flying lessons and to buy a cropduster. Despite having a blackeye, threatening the loan officer, and talking of attacking Washington, he provoked no suspicion; he was denied the loan because he did not meet criteria for foreign nationals. *The Times*, 8 June 2002.

5. *Financial Times*, 4 June 2002, p. 6; and 20 Sept. 2002, p. 20.

6. Larry Elliot and Heather Stewart, 'The Cost of War?' *The Guardian*, 22 Sept. 2001.

7. 'A Nation Challenged: President Bush's Address on Terrorism Before a Joint Meeting of Congress,' *New York Times*, 21 Sept. 2001.

8. John Hooper and Kevin O'Flynn, 'Russia Exploits the War Dividend,' *The Guardian*, 26 Sept. 2001, p. 6.

9. Among other features, Resolution 1373 (2001), stipulated that 'all States shall: … (c) Deny safe haven to those who finance, plan, support, or commit terrorist acts, or provide safe havens; (d) Prevent those who finance, plan, facilitate or commit terrorist acts from using their respective territories for those purposes against other States or their citizens.'

10. Cited in John F. Burns, 'Taliban Say They Hold Bin Laden, for His Safety, But Who Knows Where?' *New York Times*, 1 Oct. 2001.

11. *The Guardian*, 2 Oct. 2001.

12. Bush's speech was widely reported. The official website is: http://www.whitehouse.gov/news/releases/2001/10/20011007-8.htm/

13. 'Bush Says U.S. Will Solve Anthrax Crimes,' Radio Address by the President to the Nation, The Oval Office, Radio Transcript, Office of the Press Secretary 3 Nov. 2001.

14. [No author] 'Winter is Coming and the Taliban are Strong as Ever. What Now for the War on Terror?' *The Guardian*, 3 Nov. 2001, p. 6.

15. *New York Times*, 8 Nov. 2001.

16. *Daily Telegraph*, 14 Nov. 2001.

17. Reuters, 14 Nov. 2001.

18. Transcript posted at http://www.news.bbc.co.uk/hi/english/world/south_asia

19. *Washington Times*, 23 Nov. 2001.

20. Quoted in *The Scotsman*, 7 and 8 Dec. 2001.

21. *The Times*, 25 Jan. 2002.

22. Quoted in *Financial Times*, 14 May 2002.

23. Catherine Philip, 'Taleban Offers Reward for Westerners,' *The Times*, 6 April 2002.

24. *The Times*, 18 May 2002.

25. Cited in Charles Glover and Richard Wolffe, 'Friends and Foes,' *Financial Times*, 6 March 2002, p. 18; emphasis added.

26. 'Philippines Bomb Kills 13, Wounds 12,' *New York Times*, 24 Dec. 2002.

74

9

Rethinking small places-urban and cultural creativity

Examples from Sweden, the USA and Bosnia-Herzegovina

By Tom Fleming, Lia Ghilardi and Nancy K. Napier

Over the past 25 years, the disappearance of local manufacturing industries and periodic crises in government and finance have increasingly made culture and the broader *creative economy* the business of cities and the basis of their tourist attractions and their unique, competitive edge (Zukin 1995). During the 1990s, in particular, notions such as the network society, the experience economy, creative cities and globalization were used to define new modes of production and consumption within the 'new economy' (Kelly 1998) and emphasis was put on the interplay between the economy and culture, as well as on creating crossovers between media and technologies (Amin and Thrift 2005). The result for urban policies was that, rather than selling just goods or services, even small cities began to mobilize tourism, the retail trade, architecture, event management and the entertainment and heritage industries, as well as the media and the wider creative industries, in order to produce and sell 'experiences' (Pine and Gilmore 1999).

This is true today of large cities but even more so for small or 'second tier' cities such as those presented in this chapter.[1] Essentially, the more outside competition these cities confront, the smoother must their operations be in order to harness their internal resources or their 'creative capital'. In this scenario, a dynamic and creative-led urban policy becomes part of the image of a city and acts as a catalyst for its symbolic economy (Verwijnen and Lehtovuori 1999). Thus, tourism, culture and the

creative industries—the fastest-growing industries in Europe—play an important role in the urban image-creation processes, providing a major rationale for the aestheticization of city landscapes and the creation of new urban identities. This understanding of the complex and often contradictory nature of urban space is explored in Henri Lefebvre's notion of 'the production of space':

> Space is permeated with social relations; it is not only supported by social relations but it is also producing and produced by social relations (1991: 286).

To this he also adds that every society in history has shaped a distinctive social space that meets its intertwined requirements for economic production and social reproduction. This social notion of space—applied to the current concerns of small cities—will form the basis for the analysis of the three case studies presented in this chapter. In particular, we will argue that while new narratives of regeneration, urban culture and heritage have been employed in the conversion of these places into post-industrial, knowledge-oriented creative hubs, the process of implementing this regeneration has not been unproblematic. As more small cities compete (using similar mechanisms) in (re)producing and promoting themselves to attract a globally mobile middle class and other forms of flexible capital, their ability to create uniqueness diminishes, the economic benefits turn out to be short-lived and the 'creativity potential' is depleted. In *The City and the Grassroots*, Manuel Castells (1983: 314) has noted that the problem with this new 'tendential' urban meaning is that it creates the spatial and cultural separation of people from their product and from their history. The implication here is that these policies can have an effect not just on the urban form but also on governance and, ultimately, on social justice.

This chapter draws together case studies from three contrasting regions—southern Sweden, Idaho USA, and Bosnia-Herzegovina—to explore the divergent approaches to urban development policies and the broader 'creative economy approach' that smaller, 'second tier' cities adopt, according to different levels of political and economic stability, cultural integration and metropolitan aspiration (see Table 9.1). The three case-study cities— Malmö, Boise and Tuzla—are each going through a process of re-thinking their position in the urban hierarchy through a focus on creativity, new forms of governance and partnership—each with varying levels of success. These responses are provided, variously, against a context of political upheaval, cultural inferiority, low levels of economic capital, bureaucracy and relative prosperity. The contrasts between the case studies are marked, yet the ambition to steer each of these cities towards international competitiveness and local harmony—based upon innovative approaches to cultural planning and regeneration—reveals what these very different 'smaller cities' have in common.

LEARNING TO BE CREATIVE THROUGH REGENERATION: THE CASE OF MALMÖ

With a population of 270,000 inhabitants, Malmö is Sweden's third largest city and the commercial centre of southern Sweden. It is a cosmopolitan and multicultural city where high-tech and knowledge-intensive activities are slowly replacing the old, traditional industrial structure that had given it its 'working-class' character since the 1960s. In particular, the integration of the Öresund region, brought

about by the link with Copenhagen, plus other major infrastructural investments, is putting the city on the map along with the most advanced European 'second tier' centres such as Rotterdam or Lille.

Table 9.1 A brief introduction to the case-study cities

• •

Malmö, southern Sweden is a progressive and forward-thinking city, with an increasingly qualified workforce, where high-tech and knowledge-intensive activities are replacing the old, traditional industrial structure. The expansion of Malmö University College, the opening of the Öresund fixed link between Malmö and Copenhagen, in neighbouring Denmark, and the regeneration of the Western Harbour symbolize how the city is aggressively repositioning itself as a player in the global urban competition game. An additional ingredient in this process of identity building is the (still ongoing) implementation of a number of housing and regeneration projects in the area of the Western Harbour. However, as the Malmö section will show, this process of identity rebuilding—from an industrial centre to a sophisticated, high-tech, new-economy-driven hub—poses a number of challenges which even a relatively successful city such as Malmö cannot ignore.

Boise, Idaho is by many measures a most unlikely place for urban creativity and the strategic pursuit of a creative agenda—it is relatively small, remote and, for many people even in the US, little known; it is prosperous and increasingly so; and it is located in a region not recognized for its creativity and the progressiveness this implies. And yet Boise is developing into a small urban creative city on the move. Unlike many cities, Boise is facing no serious economic crisis that pushes it towards embracing a creative-led agenda. Unemployment is typically below four per cent, housing starts and price increases are among the fastest growing in the US, and the city and state continue to rank high in top business, recreation and retirement reports. However, key people in business, arts, government and education are increasingly realizing the importance of creativity as a crucial part of maintaining the city's quality of life while also preserving a strong economic base. This is in some part linked to the city's long tradition of entrepreneurship: the city's key companies (many of which have been on the Fortune 500 list of the country's largest) stemmed from the pioneering efforts of a few hard charging individuals. Thus, the notion of moving forward, trying new ideas and accepting failure, has a precedent.

Table 9.1 *continued...*

In **Bosnia-Herzegovina**, small cities are struggling to 'break into' international networks and to undertake calculated risks that advance their status and profile. Key strategic considerations often centre on re-building civic identity and intercultural pride from the 'bottom up', with memories from the 1990s war too painful and divisive to allow a more progressive international focus to take hold. For some, building an international role and profile is seen as a relative luxury; yet for many it is increasingly recognized as a necessary move if cities are to shed their internal parochialism and its dangerous consequences and climb inter-regional and international urban hierarchies. Vital is the contribution of relatively young leaders and intermediaries, less implicated in the war, more open to the cultural and creative opportunities of inter-city connectivity, and critically aware of the positive impact this 'openness' will bring to the political process and community. This section will introduce the ways the northern Bosnian city of **Tuzla** is basing its future harmony and success on a broad approach to 'cultural democracy', where every project, service or intervention is positioned as part of a wider cultural plan to raise the profile of the city to the 'outside world' while connecting locally to the aspirations of a local population which is for the most part keen to move on from the torment of recent history.

. . . .

The expansion of Malmö University College (with a student population of 21,000) and the development of the Western Harbour area, with housing and innovative workspaces such as the incubator MINC, has brought an atmosphere of youthful creative energy to the city. Cafés, open spaces, galleries and shopping areas are dotted all around the city and the overall feel is that of a compact, lively place. What was once a brash, blue-collar city, is now in the process of becoming an acknowledged centre for information technology and biotechnology. This transition, however, does not appear to have been an easy one to achieve for a city that still carries the burden of recent industrial failures on its shoulders. The 1990s recession hit

Malmö harder than any other city in Sweden, with 27,000 jobs disappearing during a period of three years in the mid-1990s. As a port and business city, with roots going back to the Middle Ages, Malmö seems to have a peculiar 'genetic code' that makes it prone to constant swings between periods of growth and prosperity and decades of relative decline.

From an urban sociology perspective, one could argue that this is a cycle often observed in medium-size European port cities, and here the names of Hamburg, Bilbao, Rotterdam, Bristol and Glasgow come to mind. These are all cities that had a great history of commercial and urban development and then hit the rocks of recession in the 1970s. But, since then, they have all been able, to a certain degree, to reinvent themselves. This successful 'remaking' of smaller cities is often underpinned by a focus on the resilience, creativity and cultural mix of these urban centres. In the case of Glasgow, it was its internationalism as well as its urban and cultural heterogeneity that made it possible for the city to successfully begin—in the early 1990s—to reverse the cycle of decline which, until then, seemed intractable.

Similarly, early commercial development brought cultural variety to the city of Rotterdam, so much so that it was precisely this successful cosmopolitan mix of skills and potential that saved the city in the early 1980s from the decline of the shipbuilding industry and encouraged the planners and policymakers to design a new regeneration plan (the Binnenstadsplan). This, in turn, was the first step towards the successful creation of a new identity for the city. This notion of urban and social mix, along with the importance for cities of having a creative milieu, are increasingly seen by urban commentators as central in the making of successful and competitive cities. In particular, the argument put forward by economic development experts such as Allen Scott (1998), Jeremy Rifkin (2000) and, more recently, Richard Florida (2002), is that today's economy is fundamentally a 'creative' economy.

In his study of what makes cities and regions grow and prosper, Florida observes that, rather than being exclusively driven by companies, economic growth is occurring in places that are tolerant, diverse and open to creativity, mainly because these are the places where creative people of all types want to live. Scientists, engineers, architects, designers and artists are all part of a new creative global class that cities need to nurture in order to be able to compete internationally (Florida 2002). So, by extension, Florida's message is that development policies need to be aware of the benefits of creating an environment in which tolerance of different lifestyles and a good quality of life for everybody living in a particular place go hand in hand.

In the Swedish panorama of old industrial cities attempting to recover new functions, Malmö seems to have done better than other cities. From its thirteenth-century origins, rooted in the herring trade, to the splendours of its Danish period and the great developments of the nineteenth century, characterized by the expansion of the textile industry and the shipyards, Malmö is a city open to external influences, proud of its achievements and not afraid of taking risks.

Now that its once-thriving docks are being redeveloped into both University Island and the new housing and business district of the Western Harbour, Malmö is learning to develop new ways of dealing with planning and governance. This new approach is the result of a process of 'learning by doing' which has its roots in recent attempts by the city to implement large regeneration projects using the tools of masterplanning and welfare policies—typical of an old utopian Swedish tradition—despite the 'discovery' that these tools don't work any more in an environment in which cultural diversity, fragmentation of interests and new forms of democratic representation dominate.

Learning to be creative

The big issue for Malmö is recreating its identity. The image of an old industrial city belongs to the past; we now have to come up with a major project for the future, something indicative of a shared vision.

With these words, back in 1999, the City Director, Ilmar Reepalu, articulated Malmö's aspiration to join Copenhagen in the new Öresund region while at the same time sending out a message that the city needed to be bold in its thinking about the future. The response of the city came in the shape of the Draft Comprehensive Plan published less than a year after Reepalu's speech. The Plan singled out a number of mainly infrastructural projects for implementation—such as the expansion of the University and the transformation of the Western Harbour—which in the minds of the planners were to give tangible benefits to the whole of the city's economy. However, these projects ran into difficulty as soon as they started, because of a number of social and economic reasons, the most important of which was the underestimation by planners and policy makers alike of the social changes the city was undergoing at the time.

The late 1990s was a period of great upheaval for the city and while refugees from Kosovo and other European war zones were increasingly choosing to settle in the city—putting a strain on Sweden's legendary liberal ideals of social and housing policy—unemployment (particularly in the public sector) was rising as the spatial segregation between the new middle classes and the old inhabitants increased. The launch of the regeneration of the Western Harbour (spearheaded by the 2001 Housing Expo Bo01) came right in the middle of these changes and, with mounting controversy in the press about the ability of regeneration to deliver benefits for the whole of the community and not just for the new middle classes, it looked as if, for a time, the success of the plan was in danger.

The root of the problem was later identified as the lack of support given by the local community to this big regeneration plan. In particular, the language adopted in the marketing literature for the Western Harbour prompted community leaders to criticize those in charge of the delivery of the plan for bypassing the basic principles of democratic accountability.[2] This reaction can only be understood by looking at the past 40 years of Malmö's history, whereby since the 1960s (a time of great urban expansion for both the inner city and the suburbs), economic growth and urban expansion were achieved through carefully nurtured relations between the political establishment (mainly the Social Democratic Party), the public sector, the banks and the construction industry. Thus, while in the past such transformations were the result of a shared, top-down, carefully planned long-term vision, today they seem to happen more as an urgent, 'ad hoc', response to perceived outside threats.

For any small city to go from an essentially industrial economy to a 'creativity and knowledge-driven' mode of production and consumption, all in little more than a decade, would be a challenge, but for Malmö the stakes are even higher. There are two reasons for this. The first, as mentioned earlier, is the 'historic baggage' of welfare and democratic accountability to which the city is still tied and the second is the rapidly changing social, economic and cultural environment in which policy makers were and are trying to operate.

With more than a quarter of the population having foreign roots, Malmö is the most multi-ethnic city in Sweden. Here, diversity also extends to a highly visible variety of lifestyles, political and ethical allegiances, consumption patterns and sexual orientations. This richly diverse environment requires constant renegotiations of trust along with redefinitions of legitimacy by local government. This is the task that local politicians and policy makers alike are learning to perform and the testing ground is the completion by 2010 of the cultural and housing redevelopment of the Western Harbour. The redevelopment will involve turning 160 hectares of harbour-front brownfield land into a fully developed new, ecologically sustainable, 'neighbourhood' of 10,000 inhabitants. Malmö's 'City of Tomorrow' is made up of the old Swedish ingredients of meticulous planning and a quality of housing and urban design of such standard that the 'new neighbourhood' has already been heralded as a prototype for the new European urbanism.[3]

So far, the city appears to have turned what could have been a 'high risk' development into a successful tool to attract interest and investment from Sweden and elsewhere, but what is interesting here is to look at the management and governance components

of this success. In particular, it is worth noting a precondition, which is that, over the past ten years, Malmö City Council has increasingly assumed responsibility for urban and economic growth. This 'decentralization' of responsibility was implemented through the establishment, in 1996, of a 'Districts' Reform'. The Reform involved the division of Malmö into ten city districts with their own councils and administrations. The result was a much leaner government with the ability to respond quickly and flexibly to local needs. This new 'culture of flexibility' prepared the ground for the establishment of the public–private partnership that is currently presiding over the development of the Western Harbour. Although the lead organization is the City of Malmö (backed by the Swedish government), this partnership includes private development companies (a total of 13 developers), the university, business leaders and residents' associations. The partnership is a flexible mechanism that is allowing the city to shorten the time span considerably between planning and implementation and it is a strategic mechanism capable of delivering on issues ranging from the infrastructure for the creative economy to education and training and housing.

Examples of the projects implemented recently through the partnership include the creation of MINC, an incubator for high-tech start-ups, now expanding into a key support mechanism for local design companies, and the creation of University Island (the new university campus which specializes in new media and communication). These two projects were achieved in parallel with the creation of 500 ecologically-sustainable residential units, which are currently rented or sold to occupants working in creative jobs in the Western Harbour. Though implementation has turned out to be quite a steep learning curve for the city, this level of regeneration and risk-taking in a 'small town' such as Malmö is still unprecedented in Sweden and especially as far as 'governance' is concerned. Here, too, Malmö is experimenting with new mechanisms aimed at ensuring democratic participation and a higher degree of transparency in the decision-making process in relation to large regeneration programmes. One such mechanism is the City

80

Planning Forum set up two years ago. The Forum is a permanent place where the planning department can hold exhibitions, meetings and seminars on the subject of Malmö's urban developments (especially those in the Western Harbour). This is a strategic tool put in place not only for the dissemination of information to the general public, but also as a way of inducing a collaborative approach to the design and planning of the areas in need of transformation.[4]

In conclusion, the key lesson from this example is that 'little to lose', upstart, ex-industrial cities such as Malmö are performing a 'trailblazer' role in Sweden by challenging traditional, top-down approaches to urban and cultural development. In this case, a mix of risk-taking, flexible management, cross-disciplinary work and democratic participation combine to establish a broader understanding of the city's cultural resources that put Malmö on the map of cities to visit, invest and live in. Finally, Malmö's quintessentially 'adaptive' quality has opened the way to experiments in governance which other cities in Sweden and elsewhere may wish to follow.

THE PIONEER MODEL: MOVING TOWARD THE CREATIVE ECONOMY IN BOISE

Boise, Idaho, is a most unlikely place for a creative-led approach to urban development—it is relatively small, remote, little-known and growing very quickly. Malmö is a more 'obvious' location for creative-oriented growth: it is closer to the metropolitan core of the continent, it is more diverse and it has a long history of industrial development. And yet, for several reasons, Boise is developing into a small urban creative city on the move, with several characteristics similar to Malmö. For example, Richard Florida's (2002) rankings have shown Boise, Idaho, to be one of the top US cities that are attractive to creative people (and Malmö is an increasingly promising propositon for aspiring creative people in Sweden). With such confirmation of an already strong position, Boise's decision makers and urban strategists recognize that a valuable intellectual market will be available only if the city grows its economic strength and remains an attractive place

in which to live: creativity is thus an investment in future competitiveness and prosperity. This section explores how Boise is investing in its future by adapting approaches that contributed to its very existence: it was once a pioneer city on the edge of the American West, a place where only the most adventurous settled and invested. Today, new pioneers are seeking to establish a creative city for the future.

Conditions defining Boise

Boise and Idaho are known for odd reasons or not known at all. Potatoes, racists and 'where's that?' are the most common image challenges. It is remote—Boise is the state's (only significant) population centre, with nearly 400,000 in a 50 by 30-mile valley. It has been know for being the 'potato state' (as the major supplier of McDonald's French fried potatoes), as a (former) neo-Nazi haven, until 2000 when the Aryan Nations lost a major legal battle and left the area, and for having 'no image', since people confuse it with states having similar sounding names (for example, Iowa, Ohio). The negative (or lack of) images of Idaho and Boise are fast being replaced by one of a high quality of life, a good business environment and an attractive retirement option. In the last few years, Boise has received much positive attention in a variety of press outlets as a place to do business, retire, or enjoy recreation. For example, it has attracted a collection of large firms (for example, Micron Technology) and start-ups and the state's largest university (more than 18,000 students).

However, remoteness continues to scare off potential employees and employers ('why would I move to the end of the world?') and makes some aspects of business life (international travel) slightly more challenging. The CEO of one of the city's top software firms—small, but with clients worldwide—recently commented that as his firm grows, it becomes harder to recruit. Without a large cluster of software firms in the city, high-tech experts are reluctant to move from areas like Silicon Valley, where their career options are broader. However, remoteness in Idaho does have its positive sides. Because of the lack of amenities, original settlers—and modern-day pioneers as well—have created a

81

full spectrum of cultural, economic and social fabric in the city. In addition, having major corporations based in the city means that many managers have come from more cosmopolitan settings, and hence expect access to cultural and related activities. The city has its own philharmonic, ballet, modern dance and opera companies; it has two professional theatre groups—a nationally recognized summer Shakespeare Festival and a highly regarded contemporary theatre. While the city lacks the range of options of a metropolis like Seattle or San Francisco, it has cheap and accessible parking, relatively low event ticket prices and high-quality performances.

Today, Boise sits at the state's political, (newly developing) educational and business centre. It hosts the state capital, state agencies, branch offices of several federal agencies and even headquarters of selected federal agencies, such as the National Interagency Fire Centre, which coordinates all forest fire efforts for the country as a whole. Boise State University leads the state in the rate of growth of student numbers, with lead programmes in engineering, business and public affairs. Finally, as introduced above, the business centre of the state is undoubtedly in Boise. Many firms, like Micron Technology, have their headquarters in Boise, or their major divisions, such as Hewlett-Packard. The actual number of spin-offs from the larger technology firms is unknown but estimated to be about 300. Such conditions lead to questions of why and how such a small urban community should move towards a more robust, creativity-based economy. The 'why' is born out of a lack of complacency and a realization that for the city to grow beyond its small-city status it requires a broader range of creative assets and approaches; the 'how' is through an emerging model that differs from any other non-East-Coast US city and has more in common with cities in Europe: the pioneer model.

The Pioneer Model of Small Urban Development

Compared with the US, cities in Europe have led the wave of interest in and development of creative industries and creative communities. Only in the past few years have pockets of creative-led urban strategies begun to emerge in the mid- and western-US. Much of the initial deliberate efforts have come in the eastern part of the US, especially in New England, the south-east (for example, Georgia and Florida) and south (for example, Memphis, Tennessee and Louisiana). In the UK/ Europe and eastern US, efforts appear to be primarily driven or led by key champions, often government or political officials. For example, the Department for Culture, Media and Sport in the UK spearheaded early work on creative industries; and the mayors of cities in the UK (for example, Huddersfield) and Europe (for example, Freiburg, Germany), helped lead work to distinguish their cities. Likewise, governors of Maine, Vermont and Louisiana have made the creative economy and creative industries a key focus for economic development. On the other hand, a top-down, champion-driven model, common in Europe and the eastern part of the US, may not always be appropriate or desirable, especially in the western part of the US. The 'pioneer' metaphor helps to illustrate an alternative model of how creative economies and creative industries may evolve, at least in one part of the 'Wild West'.

The notion of pioneers is fundamental to American culture and identity. It suggests migration of a group of nameless adventurers, who see themselves as highly independent and set out (mostly) together on a journey to a generally unknown destination (and they shape it as they go), where they use external guides (like experts on creative industries). Boise's pioneers are just beginning the trek. Despite no clearly identified pathway, signs already exist to suggest some of the outcomes for Boise, especially ways to blend different disciplines to support high-tech, the arts and educational endeavours. For example, an informal group has formed (TekKlatsch) that brings together people from business, government and education to share information and ideas about how to build the high-technology industries within the region. In particular, there is growing interest in creating a Media Centre that would house high-tech, arts, educational and meeting points for people from a whole range of disciplines. In addition, state-level effort has begun to find ways to bring film industry production to the state as well as ways to support the budding local, indigenous, independent film industry: the acclaimed 2004 film *Napoleon Dynamite* is a case in point.

The pioneer model is at an early stage of development, yet it is already clear that there are at least four reasons why the model may be appropriate for a remote, small urban community like Boise, Idaho. First, a lack of clear 'leaders' or champion(s) *can* be an advantage because it allows creative community development to emerge organically, permitting unexpected pathways and options to arise. Second, with no clear champions on the horizon in the city, a group of nearly invisible or quiet 'guides and translators' is appearing. These people are quietly guiding groups to move in similar directions and are helping 'translate' knowledge from outside sources for usefulness to the Boise community. They have formed no coordinated group, have no official name, but rather 'nudge' quietly in their respective areas. A third reason for the Pioneer Model's success is the notion of being able to 'find new veins', in this case creativity—a renewable and distributed resource. Finally, the model seems to work because the pioneers are willing to create pockets of change or 'forts' as the community develops. The quiet guides are creating formal and informal discussion groups, websites with access to information and experts, and advocacy teams to work towards building certain industries.

Boise, Idaho, a remote city in what many (still) consider to be the frontier of the US, may offer a model for how smaller creative cities develop over time. The mix of location, people and history has blended to yield a more pioneering (bottom-up) potential model. To succeed, several factors are critical. First, eventually, the community will need a champion(s) to offer cohesive vision. In addition, the model allows opportunities for many trails or directions. Yet, eventually, the community must decide whether it can (or should) sustain all of the 'good ideas' or creative industries or whether it should focus on a few. At present, emerging areas range from biosciences to film to media centres to high-tech to agribusiness and beyond. Will the

state, the community, or organizations want to support all (in time, money and other resources)? Such questions and longer-term monitoring may reveal the Pioneer Model as an emerging alternative approach to creative community development and the revisioning of cities at the margins.

REVISIONING THE SCARRED CITY: CULTURAL DEMOCRACY, LEADERSHIP AND THE YOUNG VOICE OF TUZLA

Tuzla, in north-east Bosnia-Herzegovina, provides an example of how a relatively small, undistinguished city in a marginal and stricken part of the world, can invigorate change that is innovative, empowering and distinctive. Through undertaking a 'cultural democracy' approach to city planning, Tuzla has managed to transform its decaying industrial heritage into a new economy asset; it has translated a negative identity based on this industrial heritage into a progressive forward-looking sense of place; and it has used the shock and pain of war to galvanize citizens into building cohesively for the future good of the city. Tuzla remains relatively poor, isolated and negatively received/portrayed; but the city has set in motion a process of change that is gradually transforming the physical and psychological landscape to configure a new city that is youthful, bold, international, innovative and increasingly intercultural. This process of change is led by a genuinely visionary mayor and supported by a population that has shown ambition, tolerance and huge appetite for a better and more connected city. The increased engagement and commitment of the city's younger citizens has been vital.

There's no avoiding salt

Tuzla is Bosnia-Herzegovina's fourth largest city, with a population of 165,000.[5] It is one of Europe's oldest continuously populated settlements and can attribute its growth to coal and salt extraction, which has established the city as a centre for heavy industry, with a strong presence of complementary chemical and energy production.[6] It is this industrial

83

city image that dominates notions of Tuzla, plus the tragic events of recent history, when in 1995, 72 young people were massacred by a Serb mortar attack. It is very much a scarred city: physically and psychologically scarred by industry and war.[7] For example, there is no escaping salt: the name Tuzla is derived from the history of salt extraction;[8] the city has a 'Salt Square' and, until recently, the old salt mines were subsiding, sinking parts of the city by more than 10 metres, scarring the landscape and city identity, leading to regular salt-water flooding and prompting a range of disincentives to invest in or think positively about the city.

However, there is more to Tuzla than salt and war. For example, the city has a strong cultural heritage. It is the birthplace of possibly the greatest artist in Bosnia, Ismet Mujezinovic, and home to one of its foremost living writers, Semezdin Mehmedinovic. It has Bosnia and Herzegovina's oldest theatre. It is also a university city, with a relatively young population for a country losing a high proportion of its youth through international migration. It is the energy, resourcefulness and vision of Tuzla's young people that provides the focus for change in the city: their capacity to reinterpret the past—the salt, the war—to create new identities and opportunities is crucial to future prosperity, competitiveness and, quite possibly, peace.

Unlike a range of other small cities in marginal, often fraught locations, Tuzla is grappling with change as a positive challenge. Three key themes are vital to constructing new positive opportunities, ideas, identities and infrastructure:

- building cultural democracy: engaging, listening, willingly accountable;
- maximizing the value of a past that won't go away: from salt and war come positive ways forward;
- developing new markets and a new voice: youth, ideas and the creative industries.

Together, these themes contribute to a nascent toolkit for Tuzla that has attributes transferable to other small, struggling, even marginal cities. Indeed, Tuzla teaches us that a city can never be totally reinvented, for the past cannot be destroyed; it shows us that a genuine engagement with local people can lead to both innovation and stronger, more creative communities; and it warns us that without allowing younger and diverse voices to take a lead, the city will cease to be a city.

Building Cultural Democracy

In few other countries in Europe is cultural policy and engagement more important than in Bosnia and Herzegovina. Issues of culture and identity are both the cause and the solution to its problems. Landry (2002) explains that they are the cause, because cultural arguments were used to divide the country and to turn the different groups against each other in an 'orgy of destruction'; and they are the solution because culture might be able to bring people back together again through initiating cultural programmes and activity that increase mutual understanding. In Tuzla, a re-engagement with culture has been at the forefront of public policy rationale, with almost every policy action and its causative challenge or question understood in terms of its cultural impact or meaning: 'what will this do *for* Tuzla?'; 'how can we build a more open Tuzla?'; 'what are our disadvantages and how can we turn them into advantages?'. Crucial here has been the role of the Mayor and his office, asking difficult questions and seeking culture-based solutions. Mayor Imamovic represents a new type of politician in Bosnia-Herzegovina. In a country previously crippled by corruption, bureaucracy and ethnic-based fragmentation, Mayor Imamovic has built a persuasive vision for Tuzla based on the phrase: 'No one is as smart as everyone together'. Whilst sounding a little idealistic—especially in a recent war zone—there is genuine substance to this phrase, a substance developed through a practical engagement with local residents.

Put simply, in 2000 the Mayor introduced a two-year process of in-depth public consultation as the first stage in his *cultural democracy programme*. This was driven by two main agendas: to find out the needs and aspirations of local people;

and to ensure that future corresponding actions have a relevance to, and ownership for, local people as the basis for civic pride. The consultation was and continues to be based upon in-depth engagement with over 40 local communes and voluntary organizations; the creation of a Mayoral Advisory Council of 25 unelected advisers that cut across religious, ethnic and gender boundaries; a six-monthly citywide survey of public opinion; and an ongoing process of civic engagement, triggering informal debate and targeting themes that progress new ways of thinking about the city and its potential.

However, conviction, persuasiveness and a determination to build consensus around genuine reform rather than stasis, are insufficient to exact change by themselves. This is because a city such as Tuzla needs more than collaboration and strength of character if it is to progress as a growing internationally focused city. It requires good ideas. This is where the most significant strength of Mayor Imamovic lies: his ability to stimulate ideas from the population and to identify those ideas that will work to transform the city from economic decline and painful memories to an outward-looking city with real reasons for renewed civic pride. This requires an assured approach to the delivery of essential services; the development of a mix of high-profile projects that genuinely 'raise the game' of the city; an ongoing and deeply embedded relationship with local people—especially young people; and an outwardness, fostered through nascent relationships with other cities. Tuzla has now cultivated international links with cities as diverse as Götheburg and Bologna, Osijek and Ravenna. The city has gained membership of several pan-European and international networks and thus actions in the city are seen by local people as actions within a network of cities, impelling Tuzla to be more bold and creative than perhaps a provincial approach might produce.

Maximizing the value of the past: The Salt Lake

Tuzla remains a city famous for salt. However, today the city is famous for a salt lake rather than a declining industry that was literally and psychologically sinking and undermining the city. Mayor Imamovic, through his consultation processes, identified a series of options for the area of Tuzla most damaged by salt-water flooding—an area adjacent to the city centre. In short, the solution agreed was both simple and brilliant: to capture the water through the construction of a salt lake that, in turn, acts as a resort in the heart of the city. The newly formed Lake Pannonia is a masterstroke of civic planning and cultural democracy: forged through a positive translation of local connections to salt, providing employment for workers who previously mined the salt, introducing a new unique leisure opportunity for people from across the region and beyond, and establishing an iconic feature that affirms the transformation of Tuzla into a progressive and innovating city.

No other city has a salt lake and surrounding beach that provides coastal features despite the great distance from the sea. Over 300,000 people visit the shores of the lake every year, bathing, sunbathing, using the lake as a base from which to visit other attractions such as the Peace Flame Centre. At least 300,000 people are changing their perception of Tuzla. Indeed, an Austrian Bank Director was so impressed by the lake and what it signified that he established the Bank's national headquarters in Tuzla. The Mayor and his growing networks of city visionaries have shown great understanding of the importance of effective branding and positioning with increasing inter-city competition, while realizing that it is crucial for high-quality, effective and convincing policy and action to underpin that brand. What's more, the city is no longer sinking.

Further initiatives are underway that re-engage with the past to establish a contemporary, outward-focused identity for the city. They include the Peace Flame—a collaborative international programme intent on maintaining dialogue and nurturing positive outlooks from the memories of atrocity and hate. This is physically expressed through the Peace Flame Centre, close to the salt lake, which operates as a type of community and arts centre, undertaking initiatives aimed at bringing local people together through creative practice. In addition, the Mayor has championed a range of cultural and creative initiatives and programmes, including an annual literary festival and a series of high quality public art and public realm schemes. These have included a streetscape re-fashioned to represent 'symbols of humanity' (such as Nelson Mandela, Shakespeare and The Beatles). The Mayor often seeks support from cities abroad—requesting that a piece of art be donated or access be made available to the cast. A focus on international connection is coupled with a focus on translating the pain of war into a positive affirmation of humanity with a revitalized, inclusive, tolerant and connected Tuzla being the primary aim.

Yet, despite the considerable success of the cultural democracy approach of Mayor Immamovic, it is clear that Tuzla's future prosperity and peace depend on a more sophisticated engagement with an even wider range of voices and a more focused and nuanced approach to determining opportunities in the 'new economy'. *A prosperous and inclusive society can't be built on cultural gestures and iconic developments only*: for the young people to stay (and they continue to leave in large numbers), feel engaged and become economically active, will require the development of new home-grown markets for creative products and experiences.

Moreover, by collecting and negotiating around the production and consumption of new cultural forms, young people will be able to explore their identities without recourse to remember the war or even salt as the primary drivers of their identities: new cultural markets will bring a new type of cohesiveness that is spared the pain and embarrassment of the past. There is a growing realization—borne out through connections with other cities—that for Tuzla to be competitive and progressive, it needs to develop its own new, distinctive cultural products and services, and it would benefit most from undertaking these activities on a commercial and entrepreneurial basis: developing new local creative industries markets and connecting these emergent taste communities to a huge potential market across the Bosnian diaspora and beyond.

Ongoing challenges

Tuzla is far from a fast-growing, well-connected and respected international city. It remains very much a city on the margins of a wider European context: unemployment is high; many people are leaving the city (while many displaced people still arrive); negative self-identity is commonplace; post-war hatred and suspicion remain; and the cultural economy is far weaker than state-developed cultural programmes. In addition, culture remains too overtly politicized (often on ethnic terms); piracy is stifling commercial potential in the music industry; there is a severe lack of legal expertise to coordinate change; and the learning and skills sector is too didactic and narrow, discouraging students from thinking laterally and creatively. However, Tuzla *is* a model for other cities blighted by war and industrial decline because it is confronting these and many more issues in a direct and far from complacent manner.

John Kao (1996) defines creativity as:

> The entire process by which ideas are generated, developed, and transformed into value. It encompasses what people commonly mean by innovation and entrepreneurship … (I)t connotes both the art of giving birth to new ideas and the discipline of shaping and developing those ideas to the stage of realised value.

Tuzla has embraced this broad definition of creativity to begin to address a range of city development challenges. Through history, cities have thrived where the management of creativity and innovation is paramount (Hall 1998). In contemporary society, Florida (2002) and Landry (2000) highlight how cities are increasingly operating as providers of cultural currency, as key determinants in generating and attracting creative talent. Tuzla is currently grappling to establish the climate and ecology for the development and release of its creative talent, which in turn will be followed by the attraction and retention of creative talent. It is extending its organizational capacity (such as through networks and fora), engaging deeply to engender participation and ideas generation (a cultural democracy), introducing catalysing projects (such as the salt lake) and placing its bets firmly on its strongest card (the talent, energy and aspiration of young people working with new content and technology).

According to an UN survey, 62 per cent of young people now want to leave Bosnia and Herzegovina and most want to leave forever.[9] The best and the brightest are finding it easiest to leave. Without a direct commitment to building creative opportunities at a local level while ensuring the city is connected internationally, cities such as Tuzla will continue to lose the creative talent on which their future depends. In her groundbreaking book *Towards Cosmopolis*, Leonie Sandercock (1998) notes the focus for decision-makers in cities, regions and countries is how they can 'organize hope', 'negotiate fears' and 'mediate memories'. The youth-focused cultural democracy embraced in Tuzla is helping to arrest trends in youth departures, giving them a powerful, hope-provoking stake in the revisioning of their particular small but very significant city.

CONCLUSION: THREE CITIES, COMMON CHALLENGES

This chapter has explored how three very different small cities are engaging with creativity agendas in pursuit of stronger and more distinctive identities, greater connectivity, higher levels of creative entrepreneurship and governance and thus more competitive economies. Each city is faced by divergent sets of challenges and opportunities. For example, Malmö is moving from an atmosphere of constant crisis, bureaucracy and top-down policy making to implement more adaptive structures that deal on a project-by-project basis to reorientate the image of the city, transform its physical landscape

and build on its existing and incoming creative population. Boise is responding to a history of pioneering development to focus on the new creative pioneers—networks of forward-thinking individuals unsettled by the 'comfort zone' of a successful economy and increasingly skilled workforce: there is a recognition that for Boise to adapt productively and for it to match its increasing size in dynamism, it needs to raise the stakes and build a strong and distinctive creative economy. Tuzla continues to struggle with a fraught political and economic context and is in a painful transition from conflict and economic decline; yet the city is proactively seeking new ways to adapt old problems into new economy assets, to galvanize and engage a population that lost its way and in many cases moved away, and to move forward, emboldened through a direct embrace with its creative potential.

Though very different, each city has recognized the value of exploring its creative potential as a way to climb urban hierarchies while retaining existing strengths—whether through a direct development approach to the creative industries or through a creative approach to governance and place-building. This is not an 'empty gesture' approach to creativity where the creativity of a city is proclaimed as little more than an exercise in civic boosterism. This is a brave and risky engagement with often disenfranchised populations, inflexible and dying businesses, or at times complacent and insular politicians. Each city has recog-nized that continuing to decline, to stagnate or even—in Boise's case—to sit pretty, is not an option given the ruthlessness of contemporary inter-city competition, where investment and people are increasingly mobile and unflinchingly promiscuous until they find and settle in progressive, innovative, inclusive places with a strong mix of commercial and cultural opportunities and strong distinctive identities. The small cities of today that face this critical reality face-on are likely to be the big cities—in approach and reputation, if not size—of tomorrow.

NOTES

1. For a definition of second tier cities see: Ann Markusen *et al.* (eds.) (1999) *Second Tier Cities:Rapid Growth Beyond the Metropolis*, Minnesota: University of Minnesota Press.
2. See City of Tomorrow Brochure, 1999.
3. See City of Tomorrow Brochure, 1999.
4. For an analysis of the City Planning Forum's role in the regeneration of the Western Harbour, see case study: Building a Collaborative Design Approach for the Development of the Western Harbour, in the dissertation by Maria Lundgren (2004) Malmö University, Department of Media and Communication.
5. Tuzla is the seat of the Tuzla Canton, which is a canton of the Federation of Bosnia and Herzegovina, as well as of Tuzla Municipality, which is one of the 13 municipalities that together constitute the Tuzla Canton. Administratively, Tuzla is divided into 39 mjesne zajednice (local districts).
6. For example, in AD 950, the Byzantine historian and cezar Constantine Porfirogenet mentions the existence of Tuzla's saltwater springs and settlements surrounding them.
7. During and after the war, over one million people left the country, around 25 per cent of the total population, including a large proportion of the professional classes—the intellectual and knowledge infrastructure of the country has been decimated. Over 300,000 people were killed—the majority Bosnians. Forty per cent of the population remains displaced—creating immense problems of community building (see Landry 2002).
8. It is derived from the Turkish word *tuz* meaning salt.
9. See Landry 2002.

10

Australia's Millennium Drought: Impacts and responses

By Matthew Heberger

As this edition of *The World's Water* goes to press in early 2011, eastern Australia is recovering from devastating floods that claimed more than 20 lives and destroyed hundreds of homes. The heavy rains of 2009 and 2010 that caused so much destruction also marked the end of Australia's decade-long Millennium Drought. Beginning in about 1997, declines in rainfall and runoff had contributed to widespread crop failures, livestock losses, dust storms, and bushfires. Such are the vagaries of water on the continent with the world's most uncertain and variable climate.

The "Big Dry," as the long drought is commonly called by Australians, has profoundly affected the continent's environment, economy, and national psyche. It has prompted changes to the way Australia manages water and has accelerated reforms that were already under way to modernize its water laws and institutions. Modern Australia, shown in FIGURE 10.1, is home to 22 million people, and is an industrial, developed society with among the highest standards of living in the world. Most of its citizens live in cities near the coast, and much of the food they eat and products they buy are imported from overseas, insulating them somewhat from the worst effects of drought.

Australia's farmers are even more vulnerable. Agriculture, once the country's dominant industry, now makes up only 2.5 percent of the economy, yet it uses two-thirds of the water supply. For most of the 20th century, irrigation policies were designed to encourage settlement in the dry, sparsely settled outback. As part of a sweeping package of economic reforms in the 1990s, the Australian government began signaling to farm communities that they should no longer rely on government drought relief. The duration and severity of the latest drought, however, has caused the government to soften this policy—thousands of farmers received "exceptional circumstances" payments over the past ten years.

Drought has caused many other changes over the past decade. Australia's sheep population, which once outnumbered humans 10 to 1, has been halved in the past 10 years. Other agricultural sectors were also hard hit: rice production collapsed in some years, as did cotton. City dwellers have learned to live with frequent water restrictions, prompting creative ways to reuse water and spawning new industries in water conservation technology. Drought has also increased Australians' awareness of climate change and the fragility of their country's ecosystems. The lessons learned in recent years in Australia may soon be of interest to other parts of the world as water management challenges grow.

WATER RESOURCES OF AUSTRALIA

It is often written that Australia is the driest inhabited continent. This simple description, correct in the aggregate, belies Australia's relative water wealth. Australia's per-capita renewable water resources

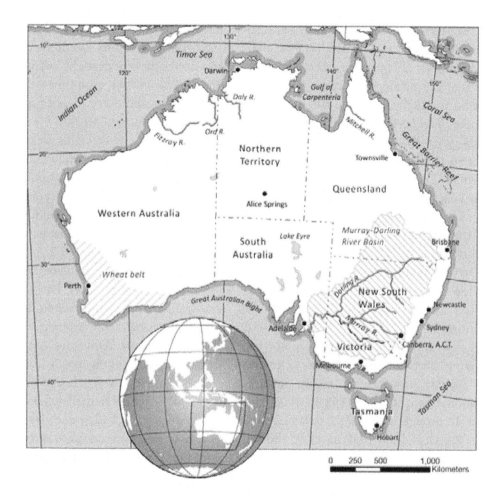

Figure 10.1 Map of Australia.

Source: Map created by the author using data from Natural Earth, www.naturalearthdata.com.

average 25,000 cubic meters per year, a level higher than France, Germany, or Japan (UNESCO 2009). Surrounding Australia's vast inland deserts, where rainfall averages less than 20 centimeters per year, a variety of climates exist on and near the coasts. These range from subtropical rainforests in the northeast where rainfall can exceed 3 meters per year, to Mediterranean climates on the southwest coast marked by winter rains and hot, dry summers. Much of this precipitation is unavailable for human use—88 percent of rainfall re-enters the atmosphere via evaporation or transpiration by plants, with only 12 percent left to penetrate the ground, replenish aquifers, or flow in rivers (Cooperative Research Centre for Water Quality and Treatment 2006). In southeastern Australia, the country's most productive agricultural zone, the peak of the summer growing season in December and January coincides with the lowest streamflows under natural conditions, and hence the least water availability. Throughout this chapter, statistics are reported by Australian water years, which run from July 1 to June 30.

As Australia's first European settlers learned, averages mean far less in Australia than in the north. In temperate climes, the average tells one what to expect, while in a highly variable climate like Australia's, the calculated mean does little to indicate how much rainfall to expect in a given year. Australia's latitude means it is subject to the atmospheric phenomenon called the subtropical high (Figure 10.2). Circulation patterns create long-lasting zones of high air pressure over the continent, leading to clear skies and low rainfall. And unlike temperate regions where rain is driven by seasonal patterns that recur every year, Australia's precipitation is heavily influenced by ocean and atmosphere conditions that can persist for several years, such as the El Niño Southern Oscillation and the Indian Ocean Dipole (Verdon-Kidd and Kiem 2009). El Niño events generally coincide with low rainfall, while the associated La Niña often brings floods (Nicholls 2008). Recent work by the University of New South Wales indicates that warm sea-surface temperatures in the Indian Ocean are significantly correlated with drought in southeastern Australia and that this effect may be even more important than El Niño (Ummenhofer et al. 2009).

Since 1860, when reliable records began, Australia has had a major drought somewhere on the continent in 82 out of 150 years (Lake 2008). It is now known that drought is a normal and recurring feature of Australia's climate. The most serious droughts on record include the Federation Drought from 1895 to 1902, the World War II drought from 1937 to 1945, and the recent "Big Dry" from 1997 to 2009. Shorter droughts appear throughout Australia's recorded history, for example in 1914–1915, 1965–1968, and 1982–1983. "Australia should be used to the death and destruction of drought," wrote the newspaper *The Australian*, "but each time we are surprised by its ferocity—and every disaster seems worse than the last" (McKernan 2010).

While previous droughts were usually limited to specific regions, the Millennium Drought differed in that it covered much of the continent over the course of several years (Lloyd 2010). Each of Australia's most populous cities—Sydney, Melbourne, Brisbane, Adelaide, and Perth—has been affected (Figure 10.2), along with the nation's major food-producing regions, primarily the Murray-Darling River Basin in southeastern Aus-tralia, and the wheat belt in the southwest.

The short but acute drought of 1982–1983 was among the most damaging on record. Rainfall deficiencies (amount below the long-term average) were the greatest ever recorded (Verdon-Kidd and Kiem 2009). While rainfall deficiencies were not as severe during the Millennium Drought, climatologists have rated it even more severe in terms of its duration and spatial extent. Anecdotes abound

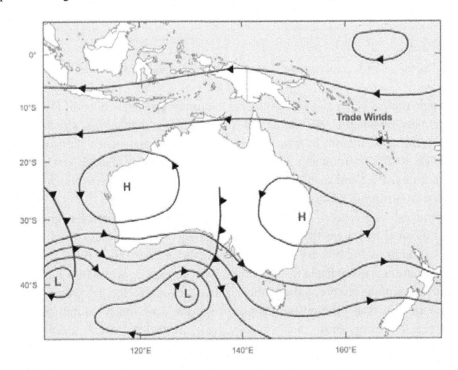

Figure 10.2 Stable high-pressure air masses over Australia leading to long, warm, dry periods.

Source: Redrawn from Australian Bureau of Meteorology undated

verifying their conclusion. A grazier in Central Queensland with records going back 120 years told interviewers: "What we have just been through is more than twice as bad as the worst drought previously recorded which was in 1902.... [In] this drought, we have had trees dying here. Those trees were here when Captain Cook sailed up the coast [c.1770] so when you have got briga-low trees dying it is a drought—there is no doubt about it" (quoted in Stehlik 2005).

A number of definitions of drought have been put forth by different authorities, and these definitions vary depending on their purpose (Cooley 2007). Hydrologists define droughts based on changes in environmental water, such as lake levels or river flows. A meteorological drought refers to a deficit of precipitation. Agricultural droughts are declared when soil moisture is depleted below levels needed for healthy crops. A water management drought may be declared when reservoirs fall below a certain level.

Drought relief in Australia has been tied to official drought declarations, and drought triggers were inconsistent among the states and frequently politicized. As a result, the Australian government moved to create a standard national definition of drought in the 1990s. Drought is now defined by comparing rainfall for a given period to the long-term average for that same period. Rainfall totals in the lowest decile (lowest 10 percent of records) are termed a "serious" rainfall deficiency. When rainfall is in the lowest 5 percent of observations, it is classified a "severe" rainfall deficiency. The Bureau has not, however, created a clear definition to mark the end of a drought (Botterill 2005).

Discussion of the Australia's Millennium Drought often glosses over the fact that the entire country was not in a drought for the past decade. In fact, in some years, good rains in certain regions allowed water restrictions to be lifted and some agricultural enterprises to prosper. In 2008–2009, a year before the drought lifted, planting of cotton and canola were up nearly 50 percent in response to good growing conditions in some regions. Figure 10.3 shows drought conditions in Australia indicated by rainfall deficiencies for the water years

from 1997 to 2010. Rainfall in the lowest decile occurred in some regions repeatedly over the last decade, much more often than one would expect based on a 10 percent chance in a given year.

The Millennium Drought has had observable effects on much of the continent's flora and fauna. Along the Murray River, salty and acidic water is causing the death of beloved red gum trees along 1,500 kilometers of the river. The condition of the Menindee Lakes along the Murray River, and the Coorong Wetlands near its mouth, have deteriorated during the drought due to lack of freshwater inflows, causing the near disappearance of iconic shorebirds, including pelicans, black swans, and fairy terns (Ker 2009). In 2007, National Geographic noted that kangaroos had become a common sight in the parks and streets of cities in southeast Australia, "invading" cities in search of food and water (Peatling 2007). Koala are also at risk as drought is killing off several species of eucalyptus trees, the animals' main food source (Sohn 2007).

In the future, climate change is likely to exacerbate drought conditions. Some argue that it already has. Scientists at the Commonwealth Scientific and Industrial Research Organization (CSIRO) found that, since the middle of the 20th century, rainfall has decreased by 15 percent, and temperatures in the first decade of the 2000s were 0.3–0.6°C above the long-term average. These changes combine to increase potential evaporation (Nicholls 2008, Ummenhofer et al. 2009). The combination of higher evaporation and lower precipitation depletes soil moisture and runoff and raises the prospect of more frequent and intense droughts in the future. A 2008 CSIRO report forecast a 35 to 50 percent decline in water availability in the Murray-Darling by the year 2030, and predicted that flows to the Lower Lakes near the Murray's mouth could drop by up to 70 percent (CSIRO 2008). A number of Australians now believe that their country is a "canary in the coal mine" when it comes to climate change and that drought conditions are an early indication of changes that other regions of the world are likely to experience in the future.

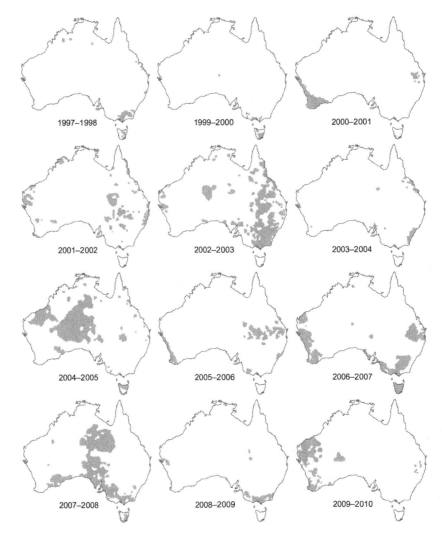

Figure 10.3 Extent of drought in Australia during the big dry. Shaded regions indicate serious water deficiency (rainfall in the lowest decile) for the Australian water year July 1–June 30. (The year of 1998–1999, in which few regions experienced serious deficiencies, is not shown.)

Source: Data from the Australian Bureau of Meteorology undated

IMPACTS OF THE MILLENNIUM DROUGHT

The most apparent effect of drought has been on Australia's landscape and watercourses; images of dry lake and riverbeds have become common in newspapers and on television. The drying of soils and lowering of water tables has had a discernible effect on the continent's plant and animal life, and has led to an increase in wildfires and dust storms over the past several years. Further, decreased river flows and reservoir levels have dramatically curtailed irrigation in some years, causing loss of income and economic hardship in rural communities. These impacts of the drought and others are discussed in the sections that follow.

Agriculture

Ten years of drought have affected nearly every aspect of Australia's rural economies. Considering only one of the worst years of the Big Dry, the Australian Bureau of Statistics estimated that drought in 2002–2003 caused a $7.4 billion drop in agricultural production and a loss of around

70,000 jobs (Lu and Hedley 2004).[1] For that year, losses were equivalent to 1.6 percent of Australia's gross domestic product. While some question the logic of such assessments (i.e., does it make sense to assign a theoretical value to crops never planted or harvested?), drought has clearly had a major effect on agricultural output, as shown in Figure 10.4. The figures plotted here do not paint a picture of uniform devastation. Some industries enjoyed good years in the past 10 years, while others expanded production overall. Among the hardest-hit sector has been Australia's well-known sheep industry. By the end of the drought, sheep populations declined by half, to 72.7 million, their lowest levels since 1905. The wool clip had fallen by 40 percent (Wahlquist 2010). Sheep numbers had already been declining steadily since they peaked in 1970 (at 180 million—there were 14 sheep for every person), but drought appears to have contributed to an even steeper decline in the past decade.

Australia's second-most-important livestock industry—cattle for beef and dairy— also suffered during the drought, although its decline was not as precipitous as with sheep. The number of dairy cows decreased 25 percent during the drought. Milk production declined less due to higher milk production per cow, and the dairy industry actually increased in value. Australia's cotton production before the drought reached a high of 795,000 tonnes in 2000–2001, valued at $1.8 billion. By 2007–2008, production fell to just 133,000 tonnes, worth $254 million.

Crop production also declined during the drought. The widest fluctuations occurred among annual crops, such as rice and wheat. Rice, which is especially water intensive, saw the most dramatic declines. The start of the decade brought a record crop of 1.6 million tonnes, worth $350 million. In 2007–2008, the rice harvest contracted to the smallest levels on record, at 18,000 tonnes. Upon hearing suggestions that perhaps Australia should not grow a crop that requires flood conditions in an arid country, rice farmers are quick to point out

that they achieve among the highest yields in the world, averaging 10 tonnes per hectare in 2006, and grow high-quality strains that fetch premium prices on the international market. And, as an annual crop, rice fields can be fallowed during dry years. Indeed, some rice growers took advantage of newly created water markets to sell their meager water to downstream water users.

Dry years can mean a halving of Australia's wheat production. Because it accounts for 15 percent of the world's total production, this can affect markets and food prices globally (Berry 2008), raising the prospect of food shortages. Meanwhile, Australians have discovered that grocery shopping and restaurant dining have become much more expensive, especially the cost of fruits, vegetables, and meat.

Australia's prominence as a global wine producer is also threatened by drought. In recent years, Australia has become a major wine exporter, with exports valued at $3 billion per year. The country has become the number one supplier of imported wine in England and lags only France and Italy in supplying the United States' import market. All of Australia's grape growers rely on irrigation, and as water has become more expensive, their profit margins have decreased. Wine industry groups have estimated that 1,000 out of Australia's 7,000 wine growers may leave the industry because their vineyards are no longer profitable (Thieberger 2008). Research by CSIRO indicates that climate change is likely to further stress Australia's wine-growing regions, making 44 percent of viticultural areas unsuitable for grape growing by 2050. Others suggest that people's tastes will have to adapt along with a changing climate. In the meantime, drought may end up benefiting Australia's wine industry by driving up prices and quality. Paul Dalby of Australia's Center of Excellence in Water Management says, "The drought has increased grape prices overall because supply has dropped, wiping out a glut of product that had been keeping prices low" (quoted in Beasley 2009).

The drought has accelerated major structural changes already under way in Australian agriculture. The largest and smallest farms fared best during the drought. It is estimated that the

---

1 Throughout this chapter, costs are reported in Australian dollars. In 2010, it was roughly equivalent to the US dollar.

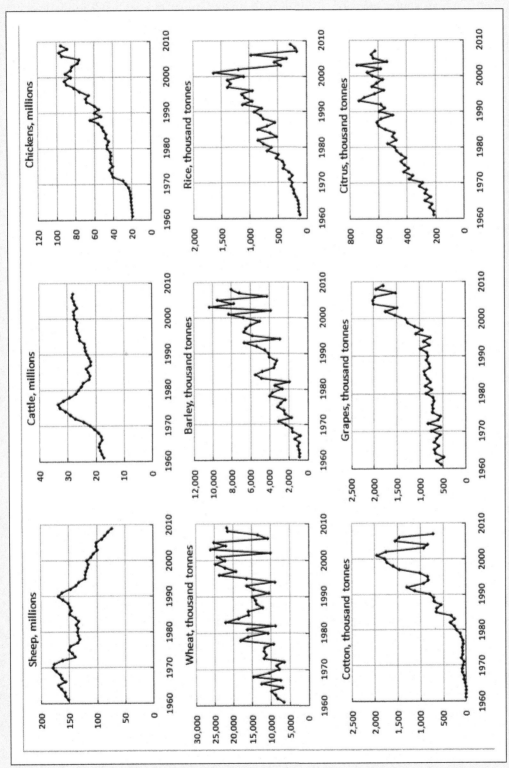

Figure 10.4 Production of Select Commodities in Australia, 1960–2009. The top graphs show the number of animals in millions, while the remaining graphs report annual harvests in thousand tonnes.

Source: Data for 2008–2009 from Australian Bureau of Statistics, publication 7121.0, Agricultural Commodities, Australia, 2008–09, http://www.abs. gov.au/AUSSTATS/abs@.nsf/DetailsPage/7121.02008-09 (download link for Publication tables, .xls). Data for 1961–2007 from the UN Food and Agriculture Organization, via UNdata, http://data.un.org/Explorer.aspx?d=FAO

Datasets > FAO Data > Crops or Livestock (custom queries for various agricultural commodities, filtered to show only Australia).

top 25 percent of producers remained profitable during the drought, while small farms with under $100,000 in sales are buffered because some of their income comes from off-farm employment. According to the director of the Australian Farm Institute, Mick Keogh, mid-size "mum and dad farms" were the most vulnerable to drought, as they are "too small to get the economies of scale they need, and too big to leave the farm to work." Mid-size farmers received the majority of the $4 billion in government drought relief since 2001 and were the most likely to quit farming altogether (Wahlquist 2010).

During the worst years of the drought from 2001 to 2006, 10,636 families gave up farming (Berry 2008). Many other farm families turned to other sources of income, taking jobs off the farm or searching for other ways to supplement their income. Farm debt has tripled over the past 10 years, to the point where the average farmer owes $400,000 (Byrnes 2007). The drought has also discouraged a generation of young, would-be farmers. Today, only 29 percent of farm families expect their children to take over the farm (Diamond 2005). A potential consequence of farm closures is to further depopulate already sparsely settled areas, making it more difficult for the government to maintain public services (Botterill and Wilhite 2005).

BUSHFIRES AND DROUGHT

Fire has always been a feature of the Australian landscape. For thousands of years, Aboriginal Australians have practiced "firestick farming." Land was burned to clear it of tall, dry grass. New green grass that sprouted up in its place supported kangaroos and wallabies, food sources for the native hunter-gatherers (Cathcart 2010, Diamond 1999). Today, there are wildfires every year in Australia, but they are more widespread and severe during drought years. The worst fires in Australia's history have been associated with droughts, such as the Black Friday fire of 1939 and the Ash Wednesday fire of 1983 (Lake 2008). Since 1851, fires have been blamed for more than 800 deaths and damages of $1.6 billion.

Some of the most destructive fires in Australia's history have occurred in the past 10 years. The Black Christmas fire that struck New South Wales in 2001 and 2002 is blamed for the destruction of 121 homes. On the Eyre Peninsula, bushfires in 2005 were responsible for 9 deaths and the loss of 93 homes. In 2009, dry conditions and an intense heat wave contributed to the deadliest fires in Australian history. Beginning on March 7, around 400 fires raged across 450,000 hectares (450 square kilometers) in Victoria, burning more than 4,000 homes and other buildings. Most tragically, what has come to be called the Black Saturday bushfires claimed 173 lives and caused 414 injuries (Romsey Australia 2010). The proximate causes of the fires were either arson or falling power lines, but the 10-year drought contributed to their severity.

A panel of experts convened to prevent future disasters recommended against allowing residents to rebuild destroyed homes or resettle in fire-prone areas. They recommended a "large scale government buy back" of land in "areas of unacceptably high bushfire risk" (Rintoul 2010), mirroring government efforts to buy back water entitlements from irrigators to restore the health of rivers, described later in this chapter in the section on water management in the Murray-Darling.

97

Dust Storms

In the 1930s and 1940s, there was a widespread fear that severe droughts could cause "desert outbreaks" in Eastern Australia, what today would be called desertification. Generations of experience would reveal the true causes of soil degradation: overgrazing, deforestation, invasive rabbits, and unsuitable agricultural practices. Dry soils with no vegetative cover are liable to be carried off by wind or rain, resulting in soil erosion and dust storms. Melbourne was blanketed in dust in 1902 as thousands of tons of topsoil from hundreds of kilometers inland blew past on its way out to sea. This would be repeated in 1983 and again during the Millennium Drought.

On September 22, 2009, a massive cloud of dust 500 kilometers wide by 1,000 kilometers long spread from the outback into eastern Australia. In Sydney, it darkened skies, canceled flights, and forced people indoors for shelter from the hazardous air (Boston Globe 2009). The Bureau of Meteorology reports that it was the worst dust storm since the 1940s, with air pollution up to 10 times worse than ever recorded (O'Loughlin 2009). Across New South Wales, there were reports of people being hospitalized due to asthma (Riebeek 2009).

RESPONSES TO DROUGHT

The Millennium Drought has prompted unprecedented changes in the way Australia manages water and has reinvigorated water reforms already under way by the states and the Commonwealth government. Recent developments in water policy grant more power to the national government and have accelerated the development of water trading and other market-based initiatives. Institutional reforms have been aimed at improving long-term water resiliency and mitigating the economic damage from drought. Meanwhile, urban water suppliers faced with dwindling supplies imposed restrictions and moved forward with projects to increase supplies, such as desalination, water recycling, and stormwater capture, and to reduce demand by improving water-use efficiency and changing water-use practices.

Water reforms have been influenced by the so-called neoliberal political philosophy that favors fiscal conservatism and application of free market economics, causing some to contend that economists have been given disproportionate influence over water policy (Thompson and Price 2009, Lockie and Higgins 2007). Throughout the 1990s, Australian policy makers pursued policies that focused on using economics and free market ideals to improve public services. This followed on a wave of privatization of government services, under the assumption that "when businesses compete, consumers get the best deal" and that enterprises will be run more efficiently and at lower cost. The water reform process has been closely tied to economic

reforms designed to remove restrictions on competition. The goal has been to promote "competitive neutrality," the idea that government should not enjoy an advantage over private service providers by virtue of public sector ownership.

Development of National Water Policies

The Australian constitution vests most water management responsibility to the states: "The Commonwealth shall not, by any law or regulation of trade or commerce, abridge the rights of the States or of the residents therein to the reasonable use of waters from conservation or irrigation" (Section 100 of the Australian constitution). Yet there has been a trend toward consolidation of power, exemplified by the "new federalism" under Prime Minister Bob Hawke in the early 1990s. Much of the water reform agenda has been pursued through the Council of Australian Governments (COAG), an organization consisting of the federal government, the six states and two territories, and the Australian Local Government Association, with a stated purpose to "develop and monitor the implementation of policy reforms that are of national significance and which require cooperative action by Australian governments" (COAG 2009).

Until the 1990s, state and federal government responded to drought with emergency relief efforts and funding, in much the same way they did for other disasters, such as cyclones, earthquakes, or floods. With the realization that drought was an inevitable and recurring threat, governments at all levels agreed to a National Drought Policy in 1992, based on principles of self-reliance and risk management.

In 1994, the COAG agreed to the Water Reform Framework, a key goal of which was to establish a market-based water management system by 2005. Elements of the Framework included allowing prices to reflect the full cost of resources, ending most subsidies, and making remaining subsidies more transparent. Conflicts of interest were to be removed by taking regulatory functions away from agencies also involved with supplying water. Lastly, trading and selling of water rights was to be introduced nationally. Difficulties were encountered in implementing the ambitious reform package, in part due to lack of cooperation between states, each having separate jurisdiction over portions of watersheds and competing for the same resource (Thompson and Price 2009).

Disappointed by slow progress, governments made a new attempt to accelerate reforms with the National Water Initiative (NWI) in 2004. Under the Initiative, signed by all the states and territories between 2004 and 2006, states agreed to conduct water reforms and move toward "integrated management of water for environmental and public benefit." The agreement built on the 1994 Water Framework, and its purpose was to develop a more cohesive approach to the way that Australia manages, measures, plans for, prices, and trades water. In December 2004, the Australian government created an independent body, the National Water Commission (NWC), to oversee implementation of the NWI.

As a part of the NWI, the government also created a $2 billion Water Fund to invest in water-efficiency upgrades (discussed later in this chapter). The largest of these programs, Water Smart Australia, was a competitive grant program funded at $1.6 billion. Two smaller programs included Raising National Water Standards ($200 million) and Community Water Grants ($200 million). The NWC was given responsibility for administering the latter programs, whereas Water Smart Australia has since been transferred to the Department of the Environment, Water, Heritage and the Arts (Cull et al. 2010).

In January 2007, faced with growing water shortages and seeing a need for swift action, Prime Minister John Howard announced the National Water Plan, extending the powers of the federal government over water management and committing $10 billion to various water projects. The plan was called "hurriedly prepared and ambitious," launched during the administration's last year in a bid to be seen as taking action on water, which had proven vexing to many politicians (Connell and Grafton 2008, Watson 2007). However, the plan was enthusiastically taken up by the newly elected

Labor Party administration of Kevin Rudd in 2008. Under the 2007 Water Act and amendments passed by the Parliament in 2008, Australia established a new authority to manage the waters of the distressed Murray-Darling Basin and restore water to the environment. Further, the act committed the federal government to spending $12.9 billion, with the majority of funds for infrastructure improvements and irrigation efficiency projects, and to "buy back" water from irrigators and dedicate it to the environment.

AGRICULTURAL WATER MANAGEMENT

It has been said that Australia rose to prominence on the backs of sheep. In the 19th century and first half of the 20th century, agriculture formed the basis of the economy and wool was the number one export. In recent years, agriculture has contributed to only 3 percent of the nation's economy (Hamblin 2009). Yet agriculture takes up 54 percent of Australia's land and 65 percent of its human water use (Australian Bureau of Statistics 2010b). In his bestseller *Collapse* (2005), Jared Diamond states that "only tiny areas of Australian land currently being used for agriculture are productive and suitable for sustained agricultural operations." Behind his contention is the fact that 80 percent of agricultural profits come from only 0.8 percent of the country's agricultural lands and that up to half of farms are unprofitable (DSEWPC 2002).

In effect, government subsidies, including low-cost water, prop up an industry that would not otherwise be profitable. Diamond enumerates the environmental advantages of phasing out unprofitable agriculture but acknowledges it would be a "first" in the modern world if any government decided to do so. The debate on agricultural water use and the extent to which government should "bail out" farmers struggling due to drought illustrates the dilemmas of this policy decision. On the one hand are the neo-liberal political ideals and policies idealizing the free market and competition. On the other is Australians' deep nostalgia for their

99

agrarian roots and sympathy for hardworking farm families.

According to the Australian Bureau of Meteorology: "The 1990s saw formal Government acknowledgement that drought is part of the natural variability of the Australian climate, with drought relief for farmers and agricultural communities being restricted to times of so-called 'exceptional circumstances.' In other words, the agricultural sector was expected to cope with the occasional drought, and relief would be available only for droughts of unusual length or severity" (Australian Bureau of Meteorology 1999). Changing attitudes have led to the gradual reversal of long-standing policies intended to increase irrigation water use and foster settlement in rural Australia. "In 1992, the Commonwealth government insisted that farming be considered a business—a central element of which has to be the ongoing management of risk—and subsequently removed farm welfare provisions from agricultural adjustment programmes" (Mercer et al. 2007).

This new policy was bound to be unpopular with farmers. A female grazier in Central Queensland told interviewers: "I think [the government's position] is absolutely stupid. It is a disaster. We haven't created it. It is the same as the cyclone or earthquake. It is the elements [that are] beyond us." Another stated: "Everybody else gets assistance if there is a flood or a fire. Why shouldn't the farmers get assistance? We are feeding the nation" (quoted in Stehlik 2005). It has been difficult for the government to maintain a disciplined stance in the face of obvious suffering. Between August 2001 to September 2010, the Australian government spent more than $4.5 billion on "exceptional circumstances" payments to support farmers and small businesses affected by the drought (Lloyd 2010). In 2007, the government doubled to $150,000 the amount it would pay to a farmer to simply leave his or her land (Hamashige 2007).

Public pressure and Australian attitudes contribute to this difficulty. Despite the fact that most Australians live in cities and suburbs, images of the outback and the hard-working farm families are an important part of the Australians' self-image. Linda Botterill, director of the National Institute for Rural and Regional Australia, cites as an example cultural representations of the "real Australia" in the opening ceremonies of the Sydney 2000 Olympics, and the popularity of television programs with rural settings, such as *McLeod's Daughters, Flying Doctors,* and *Blue Heelers* (Botterill 2003). As desert specialist Mark Stafford Smith puts it, the "almost mythological place that the outback has in the heart of urban Australia enables a small rural electorate to have a disproportionate influence on the political process through the emotional ties of the urban populace" (Botterill and Wilhite 2005).

The Australian government is investing heavily in infrastructure to improve agricultural water efficiency, committing the largest portion of the $12.9 billion in the 2007 Water Act to infrastructure improvements and grants to support on-farm irrigation efficiency. Not everyone agrees with the wisdom of investing in irrigation infrastructure. A number of environmentalists and economists argue that much of Australia's irrigated agriculture harms the environment and is losing money, and that the country needs *less* irrigated land. Savings from agricultural efficiency improvements are difficult to quantify, and equivalent savings could frequently be obtained more cheaply by simply purchasing water entitlements and retiring marginal lands (Collins 2008).

At the farm-field scale, many more farmers are now using water-saving management practices, such as no-till planting and improved irrigation methods. Zero-till has been described as a revolution in wheat farming in Australia in the past decade. Using zero-till methods, farmers plant directly into undisturbed soil, leaving stubble from the previous crop in place. This method conserves soil moisture and organic matter, allowing farmers to achieve small but economic harvests with as little as 100 millimeters (4 inches) of rain (O'Neill 2010). Mick Keogh, executive director of the Australian Farm Institute, says that cropping technologies such as minimum tillage have had a huge impact: "In terms of labour and time, the technology is light years from where it was 20 or 30 years ago and with that comes flexibility" (quoted in Wahlquist 2010).

Drought forecasting is another strategy to help farmers improve water management and farm income. The variability of Australia's climate from one year to the next poses challenges to farmers in deciding what crops to plant and when to plant them. For those whose livelihoods depend on rainfall, it is troubling to find that "seasons are poorly defined" and are not "fixed in either amplitude or timing" (Botterill and Wilhite 2005). At the federal level, Land and Water Australia has conducted research to create monthly, seasonal, annual, and longer-term forecasts to help farmers make better decisions about planting and managing water (Land and Water Australia 2009). Colin Creighton, the Managing Climate Variability coordinator at Land and Water Australia, says, "Our research success will mean the agricultural sector can make better decisions on dryland production mixes and practices by linking their on-farm decisions to risk analysis and predictions for key attributes such as plant-available water, frost frequency, heat events, and forage availability."

The Australian government is also sponsoring research to develop drought-resistant varieties of important crop species. These efforts are not new: Australia's wheat industry burgeoned after introduction of early-maturing and disease-resistant Federation wheat in 1901. Today, CSIRO's Plant Industry division has an annual budget of $84.4 million and 700 staff at nine facilities around the country. Recent research there has focused on developing the world's first drought-tolerant strain of wheat, Australia's most important export crop. Progress has been slowed by the size and complexity of wheat's genome— there is no single gene that controls for drought tolerance (O'Neill 2010).

Government and corporate researchers, working in a public-private partnership dubbed "Graingene," have so far released two varieties, Drysdale and Rees. These are sold by the agribusiness company AWB and are protected by Australian intellectual property law, making it illegal for "any unauthorized commercial propagation or any sale, conditioning, export, import or stocking of propagating material" (CSIRO Plant Industry 2010). Another potential obstacle faced by plant breeders is that the Australian public is generally untrusting of genetically modified (GM) food, and several states have placed moratoriums on growing GM food crops. GM cotton, however, introduced in Australia in 1996, made up 95 percent of the cotton crop in 2010 (GMO Compass 2010).

Companies have also developed products that reduce evaporation from water surfaces such as farm ponds. Products in use in Australia include specially made shade cloths that float on top of water; a variety of floating, modular devices that are effective (and expensive); and monolayers, which are chemical films that float atop water. These chemicals need to be reapplied frequently and are less effective when wind disturbs the water surface (Short 2007). Some members of the public have also expressed concern about the safety of introducing these new, patented chemicals into the environment and food supply. Agricultural extension services recommend other practices that are more natural, such as planting trees as windbreaks or adding compartments to farm ponds to reduce the surface area when it is less than full.

The government has also invested to improve the measurement of water deliveries to irrigators. In many locales, measurement was impossible due to lack of measurement devices and staff. According to writer Michael Cathcart: "During the 1990s, I met irrigators who confessed to jamming their meters or to secretly pumping directly from the river in the dead of night" (Cathcart 2010). A portion of the government's spending under the National Water Plan has been to improve water metering. In 2008, $417 million was dedicated to begin building the Australian Water Resources Information System, which will employ 120 hydrologists and information technology professionals (Woodhead 2008). Accurate water metering is also a prerequisite to creating working water markets.

A great deal of international attention has focused on water trading in Australia. The creation of water markets has been the government's most important strategy for dealing with drought and restoring the environment in the Murray-Darling River Basin, as described in the following section.

101

Water Management in the Murray-Darling

The Murray River Basin in southeast Australia covers one million square kilometers (14 percent of Australia's area), a size equivalent to France and Spain combined. It is home to 39 percent of the nation's agricultural production and 85 percent of the irrigated area. The watershed also contains 30,000 wetland areas, 16 of which are recognized under the Ramsar Convention (an international treaty signed in Iran in 1971 governing the protection of wetlands of international importance, especially as waterfowl habitat). Due to overextraction and drought, the Murray River failed to flow to the sea in 2002. For decades prior, the poor health of the river and the growing environmental movement led to calls to restore the river through better water management.

In response to evidence that the river system was overallocated, governments and irrigators agreed in 1992 to cap diversions, preventing more water from being taken out of the rivers. The "Murray-Darling Cap" was meant to allow greater environmental flows (which farmers dismissively called "duck water"), but it became clear that restoring the health of the river would require much bigger cuts (Cathcart 2010). In 2002, a group of prominent environmentalists released a series of statements including the *Blueprint for a National Water Policy*, calling for a halving of withdrawals from the river (Cosier et al. 2003).

In 2006, flows on the Murray fell to unprecedented lows, prompting the administration of Prime Minister John Howard to come up with a plan. He tasked the Basin Authority with setting "sustainable diversion limits," the level of consumptive water use in the river system in line with restoring the health of ecosystems. The result, a draft plan released in October 2010, calls for cuts of 22 to 29 percent in water use in the basin by cities and farms. Water expert Sandra Postel called it "perhaps the boldest water reform of this type ever proposed" and one that "few in the world have had the courage to undertake: asking farmers and communities to adapt to a future with less water in order to restore failing rivers, lakes, and wetlands" (Postel 2010).

The Commonwealth government has committed $12.6 billion over the next 10 years to ease the transition. About half of the funds ($5.8 billion) are targeted toward water-efficiency projects, for example, improving on-farm efficiency by installing drip irrigation. This approach has been criticized on several grounds. On the one hand, such subsidies are at odds with the stated goals of the National Water Initiative of full-cost pricing of resources and eliminating subsidies, leading some to call water policies "schizophrenic" (Crase 2009). Others point out the unfairness to irrigators who have already invested in on-farm efficiency improvements and will not benefit from government payments, while those who lagged behind receive assistance.

Reaction to the Basin Plan among farming communities has been overwhelmingly negative, as farmers already stressed by years of drought are worried about future cuts. The plan reflects the growing political power and influence of the environmental movement in the face of what Australian economist Lin Crase has described as "the long-standing vested interest from irrigated farming to maintain the status quo," and ability to "cushion its constituents from the impacts of any reallocation of the resource" (Crase 2009).

Water Markets

Market mechanisms have been explored as a way to reallocate water use in the Murray-Darling Basin, beginning in the 1980s when water trading was introduced in the state of South Australia. Among the obstacles to more widespread trading was that entitlements (the quantity of water a farmer has a right to use) were not always well established or well documented. A second barrier was the inability to measure water deliveries and extractions in rural districts. Further, the Murray-Darling Basin is divided among four states, each with separate jurisdiction over water allocation, and often competing for use of the same resource.

Reforms in the mid-1990s and again in the mid-2000s dealt with some of these issues, clarifying and documenting entitlements and permitting interstate water trading. A key provision of the 2007 Water Act was to give the Australian Competition and Consumer Commission expanded powers to develop and enforce water charges and water-market

102

rules. The government moved to expand water markets "based on the premise that trading provides economic benefits to buyers and sellers, and to society as a whole, by reallocating scarce water resources to higher valued uses" (NWC 2010).

As the thinking went, the "discipline of the market" would drive up the cost of water, forcing irrigators to use it efficiently and reduce waste. A farmer with a tradition of using water is granted a water-access entitlement that he can lease or "transfer" for six months to another water user. Policy makers and economists talk of "willing buyers" and "willing sellers": a farmer is motivated to trade when he believes he can make more money by selling his water entitlement rather than using it himself. Trades are usually handled through brokers, such as Adelaide-based Waterfind. Entitlements can also be sold outright, in which case the irrigation block is stripped of its water. The "unbundling" of water from the land has been a key reform at the state level—previously licenses allowed for only certain uses (e.g., irrigating a particular parcel of land). The result of reforms has been to make trading faster and easier; irrigators can now buy and sell water over the phone or even via text messaging.

Although economists admit that freer trade will not benefit everyone, they argue that "gains will outweigh losses on average and that, if necessary, losers can be compensated" (Quiggin 2006). But water markets by themselves do not necessarily benefit the environment. In order to restore water to ecosystems, the Australian government in 2008 committed $3 billion to buy back water from the overallocated Murray-Darling. It created the Commonwealth Environmental Water Holder to purchase and retire existing water rights and dedicate water to instream flow or to refill lakes and wetlands (Postel 2010). As of 2009, the government had already purchased 766 billion liters worth of entitlements. The Basin Authority estimates that water buybacks and efficiency improvements can save up to 2 trillion liters per year, or up to two-thirds of the reductions needed to meet restoration goals. Buybacks have become the main element in the government's efforts to restore aquatic ecosystems. Australia's decision to use buybacks as a strategy partly reflects the limited power granted to the federal government by the Australian constitution; with regard to water, the government's powers are generally limited to taxation and spending. However, when compared to alternatives such as desalination or funding water-efficiency upgrades, analysts have called buybacks "the cheapest and most feasible mechanism for dealing with over-allocation problems" (Crase 2007).

To date, water trading has received broad support from politicians, environmentalists, and the agricultural community in Australia, but it is not without detractors. General concerns raised by human rights campaigners condemn markets as a corporate takeover of water. Taxpayers wonder whether the only way to guarantee river flows is to spend billions in taxpayer dollars. If water is a public good, why should the public have to pay to keep rivers flowing? Another concern is that water trading could activate unused water rights (called "sleepers"), worsening the problems that markets were to help resolve (Quiggin 2006).

Many have also expressed concern about the effects of water trading on rural communities, frequently focused on the concept of "stranded assets" (NWC 2010). Within an irrigation district, each subscriber's payments help fund operations and infrastructure maintenance. When individuals sell entitlements, there are fewer subscribers in the district, placing a greater financial burden on the remaining irrigators. Government regulators have attempted to mitigate such "third-party effects" of trading by setting caps on the amount of water that can be sold outside of an irrigation district. For example, Victoria and New South Wales set a 4 percent annual limit on the volume of water entitlements that could be traded out of a district. Such limits to trading proved unpopular with irrigators, and were removed at the beginning of the 2009–2010 season. Regulators have also contemplated adding "termination fees" to compensate irrigation districts for lost revenue and help manage the stranded assets problem.

University of Queensland economist John Quiggin writes that "the idea of stranded assets may be extended further, to encompass social infrastructure such as schools, hospitals and banking services." Some economists have dismissed this argument, arguing that "sunk costs" should be disregarded in investment decisions. Regardless of this logic, it is small consolation to a farmer who has recently invested in laser leveling and drip irrigation. Quiggin argues that transitioning to a sustainable rural economy will involve adjustment costs, and "the appropriate response is to mitigate those costs rather than to prohibit trade altogether" (Quiggin 2006). Throughout the reform process, there has been pressure on government to mitigate the negative effects on rural communities. For decades, official policies encouraged irrigated agriculture that is now seen as unsustainable, and some argue that it is only fair to compensate those dealing with the results of these policies. "The persuasiveness of the stranded assets argument and the accompanying hysteria about water leaving agricultural districts undoubtedly explains the return to favor of engineering solutions in policy circles. After all, renovating irrigation districts and subsidizing on-farm capital investments is hardly likely to draw criticism from the agricultural sector" (Crase 2009).

Critics have also raised concern about manipulation of water markets and hoarding by "water barons." A recent series of articles have focused concern on the involvement of large international investors getting involved in the Murray-Darling's water markets. Regulations were written so that markets are not limited to bilateral trades among bona fide water users. In other words, third parties—even those who have no intention or ability to use Murray water—can participate in the market. This increases a market's "liquidity" and efficiency, increasing the chance that one can make a transaction quickly, rather than waiting for a willing buyer or seller to appear. However, it also sets the stage for speculation, market manipulation, and instability. Andrew Gregson of the New South Wales Irrigators Council told the *Sydney Morning Herald*, "We don't have a problem with investment, or indeed, speculation in the water market. We are concerned about market dominance. It's a recently developed, relatively fragile market" (Circle of Blue 2010).

In a review of the Murray-Darling water trading scheme, the NWC concludes that water trading has played a role in reducing financial hardships to farmers during the drought: "Although water trading out of a region may in some cases accelerate existing social and economic changes, without the financial cushioning effects of water trading the impacts of the drought would undoubtedly have been worse" (NWC 2010). The government audit found that trading resulted in the movement of water within regions, as well as transfers between states and regions, with the volume of trading increasing in 2008–2009 to the point that nearly one in four water deliveries consisted of traded water.

Since trading was initiated in 2001, it has contributed $370 million in the Southern Murray-Darling Basin. From 2001 to 2006, the value of agricultural production in the region increased by 2 percent despite a 14 percent reduction in water use. This appears to be driven by a decrease in area cultivated in rice, and by slight increases in higher-value crops such as vines and citrus. Not all regions benefited, however; the rice-growing region along the Murrumbidgee River saw decreases in water use and declines in agricultural output. On a national scale, the benefits of trading appear to have exceeded the costs, with analysts concluding that water trading contributed an additional $220 million to Australia's gross domestic product. The NWC has concluded that water trading can play an increasingly important role in mitigating the future impacts of drought, climate change, price fluctuations of agricultural commodities, and diversion limits imposed by regulators. In fact, the Commission is so confident in the benefits of trading that it has recommended expanding the system of water markets to the nation as a whole, and for the government to move forward quickly with further reforms to make water trading faster, easier, and more efficient.

Urban Water Management

Drought-induced water shortages have renewed focus on the water needs of Australia's growing cities. The Australian government has been working with states and territories to reform urban water management, with the goals of enhancing water-supply security, adapting to changes brought on by climate change, and decreasing overall water use. A number of these programs are being developed through the Council of Australian Governments—a coalition of federal, state, and local governments.

To date, most urban water suppliers have been reluctant to purchase water from irrigators to augment their supply. For example, Sydney has pursued expensive desalination, recycling, and a dam-raising project ahead of purchasing cheaper water from irrigators served by the Tantangara Dam (Collins 2008). While transfers from agriculture are feasible for many of Australia's cities, and are in many cases cheaper and more environmentally friendly than the alternatives, a range of government policies discourage such transfers (Quiggin 2006). Other reasons put forth are Australians' sympathy for farmers, and the reluctance of politicians to disrupt the status quo in the absence of a strong demand from the electorate. Ultimately, however, water suppliers have only two options for dealing with shortages: to increase supply or to decrease demand. The ways in which Australia's urban water suppliers have moved forward with both of these strategies are described in the sections that follow.

Recycling and Desalination

The use of reclaimed water, or recycled water, has become more common in the past decade. Water recycling refers to reusing treated wastewater. Depending on the level of treatment, water may be suited for nonpotable use, in irrigation or for flushing toilets. In other cases, highly treated water is suitable directly for drinking (called direct potable reuse). An example of the latter is the $90 million water recycling facility under construction in Geelong, Victoria, toward which the Australian government is contributing $20 million. The facility expected to produce 2,000 million liters a year of potable water, enough to supply about 10,000 homes, or about 5 percent of the city's annual water use. At the plant, sewage undergoes conventional wastewater treatment, followed by ultra-filtration, and passes through two rounds of reverse osmosis membranes. In pilot tests, the water removed all pathogens and viruses and passed all government regulations for Class A drinking water (Barwon Water 2010). Despite reassurances that the recycled water is fit for drinking, recycled water in Victoria will be distributed via "purple pipe" for watering gardens, washing cars, and flushing toilets. The public has been slow to accept direct potable reuse, causing suppliers to discharge recycled water to surface reservoirs or aquifers or to create "dual reticulation" systems like the one in Victoria.

Drought has encouraged more cities to consider desalination as a new source of water supply. In 2006, the city of Perth opened the Kwinana Desalination Plant, the first seawater desalination plant for urban water supply in Australia. A second plant is already under construction in Perth. A number of other plants are either being planned or already under construction in Sydney, Melbourne, Adelaide, and on the Gold Coast. Together, the country's five largest cities are spending $13.2 billion and installing sufficient capacity to meet 30 percent of their current water needs (Onishi 2010). As of 2009, there were a total of 46 desalination plants in Australia with a capacity of at least 10,000 liters per day, and by the year 2013, the total capacity is expected to double (Hoang et al. 2009).The government has also dedicated $20 million over five years to create a desalination research center in Perth and a center for research on water recycling in Brisbane (DSEWPC 2010).

While the official government policy is that 100 percent of water infrastructure and delivery costs should be passed on to customers through water rates, the Australian government has provided millions in incentives and subsidies for the construction of desalination and water recycling plants. Desalination is among the costliest of water-supply options, and critics contend that investments in water conservation and efficiency are far less expensive. To finance construction, suppliers have been forced to raise water rates, passing on the expense to customers. Others oppose desalination for its environmental impact. Up to half the cost of operating desalination plants is for the purchase of electricity. And because most of Australia's electricity is

105

produced from coal, desalination contributes to the emission of greenhouse gases.

Restrictions

Australian cities' demand management efforts have been largely successful; between 2002 and 2008, per-capita urban water use declined by 37 percent (Kendall 2010). The predominant approach that cities have used to limit water demand has been to impose water restrictions. Restrictions can be either permanent or temporary, and they may subject certain uses to an outright ban or put in place rules to promote efficiency. An example of one such rule is requiring hoses to have a nozzle with a shutoff trigger. Another category of rules discourages watering by making it more inconvenient and time-consuming, for example, by banning sprinklers but allowing buckets for hand watering. Table 10.1 shows the drought stages in the Australian Capital Territory (ACT), home to Canberra, which is Australia's capital and eighth-largest city (ACTEW Corporation Limited 2010). Stages are tied to reservoir levels and water-supply outlooks; managers announce progressively greater restrictions as supplies dwindle.

Temporary restrictions are the most common urban drought management policy, and they have been implemented by nearly all municipalities across Australia over the past decade. Although the

Table 10.1 Water Restrictions in the Australian Capital Territory

	Stage 1	Stage 2	Stage 3	Stage 4
Target annual reduction	10%	25%	35%	55%
Sprinklers and irrigation	Alternate days, 7–10 a.m. and 7–10 p.m.	Drippers only, 7–10 a.m. and 7–10 p.m.	No reticulation	
Hand-watering gardens and lawns	No restrictions	Alternate days, 7–10 a.m. and 7–10 p.m.	No watering lawns; watering plants alternate days, 7–10 a.m. and 7–10 p.m.	Graywater only
Swimming pools	No emptying or filling; topping up allowed		No topping up, emptying, or filling	
Car washing	Once a week, or at commercial car wash	Once a month, or at commercial car wash	Only at commercial car washes	No car washing
Window cleaning	Only with bucket or high-pressure, low-volume cleaner	No window cleaning		

The term *reticulation* refers to the use of piped irrigation systems, including sprinklers and drip irrigation systems (drippers).

Source: ACTEW Corporation Limited 2010, Wikipedia 2010.

restrictions vary widely, authorities typically first target outdoor water uses that are most visible and consumptive, such as lawns, gardens, swimming pools and spas, car washing, and washing hard surfaces. Permanent restrictions have often grown out of temporary ones, as some districts decide to keep certain rules in place even after the drought has ended. To date, permanent restrictions have been put in place in cities in Victoria, South Australia, and the ACT. The most typical permanent restriction is on daytime sprinkler use, which utilities estimate have resulted in savings of 4 to 9 percent (Chong et al. 2009).

Restrictions on outdoor water use have made it harder to keep recreational areas green and attractive. This has been blamed for a number of social ills, including "loss of participation in sports and associated impact on community health, community pride and spirit; rise in antisocial behaviour, and a loss of employment" (Chong et al. 2009). Australia's professional sports leagues have been latecomers to water conservation. After three years of deliberation, the Australian Football League and Cricket Australia have agreed to standards for synthetic turf, and they began constructing the first synthetic turf oval in Wyndham City, Victoria, in February 2011 (Edwards 2011).

The Australian public has been generally supportive of water restrictions. A 2008 survey of community attitudes toward water restrictions found that most Australians understood the need for restriction but noted that attitudes may change as restrictions become more severe or long-lasting, such as total outdoor watering bans that last an entire summer. Indeed, an engineering study conducted for the ACT government quoted complaints from elderly customers who had difficulty "hand watering during early morning or late evening times, particularly during winter" (Hughes et al. 2008).

In practice, some restrictions are difficult or impossible to enforce, and they rely on the cooperation and goodwill of the public for their success. One Melbourne resident explained people's cooperation as a sense that "we're all in this together." Others have suggested that this kind of social cohesion

and cooperation is part of the Australian character. "Mateship" is a traditional term for friendship but also connotes a code of conduct stressing equality. The public's overall acceptance clashes sharply with the rhetoric of some politicians, who describe restrictions by water suppliers as "draconian impositions on individual freedoms":

> The simple fact is that there is little or no reason why our large cities should be gripped permanently by water crises. ... Having a city on permanent water restrictions makes about as much sense as having a city on permanent power restrictions. (Prime Minister John Howard, July 17, 2006)

> I think Melbournians have had a great amount of goodwill in saving water but I think, with the Government threatening to introduce some very draconian measures that the Government is at risk of eroding community goodwill. (Louise Asher, member of the Victorian Legislative Assembly, Shadow Minister for Water) (each quoted in Chong et al. 2009)

So far, in spite of Australians' dislike for "pollies" (politicians), they have for the most part gone along with restrictions ungrudgingly. Perhaps cooperation is related to awareness of environmental issues; 98 percent of Australians participate in recycling programs, a far greater proportion than in either Europe or the United States. Melbourne authorities have sought to prevent water restrictions from becoming "an avenue for expression of neighbourhood disputes" by designing an enforcement program to minimize risks (Chong et al. 2009). For example, meter readers wear "water patrol" vests; even though they do not have authority to issue fines, their presence creates community confidence and provides a visual reminder of restrictions. When a neighbor calls to report a violation (a so-called "dob in" call), the city first sends an educational letter to the alleged violator. Only a second call results in a site visit. Melbourne authorities have recently stopped accepting such calls altogether, requiring complainants to fill out a witness form and provide written details of the violation.

Some states have deputized "water inspectors" to issue penalties to water wasters. On-the-spot fines range from $100 to $500 but are generally not issued until the second or third offense. Perhaps surprisingly, a government review of the program found little opposition to fines among community representatives (Chong et al. 2009). There is also anecdotal evidence of community policing, which unfortunately has led to a few instances of confrontations, violence, and even one death (Australian Broadcasting Corporation 2007).

Communicating information to customers on restrictions is obviously of prime importance. Utilities have communicated with customers mainly through mailings or inserts in water bills on restrictions, via the utilities' websites, and using public advertising. Messages encouraging compliance with restrictions are generally included in a broader campaign to promote water conservation and efficiency. Hence, messages about restrictions are accompanied by information on rebates for water-efficient appliances and devices, showerhead exchanges, and more general educational information (Chong et al. 2009).

Some analysts have urged greater use of economics, emphasizing the use of price incentives for conservation, rather than prescribing when and how people use water. One economist noted that "water restrictions are a relatively limited and inefficient method of rationing demand, imposing inconvenience costs and allocative efficiency costs and also involving significant enforcement costs" (Hughes et al. 2008). Water pricing, some argue, is a better economic tool, and that approach has also been tested in Australia.

Water Pricing

Among other reforms passed during the Millennium Drought, the National Water Commission has created a set of nationwide principles for pricing urban water. The national guidelines require utilities to put water rates for all types of customers on a rational footing, removing pressure on politicians to underprice water to win favor with voters. Reformers have stressed that consistent pricing policies would lead to efficient water use and help create more-efficient and viable markets for water trading between jurisdictions (NWC 2010). Under the NWI, the national government has directed state and local administrations to use best practices in water pricing. Broadly, rates should be set to recover costs (including mitigation of environmental harm) while precluding excessive profits by monopoly service providers.

The new policy, finalized in February 2010, stipulates that all municipalities should move to full-cost pricing of water, or "upper bound pricing," in which all aspects of water service delivery and infrastructure are covered by ratepayers, rather than through subsidies or transfers from other government revenues. Policy makers have acknowledged that, especially in rural areas, "some small community services will never be economically viable but need to be maintained to meet social and public health obligations" and will require continued subsidies, but these are to be publicly disclosed and transparent (DEWHA 2010).

The new pricing policies are intended to promote efficient, sustainable use of water and continued investment in infrastructure. The policy requires consumption-based pricing (the more you use, the more you pay) but stops short of requiring tiered rates. Many Australian cities charge two-part tariffs, where users pay a connection fee as well as volumetric water charge, but tiered rates are much less common in Australia than in other industrialized countries. Under tiered rate structures, customers pay increasingly high rates when their consumption increases to higher levels. Such rates are intended to make water service affordable to everyone while charging a premium to big consumers and discouraging waste.

The concept of "staged" scarcity pricing has also been promoted by the NWC and backed by a study from the Australian Bureau of Agricultural and Resource Economics (Hughes et al. 2008). Water rates are currently set by regulators to match estimates of the costs of running the water system. Suppliers lack the ability to quickly change prices to send economic signals for conservation when supplies are low. With scarcity pricing, water prices would go up when supplies are low, for example, by tying rates to reservoir levels. Government economists argue that scarcity pricing is more flexible and less costly than imposing restrictions, but they acknowledge that it raises equity concerns and that attention should be paid to how such schemes may affect the poor. Potential ways to address these concerns are through subsidies to low-income families, or rate designs in which the lowest tier of consumption is made very inexpensive or even free—a practice that has been implemented in other countries.

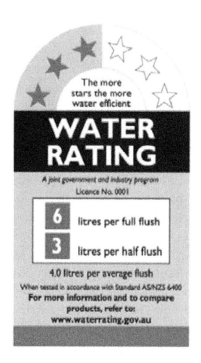

Figure 10.5 Wels (water efficiency labelling and standards) rating label.
Source: Courtesy of Caroma, http://www.caroma.com.au

Labeling and Education

In 2006, Australia introduced the Water Efficiency Labelling and Standards (WELS) Scheme to promote water-efficient appliances and fixtures. Backers emphasize the program's financial savings and greenhouse gas reductions as well. The program's website declares: "By 2021, Australians could save more than one billion dollars through reduced water and energy bills by simply choosing more efficient products." As of July 2006, all products in the following categories must carry a WELS rating label (like the one in Figure 10.5): faucets (with some exceptions), showers, toilets, urinals and flow controllers, clothes washers, and dishwashers.

Key components of the program include a labeling scheme, product testing, and enforcement. Besides helping to reduce domestic water consumption, it also allows manufacturers to showcase their most water-efficient products. Australia has become the world leader in the labeling of water-efficient appliances. Similar systems have been adopted in the United Kingdom, New Zealand, Singapore, and Hong Kong. The program has influenced the United States' WaterSense program and has prompted discussion about creating a similar scheme for the European Union (Benito et al. 2009).

Rebates are not offered through the WELS program, but many local councils and water authorities give rebates for WELS-registered products with

specific star ratings. The Australian Department of Climate Change and Energy Efficiency maintains the Living Greener website (www.livinggreener.gov.au), where residents can search for rebates and other assistance available in their area.

In addition to rebates, some utilities offer direct installations, usually of toilets, the biggest indoor water use. For example, Sydney Water offers a Toilet Replacement Service that takes up to $370 off the cost of installing a modern, efficient toilet. The program is designed to make it easy for low-income residents and renters to participate in the program. Participants choose from among three different four star–rated, water-efficient, dual-flush toilets, each of which is installed with a 10-year warranty. Residents can choose to make a single payment or have the cost spread out over several water bills.

Conservation Incentives

Many Australians have taken advantage of government incentives to purchase water-efficient appliances and fixtures in the past 10 years. According to a report by the Australian Bureau of Statistics, 251,000 households received a rebate or incentive in 2009–2010 for washing machines and dishwashers. These were followed closely in popularity by water-efficient taps and showerheads (225,000). The market for dual-flush toilets was not as robust (32,800), probably because they have already been installed in 86 percent of households. Over the past decade, the market penetration of water-efficient products has increased substantially (Australian Bureau of Statistics 2010a), as shown in Figure 10.6.

With drought-imposed water restrictions, interest in rainwater and graywater use has grown. *Graywater* refers to household water that has been used in sinks, showers, and the laundry (toilet water is referred to as *blackwater*). As of the late 1990s, graywater reuse was illegal in every state in Australia, although it was already widely used in many households (Marshall 1997). Today, graywater use has become more common and ranges from fully plumbed systems to simply placing a bucket in the shower to catch runoff for watering flowers.

As recently as the early 1990s, rainwater tanks were a common sight in Australia, where as many as 16 percent of homes had tanks and 13 percent relied on them even for drinking water. However, they had mostly disappeared by the 2000s. The drought and water restrictions renewed interest in rainwater tanks, and utilities and state governments began encouraging residents to install rainwater tanks, often with the offer of a financial rebate or incentive.

The National Rainwater and Graywater Initiative promotes these technologies and provides financial incentives to residents. Rebates can range from $150 to $1,500 for the installation of a rainwater tank, depending on the size of the tank and whether it is connected to the house's plumbing. Because the cost for an average tank is around $4,000, it is a substantial investment for residents, yet 104,600 people received a government rebate in 2009–2010 alone.

CONCLUSION

Heavy rains and flooding in the austral spring of 2010–2011 prompted journalists to declare an end to the Millennium Drought. The nation's largest newspaper, the *Australian*, confidently declared, "Fresh Hope for Nation as Drought Breaks" (Lloyd 2010). Indeed, high rainfall across southeastern Australia refilled dams and restored river flows across Queensland, New South Wales, southwestern Victoria, and parts of South Australia. However, Australia's National Climate Center was more cautious, stating that "Australia's wettest September

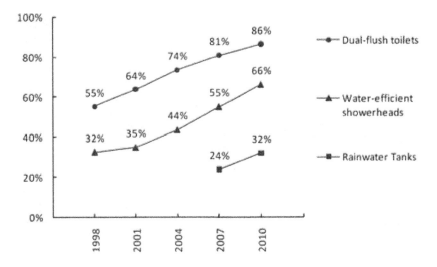

Figure 10.6 Households with water-saving products, 1998–2010.

Source: Australian Bureau of Statistics 2010a

on record is not enough to clear long-term rainfall defi-cits" (National Climate Center of Australia 2010). Although rains restored soil moisture and give irrigators at least a temporary reprieve from drought, water suppliers' troubles have not ended, as the rains were not sufficient to restore all of the country's depleted reservoirs and aquifers. And, as history shows, droughts return.

Also worrisome, climate scientists warn that climate change will continue to worsen the risk of droughts, as temperatures rise and precipitation and water availability decrease. Some Australians speak of having already experienced a "step change" in climate and of being among the first nations to experience the negative consequences of global warming. How well Australia manages water will largely determine how well the country adapts to a warmer, drier, and more uncertain future.

The Big Dry will be remembered as the longest and most serious drought in Australian history. It has had a lasting effect on Australians' attitudes toward water, climate change, and the environment. It has profoundly affected rural economies, stimulated changes in the agricultural sector, and prompted critical thinking about how to modernize Australian agriculture and make it sustainable. The drought has set off a building spree of desalination plants on the nation's coasts and has increased Australians' awareness of water conservation. It has turned the humble rainwater tank into a fixture of more and more homes and has made newfangled dual-flush toilets the norm. Finally, it has set Australian water management on a new course, the success of which will not be fully understood until the next major drought.

REFERENCES

ACTEW Corporation Limited. 2010. Scheme of Temporary Restrictions on the Use of Water from

ACTEW Corporation Water Supply System. http://www.actew.com.au/publications/TemporaryWater RestrictionsScheme.pdf

Australian Broadcasting Corporation. 2007. Man Charged with Murder After Lawn Watering Dispute.

http://www.abc.net.au/news/stories/2007/11/01/2078076.htm (accessed December 30, 2010).

Australian Bureau of Meteorology. 1999. Climate Education: Drought. http://www.bom.gov.au/lam/climate/levelthree/c20thc/drought.htm (accessed January 3, 2011).

Australian Bureau of Meteorology. Undated. Drought, Dust and Deluge. Climate Education website. http://www.bom.gov.au/climate/environ/drought.shtml (accessed February 19, 2011).

Australian Bureau of Statistics. 2010a. *Environmental Issues: Water Use and Conservation, Mar 2010.* Canberra: Australian Bureau of Statistics. http://www.abs.gov.au/AUSSTATS/abs@.nsf/DetailsPage/4602.0.55.003Mar%202010?Open Document (accessed February 5, 2011).

Australian Bureau of Statistics. 2010b. *Year Book Australia, 2009–10.* Canberra: Australian Bureau of Statistics. http://www.abs.gov.au/AUSSTATS/abs@.nsf/Lookup/1301.0Chapter16012009%E2%80%9310 (accessed February 20, 2011).

Barwon Water. 2010. Barwon Water Northern Water Plant. http://www.barwonwater.vic.gov.au/projects/nwp (accessed February 6, 2011).

Beasley, D. 2009. Lessons From Australia: Drought Can Help Georgia Economy. http://www.globalatlanta.com/article/17131/ (accessed January 6, 2011).

Benito, P., et al. 2009. Water Efficiency Standards. Bio Intelligence Service and Cranfield University, Report for European Commission (DG Environment).

Berry, C., 2008. Australia's long drought withering wheat, rice supplies. *National Geographic News.* http://news.nationalgeographic.com/news/2008/05/080529-food-australia.html (accessed February 1, 2011).

Boston Globe. 2009. Dust storm in Australia. The Big Picture, Boston.com. http://www.boston.com/bigpicture/2009/09/dust_storm_in_australia.html (accessed February 6, 2011).

Botterill, L.C. 2003. Uncertain climate: The recent history of drought policy in Australia. *Australian Journal of Politics and History* 49(1): 61–74.

Botterill, L. 2005. Late twentieth century approaches to living with uncertainty: The national drought policy. In: *From Disaster Response to Risk Management: Australia's National Drought Policy.* L. Botterill and D.A. Wilhite, editors. New York: Springer, pp. 51–64.

Botterill, L., and Wilhite, D.A., eds. 2005. *From Disaster Response to Risk Management: Australia's National Drought Policy*. New York: Springer.

Byrnes, M. 2007. Australian farmers face bankruptcy from drought. *Environmental News Network*. http://www.enn.com/climate/article/24066 (accessed February 7, 2011).

Cathcart, M. 2010. *The Water Dreamers: The Remarkable History of Our Dry Continent*. Melbourne: Text Publishing Company.

Chong, J., et al. 2009. *NWI parties review of water restrictions*. Canberra: Australian Government National Water Commission.

Circle of Blue. 2010. Foreign Investors Are Becoming Players in Australia's Water Market. http:// www.circleofblue.org/waternews/2010/business/foreign-investors-are-becoming-players-in-australia%E2%80%99s-water-market/ (accessed February 7, 2011).

Collins, D. 2008. Threats to effective environmental policy in Australia. In: *Promoting Better Environmental Outcomes, Roundtable Proceedings*. Melbourne: Australian Government Productivity Commission. http://www.pc.gov.au/research/confproc/environmental-outcomes Commonwealth Scientific and Industrial Research Organization (CSIRO). 2008. *Water Availability in the Murray-Darling Basin Report. A Report to the Australian Government from the CSIRO Murray-Darling Basin Sustainable Yields Project*, Australia: CSIRO. http://www.csiro.au /resources/WaterAvailabilityInMurray-DarlingBasinMDBSY.html (accessed February 5, 2011).

Commonwealth Scientific and Industrial Research Organization (CSIRO) Plant Industry. 2010. Drysdale: A World's First. http://www.csiro.au/files/files/pl27.pdf

Connell, D., and Grafton, R.Q. 2008. Planning for water security in the Murray-Darling Basin. *Public Policy* 3(1): 67–86.

Cooley, H. 2007. Floods and droughts. In: *The World's Water 2006–2007, The Biennial Report on Freshwater Resources*. P.H. Gleick, editor. Washington, D.C.: Island Press, pp. 91–142.

Cooperative Research Centre for Water Quality and Treatment. 2006. *Consumer's Guide to Drinking Water*. Adelaide. http://www.wqra.com.au/_dyn/media/r396/system/attrib /file/337

Cosier, P., et al. 2003. *Blueprint for a National Water Plan*. Sydney, Australia: The Wentworth Group of Concerned Scientists.

Council of Australian Governments (COAG). 2009. Council of Australian Governments Water Reform Framework. http://www.environment.gov.au/water/australia/coag.html (accessed February 25, 2011).

Crase, L. 2007. Water markets and the chimera of price distortions. *Connections: Farm, Food and Resource Issues*. http://www.agrifood.info/connections/2007/Crase2.html

Crase, L. 2009. Water policy in Australia: The impact of drought and uncertainty. In: *Policy and Strategic Behaviour in Water Resource Management*. A. Dinar and J. Albiac, editors. London: Earthscan, pp. 91–107.

Cull, S., et al. 2010. *Administration of the Water Smart Australia Program*. Canberra: Australian National Audit Office.

Department of Sustainability, Environment, Water Population and Communities (DEWHA). 2010.

National Water Initiative Pricing Principles Regulation Impact Statement. http://www .environment.gov.au/water/publications/action/pubs/ris-nwi-pricing-principles.pdf

Department of Sustainability, Environment, Water, Population and Communities (DSEWPC). 2002. *Australians and Natural Resource Management 2002: National Land and Water Resources Audit, Commonwealth of Australia*. Canberra: DSEWPC.

Department of Sustainability, Environment, Water, Population and Communities (DSEWPC). 2010. Policy and reform in the area of urban water. *Australian Government*. http://www .environment.gov.au/water/policy-programs/urban-reform/index.html (accessed February 2, 2011).

Diamond, J. 2005. *Collapse: How Societies Choose to Fail or Succeed*. Later printing. New York: Penguin (Non-Classics).

Diamond, J.M. 1997. *Guns, Germs, and Steel: The Fates of Human Societies*. Later printing. New York: Norton.

Edwards, N. 2011. AFL breaks ground on full-sized synthetic oval. *AFL News*. http://www.afl.com .au/news/newsarticle/tabid/208/newsid/107237/default.aspx (accessed February 22, 2011).

112

GMO Compass. 2010. Genetically Modified Cotton: Global Area Under Cultivation. http://www.gmo-compass.org/eng/agri_biotechnology/gmo_planting/343.genetically_modified_cotton_global_area_under_cultivation.html (accessed February 25, 2011).

Hamashige, H. 2007. Worst drought in a century hurting Australian farmers. *National Geographic News.* http://news.nationalgeographic.com/news/2007/11/071108-australia-drought.html (accessed February 1, 2011).

Hamblin, A. 2009. Policy directions for agricultural land use in Australia and other post-industrial economies. *Land Use Policy* 26(4): 1195–1204.

Hoang, M., et al. 2009. Desalination in Australia. CSIRO. http://www.csiro.au/resources/Desalination-In-Australia-Report.html

Hughes, N., et al. 2008. *Urban Water Management: Optimal Price and Investment Policy Under Climate Variability.* Canberra: Australian Bureau of Agricultural and Resource Economics.

Kendall, M. 2010. Drought and Its Role in Shaping Water Policy in Australia. http://www.nwc.gov.au/resources/documents/Kendall_International_Drought_Symposium_FINAL_mbk_260310.pdf

Ker, P. 2009. The Coorong is dead but can be revived. *The Age.* http://www.theage.com.au/environment/the-coorong-is-dead-but-can-be-revived-20090722-dtl3.html (accessed February 9, 2011).

Lake, P.S. 2008. Drought, the "creeping disaster": Effects on aquatic ecosystems. Land and Water Australia. http://lwa.gov.au/files/products/innovation/pn20677/pn20677.pdf

Land and Water Australia. 2009. Farmers beat the dry times. *Land and Water Australia.* http://lwa.gov.au/news/2009/mar/04/farmers-beat-dry-times (accessed January 10, 2011).

Lloyd, G. 2010. Fresh hope for nation as drought breaks. *The Australian.* http://www.theaustralian.com.au/national-affairs/the-drought-breaks-story-fn59niix-1225952583089 (accessed January 3, 2011).

Lockie, S., and Higgins, V. 2007. Roll-out neoliberalism and hybrid practices of regulation in Australian agri-environmental governance. *Journal of Rural Studies* 23(1): 1–11.

Lu, L., and Hedley, D. 2004. The impact of the 2002–03 drought on the economy and agricultural employment. *Economic Roundup*, pp. 25–43. http://www.treasury.gov.au/documents/817/HTML/docshell.asp?URL=03_article_2.asp (accessed May 23, 2011).

Marshall, G. 1997. Greywater re-use: Hardware, health, environment and the law. *Permaculture Association of Western Australia.* Available at: http://permaculturewest.org.au/ipc6/ch08/marshall/index.html (accessed February 3, 2011).

McKernan, M. 2010. Coming to terms with the reality of a land burnt dry. *The Australian.* http:// www.theaustralian.com.au/national-affairs/coming-to-terms-with-the-reality-of-a-land-burnt-dry/story-fn59niix-1225952595679 (accessed December 30, 2010).

Mercer, D., Christesen, L., and Buxton, M. 2007. Squandering the future—climate change, policy failure and the water crisis in Australia. *Futures* 39(2-3): 272–287.

National Climate Center of Australia. 2010. Special Climate Statement 22: Australia's wettest September on record but it is not enough to clear long-term rainfalldeficits.

National Water Commission (NWC). 2010. *Impacts of Water Trading in the Southern Murray–Darling Basin: An Economic, Social, and Environmental assessment.* Canberra: Australian Government. http://www.nwc.gov.au/www/html/2816-impacts-of-water-trading-in-the-southern-murraydarling-basin.asp?intSiteID=1 (accessed January 11, 2011).

Nicholls, N. 2008. Recent trends in the seasonal and temporal behaviour of the El Niño–Southern Oscillation. *Geophysical Research Letters* 35(19): L19703.

O'Loughlin, T. 2009. Australia engulfed by dust storms. *The Guardian.* http://www.guardian.co.uk/world/2009/sep/23/australia-dust-storm-sydney (accessed February 6, 2011).

O'Neill, G. 2010. Designing drought tolerant crops. *Australian Life Scientist.* http://www.lifescientist.com.au/article/368007/feature_designing_drought_tolerant_crops/ (accessed February 7, 2011).

Onishi, N., 2010. Arid Australia turns to desalination, at a cost. *New York Times.* http://www.nytimes.com/2010/07/11/world/asia/11water.html (accessed February 7, 2011).

Peatling, S. 2007. Kangaroos invading Australian cities as drought worsens. *National Geographic News.* http://news.nationalgeographic.com/news/2007/07/070718-roos-drought.html (accessed February 1, 2011).

Postel, S. 2010. Australia takes a bold step to shape its water future. NatGeo News Watch. *National Geographic News.* http://blogs.nationalgeographic.com/blogs/news/chiefeditor/2010/10/australia-water-allocations.html (accessed February 1, 2011).

Quiggin, J. 2006. Urban water supply in Australia: The option of diverting water from irrigation. *Public Policy* 1(1): 14–22.

Riebeek, H. 2009. Dust Over Southeast Australia: Image of the Day. http://earthobservatory.nasa.gov/IOTD/view.php?id=41458 (accessed January 10, 2011).

Rintoul, S. 2010. Ban development in fire-prone areas, experts tell royal commission. *The Australian.* http://www.theaustralian.com.au/news/nation/ban-development-in-fire-prone-areas-experts-tell-royal-commission/story-e6frg6nf-1225830521084 (accessed February 6, 2011).

Romsey Australia. 2010. Summary of Major Bush Fires in Australia Since 1851. http://home.iprimus.com.au/foo7/firesum.html (accessed February 6, 2011).

Short, R. 2007. Rural Water Note: Reducing Farm Dam Evaporation. http://www.water.wa.gov.au/PublicationStore/first/76927.pdf

Sohn, E., 2007. The Big Dry: Prolonged drought threatens Australia's people, wildlife, and economy. *Science News* 172(17): 266–268.

Stehlik, D. 2005. Managing risk?: Social policy responses in time of drought. In: *From Disaster Response to Risk Management: Australia's National Drought Policy.* New York: Springer, pp. 65–97.

Thieberger, V. 2008. Drought forces wine makers in Australia to think again. *New York Times.* http://www.nytimes.com/2008/03/25/business/worldbusiness/25iht-wine.1.11395929.html (accessed January 6, 2011).

Thompson, W., and Price, R. 2009. Australia: Water reform, 1994–2004. In: *The Political Economy of Reform.* Organisation for Economic Cooperation and Development. http://www.ingentaconnect.com/content/oecd/16815378/2009/00002009/00000007/1109011ec019 (accessed February 8, 2011).

Ummenhofer, C.C., et al. 2009. What causes Southeast Australia's worst droughts? *Geophysical Research Letters* 36(4): L04706.

United Nations Educational, Scientific and Cultural Organization (UNESCO). 2009. The state of the resource. In: *The 3rd United Nations World Water Development Report: Water in a Changing World.* Chapter 4. London and Paris: UNESCO and Earthscan. http://www.unesco.org/water/wwap/wwdr/wwdr3/

Verdon-Kidd, D.C., and Kiem, A.S. 2009. Nature and causes of protracted droughts in southeast Australia: Comparison between the Federation, WWII, and Big Dry droughts. *Geophysical Research Letters* 36(22). http://www.agu.org/pubs/crossref/2009/2009GL041067.shtml

Wahlquist, A. 2010. Rural incomes rocket from reform. *The Australian.* http://www.theaustralian.com.au/national-affairs/rural-incomes-rocket-from-reform/story-fn59niix-1225952593371 (accessed December 30, 2010).

Watson, A. 2007. A national plan for water security: Pluses and minuses. *Connections—Farm, Food and Resources Issues* 7(1).

Wikipedia. 2010. Water Restrictions in Australia. http://en.wikipedia.org/wiki/Water_restrictions_in_Australia (accessed February 2, 2011).

Woodhead, B. 2008. National water plan advances. *The Australian.* http://www.theaustralian.com.au/australian-it/national-water-plan-advances/story-e6frgamf-1111115367518 (accessed February 8, 2011).

11

China's Security, China's Demographics

Aging, Masculinization, and Fertility Policy

By Valerie M. Hudson and Andrea den Boer

With 1.3 billion people, China is the most populous state in the world and comprises approximately 20 percent of the total world population. In March 2006, Zhang Weiqing, head of China's National Population and Family Planning Commission, announced that China's family planning policy had helped to prevent 400 million births since its inception three decades ago.[1] China's population policy is often heralded as a success story for achieving a growth rate similar to that of developed states. But at what cost? In earlier work, we argued that China should alter its family planning policy in order to reduce the social instability and security risks that could result from the imbalance in China's sex ratios.[2] In this article we extend the analysis by further examining the relationship between China's family planning policy and the demographic shifts taking place in its age and sex structure.

FAMILY PLANNING IN CHINA

China's family planning policy, often referred to as the "one-child policy," has undergone numerous modifications since it was first introduced in 1979, rendering it more complex than its name suggests. The large increase in the population between the 1950s and early 1970s, coupled with a decline in China's economic growth, led to government fears that China faced a population crisis that would greatly hinder its economic and political development.[3] These fears culminated in concrete policy action in 1979, when China introduced the one-child policy. Although the one-child policy did not become an official law until September 2002, the government at all levels throughout China acted as though the policy were law and attempted to enforce its rules and penalties.[4] In the initial phase of the one-child policy (1979–1983), the government followed a policy of strict enforcement of the one-child norm; failure to comply in some areas led to the imposition of fines; removal of benefits such as subsidized day care, health care, housing, and education; use of psychological intimidation of co-workers or co-villagers; as well as violence, including detention, beatings, forced medical procedures, and destruction of property.[5] Following the peasant backlash against the 1983 campaigns of forced sterilization and abortion the government "relaxed" the policy in 1984 to a 1.5 policy (parents whose first child was a girl in some poor rural areas were permitted to apply for a permit to have a second child after a suitable period).[6] Although family planning was a national goal supported by the 1980 Marriage Law and the 1982 Constitution, the Chinese Communist Party acknowledged that the one-child policy could be adjusted to meet local demographic and socioeconomic conditions, which resulted in a variety of provincial and local policies regarding fertility. According to regulations at the provincial level, the one-child rule is enforced in all urban areas as well as six provinces, the 1.5-child rule applies to 19 provinces, and a two-child rule applies to five provinces, although there are further exceptions and local variations within these provincial rules.[7] The overall effect of these variations at local and provincial levels is that China has an average fertility policy of 1.47, which may be close to calculations for the actual fertility, which is estimated to be between 1.5 and 1.8.[8]

The fertility decline in China has had some positive effects beyond simply reducing the population growth rate and aiding economic development. Mortality rates for women, for example, have decreased in part because of the low fertility rate. A later age for marriage, greater birth spacing, and giving birth to fewer children, has led to lower incidences of maternal mortality with a subsequent rise in women's life expectancy.[9] This benefit is offset, however, by the structural violence against women resulting from the renewal of cultural beliefs in the value of sons over daughters supported and sustained by China's fertility policy.[10]

CHINA'S TWO MAJOR DEMOGRAPHIC SHIFTS

The 2000 census in China provides the most recent comprehensive statistics for China's population. According to the census there were 653 million men and 612 million women with an overall sex ratio of 106.7 males per 100 females.[11] In 2007, Zhang Weiqing, director of the National Population and Family Planning Commission, indicated that the national current birth sex ratio had risen to 119.6 (122.9 in rural areas); in contrast, the birth sex ratio in 1981 was 108.5.[12] The high birth sex ratios are an indication of gender selection through the use of sex-selective technology, resulting in a gender imbalance in China's population. High birth sex ratios result in high sex ratios in subsequent age cohorts: high sex ratios are observed in all age groups born since 1980.[13] High sex ratios observed among China's youth are also due to the neglect of female infants in the first days or years of life. Mortality figures from the 2000 census reveal that females in China die at higher than expected rates during

the first four years of life.[14] The high sex ratios at birth, coupled with differential infant and childhood mortality patterns in China, has resulted in a severe gender imbalance in the population: men outnumber women by 41 million.

While the Chinese government is aware of the gender imbalance, officials blame traditional son preference for the gender imbalance rather than China's fertility policy. In a statement to the press

> Officials blame traditional son preference for the gender imbalance rather than China's fertility policy.

in April 2006, Zhang Weiqing stated that technology and son preference are to blame for the high sex ratio, and that there was "no direct connection" between the sex ratio and family planning.[15] The causes of the rising sex ratio and resulting imbalance are complex, resulting from traditional son preference, economic reforms, and China's fertility policy. In areas of patrilineality, in which daughters seldom inherit land or other resources and do not continue the family line, and patrilocality, in which daughters leave their home upon marriage and are therefore "lost" as a resource to the family, sons are more highly valued.[16] A preference for sons is particularly strong in rural areas, where male labor is more highly valued. Whereas many urban families are protected by pensions (78 percent in 2006), few rural families have access to state or other forms of pensions (only 4.8 percent in 2006).[17] Thus, many rural families view a son as essential to take care of them in their old age.

However, it is fair to say that contrary to the view of the Chinese government, China's family planning policy has played a key role in the establishment and perpetuation of the current high sex ratios in China. China's fertility policy affects all aspects of life; it permeates society, filters down into the home and affects family and individual decisions regarding family size, health, and economics. The widespread availability of sex-selective technology—even in the most remote

117

parts of China—is a direct result of the nationwide enforcement of birth control: ultrasound machines were used to monitor IUD insertion and verify that the devices had not been removed illegally. The increasingly widespread availability of ultrasound technology in the mid-1980s to control fertility, however, also enabled parents to manipulate the sex composition of their small families. Other countries in Asia in which son preference is high have also experienced a rise in sex ratios, but none exhibit ratios as high as those in China (not even in ethnically Chinese Taiwan where the 2006 birth sex ratio was 109.7).[18] The Chinese government in fact gave support to the belief that sons are more valued than daughters, when, in 1984, it permitted families in rural areas who had given birth to a daughter to have a second child, because they were taking "into account the difficulties (such as the shortage of household labor) of peasants who have one daughter."[19] By adopting this 1.5 child policy, the government reinforced the idea that a female was worth less than a male in terms of her contribution to household labor.

Families in provinces or rural areas in which a second child is permitted generally do not resort to sex-selection with the birth of their first child: in rural areas, the sex ratio of first births in 2000 was 105.7, which is within a normal range.[20] First birth sex ratios in towns and urban areas, where fewer second births are permitted, were much higher, at 110.4 and 108.9. The majority of families apparently take advantage of sex selection to ensure that their second child is male, as shown by the high sex ratios for rural, town, and urban areas of 152.1, 154.6, and 147.6 for second child births.[21] Further links between China's fertility policy and the high sex ratios can be seen in the form of discriminatory treatment of female infants and children at higher birth orders. In their examination of infant and child survival in rural China, Shuzhuo Li, Chuzhu Zhu, and Marcus W. Feldman found that excess deaths were not found equally among all daughters; rather, second and higher birth order daughters were more likely to experience differential care resulting in higher mortality patterns. The authors further found that excess female deaths are more

likely to occur when a birth takes place without a "birth quota" (i.e., without permission from the Family Planning Commission): 79 percent of deaths occurring in the first day of life for infants born without a birth quota were female.[22] The restrictions placed on families regarding the number of permitted births may lead some parents to choose not to spend precious resources on a female infant when these resources might be used for a son. Recognizing the effect of China's fertility policy is crucial to improving survival rates for females and quality of life for women in general, because birth quotas imposed by the family planning policy make it more likely that higher order births, or out-of-plan births, are more likely to take place at home and that daughters may have a lower survival rate

> The one-child policy is also causing China's population to shift towards an aging societal structure.

regardless of investments in healthcare.[23] Son preference, the availability of sex selective technology, economic factors such as the lack of pension for the elderly, and the one-child policy are interrelated factors that have contributed to the gender imbalance in China today.

The one-child policy is also causing China's population to shift towards an aging societal structure that resembles that of many industrialized nations. While fertility declines typically accompany economic modernization, in China's case this shift has arrived prematurely; the prevention of over 400 million births since 1980 has hastened the aging of China. The 2000 census recorded 88 million persons aged 65 and older, which constituted 7.1 percent of the total population.[24] If the current 1.5 child policy is continued, then China's aging population (those aged 65 and over) will constitute 10 percent of the population in 2010 and 25 percent of the population in 2040. A significant percentage of the population (which includes both dependent elderly and children) will then be reliant on a decreasing labor force:

118

China will experience a decline in its labor force (those aged 15–64) of 100 million in each decade between 2030 and 2080.[25]

THE CONSEQUENCES OF MASCULINIZED SEX RATIOS

The high sex ratios in China will have the greatest impact on its population and societal stability. Men currently outnumber women by 41 million, but the majority of the "excess men" are currently found among the juvenile and youth population (31 million of them are aged 0 to 34). In colloquial Chinese, excess men are referred to as "bare branches" on the family tree because they will not marry and bear children. Chinese society is already beginning to experience the effects of the bare branches as male youths enter the marriage market and are unable to find partners, but the problem is expected to worsen with each passing year. In December 2007, Zhang Weiqing stated that "by 2020, males aged between 20 and 45 are forecast to outnumber females by 30 million."[26] In 2004, demographer Li Weixiong put the figure somewhat higher and warned that the Chinese government China faces a future of "crime and instability as a generation of 40 million men is left frustrated by a lack of brides" due to the numbers of women missing from the population.[27] Chinese scholars have recently focused on the effect of the dearth of women on a marriage squeeze; one report co-authored by the China Youth and Children Research Center and Renmin University in 2007 states that, in particular "it will become more difficult for low-income men to find suitable spouses as they get older."[28] The report added that a large population of unmarried males would lead to increased violence, crime, and instability, pointing to the increasing incidences of the abduction of women and human-trafficking in areas with the highest sex ratios.[29] Social instability and the outbreak of violence associated with large numbers of bare branches has historical precedence in China, most prominently in the Nien Rebellion of 1851

to 1863, but China has never had to mitigate the effects of such large numbers of bare branches.[30]

In many ways, China's floating population (unregistered temporary migrants who travel to urban areas in search of employment) exhibits some of the behaviors of a bare branch community. The floating population of China reached 147.45 million in 2005.[31] More than 10 percent of China's population is composed of migrants living in or around China's urban centers. Because these migrants have left their homes without government approval, they are denied social benefits such as subsidized housing, education, and health care. The size of the floating population has increased greatly in recent years due to economic reforms in the countryside that have forced formers to seek work elsewhere.

Concomitantly, the increasingly high sex ratios in rural areas have resulted in a large number of men who join the ranks of the floating population in search of work and the financial capital required to secure a wife. Floaters work in jobs that are dirty, dangerous, and demeaning.[32] While the floating population also includes some women and married men, studies suggest that the population is primarily youthful (70 percent are aged 15 to 35), predominantly unmarried, underemployed males with low education, living in slums or slum-like conditions.[33] The members of the floating population often find themselves exploited by their employers, and "as temporary residents they have little recourse against exploitation and sometimes resort to collective violence to help themselves."[34]

The Chinese government blames the "peasant migrants," whom they class as criminals, for the increase in crime in China: they are believed to be responsible for more than 50 percent of all national crime, and in coastal areas this figure is 70 percent.[35] A recent study of the relationship between sex ratios and violent crime and property crime in China found a correlation between an increase in the number of unmarried males and the rise in crime.[36] During the period under study, the sex ratio for males aged 16 to 25 rose by .04 (from 1.053 in 1988 to 1.095 in 2004) resulting in a 20 to 25 percent rise in crime rates, accounting for 25 to 33 percent of the overall rise in crime. The authors

119

find that it is not just an increase in the number of males that raises the crime rate, but suggest that the magnitude of the rise in crime "is suggestive of the possibility that higher sex ratios (and the reduced probability of marriage or partnership) have raised male propensity to commit crime (conditional on marital status)."[37] The rising crime associated with the presence of floaters on the outskirts of urban centers has created problems for authorities, and, because of the elusive nature and size of the population, many argue that "the traditional system of social control cannot resolve this problem."[38] The floating population operates within "a 'vacuum of authority' that is institutionally unreachable to both the rural and urban governments."[39]

Some floaters find themselves banding together in either temporary, or more permanent and organized gangs. One study estimates that "10 to 30 per cent of the floating population gets 'dragged into the spreading urban criminal underworld, where they provide both the muscle and the prey of crime and vice-gangs.'"[40] As of 2001, the number of criminal secret societies (referred to in China as *hei bang* or *hei shehui*—"black gangs" or "black societies") was believed to be 11,300, with membership of over 20 million.

Violent protests and membership in criminal gangs have both increased in recent years. An Chen suggests that these protests are motivated more by economic and social deprivation rather than any desire to democratize the country. The protests and mob actions are fuelled by a strong anti-state sentiment created by "a sense of relative deprivation that, accompanying the deteriorating socioeconomic polarization, is perhaps far stronger and more anti-government than in democratic societies."[41] Through their everyday acts of random

> Violent protests and membership in criminal gangs have both increased in recent years.

violence, violent protests, and organized criminal violence, these gangs "have produced a significant impact upon Chinese society. They disrupt the buildup of a new socioeconomic order, impede the process of the rule of law, and jeopardize the routine lives of ordinary citizens. They have posed an organizational and potentially political threat to the communist regime as well."[42]

It is also worth noting that an increasingly masculinized society may also be a society more prone to certain types of disease. It has recently been noted that the surplus young adult males of China provide what epidemiologists call a "bridging population" for transmission of HIV/AIDs into Chinese society.[43] Researchers have found that surplus males engaged in riskier sexual behavior (multiple partners, use of prostitutes, non-use of condoms), increased the sale of blood, and increased use of illicit drugs. All of these behaviors increase the likelihood of contracting HIV, and since China has only rudimentary screening and care of HIV patients, HIV infection portends almost inevitable development of full-blown AIDS. China's AIDS problem, only recently acknowledged by the national government, will almost certainly be worsened by its abnormal sex ratios.

THE CONSEQUENCES OF AGING

The impact of China's bare branches must also be examined alongside the demographic shift in China's age structure. Most of the developed nations of the world are aging, but China is unique in that it is still developing. Its aging comes prematurely, hastened by the one-child policy. Robert Stowe England notes that by 2055, China's elderly population will exceed the elderly population of all of North America, Europe, and Japan combined.[44] Furthermore, the working age population of China is expected to peak in 2025, and begin to decline thereafter, if China continues to pursue its current fertility policy.[45]

Aging—even in the context of normal sex ratios—has numerous important economic effects, which are already beginning to be felt in Europe and Japan. Declining working-age populations are a drag on economic growth. Consumption patterns between workers and the elderly are quite different, with the elderly consuming much less than workers (especially in the area of durable goods) except in the area of health care. According to Steven A. Nyce and Sylvester J. Schieber, for nations with shrinking populations to maintain their current standards of living, they have to import more or produce more; if consumer spending falls, there are likely to be lay-offs and rising unemployment.[46] Aging societies also have significantly lower savings rates, as the elderly must divest themselves of their assets to maintain their standard of living in a context of rising health care costs. As a result, capital investment both at home and abroad may be compromised. Businesses may experience a lower return on investment in their homeland, but increasing investment abroad may lead to a net capital outflow, which may result in the weakening of the currencies of aging societies. Nyce and Schieber also note that if aging brings with it higher pension costs, this will lead to fewer low income jobs, wage depression, slowing economic growth and job creation, declining interest from foreign investors, lower entrepreneurship, and higher budget deficits.[47]

The Center for Strategic and International Studies (CSIS) Commission on Global Aging suggests that aging societies will shift their spending priorities, with a lower priority placed on infrastructure, defense, and education. Labor force declines also translate into lower tax revenues for governments, and if these governments are tempted by deficit financing, global financial stability may be compromised. The commission feels that there may be a shift in global economic, political, and perhaps even military power away from aging societies. The lack of savings may cause interest rates to rise globally, perhaps even prompting a global recession.[48]

Interestingly, this commission also predicts that the position of China could be quite crucial in the context of global aging. China has increasingly become a repository for pension wealth from developed countries, and the commission wonders if this means that China can continue its high economic growth even in the context of its own aging, or if China would begin to act in a more mercantilist fashion, which might lead to a new global depression.[49]

Nyce and Schieber remind us that economic slowdowns are accompanied by significant domestic unrest.[50] Unemployment in general may be China's greatest internal security threat as losses in different sectors of the economy increase unemployment. Many of the men comprising the floating population were once workers for state-owned enterprises, 300,000 of which are currently operating at a loss each year. This threatens the livelihood of millions of workers, over one million of whom are soldiers and officers in China's military's reserve force. Rising costs, new technologies and increased competition are endangering town and village enterprises employing 135 million, and there are fears that the rural "army of jobless will soon reach 120 to 140 million."[51] Nicholas Kristof writes that, "Wildcat protests, some violent and involving thousands of people, have been exploding around the country. By the Chinese government's own count, there are now more than 200 protests a day, prompted by everything from layoffs to governmental seizures of land. The protests may grow if, as seems likely, China's economic model appears less miraculous in the years ahead."[52]

THE INTERSECTING FORCES OF AGING AND MASCULINIZATION

When we look at the effects of aging and combine that with an analysis of the effects of abnormal sex ratios on a society, the synergistic effects are likely to be quite dangerous for the Chinese government. There appears to be an economic slowdown approaching in the global economy that will likely be extended and deepened by aging in the most advanced economies[53] This global slowdown is likely to amplify the economic storm clouds already looming for China. A society with a masculinized young adult population, such as China's, is likely to respond to significant economic hardship with severe domestic instability and crime. The Chinese regime will be hard-pressed to maintain its usual control over society as a result, and it will likely become more authoritarian to meet this internal security challenge.

> A society with a masculinized young adult population is likely to respond to significant economic hardship with severe domestic instability and crime.

An important question for the government will be, how can it attract the allegiance of its bare branches, and channel them towards less internally destructive deeds? One temptation may be to play the card of nationalism, and it is here that we must examine some elements of Chinese culture for clues to the future.

It has often been noted by psychologists that youth take their understanding of their nation and its place in the world from the experiences of their forebears, typically the generation of their grandparents.[54] What types of vivid experiences will the grandparents of today's young adults in China tell them about? This generation of forebears would have been born around 1935. They would have lived as young children through the invasion of Japan, which would have left them with deep-seated animosity towards the Japanese. But they would also have seen in their youth the corruption of the Nationalists during the civil war period, and feel a sense of unfulfillment that the regime escaped to Taiwan, preventing the complete unification of China. They would feel a great deal of ambivalence about U.S. support of the regime on Taiwan. At the same time, they would have been starting their careers during the Cultural Revolution, and may have seen their own families, especially their parents, devastated by ideological extremism. This generation, then, is highly nationalistic, anti-Japanese, has strong feelings about the reunification of Taiwan with the mainland, is ambivalent towards the United States, and may be more inclined to respect authoritarian measures to ensure social stability.

It may be that the Chinese government would be able to play upon these themes to maintain power in the context of an aging, more masculine society experiencing a profound economic slowdown. The government could use anti-Japanese, anti-Taiwan independence themes to galvanize not only the elderly generation, but more importantly, the younger

generation. Masculine societies are very susceptible to political campaigns stressing national pride vis-

> Masculine societies are very susceptible to political campaigns stressing national pride vis-à-vis a competing nation.

à-vis a competing nation. But masculine societies are a double-edged sword, for if the government is perceived as weak or unsuccessful in contests of national pride, it will be very vulnerable to internal dissension that would bring a stronger government to power.

OVERALL ASSESSMENT OF CHINA'S SECURITY DEMOGRAPHICS

The combination of China's abnormal sex ratios and its premature aging do not bode well for its future. Even if sex ratios were rectified today (which they will not be), young adult sex ratios in China will result in a significant percentage of bare branches for the next 30 years. Economists warn us that a global economic slowdown will almost certainly occur by approximately 2020. In 2020, China will still be increasing its labor force population, while the richest nations of the world fade from global dominion due to aging. By about 2040, the economic effects of aging will catch up to China as well. In the period 2020 to 2040, the pain China will experience from the economic slowdown, accompanied by the opportunities afforded by the fading of the West and Japan, will create a unique crucible for possible dramatic change in China's security situation.

Our analysis suggests that the projected economic slowdown will create massive unrest and instability in China, made worse by its abnormal sex ratios. Regionally based threats to the national government's primacy may arise. Gang-based violence, already worsening, may coagulate into larger threats, as gangs combine to augment their power vis-à-vis the government. China may be tempted to improve its situation with mercantilist policies, but economists feel this would more likely lead to a prolonged global depression, which would only worsen China's outlook.

Faced with worsening instability at home, and an unsolvable economic decline, China's government may well be tempted to use foreign policy to "ride the tiger" of domestic instability. The twin themes of anti-Japanese feeling and dissatisfaction concerning the lack of progress in China's quest for reunification with Taiwan will resonate with much of the population of China at that time. In fact, these may be the only themes left that could unite the Chinese population behind the national government. In addition, the government will be searching for contests of national pride involving martial prowess, which will be highly attractive to the bare branch population that will be causing it severe internal problems. The threat from within at this time may be seen by the government as much more pressing than the forces of international deterrence, which may be fading due to the aging-related weakening of the West. The government may see a way to kill two birds with one stone, seizing a greater share of international power through successful international use of force, while also thinning the ranks of its bare branches through attrition warfare. The alternative may be to see China disintegrate into smaller geographical units, an alternative the Chinese Communist Party is unlikely to accept.

There are also opportunities to the north. The Russian Far East is rapidly depopulating, and is at the same time the site of most of Russia's great mineral and oil wealth. There has been a tremendous influx of Chinese into this area, with the result that over 8 percent of the population of the Russian Far East is, in fact, Chinese. Bare branches have traditionally been the first colonizers sent abroad, and it may be that Chinese bare branches will play an important role in the Sinification of the Russian Far East. Economic control of these natural resources would place China in a much better position to lighten the effects of an economic decline, but it would also have grave geopolitical consequences for the international community. Would Russia countenance this demographic colonization of the seat of its wealth? Could Russia stop this trend, even

if it wanted to do so? What would be the economic consequences for the West?

In the next two to three decades, we are likely to see observable security ramifications of the masculinization of China's young adult population in combination with Chinas premature aging; the consequences of global aging, the particularities of Chinese nationalism, and the epidemiology of pandemics such as AIDS will be the driving forces of these implications.

THE MANIPULABLE VARIABLE OF FERTILITY POLICY

It is not difficult to see how crucial a role China's one-child policy plays in the demographic shifts toward masculinization and aging. In this case, the centrality of China's fertility policy to its security demographics constitutes a problem for China's policy makers. But it also represents an important opportunity: policy can be changed. Our analysis of the intersection of aging and masculinization on China's future security provides a strong rationale for our position that now is the time for China to change its fertility policy. Even the delay of one decade could have troubling implications for China's future stability.

Such a change in fertility policy is not unthinkable. Alternatives to China's one-child policy were proposed even in 1979, when the policy was promulgated by the state. Scholars suggested that a two-child policy would have fewer negative consequences than a one-child policy.[55] Similarly, when the policy was relaxed in 1984 after a period of strict enforcement, Chinese demographers again proposed a two-child policy alternative.[56] In the years since 1984, scholars have appeared to accept China's fertility policy and have not renewed calls for its change until 2004, when a research consortium of the China Population Association presented arguments for gradually moving toward a two-child policy.[57] According to demographer Zeng Yi, most Chinese demographers now agree that China's family planning policy must be changed, but they disagree on the timing and nature of an alternative strategy.

In his analysis of the three major proposed policies (retaining the current 1.5 policy with long birth spacing and the option of two children for only-child couples, retaining the current policy but with relaxed spacing and transition to a two-child policy at a later date, or moving to a universal two-child policy with incentives to encourage long birth spacing) using a population projection model, Zeng demonstrates that the economic and social costs of the first and second options are too high. Retaining the current policy results in a continued high birth sex ratio with its consequences for gender inequality, high economic costs for the government project to support the rural elderly who have only one child or two daughters (these costs would increase from 1.2 billion yuan in 2005 to 25.4 billion in 2050), high economic costs in terms of a shrinking labor force and pension deficit, and the social costs of increasing numbers of excess men.[58]

If the Chinese were to move towards a two-child policy now, Zeng suggests that the sex ratio at birth would normalize by 2030, the number of excess men aged 20 to 49 would reach a lower peak (just below 11 percent) in 2040, and the number of men would become close to normal by 2050. The economic costs to the government would be greatly reduced as the number of elderly dependent on the state would peak in 2021 and decline to almost zero in 2050, the labor force would be substantially larger and the pension deficit would be greatly decreased.[59] In other words, the results will make a difference in that dangerous time period of 2020 to 2040 we identified previously.

Zeng is optimistic about the possibility of reversing some of the negative consequences of China's fertility policy if the state acts now. But official statements suggest that China remains committed to its current policy for the foreseeable future.[60] It is also doubtful whether, as Zeng believes, the introduction of a two-child policy would normalize the sex ratio. A two-child policy is currently in effect in most of rural China, where the birth sex ratio is currently at a high of 122.9. While a rise in fertility to 2.0 for the total population may help to improve some features of China's demographic future, it may not have much effect on the gender imbalance and its consequences.

In the late 1970s, a team of Chinese scientists, led by China's leading missile scientist, drew on the resources and discourse of defense science to argue convincingly that China's population was a matter of national security and proceeded to design what would become China's one-child policy. The Chinese doubtless did not expect that the policy designed to forestall a national security crisis might in the end cause one.[61] Population growth may indeed have posed a threat to China's development and security, but its current and future demographics may pose an even greater threat if current policies persist. China's contempt for its daughters may lead to a more dangerous world not only for the Chinese themselves, but for everyone.

NOTES

1. "Policy reduces 400 million births," Xinhua, 21 March 2006.
2. China is one of several Asian countries to have an imbalance in the sex ratio of the population, but it is the only country whose gender imbalance is due, in part, to a national fertility policy. For further information see Valerie M. Hudson and Andrea M. den Boer, "Missing Women and Bare Branches: Gender Balance and Conflict," *Environmental Change and Security Report* 11, (2005): 20–24; Andrea M. den Boer and Valerie M. Hudson, "The Security Threat of Asia's Sex Ratios," *SAIS Review* 24, no. 2 (Summer–Fall 2004): 27–43; Valerie M. Hudson and Andrea M. den Boer, *Bare Branches: The Security Implications of Asia's Surplus Male Population* (Cambridge, MA: MIT Press, 2004).
3. For an in-depth analysis of China's decision to adopt the one-child policy, see Susan Greenhalgh, "Science, Modernity, and the Making of China's One-Child Policy," *Population and Development Review* 29, no. 2 (June 2003): 163–196.

4. The one-child policy is outlined in a number of Chinese Communist Party directives, provincial regulations and finally national legislation. See Xiaorong Li, "License to Coerce: Violence Against Women, State Responsibililty, and Legal Failures in China's Family Planning Program," *Yale Journal of Law and Feminism* 8, no. 1 (1996): 145–191.

5. Xiaorong Li, "License to Coerce," 154–155. See also Nicholas D. Kristof and Sheryl WuDunn, *China Wakes: The Struggle for the Soul of a Rising Power* (New York: Vintage, 1994).

6. There were some provincial or local variations of the policy. In addition, minorities were permitted to have two or more births. For further information about the mass sterilization of the early 1980s, see Tyrene White, *China's Longest Campaign: Birth Planning in the People's Republic, 1949–2005* (Ithaca, NY: Cornell University Press, 2006).

7. In their study of provincial regulations adopted by provincial People's Congresses, Gu Baochang, et. al., found over 100 different articles incorporating 22 different exceptions to the one-child rule. For example, in Ningxia and Xinjiang provinces, a second child is permitted to parents who are underground miners or fishermen, whose first child was handicapped, or if both parents are single children, among other exceptions. Gu Baochang, et. al., "China's Local and National Fertility Policies at the end of the Twentieth Century," *Population and Development Review* 33, no. 1 (March 2007): 131–136.

8. Gu Baochang, et. al. suggest that the fertility rate in the late 1990s had dropped to 1.50. Zhang, however, suggests that the rate is higher, at 1.63, but others suggest it may be as high as 1.8. See Gu Baochang, et. al., "China's Local and National Fertility Policies," 144–145.

9. Judith Banister and Kenneth Hill, "Mortality in China, 1964–2000," *Population Studies* 58, no. 1 (March 2004): 55–75.

10. Structural violence against women, which is more pervasive in rural areas than in urban areas in China, takes the form of sex-selective abortions, female infanticide, neglect of female infants and children, lower schooling for girls, as well as the denial of all state benefits to those girls born out of plan and unregistered.

11. *Population Census Office and National Bureau of Statistics of China, Tabulation on the 2000 Population Census of the People's Republic of China*, Volume 1 (Beijing: China Statistics Press, 2002).

12. "Males at marriage age 18 M more than females in China," *Xinhua*, 14 November 2007.

13. The sex ratio was highest for the juvenile population aged 1–4 (those born in the late 1990s) with a ratio of 120.8. The overall sex ratio for those aged 0–19 was 111.3 in 2000. Calculations based on census figures in *Population Census Office and National Bureau of Statistics of China, Tabulation on the 2000 Population Census of the People's Republic of China*, Volume 1(Beijing: China Statistics Press, 2002).

14. *Population Census Office and National Bureau of Statistics of China, Tabulation on the 2000 Population Census of the Peoples Republic of China.* See Table 6–4. In the first year of life, 130 male infants typically die for every 100 female infants (ratio of 1.3/1) worldwide due to the increased probability of congenital illness for the male infant; mortality rates for ages 1 to 4 are similarly higher for males with average rates of 1.11 to 1.24. The mortality rates for Chinese between ages 0–3 range from .7 to 1.0.

15. National Population and Family Planning Commission of China, "Gender Imbalance not Direct Result of Family Planning," Fresh News, http://www.npfpc.gov.cn/en/en2006-04/enews20060427.htm. Similarly, at a UN press conference in December 2006, Liu Bohong, Vice Director of the Women Studies Institute of the All-China Women's Federation claimed that the high sex ratio was the result of son preference, and "refused to accept the imbalance was connected to China's one-child policy." See "Expert blames gender discrimination for China's growing sex imbalance," *Xinhua Economic News*, 17 December 2006.

16. Monica Das Gupta, Jiang Zhenghua, Li Bohua, Xie Zhenming, Woojin Chung and Bae Hwa-Ok, "Why is Son Preference so Persistent

125

in East and South Asia? A Cross-Country Study of China, India and the Republic of Korea," *Journal of Development Studies* 40, no. 2 (December 2003): 168.

17. Percentages are the results of a nation-wide survey conducted in 2006. See "Caring for the Aged," *China Daily*, 18 December 2007.

18. Statistical Bureau of Taiwan, Monthly Bulletin of Statistics, December 2007, http://eng.stat. gov. tw/mp.asp?mp=5.

19. Zeng, "Options for Fertility Policy Transition," 229.

20. The expected birth sex ratio is between 104–107. The normal sex ratios for first births indicates that most parents are willing to take their chances with the first birth—they have a 52 percent chance of having a son. If they are one of the 48 percent who give birth to a daughter, then most will use sex-selective technology (ultrasound or amniocentesis to determine the sex of the fetus) to ensure that they have a son. This typically means aborting female fetuses. Since sex-selection is illegal in China, preconception sex selection does not occur, but prenatal sex selection is widespread despite the legal prohibition.

21. *Population Census Office and National Bureau of Statistics of China, Tabulation on the 2000 Population Census of the People's Republic of China,* Volume 2 (Beijing: China Statistics Press, 2002) Table 1–7.

22. Shuzhuo Li, Chuzhu Zhu, and Marcus W. Feldman, "Gender Differences in Child Survival in Contemporary Rural China: A County Study" *Journal of Biosocial Sciences* 36, no. 1 (2004): 92.

23. A 2005 to 2006 review of maternal and child survival rates in China conducted by the Chinese Ministry of Health, UNICEF, WHO, and UNFPA, suggests that greater access to health care facilities may have a great impact on maternal and child survival. The report does not mention China's fertility policy, nor does it disaggregate infant and child survival rates to observe the differences between male and female mortality, thus if fails to recognize the effect that China's fertility policy has on the survival of female children. See China Ministry of Health, WHO, UNICEF, UNFPA, *Joint Review of Maternal and Child Survival Strategies in China* (Beijing, China, Ministry of Health, 2006).

24. *Population Census Office and National Bureau of Statistics of China, Tabulation on the 2000 Population Census of the People's Republic of China,* Volume 2, Table 1-7.

25. Yi Zeng, "Options for Fertility Policy Transition in China," *Population and Development Review* 33, no. 2 (June 2007): 222–227.

26. National Population and Family Planning Commission, "Sex Ratio among Young Normal," 26 December 2007, http://www.npfpc.gov.cn/en/en2007-12/news20071226.htm.

27. Hamish McDonald, "Facing the Future with 40 Million Bachelors," *Sydney Morning Herald,* 10 March 2004, http://www.smh.com.au/articles/2004/03/09/1078594367697.htmljfromsstoryrhs.

28. National Population and Family Planning Commission, "Number of Young Unmarrieds in China Increases," 11 December 2007, http://www.npfyc.gov.cn/en/en2007-12/news20071211.htm.

29. Trafficking for purposes of sex exploitation and forced labor is rising, according to news reports. Trafficking in women and children is reported to be most serious in Guangdong, Fujian, Henan, Sichuan and Anhui provinces. See Wang Zhuoqiong, "More forced into labor, prostitution," *China Daily*, 27 July, 2007, 1.

30. For further information on historical examples of bare branch violence, see Hudson and den Boer, *Bare Branches: The Security Implications of Asia's Surplus Male Population.*

31. National Bureau of Statistics, "Communique on Major Data of 1% National Population Sample Survey in 2005," 16 March 2006, http://www.stats.gov.cn/English/newsandcomingevents/t20060322_402312182.htm.

32. Ingrid Nielsen, Russell Smyth and Mingqiong Zhang, "Unemployment Within China's Floating Population: Empirical Evidence From Jiangsu Survey Data," unpublished paper, http://www.buseco. monash.edu.au/units/aberu/papers/unemployment-china-floating-population.pdf.

126

33. Because many of the men and women who comprise the floating population live in temporary housing or on the streets, the exact size and composition of the population is unknown. Chinese statistics for 2003 record that of the 140 million, 98 million (70 percent) are between 15 and 35. See "Diameter of marriage selection in China under expansion," *People's Daily Online,* 8 October 2005, http://english. people.com.cn/200510/08/eng20051008_213283.html. According to China's Department of Public Security Management, the sex ratio of the floating population in 1999 was 149.8 (quoted in YuZhu, "The Floating Population's Household Strategies and the Role of Migration in China's Regional Development and Integration," *International Journal of Population Geography* 9, no. 6 (2003): 494. In Zhu's study of the floating population in Fuzhou, twenty percent of the migrants were married). One study using 1995 found that women outnumbered men in the 15–19 age category, but men outnumbered women in the 25–29 category, with a sex ratio of 259. See T. Jia, "An Analysis of the Situation of China's Floating Population," China Population Today 15, no. 5–6 (Dec. 1998): 13–14. A 1991 study conducted by the Ministry of Public Security on the floating population showed that 73.4 percent were between the ages 15 and 29 (and additional 20.7 percent were between 30 and 44), 67.4 percent were male (with a sex ratio of 207), and 40 percent had only elementary level education or were illiterate/semi-literate. See Zhang Qingwu, "A Survey of Floating Population in 50 Townships in China," Chinese Journal of Population Science 7, no. 3 (1995): 229–240. Although many of the floaters are able to find work, others remain unemployed for short or long periods: one survey in Jiangsu in 2003 found that half of the floating population had been unemployed that year, a level consistent with studies in other urban areas. See Nielsen et al, "Unemployment Within China's Floating Population."

34. Chai and Chai, "China's Floating Population," 1048.

35. Michael Dutton, "The Basic Character of Crime in Contemporary China," China Quarterly 149 (March 1997): 173. See Xiaogang Deng and Ann Cordilia, "To Get Rich is Glorious: Rising Expectations, Declining Control, and Escalating Crime in Contemporary China," *International Journal of Offender Therapy and Comparative Criminology* 43 (June 1999): 211–229.

36. Lena Edlund, Hongbin Li, Junjian Yi, Junsen Zhang, "More Men, More Crime: Evidence from China's One-Child Policy," Institute for the Study of Labor (IZA), Bonn, Germany, Discussion Paper No. 3214, December 2007, http://ftp.iza.org/dp3214.pdf.

37. Edlund, et al, "More Men, More Crime," 30.

38. Daniel J. Curran, "Economic Reform, the Floating Population, and Crime: The Transformation of Social Control in China," *Journal of Contemporary Criminal Justice* 14, no. 3 (1998): 262–280. See also, Yingyi Situ and Liu Weizheng, "Transient Population, Crime, and Solution: The Chinese Experience," *International Journal of Offender Therapy and Comparative Criminology* 40, no. 4 (December 1996): 293–299.

39. An Chen, "Secret Societies and Organized Crime in Contemporary China," *Modern Asian Studies* 39, no. 1 (February 2005): 103.

40. Chai and Chai, "China's Floating Population," 1048.

41. Chen, "Secret Societies," 101.

42. Ibid., 79.

43. Joseph D. Tucker, Gail E. Henderson, Tian F. Wang, Ying Y. Huang, William Parish, Sui M. Pan, Xiang S. Chen, Myron S. Cohen, "Surplus Men, Sex Work, and the Spread of HIV in China," *AIDS* 19 (2005): 539–547.

44. Robert Stowe England, *The Demographic Challenge to China's Economic Prospects* (Westport, CT: Praeger, 2005), 1.

45. Zeng, "Options for Fertility Policy Transition," 227.

46. Steven A. Nyce and Sylvester J. Schieber, *The Economic Implications of Aging Societies* (New York: Cambridge University Press, 2005), 166.

47. Nyce and Scheiber, The Economic Implications of Aging Societies, 226–229, 237.

48. *CSIS Commission on Global Aging, Meeting the Challenges of Global Aging* (Washington DC: CSIS Press), 2002.

49. CSIS Commission, 52.

50. Nyce and Schieber, *The Economic Implications of Aging Societies*, 179.

51. Sharif Shuja, "The Limits of Chinese Economic Reform," *China Brief* 5, no. 17 (2005): 9.

52. Nicholas Kristof, "Rumblings from China, New York Times, 2 July 2006, A29. One official suggestion to mitigate the problem of too many unemployed males is to export labor. In July 2007, Yu Xuejun, a spokesman for the NPFPC stated that China could ease population pressure by exporting labor. Yu commented that "China has 20 percent of the world's population, but accounts for only 1 percent of global expatriate laborers. In countries like the Philippines and Mexico, about 10 percent of laborers work abroad every year, which is a good inspiration for our country." See "Many free to have more than one child," *China Daily*, 11 July 2007.

53. Michael M. Grynbaum, "Investors See Recession, and Market Drops," *New York Times*, 18 January 2008.

54. See, for example, Jason Han, "Children and Nationalism in a Palestinian Refugee Camp in Jordan," *Childhood* 9, no. 1 (2002): 35–47, Sharon Stephens, "Childhood and Nationalism," Childhood A, no. 1 (1997): 5–17.

55. Zhongtang Liang, "Suggestions concerning strategies of population and development in the next few decades," 1979, cited in Yi Zeng, "Options for Fertility Policy Transition in China," *Population and Development Review* 33, no. 2 (June 2007): 215–246.

56. Yingtong Ma and Zhang Xiaotong, "Some Issues in Population Control and Policy," (policy report submitted to the Chinese central government in 1984) cited in Zeng, "Options for Fertility Policy Transition."

57. Zeng, "Options for Fertility Policy Transition," 216.

58. According to Zeng, the percentage of excess men aged 20–49 is predicted to rise until it peaks in 2040–2050 at between 12.6 and 14 and then decline gradually until 2080. Zeng, "Options for Fertility Policy Transition," 215–246.

59. Zeng, "Options for Fertility Policy Transition," 221–232.

60. "Official: Sex-ratio imbalance not a result of family planning policy," Xinhua, 23 January 2007.

61. Susan Greenhalgh, "Missile Science, Population Science: The Origins of China's One-Child Policy," *China Quarterly* 182 (June 2005): 253–276.

128

Agropolis:
The Role of Urban Agriculture In Addressing Food Insecurity in Developing Cities

By Milica Koscica

Over fifty percent of the world's population is urbanized—living in cities—and cities almost entirely depend on imported food to meet daily needs. Different factors such as population growth, urbanization, and increasing global demand for food are intensifying; urban agriculture is an important tool for enhancing food security in response to the food-related restraints faced by city dwellers. Through a historical retrospective of urban agriculture to an analysis of current practices and policies, this article explores urban agriculture's potential ability to manage the lack of land and water in cities through the development of innovative growing techniques that optimize the access, quantity, and quality of food for millions of people in developing cities around the globe.

130

As population growth, swelling food demand, and rising rates of urban poverty combine to threaten the availability of food to the urban poor, addressing food insecurity—the inability to consistently access quality food—has become increasingly important. For the first time in the history of civilization, most people now live in cities, which almost entirely depend on imported food to meet daily needs. Yet, as world population continues to grow, reaching a projected 9.6 billion people within the next thirty-five years, global food demand is similarly projected to increase between 70 and 100 percent, depending on future per capita income[1]. Current available cropland and production levels will be unable to keep pace. Meeting future demand would require either clearing an additional landmass the size of Brazil to create land on which to farm, or more extensive use of chemical fertilizers, both of which are unsustainable and environmentally harmful.[2]

As the current and unprecedented trend of rural-to-urban migration continues, the level of world urban dwellers is expected to reach 70 percent by 2050.[3] Research also indicates that the "poor have been urbanizing even more rapidly than the population as a whole."[4] Noting that most urban population growth is expected to occur in develop-

> Some see the term urban agriculture as inherently contradictory, but one could argue that urban agriculture overcomes these constraints, but also addresses them in an innovative and integrative manner to optimize access, quantity, and quality of food for the urban poor.

ing cities, the global food price crises of 2008 and 2011 underscored the extent of vulnerability and food insecurity of the poor in these areas.

In response to these trends, a debate regarding the role of urban agriculture in addressing availability and access to quality food for the urban poor has emerged. Many believe that urban agriculture struggles to produce enough food due to fierce competition for scarce urban resources such as land and water. Additionally, concerns have been raised

Milica Koscica, "Agropolis: The Role of Urban Agriculture in Addressing Food Insecurity in Developing Cities," *Journal of International Affairs*, vol. 67, no. 2, pp. 177-186.

regarding the health risks associated with urban agricultural runoff and possible soil contamination. Some consider the term urban agriculture as inherently contradictory, but on the other hand, one could argue that urban agriculture not only overcomes these constraints, but also addresses them in an innovative and integrative manner to optimize access, quantity, and quality of food for the urban poor. This paper first describes urban agriculture and its scale in the developing world regions. It then analyzes urban agricultures's main constraints—land, water, and health risks—to reveal how these constraints are transformed into opportunities that tackle food insecurity issues. Finally, the paper concludes with a look toward future possibilities and suggestions for further research.

URBAN AGRICULTURE: CHARACTERISTICS AND SIGNIFICANCE

Although urban agriculture has only recently garnered conceptual attention in international development debates, its practice is not a recent phenomenon. Cities in the Classic Maya civilization and the Byzantine Empire incorporated various forms of urban farming to address food security by building resilience against shocks and sudden interruptions in supply lines.[5] During the First and Second World Wars, countries such as the United States, England, and Canada encouraged city dwellers to plant "victory gardens" to support the war effort.[6] In 1942, more than 5.5 million gar-

> Urban agriculture accounts for an average of 15 to 20 percent of the world's food production.

deners produced an estimated nine to ten million pounds of fruits and vegetables in the United States alone.[7] Instead of painting a portrait of agriculture as innately contrary to urbanity, these historical examples—both ancient and contemporary—suggest that the practice has often been integrated into city life, debunking modernist descriptions of urban agriculture as oxymoronic.[8]

During the last decade, information showing the magnitude of urban agriculture confirms its global significance. Most recent figures estimate that approximately 800 million people around the world actively engage in the practice, and that urban agriculture accounts for an average of 15 to 20 percent of the world's food production.[9] The rate of participation in developing countries varies considerably, from 10 percent in Indonesia to nearly 70 percent in Vietnam and Nicaragua.[10] A survey sample of developing countries finds that in eleven out of fifteen countries, 30 percent of urban households participate in urban agriculture, and in eight out of fifteen countries the rate increases to 50 percent when only the low-income households are considered.[11] The large scale of existing urban agriculture demonstrates its potential to have a significant positive impact on the larger urban food system.

Although the practice of growing food in developing cities is different from region to region, certain similarities nonetheless exist. First, studies find that urban producers are predominately low-income men and women who grow food part-time for their own consumption.[12] Some studies have shown that in a number of cities in Sub-Saharan Africa, urban agriculture can provide a participating household with anywhere from 20 to 60 percent of its food supply.[n] Greater food availability and accessibility are essential elements of food security, and urban agriculture provides both to low-income households.

Second, urban cultivation involves many production systems, including horticulture, floriculture, forestry, aquaculture, and livestock.[14] Therefore, the range of agricultural output in any developing city is surprisingly diverse, including such crops as plantain, rice, potatoes, peppers, tomatoes, mushrooms, and leafy vegetables, as well as livestock products like eggs, milk, and meat.[15] What gives urban agriculture a comparative advantage over rural agriculture is its ability to produce fresh, perishable goods that might otherwise be too expensive for low-income urban consumers.[16]

Research shows that "households that engage in [urban] farming may have access to comparatively cheaper food and to a wider variety of particularly nutritious foods."[17] In terms of food security, urban agriculture therefore proves valuable since it provides participating low-income households direct access to a quality diet, rich in micronutrients.

Finally, urban agriculture can play an important role in the livelihoods of some low-income households. According to a 2011 World Bank and RUAF Foundation comparative study of Accra, Lima, Bangalore, and Nairobi, 30 percent of urban producers consider urban agriculture an important source of income.[18] Other studies have found that the percentage of income derived from the activity varies: households in African cities generate the most income, followed by Asian and then Latin American households.[19] Consequently, households that engage in urban agriculture can effectively increase their incomes either by saving money that would have been otherwise spent on food, or by increasing revenue through the sale of agricultural goods they produced.[20] In either case, the additional income translates into greater food security for the urban poor in developing cities.

Since the practice and the actors vary wildly among different regions and cities, many definitions of urban agriculture exist, and practitioners struggle to capture the essence of the activity. The most commonly accepted definition is based on the work of a leading expert in the field, Luc Mougeot, of the International Development Research Centre. Mougeot developed an inclusive definition that recognizes the integrative nature of the practice:

> [Urban agriculture] is an industry located within (intraurban) or on the fringe (peri-urban) of a town, a city or a metropolis, which grows or raises, processes and distributes a diversity of food and non-food products, (re-)using largely human and material resources, products and services found in and around that urban area, and in turn supplying human and material resources, products and services largely to that urban area.[21]

The idea of integration with the urban ecosystem—the reuse and recycle of resources—cannot be overstated. The central point of this definition allows for a reframing of the concept from one that only competes for resources to one that complements existing urban systems and needs. These synergistic relationships with land and water are explored in the following sections.

LAND: CONSTRAINTS VS. OPPORTUNITIES

Lack of land in a city is the most common argument against urban agriculture and its potential to provide food security for the urban poor. The perception is that "cities are solid with buildings, with no area to spare."[22] Indeed, land in large cities is scarce, and high population densities in developing cities create competition for land over various alternative uses with higher value, such as residential or business development. Critics assert that enough free space to grow large quantities of food simply does not exist inside a city, nor should it exist, because most modernist urban planning ideologies consider agriculture separate and "obsolete in futuristic and normative understanding of the city."[23] Therefore, most government agencies and urban planning departments do not designate any official land toward agricultural uses, and in certain cities the practice is even illegal.[24] Combined with the dearth of space, the lack of regulation regarding land allotment makes land tenure particularly ambiguous and difficult for low-income urban farmers.

But precisely because of these constraints, urban farmers have demonstrated remarkable resourcefulness, particularly where they have successfully cultivated crops and livestock. Areas for production come in all sizes, from tiny windowsills, patios and

Urban agriculture has the potential to produce large amounts of food in relatively small places.

balconies, rooftops, basements, and walls, to community gardens, vacant lots, schoolyards, roadsides, utility rights-of-way, and alongside railroad tracks and in floodplains.[25] These examples make apparent that urban agriculture integrates well within the existing city structure, and makes vacant and underused space more productive.

In light of this, it is not the size of the space that is critical in urban food production, but rather the techniques used to obtain the highest yields. Urban production methods are diverse, innovative, and geared toward optimizing the use of the available space within a city. For instance, one popular production technique used in developing cities is hydroponics.[26] Hydroponic production is the cultivation of plants in water, sand, gravel, or cinders.[27] It is highly versatile and mobile since it does not require soil, and it is energy efficient since it is a closed, controlled system that allows for the reuse of water.[28] Experimental studies have compared the vegetable yields of several production methods and found that hydroponic rooftop gardening produced three times the output of intensive gardening and nearly fourteen times the output of conventional agriculture.[29] In practice, this means that urban agriculture has the potential to produce large amounts of food in relatively small places. In fact, developing cities around the world, such as Hanoi, Dakar, Accra, Dar es Salaam, and Havana, produce more than 60 percent of their respective vegetable consumption via hydroponic production.[30] The numerous case studies of developing cities highlight the degree of self-sufficiency achieved through urban agriculture, despite the land and space constraints faced by urban farmers.

WATER: IMPROVING EFFICIENCY THROUGH REUSE AND RECYCLE

Another scarce urban resource is water. The same global trends in population growth and urbanization exerting pressure on food security also increase demand for water in cities, thus causing heightened competition between the domestic, industrial, and agricultural uses of water.[31] The UN estimates that

> Reuse of treated wastewater in urban agriculture not only reduces overall water needs but also produces better outcomes that ultimately contribute to food security of urban dwellers.

"water use has been growing at more than twice the rate of population increase in the last century," and that the rate of extraction in developing countries will increase by 50 percent by 2025.[32] Developing cities already struggle to meet increasing water demand due to a lack of infrastructure to retrieve and properly distribute water.[33] The situation is undoubtedly complex, and adding urban agriculture to the mix has led some scholars to assert that growing food in cities will only further strain already depleted urban water reservoirs.[34]

There exist several options for addressing the issue of water scarcity as it relates to urban agriculture. The first set of options involves the various production methods that urban farmers already widely employ. One of these is hydroponics, described earlier in the paper. Hydroponics not only allows for the reuse of water, but it also requires 70 percent less water in comparison to traditional soil-based farming.[35] Another production technique that requires even less water is aeroponics. This is the method of growing plants in the air and spraying only the roots with water: this method uses 70 percent less water than hydroponics.[36] Both methods are efficient and are used in a variety of settings in developing cities.

A second option involves improving urban water management systems that help to reduce the depletion of groundwater. For instance, research conducted in Beijing found that rainwater, if collected properly, could substitute for more than 90 percent of groundwater use, and therefore meet the basic water needs for urban agriculture in that city.[37]

Another solution for addressing water scarcity is to achieve resource recovery through closed-loop waste treatment systems. Growing cities generate ever-increasing amounts of wastewater, excreta, and greywater that can be treated and reused for agricultural purposes.[38] Research shows that while a sustained water supply is vital for urban

133

agriculture, drinking water is not necessarily essential, or even desirable, to faciliate successful food production in cities.[39] In reality, recycled and treated wastewater contains more of the necessary nutrients that allow for optimal plant growth and development.[40] A recent study compared the germination and growth of different vegetables and found that plants watered with ozone-treated wastewater grew bigger than those watered with regular drinking water or raw wastewater.[41] This is partly because the treated wastewater acted as a form of organic fertilizer, which produced healthy crops with high nutritional levels. In this sense, reuse of treated wastewater in urban agriculture not only reduces overall water needs, but also produces better outcomes that ultimately contribute to food security of urban dwellers.[42]

HEALTH: MANAGING RISK

Despite the positive results of water reuse and recovery, many concerns about the implementation of water treatment methods in developing cities exist due to the potential public health risks associated with using untreated wastewater for crop irrigation. The most common threat to human health from dirty water used in urban agriculture is food contamination by pathogenic microorganisms, such as by the hookworm.[43] In addition to untreated water, other risks to human health come from soil contaminated with trace amounts of toxic metals such as cadmium, nickel, and lead that are common in urban areas due to heavy industrial activity and the use of fossil fuels as an energy source.[44]

In response to these concerns, the Food and Agriculture Organization and the World Health Organization have developed a set of guidelines for assessing and mitigating health risks related to urban agriculture.[45] The guidelines focus on strategies such as crop selection, location of production, and proper hygiene[46] For example, lead concentrations in food were found to be far lower in crops cultivated away from roads, and in produce that was washed before being consumed, than in the

alternative.[47] Other strategies involve using production techniques such as hydroponics, as mentioned before, that minimize contact with contaminated soils. Lastly, technologies that effectively treat city wastewater and ensure that it is suitable for agricultural purposes already exist and should be promoted, especially in developing cities where wastewater is the most likely source of urban crop irrigation.[48] While the health risks associated with urban agriculture cannot be completely eliminated, they can certainly be managed and reduced.

LOOKING FORWARD

One innovative approach to urban agriculture that is just starting to take root is vertical farming. Located within an urban setting, a vertical farm operates much like a greenhouse, except on a larger scale: one thirty-story building has the capacity to feed 10,000 people per year.[49] Dickson Despommier, a professor of ecology and microbiology at Columbia University who developed the concept of the vertical farm, estimates that by employing hydroponic growing techniques, reusing greywater, and layering crops on each floor, it is possible for one acre of vertical farming to yield the equivalent of ten to twenty acres of conventional agriculture, depending on crop selection.[50] Since growing food indoors offers more control over various conditions, additional benefits of vertical farming include the elimination of pesticides and chemical fertilizers and a reduction in health risks associated with soil-based farming.[51] The main constraint to a wide application of vertical farms in developing cities is design and manufacture cost.[52] Nonetheless, prototypes are being constructed around the world, including Singapore, where a commercial vertical farm, Sky Greens, is currently fully operational.[53] Although cities may not have vast amounts of open land to cultivate crops, vertical farms show that the sky is the limit to growing food in the future.

Despite modernists' assumptions, urban areas have the potential to sustainably produce food. As different factors like population growth, urbanization, and increasing global demand for

134

food intensify, urban agriculture will become an important tool for enhancing the food security of the urban poor. Millions of people in developing cities already rely on the activity for better access to a diverse and nutritious diet that they otherwise may not be able to afford. Urban agriculture's success and prevalence evolved directly from the very constraints that it faces. Unrelenting competition for resources such as land and water has forced urban agriculturists to become innovative, efficient, resilient, and adaptive with their methods. Such techniques as hydroponics and the reuse of wastewater have allowed urban agriculture to integrate within the existing urban ecosystem, instead of merely competing with it. However, it should also be noted that as urban agriculture continues to increase in developing cities, so too will the health risks associated with it, unless these risks are acknowledged and managed properly. Therefore, instead of continuing to marginalize the practice, urban planners and policymakers should begin to integrate it as a legitimate urban activity. Complex questions remain regarding land use and zoning, land tenure, wastewater treatment, and the coordination of municipal departments and agencies on urban food production. Additional research on the institutional gaps that can hinder the development of the practice and exacerbate potential public health risks could expand understanding in the field. While urban agriculture is not the silver bullet for solving all the future food needs of the planet, it does significantly increase the food security of the urban poor. Therefore, its contribution should not be overlooked or undervalued.

NOTES

1. David Tilman et al., "Global Food Demand and the Sustainable Intensification of Agriculture," *Proceedings of the National Academy of Sciences* 108, no. 50 (2011), 20260–20264.

2. Dickson Despommier, *The Vertical Farm: Feeding Ourselves and the World in the 21st Century* (New York: Thomas Dunne Books/St. Martin's Press, 2010).

3. Eugenie L. Birch and Susan M. Wachter, eds., *Global Urbanization: The City in the Twenty-First Century* (Philadelphia: University of Pennsylvania Press, 2011).

4. Martin Ravallion, Shaohua Chen, and Prem Sangraula, "New Evidence on the Urbanization of Global Poverty" (World Bank Policy Research Working Paper 4199: April 2007), http://siteresources.worldbank.org/INTWDR2008/Resources/2795087–1191427986785/RavallionMEtAl_UrbanizationOfGlobalPoverty.pdf.

5. Stephan Barthel and Christian Isendahl, "Urban Gardens, Agriculture, and Water Management: Sources of Resilience for Long-Term Food Security in Cities," *Ecological Economics* 86 (February 2013), 224–234.

6. Laura Lawson, *City Bountiful: A Century of Community Gardening in America* (Berkeley and Los Angeles: University of California Press, 2005).

7. Thomas J. Bassett, "Reaping on the Margins: A Century of Community Gardening in America," *Landscape* 25, no. 2 (1981), 1–8.

8. Barthel and Isendahl, 232.

9. Jac Smit, Joe Nasr, and Annu Ratta, *Urban Agriculture: Food, Jobs, and Sustainable Cities,* (Published electronically with the permission of the United Nations Development Programme, 2001), http://jacsmit.com/book.html.

10. Alberto Zezza and Luca Taseiotti, "Urban Agriculture, Poverty, and Food Security: Empirical Evidence from a Sample of Developing Countries," *Food Policy* 35 (August 2010), 265–273.

11. Ibid., 267.

12. Ibid., 266.

13. Margaret Armar-Klemesu, "Urban Agriculture and Food Security, Nutrition and Health," *Growing Cities, Growing Food: Urban Agriculture on the Policy Agenda. A Reader on Urban Agriculture,* ed. Nico Bakker et al., (Feldafing: German Foundation for International Development, 2001).

14. Ruth Stewart et al., "What Are the Impacts of Urban Agriculture Programs on Food Security in Low and Middle-income Countries?" *Environmental Evidence 2,* no. 7 (2013), 1–13.

15. René van Veenhuizen, ed., *Cities Farming for the Future: Urban Agriculture for Green and Productive Cities* (Ottawa: RUAF Foundation, IDRC, and IIRR, 2006).

16. Rachel Nugent, "The Impact of Urban Agriculture on Household and Local Economies," in *Growing Cities, Growing Food: Urban Agriculture on the Policy Agenda,* ed. Bakker et al., 72.

17. Zezza and Taseiotti, 269.

18. Marielle Dubbeling, "Scoping Paper Feeding into the Development of UNEP's Position on Urban and Peri-urban Agriculture," *RUAF Foundation* (July 2013), http://icma.org/en/ icma/knowledge_network/documents/kn/ Document/305171/Scoping_Paper_Feeding_ into_the_Development_of_UNEPs_Position_ on_Urban_and_Periurban_Agriculture.

19. Zezza and Taseiotti, 267–269.

20. Stewart et al., 3.

21. Luc Mougeot, "Urban Agriculture: Definitions, Presence, Potentials and Risks," *Growing Cities, Growing Food: Urban Agriculture on the Policy Agenda,* eds. Bakker et al.

22. Smit et al., Chapter 4, page I, http://jacsmit. com/book/Chap04.pdf.

23. Barthel and Isendahl, 224.

24. Smit et al., Chapter 9, page 3, http://jacsmit. com/book/Chap09.pdf.

25. Sharanbir S. Grewal and Parwinder S. Grewal, "Can Cities Become Self-reliant in Food?" *Cities* 29, (2012), 2.

26. Armar-Klemesu, 107.

27. Smit et al., Chapter 5, page 8, http://jacsmit. com/book/Chap05.pdf.

28. Van Veenhuizen, 330–332.

29. Grewal and Grewal, 4.

30. Paule Moustier, "Urban Horticulture in Africa and Asia, An Efficient Corner Food Supplier," *Acta Horticulturae* 762, (2007), 145–158.

31. Dubbeling, 39.

32. "Water Scarcity Fact Sheet," United Nations Water (2013).

33. Sumila Gulyani, Debabrata Talukdar, and R. Mukami Kariuki, "Universal (Non)service? Water Markets, Household Demand and the Poor in Urban Kenya," *Urban Studies* 42, no. 8 (2005), 1250.

34. Stewart et al., 4.

35. Despommier, 208.

36. Ibid., 208.

37. Dubbeling, 40.

38. World Health Organization, "Policy and Regulatory Aspects," *Guidelines for the Safe Use of Wastewater, Excreta and Greywater* 1 (2006), 6.

39. Ibid., 8.

40. Ibid., 8.

41. M.N. Rojas-Valencia, M.T. Orta de Velasquez, and Victor Franco, "Urban Agriculture, Using Sustainable Practices that Involve the Reuse of Wastewater and Solid Waste," *Agricultural Water Management* 98 (2011), 1388–1394.

42. Ibid., 1392.

43. Ibid., 1390.

44. Grace Nabulo, Scott Young, and Colin Black, "Assessing Risk to Human Health from Tropical Leafy Vegetable Grown on Contaminated Urban Soils," *Science of the Total Environment* 408 (2010), 5338.

45. World Health Organization, "Wastewater Use in Agriculture," *Guidelines for the Safe Use of Wastewater, Excreta and Greywater* 2 (2006).

46. Ibid., 75.

47. Nabulo, Young, and Black, 5346.

48. Rojas-Valencia et al., 1388.

49. Dickson Despommier, "The Vertical Farm: Reducing the Impact of Agriculture on Ecosystem Functions and Services," *The Vertical Farm Project,* http://www.verticalfarm. com/more7essavl.

50. Ibid., 5.

51. Ibid., 145–146.

52. "Vertical Farming: Does It Really Stack Up?" *Economist,* 9 December 2010, http://www. economist.com/node/17647627.

53. Michaeleen Doucleff, "Sky-High-Vegetables: Vertical Farming Sprouts In Singapore," *NPR,* 9 November 2012, http://www.npr.Org/blogs/ thesalt/2012/11/06/164428031/sky-high vegetables-vertical-farming-sprouts-in- singapore.

13

Understanding the Cold War

By David S. Painter

This study has analyzed the Cold War as a product of the domestic histories of the great powers and of the structure and dynamics of international relations. Following World War II, changes in the global distribution of power, weapons technology, the balance of political forces within and among nations, the world economy, and relations between the industrialized nations and the underdeveloped periphery led to the Cold War. Further changes in these areas perpetuated it, and eventually brought about its end.

Throughout the Cold War, the global distribution of power influenced US and Soviet perceptions of their respective national interests and consequently their actions. Despite the upsurge in Soviet military power in the 1970s and a relative decline in US economic strength, the global distribution of power remained tilted against the Soviet Union throughout the Cold War. If popular support, industrial infrastructure, skilled manpower, and technological prowess are factored into the definition of power, the postwar era was bipolar only in a narrow military sense. By any broad definition of power, the Soviet Union remained throughout the Cold War an "incomplete superpower."[1]

This imbalance emerges even more starkly when the strength of the Western alliance is measured against that of the Soviet Bloc. Even in military terms the Soviet position had as many elements of weakness as of strength. Throughout the Cold War, the Soviet Union and its Warsaw Pact allies possessed numerical superiority in ground forces along the central front in the heart of Europe. In addition, Soviet and Chinese Communist ground forces outnumbered any possible opponent in Northeast Asia during the 1950s. In the 1970s, the Soviet Union also achieved rough parity with the United States in strategic nuclear weapons.[2]

On the other hand, the Soviet Union was never able to count on the loyalty of its Warsaw Pact partners, and after the Sino-Soviet split in the late 1950s almost a third of its ground forces had to be deployed along its border with the PRC. In assessing the nuclear balance, the Soviets had to take into account the arsenals of the other nuclear powers—Great Britain, France, and the PRC—as well as that of the United States.

The Soviet strategic position worsened over time relatively as well as absolutely. Although the weakening of German and Japanese power initially improved the Soviet Union's relative position, the defeat of these two powers along with the decline of Britain and France left undisputed leadership of the non-communist world to the United States. The successful reconstruction of West Germany and Japan, the economic recovery of the countries of Western Europe, and their incorporation into a US-led alliance meant that four of the world's five centers of industrial might stayed outside Soviet control. Moreover, the PRC's break with the USSR in the late 1950s and the growing hostility between the two communist giants put enormous demands on the Soviet military, strains that the Soviet economy eventually could not bear. The Sino-Soviet split ended any possibility of communism constituting an alternative world system that could compete with the capitalist West.

Closely related to the global distribution of power, the arms race was one of the most dynamic aspects of the Cold War. World War II accelerated dramatic changes in the technology of warfare. The systematic application of science to warfare produced weapons that reached new heights of destructiveness and dramatically expanded power projection capabilities. The development of atomic and hydrogen bombs and ballistic missiles magnified the destructive capacity of warfare and exposed most of the globe to attack and devastation. At various times, technological advances threatened to give one superpower or the other a dangerous edge over its rival, thereby triggering vigorous counter-measures and increasing the risk of nuclear disaster. The resulting arms race led to ever higher levels of military spending, more destabilizing technological competition, and constantly growing nuclear arsenals. Moreover, military expenditures tended to create constituencies that benefitted from the continuation of Cold War tensions. Established early in the Cold War, this pattern of action and counteraction continued to its end.

Although some analysts have argued that atomic weapons and the near certainty of retaliation may have helped prevent a war between the superpowers, they did not prevent numerous non-nuclear conflicts in the Third World. In addition, there were deep flaws in the command and control systems of both superpowers. As one scholar has noted, "not only were safety procedures inherently subject to error but the necessity to maintain active readiness and the capacity to respond to a nuclear attack inevitably pushed safety to the limit."[3] With both US and Soviet nuclear forces geared to "launch on warning," the danger of an accidental nuclear war was extremely high.

Gradually, the leaders of the United States and the Soviet Union came to terms with the implications of the nuclear revolution. Nuclear wars, they eventually realized, might be fought, but they could not be won.

While possession of nuclear weapons might help expand influence abroad and deter encroachments on their truly vital interests, marginal increments in nuclear weaponry did not provide commensurate additional leverage in the struggle for international influence. More and better weapons often decreased rather than increased security.

The history of the arms race highlights the impact of what international relations scholars call the security dilemma. Actions taken by one nation for its security can easily be construed by its adversary as threatening and lead to counter-measures that further reduce security for both sides. The workings of the security dilemma had an especially stark impact on the Soviet Union. Most of the measures the Soviets adopted to enhance their security resulted in less security because they provoked countermeasures by the more powerful United States and its allies that preserved or increased Western supremacy.[4]

The potential for conflict inherent in the security dilemma was exacerbated by the different social, economic, and political systems of the two main protagonists. The Cold War was an economic as well as a military and political conflict, and geopolitical alignment almost always involved a choice of economic system. The interconnected nature of international issues and domestic dynamics was one of the most distinctive features of the Cold War. During the Cold War, the direction of social and economic development was the subject of great contention. The potential impact of internal political alignments on the global balance of power invested domestic political struggles with international political and strategic significance. Changes in the balance of political forces both within and among nations took place throughout the Cold War and played a major role in initiating, prolonging, and finally ending the conflict.

The collapse of communism as an ideology paralleled the decline in the Soviet strategic position. Highly regarded by many at the end of World War II, the appeal of communism and the Soviet model of development declined sharply in most of the world over the course of the Cold War. Repression in the Soviet Union, Eastern Europe, and the

People's Republic of China tarnished communism's image. In the 1960s and 1970s some European communist parties attempted to reform themselves and to divorce communism from the harsh reality of Soviet (and Chinese) practice. These efforts failed to gain sufficient support to wrest leadership of world communism from the Soviet Union and the PRC. The faltering Soviet economy further discredited communism's appeal, as did growing international awareness of human rights and environmental abuses inside the Soviet Union, Eastern Europe, and the PRC.

Transnational ideological conflict was closely related to the development of national economies and the evolution of the global economy. Economic changes restructured power relationships among as well as within nations. The inability of the Soviet Union's economy to compete with the West restricted its citizens' standard of living, threatened its national security, and ultimately eroded the legitimacy of the communist system. Although the roots of Soviet economic problems go back at least to the emergence of the Stalinist system in the late 1920s, military competition with the United States and the PRC forced the Soviets to devote a much larger share of their smaller gross national product to defense, and siphoned off resources needed for economic modernization and development. The diversion of investment away from productive sectors and consumer goods ultimately undermined the Soviet Union's willingness and ability to compete with the United States and to maintain its empire. Economic growth in the Soviet Bloc, which had risen in the late 1940s and the 1950s, began to slow in the early 1970s and never recovered.

The failure of communism to deliver the goods contrasted sharply with Western consumer culture. Many among the new generation of Soviet citizens measured their economic status against that of their counterparts in the West rather than that of their parents, most of whom had witnessed significant improvements in living standards in their lifetimes. The 1986 Chernobyl nuclear disaster and subsequent cover-up attempts delivered a major blow to communist rule by demoralizing the few who still believed the system could be transformed from within. By the end of the 1980s, the Soviet system inspired and attracted almost no one, especially those who knew it best.

The reconstruction, reform, and relative resilience of the world capitalist system contrasted sharply with the failure of communism. On the defensive in 1945 due to the depth and duration of the Great Depression and its association with fascism, capitalism underwent significant changes and staged a remarkable comeback. The United States supported the reconstruction of Western Europe and Japan, promoted economic integration, helped forge a stable global financial order, and encouraged international trade and investment through the lowering of tariffs and the removal of other impediments to the free flow of goods and capital. Although the Western economies continued to suffer periods of stagnation and glaring inequalities in the distribution of income and wealth, they experienced unprecedented economic growth in the 1950s and 1960s and functioned sufficiently well thereafter to sustain their military might, support increasingly inclusive welfare states, and legitimize Western political and economic institutions.

While the oil crises of the 1970s caused economic difficulties and financial disorder in the West, the Soviets did not gain any lasting advantages from them. As an oil exporter, the Soviet Union benefitted briefly from higher oil prices, but the windfall distracted attention from the need for structural reforms. In the mid-1980s, when the Soviet Union finally had a government interested in economic reforms, international oil prices collapsed. The vitality of the West German and Japanese economies and the emergence of such Western-oriented "newly industrializing countries" as Taiwan and South Korea ensured the West's economic dominance over the Soviet Union and its allies, even as U.S technological and financial leadership declined and the US share of world production decreased.

The prosperity associated with the long boom stretching from the late 1940s to the early 1970s alleviated the excesses of prewar capitalism, undercut the appeal of leftist and communist parties, supported the ascendancy of moderate elites who associated their own well-being with that of the United States, and sustained the cohesion of the Western alliance. The defeat of the far right in World War II helped reduce divisions among non-communist elements, facilitating, at least in Western Europe and Japan, the emergence of a consensus supporting some form of capitalist welfare state and alignment with the United States. In addition, the Cold War provided a justification for the repression and marginalization of indigenous communist and other radical groups in the name of national security.

The Cold War distorted the process by which colonies gained their independence, and made decolonization more difficult and more violent. In addition, the Cold War polarized efforts at social, economic, and political change in Latin America. Although most conflicts in the Third World were largely indigenous in origin and their eventual success or failure was as much due to their internal histories and characteristics as to US and Soviet policies toward them, instability and conflict in the Third World fed Soviet-American rivalry.

The desire of many Third World independence movements to liberate their countries from foreign rule, to free their economies from foreign control, to overthrow repressive internal power structures put or kept in place by outside forces, and to challenge the West's cultural hegemony at times aligned some movements against the United States and its allies and with the Soviet Union. Western leaders feared that Third World radicalism could lead to the loss of access to raw materials, oil, food sources, and markets needed to rebuild the economies of Western Europe and Japan and to ensure continued US prosperity. Western leaders also feared that the Soviet Union would be able to gain ground through alliances with national liberation movements or in the turmoil that would accompany the end of Western control.

The Soviets proved unable to turn conditions in the Third World to their advantage, however. The era of decolonization (1945–75) represented a window of opportunity for the Soviet Union and a window of vulnerability for the United States and its allies. Although communist parties eventually came to power in some Third World countries (often among the poorest ones), these gains were either marginal or ephemeral as most national liberation movements proved to be beyond the control of any outside power. Soviet involvement in the Third World also galvanized Western counter-actions. By the 1980s the declining competitiveness of the Soviet economy and unpromising experience with Soviet-style planning in the Third World and elsewhere left Third World countries with little choice but to abide by the economic rules set by the Western-dominated International Monetary Fund and World Bank and to look to the United States and its allies for capital, technology, and markets. By the end of the Cold War, the threat that Third World radicalism would weaken the West and add to Soviet power had dissipated.

Although the Soviet-American rivalry that was at the core of the Cold War ended with the collapse of Soviet power and the disintegration of the Soviet Union and its empire, controversies over the meaning of the Cold War have continued. Some writers celebrate US victory in the Cold War and argue that its outcome vindicates US policies and actions during the Cold War. Others emphasize the high costs of waging the Cold War, and argue that less confrontational US policies would have brought about the same or a better outcome earlier and at a lower cost. These are very difficult issues to resolve. For one thing, the availability of Soviet documents is still very limited and incomplete. Moreover, the meaning of many of the few documents that are available is ambiguous. In many cases, as one scholar has noted, the same Soviet behavior can be interpreted as either expansionist or defensive.[5] Although many more US documents are available, especially for the 1940s and 1950s, full documentation on some key aspects of US policy, especially covert action, is still not available. In addition, the meaning of many US actions is also ambiguous. The doctrine of containment, the overarching principle of US Cold War foreign policy not only aimed at limiting the expansion of Soviet power and influence but also facilitated the expansion of US power and influence.[6] This brief book cannot resolve these controversies, which are rooted in deep, though often unacknowledged, ideological and philosophical differences. Hopefully, however, it provides sufficient information for readers to reach their own conclusions on these and other important issues.

Any assessment of the wisdom of the Cold War must take its costs into account.[7] The United States, the Soviet Union, and many other countries suffered great harm from waging it. With its insatiable demand on resources, its exacerbation of ideological and political intolerance, its emphasis on external threats, and its consequent neglect of internal problems, the Cold War deformed US, Soviet, and other societies, distorted their priorities, and dissipated their wealth. The Cold War also exacerbated such problems as chronic poverty, environmental degradation, ethnic conflict, and the proliferation of weapons of mass destruction. To paraphrase the seventeenth-century philosopher Thomas Hobbes, the Cold War was nasty, brutish, and long.[8]

NOTES

1. Philip Dibb, *The Soviet Union: The Incomplete Superpower,* second edition (London: Macmillan, 1988).

2. As Richard Betts has pointed out, however, parity itself is an elusive concept: "If it meant mutual vulnerability to unacceptable damage, parity came in the mid-1950s; if it meant nearly equal levels of civil damage, it arrived by the early 1970s; if equality in missiles or delivery vehicles, by the mid-1970s; if the measure is the balance of forces as a whole or of counterforce capacity, by the late 1970s." See Richard K.Betts, *Nuclear Blackmail and Nuclear Balance* (Washington, DC: Brookings Institution, 1987), 188.

3. Richard Crockatt, *The Fifty Years War: The United States and the Soviet Union in World Politics* (London: Routledge, 1995), 140.

4. For a similar argument, see Edward H.Judge and John W.Langdon, *A Hard and Bitter Peace: A Global History of the Cold War* (Upper Saddle River, NJ: Prentice-Hall, 1996), 312–13.

5. See William C.Wohlforth, "New Evidence on Moscow's Cold War," *Diplomatic History* 21 (Spring 1997): 229–42.

6. See Thomas G. Paterson, *Soviet-American Confrontation: Postwar Reconstruction and the Origins of the Cold War* (Baltimore, MD: Johns Hopkins University Press, 1973), 175n. Paterson and others, in particular William Appleman Williams, note that such expansion has been a central theme of US history.

7. On the costs to the United States, see Martin Walker, *The Cold War: A History* (New York: Henry Holt and Company, 1994), chap. 14; and Stephen I. Schwartz, ed. *Atomic Audit: The Costs and Consequences of US Nuclear Weapons Since 1940* (Washington, DC: Brookings Institution, 1998). On the environmental costs to the Soviet Union, see, for example, Murray Feshbach, *Ecological Disaster: Cleaning Up the Hidden Legacy of the Soviet Union* (Washington, DC: Brookings Institution, 1994).

8. I wish to thank my colleague John McNeill for suggesting this phrase.

142

14

Alternative Views of Environmental Security in a Less-Developed Country

The Case of Bangladesh

By Choudhury Shamim

INTRODUCTION

Since the end of the Cold War, there has been renewed interest in what is now called 'non-traditional' security issues. As late as 1985, the old cold warrior George Kennan wrote in *Foreign Affairs*, identifying the threat to the world environment as one of the two supreme dangers facing mankind. But it was really in the post Cold War era that the world saw a dramatic increase in international activity around environmental issues. The United Nations Environmental Program has reported that about 170 treaties have been negotiated in recent years on various issues of the global environment.[1]

The link between environment and security is still being worked out. The Stockholm Conference on Environmental Stress and Security in 1988 stated that: "So far, most of these statements of interconnections between environmental destruction and security are hypothetical. There is thus a need for sound empirical research to find out whether these hypotheses are valid or should be scrapped as only 'apparent truths'.[2] Mark Halle notes that "the relationship between environment and security feels right. It seems intuitively correct to assume a direct correlation between environmental degradation on the one hand and social disruption and conflict on the other."[3] The moderate critic" regards this linkage between security and environment as "insights without evidence" while the hard-line critic calls it "muddled thinking."[5] As stated in the Stockholm

Conference, intuition should be corroborated with empirical research.

There is, however, a sizeable literature that seeks to broaden the definition of security to include environmental concerns. Along with many others the United Nations Security Council states: "The absence of war and military conflicts amongst States does not itself ensure international peace and security. The non-military sources of instability in the economic, social, humanitarian and ecological fields have become threats to peace and security."[6]

VARIOUS INTERNATIONAL RELATIONS THEORIES ON ENVIRONMENT

A number of International Relations Theories can be applied to the issue of environment. Many of these theories only deal with the environment indirectly and peripherally. But it is useful to review the expanding literature of international-relations theory as it relates to the environment.

Realism: The two central concepts of Realist theory are power and the national interest. The international society is an anarchical *state-system*. The system is therefore a *self-help* one. Realism assumes that states and their populations need natural resources to survive. There is a competition between states for these scarce resources. War is often the result of such competition and conflict. It leads to "the struggle for power and peace," as Hans

Morgenthau put it.[7] Extreme versions of Realism, such as the geopolitical theories of major-general Karl Haushofer, look at the security implications of strategic raw materials. Both German and Japanese expansion in the 1930s was partly a search for raw materials. Some see President George Bush's intervention in Iraq as an attempt to secure the oil resources of the Middle East.

Malthusianism: Thomas Malthus, an 18th century English cleric, believed that because population grew in geometric progression and food production followed arithmetic progression, there would come a time when population growth would inevitably outstrip a country's food production and starvation would result. Although this did not happen because of technological progress, Malthusianism breathes through many arguments of global environmental politics. Some examples are The Club of Rome's *Limits to Growth* and Paul Ehrlich's famous 1968 book *The Population Bomb*. Indeed, the opposite is true today. Instead of a population explosion we see the signs of a population implosion. There is a severe decline in the fertility rate in the rich countries and also a decline in the rate of population growth in the developing world.

Liberalism: Liberalism focuses on cooperation. While liberalism sees people and states competing for scarce environmental resources, it does so in a more orderly way. Thus, "a liberal philosophy applied to global environmental politics tends to treat states as competitive participants not unlike corporations in markets they have established among themselves."[8] Private enterprise and the market produce efficiency and save nature. For example, the Stockholm Declaration of 1972 forbids states from inflicting environmental damage on each other, because this would be a violation of the state's sovereignty.

Neoliberal Institutionalism: This approach also focuses on cooperation. Here the states have a broader sense of self-interest. They focus on the public good. Their enlightened self-interest includes norms, values, principles and expectations which are the ingredients of International Regimes. The states seek mutually acceptable compromises through international negotiation. The building of International Regimes can benefit the global environment. The Kyoto Protocol of the UN Framework Convention on Climate Change is a good example of international regimes.

Ecoanarchism: This philosophy is humanistic and leftist, and Murray Bookchin is its leading proponent. Ecoanarchists believe that "the state and 'big' capital are inimical to the autonomy of humans and nature."[9] Thus to preserve nature it is necessary to break society into "small, relatively selfsufficient units." To help nature these units must practice altruism and mutual aid.

Social Naturalism: This view sees "culture and nature as bound together" in a kind of social community. Community is used in a very broad sense that includes people, animals, plants, ideas, language, history and the ecosystems. Cooperation between humans and nature is a given. The objective of social naturalism is "the creation of a cooperative ecological society found to be rooted in the most basic levels of being."[10] This philosophy strongly resembles the worldview and beliefs of certain indigenous peoples. The Navajo for example see the "world as being of an interconnected piece."[11]

Sustainable Growth: Simply stated, the growth in incomes results in economic development. As the 1990s World Bank President Barber Conable put it: "market forces and economic efficiency were the best way to achieve the kind of growth which is the best antidote to poverty."[12] So according to the neoclassical economist's dictum that "a rising tide lifts all boats" even the poor will become richer. The proponents of this theory believe that when the poor of the developing countries become richer then it will reduce pressure on the environment. For example, they will be more able and willing to pay the costs of keeping air and water clean.[13]

Sustainable Development: This phrase first appeared in a 1980 report issued by the International Union for the Conservation of Nature and Natural Resources (IUCN). It found international recognition in Our Common Future, a 1987 report published by the World Commission on Environment and Development (WCED). According to this report there was no inherent contradiction between environment and development. Yet there were limits to growth. "The concept of sustainable development does imply limits not absolute limits but limitations imposed by the present state of technology and social organizations on environmental resources, and by the ability of the biosphere to absorb the effects of human activities."[14] This approach focuses on the "needs" of the world's poor and calls for a sufficient transfer of wealth from the rich countries to the poor, so that the developing countries can deal with the problem of poverty and environmental damage.

The Steady-State Economy: Herman Daly proposed this alternative approach which focuses not on more goods, but on the durability and longevity of goods. More goods are wasteful and cause environmental degradation. It calls for recycling and the minimal exploitation of biological and physical resources. Daly's unit is the nation-state, and each country must seek to be self-sufficient and spend only its own natural resources.[15]

Radical Redistribution: Advocates of this theory believes that environmental degradation is the result of excessive wealth, the injustices of capitalism and the income inequality between the rich and the poor nations. In 2005, a typical American consumed 51 times as much energy as a typical Bangladeshi.[16] Consequently, two things need to be done. First, the rich must drastically reduce their consumption so as not to burden the earth's resources and environment. Second, the rich much transfer massive amounts of capital and technology so that the poor countries can grow economically and preserve the environment.

Ecosocialism and Eco-Marxism: Not surprisingly, ecosocialists and ecomarxists blame capitalism for environmental degradation. Capitalism is seen as inherently anti-ecological and anti-nature. By always seeking cheaper raw materials and fatter profits they impose wastes onto nature. Thus the mode of production matters for the environment. The ecosocialist program relies heavily on revolutionary action and the demise of capitalism. Given the fact that neither the state nor capitalism is about to "wither away" some proponents of this approach favor more localized, less complex and less ambitious collective efforts. They "emphasise people's collective power as producers, which directly involve local communities (particularly urban) and increase democracy, which enlist the labour movement and which are aimed particularly at economic life."[17]

Ecofeminism: Although many ecofeminists are not Marxists, they are all leftists or liberal in their philosophical orientation. For ecofeminists "the domination of women and nature are inextricably linked."[18] Some call for liberal reform while others espouse radical redistribution of resources to women, so that they can develop and protect the environment. As Ariel Salleh notes: "Feminine suffering is universal because wrong done to women and its ongoing denial fuel the psycho-sexual abuse of all Others races, children, animals, plants, rocks, water, and air."[19] For Salleh, ecofeminism offers a comprehensive progressive approach to the ecological crisis.

Ecocentrism: Ecocentrists believe that humans cannot survive without nature. They idealize nature and regard it as a source of eternal truth and beauty. Man's rapacious exploitation of nature may destroy both nature and themselves. The destruction of nature would result in both biological and spiritual impoverishment. Many ecocentrists are advocates of wilderness or "wildness." As Henry David Thoreau noted: "In wildness is the preservation of the world."[20]

Biopolitics: The origins of biopolitics can be found in the writings of Michel Foucault. According to Mitchell Dean, a follower of Foucault, biopolitics "is concerned with matters of life and death, with birth and propagation, with health and illness, both physical and mental, and with the processes that sustain or retard the optimization of the life of a population." Dean further adds that biopolitics "must also concern the social, cultural, environmental, economic and geographic conditions under which humans live, procreate, become ill, maintain health or become healthy, and die.... It is concerned with the biosphere in which humans dwell."[21] All institutions and practices concerned with exploiting, managing, and protecting the environment are expressions of biopolitics. It accepts power as an essential part of human social structures and relations.

The above are some of the basic environmental philosophies that interpret the global environment

146

and structure practices and policies. Many of these philosophies are in contrast and conflict with one another and result in very different interpretations of the reasons for environmental degradation. Some governments and countries may adhere to certain philosophies more than others. This article will focus on those environmental philosophies that the state of Bangladesh seeks to propound.

THE USE OF CASE STUDY

This first wave of research was more concerned with rewriting the security agenda. In the late nineties the second wave followed where the literature focused on empirical research based on case studies in order to understand exactly how environment and conflict are linked. The most prominent work in this field is of Thomas Homer-Dixon and Jay Blitt. In their 1998 book *Ecoviolence*, the authors produce the following eight key findings:

- Scarcities of renewable resources produce civil violence and conflict.
- The degradation and depletion of renewable resources causes environmental scarcity.
- Powerful groups capture valuable resources while marginal groups migrate to ecologically sensitive areas. Environmental scarcity constrains economic development and produces migration.
- Existing distinctions between social groups is sharpened by environmental scarcity.
- Environmental scarcity weakens governmental institutions and states.
- The above can in turn cause ethnic conflicts, insurgencies and coups d'etat.
- The International community can be indirectly affected by these conflicts generated by environmental scarcity.[22]

The use of an appropriate case study can generate a wealth of hypotheses that, when empirically tested, can create the link between environment and security.

THE CASE OF BANGLADESH: A LESS-DEVELOPED COUNTRY

Bangladesh represents a good case study of environmental security because its vulnerabilities come from both external and internal sources. Traditionally, security was seen from a military point of view. The birth of Bangladesh was a bloody affair. It seceded from Pakistan through a war of independence in which millions were killed and tens of millions fled as refugees to India. Even after the liberation of the country, guerrilla warfare and violent civil conflict continued.

Under these chaotic circumstances of the first years of independence, environmental factors were a back burner issue. The first hint of the importance of environmental security emerged when the specter of famine raged over a part of Bangladesh in 1974. The floods of 1974 had further aggravated the famine conditions. While the political regime of Bangladesh played down the famine conditions through its control of the press and media, the repercussions from such an event was not so easy to stem. The next year, in August 1975 Sheikh Mujibur Rahman, the father of the nation and President of the country, was killed in a military coup d'etat. Those who carried out the coup consisted of a few dissatisfied junior military officers of the Bangladesh Army. But there was no overwhelming protest in the rural or urban areas across the country at this sudden violent demise of democracy and a democratically elected government. I would suggest that the 1974 famine and the inability of the government to cope with the monsoon floods indirectly contributed to this political lethargy on the part of the citizens of Bangladesh.

There are a number of reasons why the links between the environment and security in Bangladesh should be studied. As the country's environment declines, it will adversely affect economic development, erode social cohesion and lead to the destruction of political institutions. Rapid population growth and the further lack of economic opportunities through environmental decline will cause demographic displacement both within the country and outside. This population migration to neighboring countries will give rise to regional tension and bilateral conflicts. Bangladesh is ethnically, religiously and linguistically very homogeneous, yet the degradation of the environment can cause various regions to become alienated from the center, giving rise to secession and even insurgency. The lack of environmental security in Bangladesh can trigger certain policy choices by the regime in power which can incite a potential conflict or aggravate an existing one. Environmental devastation caused by neighboring countries can exacerbate regional conflict and harm progress towards regional security and regional cooperation. Environmental factors also have the potential to play a debilitating effect on the domestic politics of Bangladesh. It is possible for certain narrow pressure groups like radical Muslim groups, to use a particular environmental factor like water-sharing as a political issue, especially against a neighboring country, such as India. This can upset domestic power balances and cause political instability. Thus the linkage of environment and security in Bangladesh is through economics and politics. The greater the environmental degradation in Bangladesh the greater will be the political and economic deterioration, thus leading to more national and international insecurity.

ENVIRONMENTAL CONCERNS IN BANGLADESH

The role of environmental factors in the economic and political development of Bangladesh will depend to a large extent on whether the regime in power can adapt to the changing environmental forces arrayed against it, both national and international. No one factor, but rather a combination of various environmental forces will play the decisive role in the nation's welfare and growth.

Population

The greatest problem that Bangladesh faces is an unusually large population in a small land area. It has a population density that is the highest in the world, except a few city-states like Singapore. The population grew from 42 million in 1951 to about 147 million in 2005.[23] It is projected to reach 166 million in 2015.[24] The population density is 1019 per square kilometer. When one compares this with 2 persons per sq. km. in Australia, 3 in Canada, 31 in USA, 191 in Pakistan and 324 in India, one becomes aware of the tremendous crush of population in Bangladesh. The rate of growth in the last twenty years of the 20th century was 2.1%. From 2001 to 2015 it is projected to grow 1.6% per year. The rate of growth of the urban areas is more than 7%, the fastest in the world in terms of sheer numbers. But it is often hard to grasp the meaning of these statistics. Anecdotes and imagery offer a better way to understand the population pressure in Bangladesh. One U.S. State Department official testifying before the American Congress explained that if all the people of the world came to the USA, then how crowded America would be. Bangladesh is even more crowded than that.

Because 36% of the population in 2005 was under the age of 15, the population momentum will carry it to many more millions before it comes to resemble a stable population. Yet there is some good news in the demographic field. In the last twenty-five years Bangladesh has been able to reduce the fertility rate from 7 children to close to 3.3 in 2005.[25] The World Bank reports that the population growth rate in the 1980s was 2.4%. In the 1990s it reduced to 1.6%.[26] This is in spite of the fact that Bangladesh is a conservative Muslim-majority area with a huge rural and traditional heartland, where most of the people are not only illiterate but lacking in nutrition and healthcare. It will indeed be a tremendous achievement if Bangladesh can sustain it and bring its runaway population expansion under control. The faster it does so, the less would be the negative effects on its environment. Zero population growth would be of inestimable value to the environment in Bangladesh.

Land and Soil

As noted earlier, Bangladesh covers a small area of only 144,000 square kilometers, but 63% of the total land is arable because it is located in the largest delta in the world. Formed by the three mighty rivers the Ganges, Brahmaputra and the Meghna it

148

is also "the youngest and the most active delta in the world."[27] There are hundreds of smaller rivers and tributaries that criss-cross this GBM delta; therefore, 80% of the total land area of Bangladesh consists of floodplains. Although Bangladesh is a flat alluvial plain, it does have complex soil condition and land pattern.

Erosion of land by rivers is a serious problem in Bangladesh. Every year due to strong summer winds, powerful waves and shifting rivers thousands of acres of land are eroded away, leaving thousands of families homeless and contributing to the pattern of wholesale migration towards the urban areas, mainly to the capital city Dhaka.

Deforestation

Many decades ago Bangladesh had rich tropical forests. But due to population growth and the need for firewood and timber, the forests have become rapidly depleted especially since independence in 1971. Currently the forest area comprises 13,000 square kilometers, about 10.2% of the total land space, which is much less than the universally accepted minimum of 25%.[28]

Located in the southwest of Bangladesh, the Sundarbans is a mangrove forest and covers an area of approximately 5,500 square kilometers, extending to the Indian side of West Bengal. As a whole the Sundarbans is the "largest patch of productive mangrove forest in the world"[29] and the home of the famous Royal Bengal Tiger as well as other rich flora and fauna. The United Nations has declared the Sundarbans as a world heritage site because of its rich biodiversity.

The tropical rain forests in the Chittagong Hill Tracts, home to high-value timber, rich vegetation and wild animals, is being rapidly depleted due to demand from both agriculture and industry. The Chokoria Sundarbans in the southeastern part of the country near the port-city Chittagong were completely destroyed in the 1980s and 1990s in order to facilitate shrimp farming. Similarly, the only deciduous forest located in Modhupur in central Bangladesh is facing inexorable human encroachment. A portion is now being protected as a national forest.

Despite this gloomy scenario, there is some cause for optimism. A very successful people-oriented reforestation campaign has begun. Homestead forestry is thriving. Beginning in the 1990s, every year more than 100 million saplings are planted. Taking part in the "tree plantation fortnight" has become a great new social ritual. Non-Governmental Organizations like BAPA, the Bangladesh Environmental Movement, are playing a very active role in the field of environmental public policy-making.

Floods

It is ironic that Bangladesh has too much water during the monsoon season and too little water during the winter months when no rainfall occurs. Thus the country is subject to both floods and drought. About 1360 billion cubic meters of water is discharged annually through the GBM system, 93% of which flows through Bangladesh. If all the water did not flow into the sea, the country would be under 32 feet of water. The 230 rivers with their numerous creeks and rivulets attempt to drain the water into the Bay of Bengal. But the siltation of rivers, the low river gradients in the flat plain and strong backwater effects slow the passage to the sea, giving rise to the overflowing of the river banks. Every year there are floods, in some years it becomes extreme due to extra heavy rainfall in a limited time. There is talk now of water management rather than flood-control. It may not be possible to eradicate floods, but efforts have to be made in order to ameliorate them and to live with floods by managing them.

Storms

Every year a number of storms cause damage to Bangladesh, mainly in the coastal region. About three to four severe cyclones emerge from the Bay of Bengal and the Indian Ocean. The funnel shape of the Bay increases the intensity, often blowing in excess of 240 km per hour and creating tidal bores

9 km high. One of the worst cyclones occurred on November 12, 1970, killing an estimated 300 hundred thousand people in addition to major damage to livestock, poultry, crops and vegetation.[30]

The situation is now much better owing to the implementation of the Coastal Embankment Project (CEP) with the help of the Dutch Government, under which 4000 km of high embankments were built to enclose the entire tidal flood plains in the coastal areas with 90 polders. The declared purpose of the project was to protect the lives and the properties of the inhabitants from the tidal surges that accompanied cyclones from the Indian Ocean and the Bay of Bengal. The building of many cyclone shelters in the storm affected areas has further reduced the loss of human lives.

FUTURE ENVIRONMENTAL THREATS AND INSECURITY

There are a number of factors and events on the horizon that can cause major environmental degradation in Bangladesh. Some of these issues are in the formative phase while others are quite imminent. In many ways Bangladesh is a victim unable to do much to mitigate the consequences of such looming environmental disasters.

Climate Change

Bangladesh's contribution to the global climate change is negligible. The industrial states of the Global North are the principal sources of global carbon emissions, accounting for three-fourths of global carbon dioxide emissions. The United States emits more CO_2 into the atmosphere than any other state, about 25%, five times the world average. The other chief culprits of global warming are China, Japan, Russia and the European Union.[31]

The effects of continued temperature rises could be both dramatic and devastating. Sea levels could rise up to three feet. Winters would get warmer and warm-weather hot spells would become more frequent and more severe. Rainfall would increase globally. As oceans heat, hurricanes would become

even stronger. Entire ecosystems would vanish from the planet. It would require farmers to irrigate and change their crops and agricultural practices. The combination of flooding and droughts would cause tropical diseases such as malaria and dengue fever to flourish.[32]

It is now internationally accepted that Bangladesh is highly susceptible to the impacts of global climate change and rising sea levels. If there is an increase in temperature of 6 degrees, the maximum predicted by the International Panel on Climate Change, then the greater flow of water through Bangladesh's three great rivers will inevitably lead to between 20 and 40 percent more flooding. The land available for agriculture will be significantly reduced, placing an intolerable pressure on fanners.

A three feet rise of the sea level would swamp about 16% of the total land area, destroy about 14% of the net cropped area and about 29% of the forest land, mostly in the coastal areas. In addition an estimated 10% of its projected population of 226 million in 2025 would be displaced.[33] Dr. A. Atiq Rahman, executive director of the Bangladesh Center for Advanced Studies (BCAS), warned that 20 to 25 million people of Bangladesh would become victims of climate change if adaptation measures were not taken immediately. In 2003, the Forum of Environmental Journalists of Bangladesh (FEJB) marked their 20th anniversary by organizing a seminar on climate change. They emphasized that although rich countries are causing this problem, Bangladesh would have to come up with solutions of its own.[34] A few weeks later, the Bangladesh Government undertook a high-level meeting chaired by the Prime Minister Begum Khaleda Zia, who stressed the importance of approving the proposed National Water Management Plan for optimum utilization of river waters and prevention of floods and erosion. The meeting was informed that many NGOs and local organizations, a total of 10,680 organizations, involving 40 percent women, were now working throughout the country under water-management projects. Some 639 irrigation, protection embankment, water-logging and land reclamation projects have been implemented by the Water Resources Ministry. Nearly 1.63 million hectares of land have been brought under irrigation through 28 big and 218 small-scale projects."[35]

Water Scarcity and River Linkage

Bangladesh shares 57 transnational rivers, including 54 with India and 3 with Myanmar. In 56 of the rivers, Bangladesh is the lower riparian country. The water disputes with India became aggravated when the latter started building the Farakka Barrage in the 1960s on the Ganges River, a few miles upstream from the international boundary with Bangladesh. The Farakka Dam began operations in 1975. Subsequently, a Ganges water-sharing treaty was signed between the two countries on 12 December, 1996.[36]

In 2003, the water dispute flared up again when Bangladesh was faced with India's Giant River-Link Project. The Indian government's National Water Development Agency (NWDA) has come up with a plan to take water from one basin of a river to another thus solving the water crisis in the drought-affected regions in India. For this they identified 30 connecting points in different rivers which would be connected by digging canals. The purpose of this $200 billion mega-project that India seems all set to undertake is to solve the problem of water scarcity in its various states in the northwest, including Haiyana, Gujrat and Rajasthan. These states are hundreds of miles west of Bangladesh.

The River-link plan seeks to connect the Ganges in the north and the Brahmaputra in the east, and then add to it the Kaberi and Mahanadi in the south, and from Mahanadi to Beas in the west. Again the Brahmaputra and the Teesta would be connected to take waters from the former to the latter and thence to the Farakka Barrage on the Ganges. For this purpose they need some 30 connecting canals which together would be around 10,000 km in length. In addition, 9 big and 24 small dams would be built as part of the project. Indian policy-makers such as Aijun Charan, the Indian Resource Minister, believe that the multi-faceted benefits are worth the phenomenal expenditure.

Bangladesh is totally against this river-link project. Since it will connect international rivers that flow through both India and Bangladesh, the former has flouted international law by not consulting Bangladesh about the plan. International treaties prohibit an upper riparian country from unilaterally diverting and altering the natural course on international rivers. According to the *Washington Times* report of September 20, 2003, the Indian plan would cause severe flooding during the monsoon rains and worse drought during the dry season in Bangladesh. The report cites Jayanta Bandopadhaya of the Center for Development and Environment Policy at the Indian Institute of Management in Kolkata, India, as saying that once the Indian plan is implemented, the world could lose the richest fisheries in South Asia. Bandopadhaya points out that salinity would also make inroads into the region, affecting thousands of hectares of arable land and the lives of millions of people subsisting on agriculture in Bangladesh. Mangrove forests, he says, will be disastrously affected, as they depend on the steady rise and fall of tides for their roots to breathe. Arresting the natural flow of rivers could be a death knell for the Sundarbans, the world's largest remaining coastal forest, a world heritage site, shared by the delta regions of India and Bangladesh.

The Bangladesh media and the Bangladesh Environment Movement waged a campaign against this river-link project, raising the public awareness of the adverse effects of this plan and forcing the Government of Bangladesh to take up the issue. On August 13, 2003 the Foreign Ministry summoned the Ambassador of India, Dilip Sinha and handed him a diplomatic protest note, which expressed the concern that the $200 billion river inter-linking project would threaten Bangladesh's ecology and economy."[37]

Furthermore, in February 2004, there have been reports of a proposed Chinese plan to divert waters from the upper parts of the Brahmaputra, which will have serious consequences on water flow in India and Bangladesh. The three gorges dam and the Chinese plan to divert waters from the Yangtze River illustrate the fact that China is actively pursuing the possibilities of interlinking and damming major rivers in order to divert waters from one basin to other parts of the country. This will in turn pose a threat to both

India and Bangladesh. In the future, water rather than oil will be a greater source of regional conflict.

Arsenic Poisoning

The growing trend around the world to drink water from underground sources is causing a global epidemic of arsenic poisoning. Tens of thousands of people have developed skin lesions, cancers and other symptoms, and many have died. Hundreds of millions are now thought to be at serious risk. While 17 countries are at risk around the world including China, Vietnam, India, Nepal, Argentina and the US the greatest calamity has occurred in Bangladesh.[38] Professor Willard Chappel of the University of Colorado said, "I have witnessed groundwater arsenic problem in many countries. But in terms of number of people exposed to the contamination, Bangladesh is the worst. I am sorry to say that not enough has been done to mitigate the problems."[39]

The World Health Organization (WHO) reported in September 2000 that "Bangladesh is grappling with the largest mass poisoning of a population in history because groundwater used for drinking has been contaminated with naturally occurring inorganic arsenic." Dr. Allan H. Smith, professor of epidemiology at the University of California at Berkeley, has said that between 33 and 77 millions of Bangladesh's 125 million people are at risk. In 2002, after a long debate, the United States Congress adopted the WHO recommendation of 10 micrograms per liter as the maximum contaminant level for safe drinking water. In many areas of Bangladesh concentrations are above 3000 micrograms per liter. Some experts warn that it is a matter of time before contaminated water seeps through the entire country.[40] The World Bank has recognized the problem and has allocated $44.4 million to find a remedy in Bangladesh. According to independent experts the cost for implementing the remedy itself may run into billions of dollars.

The Bangladesh Arsenic Mitigation Water Supply Project (BAMWSP) is expected to be a long-term one. The World Bank credit of $44 million was due to expire on June 30, 2003. It is anticipated that the extended BAMWSP project would receive about Taka 800 million from the government exchequer. Official sources also said that a separate fund might be allocated for mitigation of arsenic in water supplied in towns. More than 80 million people in 62 districts are now exposed to drinking arsenic-contaminated water, mostly from hand-pumped tube-wells. There are many districts where all tube-wells have been painted red to prohibit people from drinking water from the tube-wells.[41] In a big step forward to fight the dreaded arsenic contamination of groundwater, the "water quality surveillance protocol for rural water supply options in Bangladesh" was finalized in 2003. Approved by the Local Government Ministry, the department of Public Health Engineering (DPHE) would start implementing the protocol.[42]

By the middle of 2003, tube-well testing has been completed in 147 out of 268 upazila, a little bit more than 50%. But UNICEF Chief in Bangladesh Morten Geirsing asked: "We are very concerned about the quality of water samples being tested from tube-wells by some NGOs. Do the tests really attain minimum standard?"[43] In March 2004, there was an International Conference on Arsenic Contamination in Dhaka, Bangladesh, attended by 150 international and local scientists. Among other measures there was a recommendation to the Bangladesh government and international development organizations to help and rehabilitate the arsenic victims.

POLICY RECOMMENDATIONS

Some of the environmental theories and philosophies are more relevant to Bangladesh than others. The theory of Realism with its emphasis on the struggle to control nature and war over resources is less applicable for a less developed country than Neoliberal Institutionalism which seeks mutually agreeable compromises through negotiations in international regimes. The following are policy recommendations for the Government of Bangladesh:

- **Malthusianism:** Bangladesh must face the reality that it is the most densely populated country in the world. Uncontrolled population growth will have grave ecological implications for the country. It is imperative to continue with successful family planning policies to bring about a stable population of about 200 million, which is just about the carrying capacity of the land area. To feed its growing population Bangladesh must adopt new technologies such as genetic engineering and transgenetic crops. The country has been successful in adopting the Green Revolution which has enabled it to become self-sufficient in food crops. But the population may out-strip food production unless the latest technologies are adopted. Many environmentalists are against the adoption of genetically modified crops, but the government must be swift to adopt those technologies which have been proven safe for both man and the environment.

- **Neoliberal Institutionalism:** Bangladesh is going to be badly affected in the future by the activities of rich nations and the emerging countries such as China and India. Without contributing to global warming and climate change, it will be one of the sad victims of such environmental disasters. Thus, Bangladesh must seek international help. It must participate strongly in global environmental conferences in the future and put forward its views in a forceful manner. New international regimes must include remedies for the protection of the environment in Bangladesh.

- **Sustainable Growth:** In order to safeguard the environment, Bangladesh must grow faster than it has in the past. From 1993 to 2003, Bangladesh had an average annual growth in GDP of 5%.[44] In 2005, that number was 6.7%.[45] While this is better, it is still below the growth rate of both India and Pakistan at 8%, not to mention China at 10%. Many economists feel that Bangladesh can definitely grow at the rate of India and Pakistan if it can achieve political stability and curb domestic violence and terrorism. A grand coalition government involving the two main political parties, the Bangladesh Nationalist party (BNP) and the Awami League (AL), can achieve the domestic political order necessary for faster economic growth.

- **Sustainable Development:** Bangladesh cannot accept any limits to growth; rather, it should emphasize the focus of sustainable development on the "needs" of the world's poor. As one of the poorest countries of the world it should call for a sufficient transfer of wealth from the rich countries to remove poverty in Bangladesh. It should seek for international debt relief. During the 1980s when Bangladesh was under military rule, it became heavily indebted. It must seek complete debt relief or at least to renegotiate many of the corrupt loan practices of a dictatorial regime. The current debt is $18.8 billion, which is 37% of GDP and 188% of total exports.[46] Unless this debt burden is reduced, the growth of the economy will be seriously hindered.

- **Steady-state Economy:** While Bangladesh cannot be wholly self-sufficient or follow a policy of autarky, it should eschew a philosophy of over-consumption. It must focus on durable goods and materials. It must recycle materials to save the environment. It must imbibe in people the culture of conservation and saving, whether economic, physical or environmental.

- **Radical redistribution:** While Bangladesh can do little to halt the over-consumption of the rich world, it can actively work for the redistribution of wealth to the poor countries. If the developing countries are to contribute to a clean environment it will require considerable assistance and capital from the developed world. This help must be provided at no cost or under extremely favorable conditions. Poor countries like Bangladesh must have access to state-of-the-art design, technology and manufacturing. In the Kyoto Protocol, there is one such transfer method called Clean Development Mechanism.[47] This mechanism does not involve radical transfer of technology, but it does call for financing of environmentally friendly projects in poor countries through

153

foreign investment by corporations. The challenge lies in implementing such ideas and coming up with other novel methods.

- **Ecofeminism:** In the last 15 years, from 1991 to 2006, Bangladesh has been continuously ruled by women prime ministers, Mrs. Khaleda Zia of BNP and Sheikh Hasina of the AL, respective leaders of the two main political parties of Bangladesh. While neither of them are radical feminists, they have sought to increase the political power and participation of women in Bangladesh. From the National Parliament to the Union Parishad (Council) at the local government level, there are reserved seats for women. Women form an integral part of all governing structures in the country. The quota of seats for women is still fairly small. It should be increased to one-third of all seats. Some of the poorest women in Bangladesh have embarked on the path of economic development through micro-credit loans offered by such institutions like the Grameen Bank and other NGOs. Many of these poor women have also run for office in local elections. The government should actively work for the socio-economic and political development of women in Bangladesh.

CONCLUSION

The case study of Bangladesh shows that millions of people are facing insecurity from environmental factors. The findings suggest that environmental degradation often leads to economic underdevelopment, which can in turn diminish political stability. Natural disasters like floods and cyclones place a terrible burden on the government every year, whereas its inability to cope with the demands would fundamentally weaken the regime, thus contributing to potential political instability.

For the last sixteen years Bangladesh has been a democratic polity. It has two main parties, the Awami League (AL) and the Bangladesh Nationalist Party (BNP), which have alternated in holding power since 1991 but have rarely cooperated with each other. In fact, they are highly polarized and mutually antagonistic. In such a situation each party is quick to capitalize on the problems of environmental degradation faced by the government.

Thus Bangladesh not only faces global and domestic sources of environmental insecurity, it also lacks the strong political institutions necessary to cope with such dangers. The only optimistic feature is that the people of Bangladesh are very politically conscious and environmentally aware. The media and the NGOs are playing a very positive role. In 2003, the Bangladesh Environmental Lawyers Association (BELA) received the United Nations Environment Award 2003. In that same year United Nations Environment Program (UNEP) announced that BELA has been elected as Global 500 Roll of Honor for its outstanding contribution in protecting the environment. Thus, world politics and global institutions as well as democracy and private enterprise are an integral part of saving the environment in Bangladesh.

NOTES

1. J.W. Brown, "International Environment Cooperation as a Contribution to World Security" in Klare and Chandrani (eds.), *World Security* (New York: St. Martin's Press, 1998), p. 317.
2. S. Hassan, *Environmental Issues and Security in South Asia*. Adelphi Paper 261. (London: IISS, 1991), p. 5.
3. M. Halle, "Foreword" in G. Dabelko, S. Lonergan, R. Mathew, *State-of-the-Art Review on Environment, Security and Development Cooperation*, (Paris: OECD, 2000), p. 1.
4. P.F. Diehl and N.P. Gleditsch (eds.), *Environmental Conflict* (Boulder: Westview Press, 2001), p. 2.
5. D.H. Deudny, "Environment and Security: Muddled Thinking." *Bulletin of Atomic Scientists*. Vol. 47, p. 3.
6. United Nations Security Council. Note by the President of the United Nations Security Council. UN Document S/23500. (New York: United Nations, 1992).

7. Hans Morgenthau, *Politics Among Nations: The Struggle for Power and Peace* (New York: Knopf, 1948).

8. R.D. Lipschutz, *Global Environmental Politics: Power, Perspectives, and Practice*, (Washington, DC: CQ Press, 2004), p. 48.

9. Ibid. p. 56.

10. Ibid. p. 58.

11. Ibid

12. Quoted in Robin Broad, John Cavanaugh, and Walden Bello, "Development: The Market Is Not Enough," *Foreign Policy* 81 (Winter 1990), p. 144.

13. Norman A. Bailey, "Foreign Direct Investment and Environmental protection in the Third World," in Durwood Zaelke, Paul Orbuch, and Robert F. Houseman, (eds.) *Trade and the Environment: Law, Economics, and Policy*, (Washington, D.C.: Island Press, 1993), pp. 133–143.

14. WCED, *Our Common Future*, p. 8.

15. Herman Daly, *Steady-State Economics*, 2d ed. (Washington, D.C.: Island Press, 1991).

16. Pocket World in Figures, 2006 edition, pp. 116 and 234.

17. David Pepper, *Eco-socialism: From Deep Ecology to Social Justice* (London: Routledge, 1993), p. 234.

18. Ronnie D. Lipschutz, *Global Environmental Politics* (Washington, D.C.: CQ Press, 2004), p. 80.

19. Ariel Salleh, *Ecofeminism as Politics: Nature, Marx, and the Postmodern* (London: Zed Books, 1997), p. 14.

20. Henry David Thoreau, "Walking, or the Wild" (1862), part 2, para. 18, online at http://www.eserver.Org/thoreau/walking2.html#wild.

21. Quoted in Ronnie Lipschutz, Global Environmental Politics, p. 84.

22. T.F. Homer-Dixon and J. Blitt (eds.), *Ecoviolence: Links Among Environment, Population, and Security.* (Lanham: Rowman and Littlefield, 1998), pp. 223–228.

23. The Economist, *Pocket World in Figures 2006* edition, (London: The Economist, 2006), p. 116.

24. The World Bank. World development Indicators 2003. (Washington,DC: The World Bank, 2003).

25. The Economist. *Pocket World in Figures* 2006 edition

26. The World Bank. The World Development Report 2000–2001. (New York: Oxford University Press, 2000–2001), p. 278.

27. A. Najam, *Environment, Development and Human Security: Perspectives from South Asia.* (Lanham: University Press of America, 2003), p. 109.

28. The World Bank. W*orld Development Indicators 2003.* (Washington, DC: The World Bank, 2003), p. 132.

29. A. Najam, *Environment, Development and Human Security*, p. 110.

30. S. Hassan, *Environmental Issues and Security in South Asia*, p. 20.

31. C.W. Kegley, Jr., *World Politics: Trend and Transformation* (Belmont, CA: Thomson, 2007), p. 376.

32. Ibid

33. Mahtab, *Effect of Climate Change and Sea Level Rise on Bangladesh*, (London: Commonwealth Secretariat, 1989), pp. 1–10.

34. *The Daily Star*, July 24, 2003.

35. New Age, August 14, 2003.

36. "Treaty between the Government of the Republic of India and the Government of the People's Republic of Bangladesh on Sharing of the Ganga/Ganges Waters at Farakka." *World Affairs*, Vol. 1, No. 2. Apr–Jun 1997. pp. 156–159.

37. *The Daily Star,* July 14, 2003.

38. F. Pearce, "Arsenic's fatal legacy grows worldwide." *New Scientist*, August 7, 2003.

39. *The Daily Star*, February 28, 2003.

40. *The Independent*, July 2,2003.

41. *The Daily Star*, May 28, 2003.

42. *The Daily Star*, May 13, 2003.

43. *The Daily Star*, February 28, 2004.

44. The Economist *Pocket World in Figures* 2006 edition, p. 116.

45. *The Economist*, "An Ugly Alliance." (London: The Economist, 2006), September 26, 2006.

46. The Economist, *Poscket World in Figures 2006 edition*, p. 117.

47. Clean Development Mechanism, UN Framework Convention on Climate Change. Online at http://unfccc.int/cdm.

15

Economic Challenges: A Region of Disparities

By Dona J. Stewart

When widespread protests erupted across the region in the spring of 2011, news articles and expert analysis focused primarily on the role of political and social issues in creating a revolutionary desire for change. However, economic issues played a key role in the population's level of dissatisfaction with their current governments and contributed to underlying frustration in many countries. The region is marked by multiple disparities: between it and the rest of the world, among countries in the region and within countries. Despite the region's diversity many countries face common challenges resulting from population dynamics and the region's comparative disadvantage in the global economy.

PREPAREDNESS FOR THE GLOBAL ECONOMY

On the global level the region lags behind, in both its share of world exports and share of global gross domestic product (GDP). Only the sub-Saharan African region has lower economic growth than the MENA. Indeed Pamuk (2006: 810) notes that the "gap between the Middle East and high income regions of the world is roughly the same today as it was in 1913." Furthermore, despite rising oil prices the region has not kept pace with the growth rates posted by other less developed regions, including Latin America. To be fair, the region did post impressive overall growth rates between 2001 and 2006. However much of this growth was the result of unusually high oil prices and

has had little impact beyond the Gulf oil producing states. Much of these gains have also been lost amid the recent global economic downturn.

The Middle East's position in the global economy has not improved over the last century; in terms of trade, the region has declined over the last 50 years. Throughout the 1990s, exports from the region, including both oil and non-oil, grew by only 1.5 percent; far below the global average of 6.0 percent (United Nations Development Program, 2002: 4). The region produces few manufactured goods for the global market and intra-regional trade is very low. This lack of sub-regional market cooperation results in the loss of billions of dollars in potential trade.

Many countries in the MENA are heavily reliant on their agricultural sectors, both for export income as well as employment. In countries such as Egypt, Turkey and Jordan, agricultural production has traditionally been done by family farmers working small plots of land. Today, with a growing emphasis on agriculture for export to markets in the European Union, there is growing pressure to consolidate land holding into larger plots operated by commercial farms. In some countries, such as Egypt, land reform measures have encouraged consolidation, leading to more efficient farms but creating more rural unemployment. The trends identified in Table 15.1, based the most recently available data, continue to characterize the region's economic structure.

Table 15.1 Economic structure of Middle Eastern and North African countries

Country	Agriculture (% GDP)	Industry	Manufacturing	Services	Per capita GNI $ (Atlas method)
Algeria	7	62	5	31	4190
Bahrain	8[3]	61[3]	6[3]	30[3]	21,482[3]
Egypt	13	38	16	49	1800
Iraq	5[2]	84[2]	1[2]	10[2]	n/a
Jordan	3	34	20	63	3470
Kuwait	0[2]	59[2]	3[2]	40[2]	43,930
Lebanon	6	22	14	71	12,380
Libya	2	79	4	20	2520
Morocco	15	30	14	55	14,330
Oman	2[1]	56[1]	8[1]	42[1]	14,330
Qatar	2[1]	56[1]	8[1]	42[1]	n/a
Saudi Arabia	4[1]	59[1]	10[1]	5[1]	17,870
Sudan	26	34	6	40	1100
Syria	20	35	13	45	2160
Tunisia	10	33	18	59	3480
UAE	2	61	12	38	n/a
West Bank/Gaza	n/a	n/a	n/a	n/a	n/a
Yemen	13[1]	41[1]	4[1]	45[1]	960
Iran	10	44	11	45	1880
Israel	n/a	n/a	n/a	n/a	24,720
Turkey	9	28	18	64	9020
Middle East/NA	11	43	12	46	3237
Sub-Saharan Africa	12	33	15	55	1077
UK	1	24	15[1]	76	48,040
USA	1	22	14	77	47,930

All data are from 2008 as published in The World Bank, *World Development Indicators 2010,* except those indicated with[1], which are 2004 and[2] which are 2000 and[3] which are 2005.

These countries' weak manufacturing sectors are a legacy of both colonial policy and attempts during the independent period to develop domestic manufacturing. When the economies of the region were under external control by European states, the development of local manufacturing capacity was prohibited. Resources from the Middle East, such as cotton, were instead transported hack to Europe for manufacturing and processing, stimulating job growth there. At independence, therefore, these countries had little or no manufacturing capability and were heavily dependent on imports of everything from machinery, to soap, to packaged foods.

Following independence, new governments adopted import substitution policies to reduce their dependence on foreign goods and foster their own manufacturing industry. Under such policies states attempted to develop industries to domestically manufacture items they typically bought from external trading partners. Egypt and Turkey were among the earliest to embrace this policy, which was eventually adopted by Syria, Iraq, Tunisia and Algeria. State-led development through import substitution was consistent with the then popular ideologies of Ba'athism and Arab Socialism. Government-owned factories were opened to manufacture everything from cars and televisions to pasta and toothpaste.

Unfortunately, these products were often inferior in quality to those produced in the West and sometimes costlier, making them unattractive to consumers in these external markets.

Though import substitution policies often led to a stagnation or decline in the standard of living of workers and peasants (Beinin, 1999), the policies, and accompanying populist rhetoric, were in place for a number of decades. In the 1970s, as a result of rising oil prices and increased international lending to the region, most states began to acknowledge the shortcomings of import substitution. However, their economies remained heavily burdened with inefficient state industries.

Box 15.1 Oil And The Saudi Welfare State

The 1970s oil boom dramatically transformed Saudi Arabia's society. The once primarily rural, Bedouin society, characterized by animal pastoralism and loyalty to tribe, became a heavily urbanized, settled culture. The Saudi government invested heavily in infrastructure, building sleek, modern cities and creating institutions such as universities and hospitals.

The Saudi royal family used oil revenue to ensure that the Saudi population was well taken care of, citizens received subsidies and often held undemanding government jobs. In response to the Arab Spring and revolution in neighboring states, the Saudi government has used subsidies to quell domestic discontent.

Saudi Arabia relied on foreign workers to provide the skilled and manual labor needed to transform the country. No longer did Saudis lead the self-reliant Bedouin life, rather they became dependent on a luxurious, government-supported lifestyle.

Large population growth over the past three decades, to 28.6 million (including 6 million workers), and flat oil prices left Saudi Arabia unable to sustain its social welfare system at the same level. Per capita income dropped from a high of $18,000 in 1981 to $8424, rebounding to $15,711 in 2005 following sharp rises in oil prices after 9/11. The result was an increase in the number of Saudi citizens living in absolute poverty and an overall decline in the standard of living. By 2002 Saudi Arabia was running a $12 billion budget deficit. Government services, such as education and health care, were in decline. Universities, for example, could accept less than half of those seeking admittance. Unemployment worsened, especially among male youth, while simultaneously the government attempted to reduce dependency on foreign workers by 'Saudization' of their jobs.

There is growing concern over the links between the economic situation, the rise of religious extremism and the lack of support for the royal family in Saudi Arabia. The majority of the 9/11 attackers were Saudi citizens and al-Qaeda-affiliated groups have clashed violently with the Saudi government. A report by an international think tank (International Crisis Group 2004: 11), noted the instability in the kingdom:

> Over time, insufficient job creation, an ill-adapted educational system and anachronistic economic structures, particularly when coupled with the sight of thousands of princes enjoying lavish lifestyles, risk further undermining the regime's support base.

Rising oil prices, up from $10—$30 a barrel in the 1980s to $60 a barrel in 2005, have increased Saudi oil income by 48 percent. The high prices are a result of a number of factors including the chaos in Iraq, unexpectedly high international demand (especially from the US and China), production cuts by OPEC to keep prices high, instability in Nigeria and Venezuela and attacks on oil workers in Saudi Arabia. The Saudi royal family is using the oil windfall to bolster support for the regime. In August 2005, for example, the government announced a 15 percent salary increase for all government employees.

In response to the Arab Spring Saudi Arabia announced a $37 billion financial support package aimed at lower and middle income Saudis. The package included unemployment benefits, affordable housing and pay raises. In 201 1 the monarchy announced a $37 billion financial package in a move widely believed to help prevent protests like those that broke out across the region in the Arab Spring.

International Crisis Group (2004) 'Can Saudi Arabia Reform Itself?', Middle East Report 28, July 14, 2004.

Moore, B. (2006) 'Iraq's Oil and the Saudi Welfare State', *Energy Bulletin*, March 23, 2006.

The Irish Times (2011) 'Saudi king pledges $37bn in bid to avert protests, *The Irish Times*, February 24, 2011, http://www.irishtimes.com/newspaper/world/2011/0224/1224290733324.html

STRUCTURAL ADJUSTMENT AND THE MIDDLE EAST

In the 1980s, with the end of the bipolar state system, the region became more inexorably tied to global capitalism. International lending institutions such as the International Monetary Fund and the World Bank, as well as the world's only superpower, the United States, began to advocate policy for the region's economic reform. The so-called 'Washington Consensus' based on neo-liberal economic ideas focused on the development of private enterprise and an export-oriented development strategy. For many countries in the region this meant dismantling their inefficient government-run companies and scaling back their bloated government bureaucracies.

Such programs, designed to send these economies through a 'structural adjustment' process also lifted regulations on trade originally designed to

Figure 15.1 High end resort, Southern Hurghada, Egypt

protect domestic industries and cut back government debt.

The activities undertaken under structural adjustment were extensive. Public (government-owned) companies were privatized, sold to both local and foreign investors. Systems such as banking and telecommunications, once controlled entirely by the government were opened up to competition. These policies were often both difficult to implement and had negative repercussions on large portions of the populations.

Privatization, for example, often proceeded slowly as few investors were available to purchase the government-run companies. Many of the companies, saddled with obsolete or inefficient equipment, were simply unattractive investments, especially when compared to the private firms being created in the new open economic climate. Privatization also often meant a reduction in the workforce as private investors sought to increase productivity and reduce costs.

Structural adjustment also required a reduction in the state's social welfare role. Subsidies, or government discounts, on everything including gasoline, sugar and cooking oil were eliminated or slashed. Government services such as healthcare were also cut back. Though some, especially the politically connected elite, benefited from structural adjustment, its policies often caused economic hardship in the lower and middle classes. Eventually, however, increased economic growth over the long term was expected to help improve the living standard across all economic groups.

Many Middle Eastern countries, with the assistance (and often insistence) of the international

159

financial community initiated structural adjustment programs in the late 1980s and 1990s. Only in recent years have these countries, such as Egypt, begun to see a pay-off in the form of higher economic growth though this has been mitigated by the global economic downturn that began circa 2008.

FREE TRADE AND THE MIDDLE EAST

In the era of capitalism-based globalization, free trade has become the slogan of Western financial institutions. Truly free trade means that there is no impediment to the flow of goods and services across national boundaries. Tariffs and quotas that were pur in place to protect domestic industry, for example, policies that place high tax on imported cars to protect local car producers, need to be removed under a free trade regime.

According to free-trade advocates, increased trade leads to higher growth and income, thereby reducing unemployment and poverty. The removal of obstacles to free trade was often tied to economic

Figure 15.2 Windmills, Red Sea coast

packages Middle Eastern countries sought from Western governments to alleviate their large debts.

There is no doubt that the Middle East and North Africa's trade performance continues to lag. In some countries barriers to free trade remain

---

Box 15.2 Israel: Poverty Amid Wealth

In many ways the Israeli economy is quite different than that of her neighbors. Its per capita Gross National Income (GNI) of $24,720 (2008), exceeds even that of some oil exporting countries. Israel's economy is well-diversified with healthy industrial and manufacturing sectors. Israel produces high quality products that enjoy access to European and Western markets. With a wealth of human capital, Israel's high-tech sector is globally competitive. Major firms, such as Motorola and IBM, operate facilities in Israel.

And yet amid Israel's relative economic wealth, and recent economic growth, the gap is widening between the rich and the poor. A 2010 report by Israel's Central Bureau of Statistics found that 29 percent of the population in Israel is at risk of being poor. Moreover the gap between rich and poor is widening, the average net income for the wealthiest 10 percent of Israel's population was more than 7.5 times that of the poorest 20 percent.

Of greater concern may be the impact of poverty on children, as 38 percent of Israel's children are at risk of being poor.

Poverty is highly concentrated among Israeli Arabs and ultra-Orthodox Jews, both of whom tend to have large families. Critics of Israel's economic policies that have focused on reducing social services and cutting governmental costs, argue that the rising poverty figures are a result of policies that have benefited the higher classes while pushing the middle class towards poverty. In the summer of 2011 the Israeli population took to the streets protesting high prices and general discontent with the government. The 'spark' for these protests was anger over the rising cost of cottage cheese.

Poverty is even more pervasive within the West Bank (currently occupied by Israel) and Gaza Strip (occupied by Israel until September 2005). Over half the Palestinian population lives in poverty,

160

in place. Recently, the fostering of free trade has taken on a political as well as economic dimension. Believing that free trade, by reducing poverty, can reduce terrorism, the United States has brokered free trade agreements with a number of countries in the region. Those countries seeking a free trade agreement with the US agree to cooperate with the US on foreign policy and security issues, in exchange for preferential access to the US market. Presently the US has agreements with Israel (signed in 1985), Turkey (1991), Jordan (2001), Egypt (2004), Morocco (2006), Bahrain (2006), Oman (2006), and others in the planning stages (Kuwait). The number of US bilateral trade agreements with countries in the region has risen dramatically since the attacks of September 11, 2001; however, the goal of a region-wide agreement by 2013 seems to have been sidelined.

Others, however, question whether or not the Middle East, given the current state of its economies can prosper in a free trade environment or perhaps only lag further behind. If free trade increases the region's disparity with the rest of the world, more instability and violence, could be created (Looney, 2005). Critics cite the difficulties encountered by other countries with free trade agreements; many of them more developed than those in the Middle East, whose current links ro the world economy are weak. Many countries in the region are not even members of the World Trade Organization, the body that oversees global trade. Though free trade agreements with the US

Box 15.3 The Maghreb: Perilous Gateway to Europe

Morocco is a major gateway for migrants from sub-Saharan Africa seeking jobs, escape from violence, and better lives in Europe. The distance between Morocco and the coast of Spain is only 10 miles. Even more attractive to migrants seeking a foothold in Europe are the Spanish enclaves of Ceuta and Melilla, located on the coast of Morocco and surrounded by two razor-wire fences. Migrants risk death to gain entry.

The migrants come from many countries: Senegal, Gambia, Sierra Leone, Liberia, Mali, Sudan, Cameroon and others. The numbers of migrants entering North Africa is growing; an estimated 65,000–120,000 migrants from sub-Saharan Africa enter the Maghreb each year. Libya is the major crossroads for these migrants, 70 percent migrate through the country each year, this figure has likely

Box 15.3 *Continued*

increased as a result of turmoil in Libya. A further 20-30 percent make their way through Algeria and Morocco. A smaller number attempt to cross via the Mediterranean. The use of false papers and tourist visas is a common method for gaining entry into Europe.

North African countries now host large immigrant communities of people from sub-Saharan Africa who are unable to immigrate to Europe, bur do not want to return home. The sizes of these communities vary from 1.5 million in Libya to 100,000 in Mauritania and Algeria and tens of thousands in Tunisia and Morocco.

The passage of sub-Saharan African migrants through the Maghreb to Europe is a major source of friction between European governments and countries such as Morocco. European countries apply pressure to North African governments to combat this migration and accept the migrants back into the Maghreb if they are caught in Europe. North African countries, such as Morocco and Tunisia, have implemented new laws against 'irregular immigration' and human smuggling. Europe and North Africa are also cooperating on border controls.

The treatment of migrants, or suspected migrants, is of major concern to human rights organizations. They face arbitrary arrest, deportation, harassment and possible torture. The rights of migrants to request asylum are often denied. Incidents, such as the killings of five men by law enforcement officials as they attempted to climb the razor-wire fence into the Spanish enclave of Ceuta in 2005, demonstrate the risks to migrants.

Amnesty International (2005) 'Spain/Morocco: Migrant rights between two fires', 3 October 2005, http://www.amnesty.org/en/library/info/EUR41/011/2005/en [Accessed July 18. 2011].

de Haas, H. (2006) 'Trans-Saharan migration to North Africa and the EU: Historical roots and current trends', *Migration Information Source*, 1 November, http://www.migrationinformation.org/Feature/print.cfm?ID=484 [Accessed July 18, 2011].

may at first seem both politically and economically attractive, the region's great distance from the US will entail longer transit times and higher transportation costs, making the US only a remote trading partner.

DISPARITY WITHIN THE REGION

Within the region, substantial economic differences exist. The largest distinction is between the oil exporting countries, especially of the Gulf area, and the non-oil exporters. Not only do these countries have per capita GNP often many times greater than their neighbors, their natural resource base has facilitated the growth of service-related economic activity. Though not oil exporters, Israel

and Turkey benefit from their more developed manufacturing base and their close trade relations with Europe.

Figure 15.3 Skyscrapers, Dubai, United Arab, Emirates

OIL ECONOMIES AND THE CHALLENGE OF DIVERSIFICATION

While the non-oil producing countries of the region work to create strong economic bases, the oil exporting countries face a different, though in some

Table 15.2 Petroleum resources in the Middle East and North Africa

Country	Oil proved reserves 2009 (% of global total)	Natural Gas proved reserves 2009 (% of global total)
Saudi Arabia	19.8	4.2
Iran	10.3	15.8
Iraq	8.6	1.7
Kuwait	7.6	1.0
United Arab Emirates	7.3	3.4
Libya	3.3	0.8
Qatar	2.0	13.5
Algeria	0.9	2.4
Sudan	0.5	<0.05
Oman	0.4	0.5
Egypt	0.3	1.2
Yemen	0.2	0.3
Syria	0.2	0.2
Tunisia	<0.05	<0.05
Turkey	<0.05	<0.05
Morocco	<0.05	<0.05
Israel	<0.05	<0.05
Jordan	<0.05	<0.05
Lebanon	<0.05	0.0
West Bank/Gaza	<0.05	0.0

Sources: for oil proved reserves; CIA World Factbook, https://www.cia.gov/library/publications/the-world-factbook/rankorder/2178rank.html, [Accessed February 6, 2011]; for gas proved reserves: CIA World Factbook, https://www.cia.gov/library/publications/the-world-factbook/rankorder/2179rank.html, [Accessed February 6, 2011], British Petroleum, (2010), *Statistical Review* of *World Energy*, June, http://www.bp.com/productlanding.do?categoryld=6929&contentld=7044622 oil [Accessed February 6, 2011].

ways similar challenge: to diversify their economies and create jobs for their citizens, reducing the need for the state to provide economic assistance. The oil exporting countries are composed largely of Gulf Cooperation Council (GCC) members: Bahrain, Kuwait, Oman, Qatar, Saudi Arabia and the United Arab Emirates. Diversification is the attempt to develop non-oil sectors of their economy including non-oil exports and non-oil revenue sources. Such diversification is intended to guard against the day when oil supplies are depleted, as well as act as a buffer against the enormous volatility associated with oil prices.

The GCC countries have attempted to develop heavy industry, and have been successful in the area of petrochemicals. Emphasis has also been placed on bolstering their small agricultural sectors, but

Figure 15.4 Children in a computer class, Saudi Arabia

ECONOMIC CHALLENGES: A REGION OF DISPARITIES

Table 15.3 GCC economic dependence on hydrocarbons

Country	Hydrocarbon GDP as a percentage of overall GDP					
	1980 (%)	1985 (%)	1990 (%)	1995 (%)	2000 (%)	2005 (%)
Bahrain	29.20	24.44	18.11	12.35	20.75	27.65
Kuwait	83.27	54.60	46.68	50.52	64.13	68.43
Oman	64.69	52.30	52.85	40.67	55.86	67.20
Qatar	85.39	59.33	57.45	44.26	65.62	76.09
Saudi Arabia	84.36	36.47	54.42	41.52	55.81	75.93
United Arab Emirates	80.60	51.25	62.36	38.27	45.73	50.33

Coury, T. and Dave, C. (2009) 'Oil, labor markets and economic diversification in the GCC: an empirical assessment' (Working Paper), November, Cambridge, US: Belfer Center for Science and International Affairs (Harvard).

the scarcity of water resources—many rely on desalinized water—is a hindrance. In some places, such as Bahrain and the UAE, the financial services sector has been an area of growth.

Moves to attract international visitors have been especially strong in the UAE. Dubai is now home to the world's tallest building. Exclusive high-end resorts line the country's beautiful beaches, leading to an incongruous mixing of bikini-clad foreigners and veiled citizens. Dubai has become an international 'city of spectacle', hosting sporting events with outrageous prize money. In the waters off its shores, they have even created artificial marine environments stocked with a gold bar each day for a lucky diver to find. Tourism, however, is a highly volatile economic sector, political instability anywhere in the region leads to a region-wide decline in tourism.

Overall, the GCC countries have made progress in diversifying their economies. A UN report notes a steady decline in oil's contribution to GDP since the 1970s. In addition to growth in the industry and services, non-oil exports have risen steadily, though the dramatic rise in oil prices in late 2007 could change this ratio.

The Gulf diversification process in some ways mirrors structural adjustment, in that privatization of government firms and a reduction of subsidies are included in the process. In the Gulf, however, a greater amount of investment capital is available to purchase government firms and the population is wealthier and better able to withstand cuts in subsidies.

A DEMOGRAPHIC TRAP

Despite the diversity of the region's economies, some issues, such as the demographic 'trap', created by high population growth rates, effect the region overall. In all countries this population dynamic exacerbates the economic situation and creates enormous social challenges. With a present population of about 366 million, the region has the world's second fastest-growing population, lagging only behind sub-Saharan Africa. In the latter part of the twentieth century, its population increased four-fold.

In fact, with a regional population growth rate of 2 percent between 2000 and 2009, the region's

Table 15.4 Economic profiles of Middle Eastern and North African countries

Country	Economic growth rate (2005)	Economic growth rate (2010)	Population growth rate (1990–2009 average)	Total fertility rate (1990)	Total fertility rote (2010)
Algeria	1.67	0.26	1.7	4.7	2.3
Bahrain	2.54	0.39	–	–	–
Egypt	1.47	1.35	1.9	4.6	2.8
Iraq	−0.11	2.30	2.7	6.0	3.9
Jordan	3.73	−0.86	3.3	5.5	3.4
Kuwait	2.35	−0.99	1.4	3.5	2.2
Lebanon	−2.30	2.42	1.8	3.1	1.8
Libya	0.16	1.52	2.0	4.8	2.6
Morocco	−1.83	0.02	1.3	4.0	2.3
Oman	1.19	1.5	2.3	6.6	3.0
Qatar	–	–	5.8[1]	4.4	2.4
Saudi Arabia	3.08	−0.49	2.3	5.8	3.0
Sudan	4.48	1.63	2.3	6.0	4.1
Syria	0.09	1.79	2.7	5.5	3.1
Tunisia	0.80	0.15	1.3	3.5	2.1
UAE	3.70	−1.44	4.7	4.4	1.9
West Bank/Gaza	1.42	2.55	2.8	6.4	4.9
Yemen	0.34	3.33	2.7	8.1	5.1
Iran	1.25	−0.76	1.5	4.8	1.8
Israel	1.76	−0.22	2.5	2.8	3.0
Turkey	3.88	3.92	1.5	3.1	2.1
Middle East/NA	2.58	0.74	2.0	4.9	2.7
Sub-Saharan Africa	2.53	0.83	2.6	6.3	5.1
UK	−1.39	−1.91	0.4	1.8	2.0
US	−0.31	−1.29	1.1	2.1	2.1

Sources: Demographic data provided by *World Development Indicators 2010*, The World Bank, economic data from ERS annual growth rate data US Department of Agriculture, Economic Research Service (ERS), http://www.ers.usdo.gov/data/macroeconomics/Data/HistoricalRealGDPValues.xls [Accessed July 18, 2011].

[1]Qatar's high population growth rate is the result of a large number of temporary immigrant workers in the country, not a large increase in the Qatari population.

population will continue to double approximately every 34 years. The rapid population growth rate is a function not only of the large number of children being born, but also the decrease in death rates as medical advances and improved hygiene, especially in the post-World War II period, resulted in extended life expectancies.

With such rapid population growth, youth dominates the region's population. One in every three people living in the region is between the ages of 10 and 24. Demographers speak of a 'youth bulge' in reference to these countries' population pyramids. These youth need services, such as schools, and more importantly, jobs. Overall

Figure 15.5 Fruit Peddlar in Cairo

Table 15.5 Youth unemployment rates in Middle Eastern and North African countries

Youth (under age 25) unemployment rates in MENA countries	
Country	Unemployment rate (%)
Algeria	46
Bahrain	21
Egypt	26
Jordan	39
Kuwait	23
Lebanon	21
Libya	27
Morocco	16
Oman	20
Qatar	17
Saudi Arabia	26
Sudan	41
Syria	20
Tunisia	27
United Arab Emirates	6
Yemen	29

United Nations Development Program (2009) *Arab Human Development Report: Challenges to Human Security in the Arab Countries*, New York, US: Regional Bureau for Arab States.

unemployment in the region was 14.4 percent in 2005, compared with the global average of 6.3 percent. The unemployment rate among the youth, who make up 60 percent of the population, is double the global average. Typical youth unemployment figures are in the double digits, but range as high as 46 percent and 39 percent in Algeria and Jordan respectively. Job creation lags greatly behind the growing demand. To fill this demand the region needs to create 51 million jobs by 2026, an unlikely occurrence (United Nations Development Program, 2009). The large number of young people, who have few future prospects, is a growing concern for the region and the West alike.

The rate of population growth in the region has decreased in recent decades, from 3.2 percent in the mid-1980s to 2.7 percent between 1990-1995, and to 2 percent in 2005. Sharp declines in fertility are a primary reason for this decrease. Fertility is typically measured by the Total Fertility Rate (TFR), which is the average number of children born to a woman during her reproductive life. In 1960, the MENA's TFR stood at about seven, by 2006 it had declined to three. A number of countries throughout the region, most notably Egypt, Tunisia and Iran, have launched aggressive family planning campaigns in an effort to slow their population growth. However, the TFR remains high in places, especially in the Arabian Peninsula: Yemen (5.1), Saudi Arabia (3.0) and Oman (3.0). The highest fertility rates are found in countries that have the least economic ability to address the needs of a rapidly growing population: Iraq (3.9), Yemen (5.1) and the Palestinian territories of the West Bank and Gaza (4.9).

From a Western perspective the decision by women to have large numbers of children may seem irrational, however within the Middle East, as well as much of the lesser developed world, child bearing brings crucial economic and social benefit to the family. Within agricultural dominated society children are an important source of labor for the family farm, helping to tend the fields and animals from even a very young age. Lacking any social security system, grown children are necessary to support the elderly. In the Middle East, family is

Table 15.6 Urban profiles of Middle Eastern and North African countries

Country	Urban Population (% of total population) 2010 projected	Urban population growth (annual %) 2009	Population growth (annual %) 2009	Population in capital city (millions) 2007
Algeria	66.5	2.48	1.50	3.30
Bahrain	88.6	1.83	2.02	0.15
Egypt	42.8	1.88	1.78	11.8*
Iran	n/a	2.06	1.3	7.87
Iraq	66.4	2.36	2.51	5.05
Israel	91.7	1.64	1.80	0.73
Jordan	78.5	3.27	2.36	1.06
Kuwait	98.5	2.43	2.41	2.06
Lebanon	87.2	0.84	0.70	1.84
Libya	77.9	2.20	1.97	2.18
Morocco	56.7	1.82	1.21	1.70
Oman	71.7	2.18	2.13	0.62
Qatar	95.8	9.64	9.56	0.38
Saudi Arabia	82.1	1.80	2.32	4.46
Sudan	45.2	4.21	2.21	4.75
Syria	54.9	3.07	2.45	246
Tunisia	67.3	1.60	1.00	0.74
Turkey	69.6	1.87	1.21	3.71
United Arab Emirates	78.0	2.57	2.50	0.60
West Bank/Gaza	72.1	2.79	2.65	0.67
Yemen	31.8	4.72	2.85	2.00

Sources: Annual urban population growth and annual population growth: *The World Bank, World Development Indicators and Global Development Finance*, retrieved from World Bank DataBank, http://databank.worldbank.org/ddp/home.do [Accessed January 30, 2011].

Urban population and population in capital city: Population Division of the Department of Economic and Social Affairs of the United Nations Secretariat, *World Population Prospects*: The 2007 Revision and World Urbanization Prospects, http://esa.un.org/unup [Accessed January 30, 2011].

*Data is for central Cairo, estimated population of Cairo metropolitan area exceeds 19 million.

the primary societal unit and the principal source of one's identity, having large numbers of children helps secure the women's role within the family and broader community. Though birth control is acceptable within Islam, religious beliefs, in which a child is considered to be a blessing from God, also contribute to high fertility rates. With increasing urbanization throughout the region, and mass migration of people from the rural countryside to the city, the economic incentive to have large families has been reduced, but the tradition of large families continues in many areas.

Despite the decline in fertility rates in recent years, the region's population will continue to increase due to 'demographic momentum' as the large number of young females entering their child-bearing years have children. By 2050, the region's population is expected to exceed 700 million.

With the growth of the region's population, its cities have swelled. The region now hosts many cities with population numbers well above the 1 million mark. Cairo's vast metropolitan area holds approximately 16 million people. It is far larger than the country's second largest city, Alexandria (3.9 million); a condition known as urban primacy, where one city, often the capital, is 'abnormally' large and dwarfs all others in the urban hierarchy. The population of Istanbul, at over 10 million, greatly exceeds that of Ankara (3.6 million) established by Ataturk as Turkey's new capital. In recent decades Tehran (7.1 million) has grown very large. These vast mega-cities contain large areas inhabited by the urban poor, such as Cairo's Imbaba neighborhood and south Tehran. Often these are newly arrived migrants, part of the large rural to urban influx that has characterized the region in the post-World War II period. Both high rates of natural increase among urban dwellers and large-scale migration combine to create massive urban growth.

Indeed the number of urban dwellers in the Middle East has increased by about 100 million in the last 35 years and is expected to increase to over 350 million by 2025. Despite the image of tents and camels, over half (57 percent) of the region's population now lives in cities. The level of urbanization is particularly high in the Gulf countries, where agricultural land is nearly nonexistent.

The loss of jobs in the Middle East's agricultural sector, and declining farm income, is a major push factor causing people, especially the youth in search of jobs, to migrate to the city. The perception of greater employment opportunities and access to more educational opportunities attract migrants from the rural area. Often, however, migrants' employment expectations cannot be met, either because they lack the skills required for urban jobs or, increasingly, enough jobs are not available. Rather than return to the rural area they remain in poor sections of city. The large influx of migrants in the last 60 years has greatly overburdened the region's cities. The infrastructure, both social and physical, is stretched and many cities have failed to keep pace with the demand for housing. The presence of large numbers of migrants, often unemployed, who lack roots in the city is a major concern for social and political stability.

168

Table 9.7 Large cities in the Middle East and North Africa

City	Population (millions)
Cairo, Egypt	7.9 (19)[1]
Istanbul, Turkey	13.1
Tehran, Iran	7.2
Baghdad, Iraq	5.4
Riyadh, Saudi Arabia	5.1
Alexandria, Egypt	4.1
Casablanca, Morocco	4.0
Ankara, Turkey	3.6
Jeddah, Saudi Arabia	3.4
Khartoum, Sudan	2.2
Rabat, Morocco	1.7
Algiers, Algeria	1.5
Aleppo, Syria	1.5
Damascus, Syria	1.5
Amman, Jordan	1.3
Beirut, Lebanon	1.3
Tripoli, Libya	1.1
Fez, Morocco	1.0

[1]Though the population of Cairo governorate is only 7.9 million, the population of the metropolitan area is thought to exceed 19 million.

THE REGION'S HUMAN CAPITAL

In 2002 the publication of the Arab Human Development Report (AHDR), written by experts from the region, focused attention on the shortcomings of human capital development in the region and its impacts (United Nations Development Program, 2009). Though the report was controversial, it offered one of the most comprehensive and well-researched assessments of the region. In essence it tried to answer , this question: Why is this oil-rich region falling behind?

The study noted the demographic issues, detailed above and further noted that the region's

Box 15.4 Islamic Finance

Recent decades have witnessed the growth of 'Islamic banks' in the Middle East as clients turn towards banking options that are consistent with their faith. Islamic banks offer products such as checking and savings accounts, loans and credit cards.

Specifically, Islamic law prohibits usury, the payment of interest. To buy a car, for example, the bank will purchase the car on the behalf of the individual and sell it to them at a higher price, giving the bank a profit, but avoiding interest. Typically the individual is allowed to pay the bank in installments, and the bank holds the title until the vehicle is fully paid for.

Similarly, savings accounts do not generate interest. Rather, clients with savings accounts are given a share of the bank's profits generated by loans and other activities, in proportion to the amount they have in the bank.

Islamic law also prohibits investing in any activities that are forbidden under the *sharia*. Such activities include the sale of alcohol or pork. Islamic banks can offer their clients investment choices, such as mutual funds or bonds, which are guaranteed to be consistent with Islamic law.

Though Islamic banks are popular in the region, they represent a very small part of the global financial system. However, interest in Islamic finance is growing in the West with an increasing number of business schools now offering this specialization. Institutions such as City University of London, Rice University and Harvard University offer courses or workshops on the subject.

Di Meglio, F. (2007) 'A Fresh Take on Islamic Finance', *Business Week Online*, March 27.

growth in income per head is lower than all regions except sub-Saharan Africa.

The AHDR argued that three major 'deficits' were responsible for the region's stagnation. These deficits were in three areas: freedom, knowledge and gender equality. These same issues, though perhaps stated differently, were raised by protesters through the region in 2011 as regimes toppled.

The AHDR argued that constraints on civil society and media, and educational systems based on rote memorization, rather than critical thinking and creative thought, were at the root of the region's 'freedom' deficit. Though many countries in the region have the trappings of democratic society, such as elections, they do not truly function as democracies. Power is tightly controlled by the central authority and often there is little accountability or few checks and balances. In these systems officials are appointed not on the basis of their skills or merit but on their loyalty or political connection. The lack of an independent media thwarts attempts to expose corruption. Such political patronage has significant economic consequences, and lowers overall economic efficiency.

Though many applauded the AHDR's willingness to confront the freedom deficit, which was well known but little talked about, the political uses of the freedom deficit added further controversy to the report. Following the report's publication, the Bush administration used the freedom deficit, and others, to justify its new interventionist policies in the region designed to bring about 'democratization', which ranged from political aid for existing authoritarian rulers to regime change in Iraq. As a result, supporters of the AHDR found it increasingly difficult to implement its suggested changes.

Noting that the Arab region was once the center of global knowledge, the report points to a current knowledge' deficit. The region produces little scientific research and has very low levels of information technology. Approximately 6 percent of the population uses the internet and only 1.2 percent own computers (*The Economist*, 2002). The report called for significant investment

Table 9.8 Female literacy and labor force participation

Country	Literacy rate adult female %	Literacy rate adult male %	Female labor force participation %
Algeria	60	80	38
Bahrain	60	80	31
Egypt	59	83	22
Iraq	64	84	n/a
Jordan	85	95	29
Kuwait	91	94	25
Lebanon	n/a	n/a	36
Libya	n/a	n/a	27
Morocco	40	66	29
Oman	74	87	24
Qatar	74	87	24
Saudi Arabia	69	87	18
Sudan	52	71	25
Syria	74	86	40
Tunisia	65	83	31
UAE	81.7[1]	76.1[1]	39
West Bank/Gaza	88	97	11
Yemen	n/a	n/a	31
Iran	70	84	41
Israel	96	98	59
Turkey	80	95	27
Middle East/North Africa	61	81	31
Sub-Saharan Africa	53	70	63
UK	99[1]	99[1]	69
USA	99[1]	99[1]	70

Literacy rates are for people aged 15 and above Literacy figures from 2006, World Development Indicators, [1] indicates 2003 data from CIA World Factbook.

Female labor force participation equals the percentage of the female population aged 1 5–64, 2005 figures from World Development Indicators.

in education, especially at the higher levels, and the infrastructure to expand knowledge acquisition and communication. A few countries have already instituted projects. Egypt, for example, initiated a project in 2001 to provide free dial-up service to all its citizens. Access to the internet is provided for free by multiple providers, no password is needed and users are billed only the charges for a local telephone call. People in Jordan can buy low cost internet access cards at grocery stores and convenience stores. At the same time, however, countries such as Tunisia and Saudi Arabia continue to block access to websites they find objectionable. In the case of Tunisia, prior to the removal of President Ben Ali in 2011, internet users reported being unable to access sites such as Amnesty International. In Saudi Arabia blocked pages range from the sexually explicit to those offering women's health advice and some popular culture sites.

The third deficit focuses on the lack of gender equality for women, with an emphasis on political empowerment, access to education and involvement in the workforce. The report notes that two-thirds of the region's 65 million illiterate adults are women, rates of illiteracy are higher than those found in poorer countries (*The Economist*, 2002). By failing to improve the status of women, the region is vastly underutilizing its available human capital and lags behind other regions in competitiveness.

Arab countries have shown the most rapid improvements in female education of any world region, female literacy rates have tripled since the 1970s (United Nations Development Program 2002, 3). This progress has often been the result of national project targets to specifically increase girls' enrollment in primary and secondary school. However, levels of illiteracy remain high, more than half of Arab women are illiterate. Female literacy is particularly low in rural areas, where girls' participation in school, even when compulsory, lags. Often girls are kept out of school in order to help at home, or the price of uniforms and books proves prohibitive. Continuation of their education onto the secondary level in rural areas is often problematic as it may require travel to a different village.

The often low quality of the education throughout the region undermines the region's competitiveness

---

Box 15.5 China's Growing Involvement in The Middle East

Historically, China has had very little involvement in the Middle East. Its great distance from the region and superpower dominance did little to encourage interaction. In recent decades China has begun to flex its economic and demographic muscle, and has adopted more activist foreign policies, forging closer relations with the Middle East. Chinese—Middle East relations are deepening each year and becoming more important.

China's new interest in the Middle East is based upon a number of factors. Firstly, given US hegemony over the region after the end of the Cold War, China may be establishing a foothold to forestall complete US dominance of the region.

More important to the rapidly expanding Chinese economy is the region's oil supply. The Middle East is now China's fourth largest trading partner. With its enormous economic expansion China became a net oil importer in 1993. By 2003 China's oil demand stood at 5.5 million barrels per day and it is the second largest international consumer of oil, second only to the United States. The Middle East now provides more than half of China's oil imports, provided mostly by Saudi Arabia and Iran.

Iran is a particularly close trade partner and signed a bilateral energy cooperation agreement in 2004. Under it, China will purchase 10 million tons of oil each year for 25 years and participate with Iran in oil exploration and development as well as the construction of power plants and cement factories. China is also becoming increasingly active in providing oil services in GCC countries as well as other parts of the Arab World.

Of major concern to the West are China's arms sales to the region, and specifically to Iran. China began supplying Iran weapons during the Iraq-Iran war when the US backed Iraq. Iran's continued international isolation, particularly as a result of its nuclear program, will likely strengthen its relationship with China. In the US, there are concerns that China will provide Iran with chemical, nuclear and biological weapons. Earlier, China had plans to sell missiles to Syria and nuclear research technology to Algeria; both deals were cancelled following US pressure and bad press. It should be noted, however, that Chinese arms sales to the region are miniscule compared to the weapons provided by the US.

Liangxiang, J. (2005) 'Energy First: China and the Middle East'. *Middle East Quarterly*. Spring.

Rubin, B. (1999) China's Middle East Strategy', *Middle East Review of international Affairs Journal*. March.

in the global economy. The educational system is often based on rote memorization and lacks 'hands on' or critical thinking skills. The educational infrastructure needs greater resources, including education technology and even basic supplies. In some countries, because of the youth bulge, schools must operate three shifts, with a shortened school day, to accommodate all students.

Finally, the report advocates increasing women's economic participation. Female labor force participation remains low, despite increasing educational attainment among women. In 2006 the overall percentage of women in paid employment was about 30 percent, well below the global average of 52 percent (Population Reference Bureau, 2007). Similarly, female rates of unemployment far exceed those of males. With job creation a major challenge for the region, increasing women's participation will require specific policies to remove gender bias from the workplace. Greater participation by women in the workforce could potentially improve the region's productivity, in the same way the youth bulge contributed to the economic boom in East Asia (Population Reference Bureau, 2007).

ECONOMIC CHALLENGES: A LINK WITH MILITANT ISLAM?

There is no doubt that the economic failure of Arab socialism, characterized by central planning, government-owned companies and guaranteed employment, has bolstered the influence of Islamist ideology. Moreover the economic transition from an agriculture based society to an urban economy based on industry and services, has historically and globally, always been traumatic and associated with social upheaval (Richards, 2002).

Militant Islamists have been able to capitalize on the region's current economic and social upheaval. According to Richards (2002: 31): "Today's basic profile for a violent militant is a young man with some education who may also have recently moved to the city. Such young people are often unemployed or have jobs below their expectations." The

> ### Summary Of Main Points
> - Second only to sub-Saharan Africa, the Middle East and North Africa lags behind in economic growth.
> - Demographic challenges, especially a 'youth bulge', both demand and hamper significant economic growth.
> - The region's youth face extremely high levels of unemployment.
> - The region's cities have grown dramatically in recent decades, receiving large numbers of immigrants from rural areas.
> - Deficits in freedom, knowledge and gender equality have been identified as barriers to economic growth.
> - Economies in the region are undergoing transformation to become more competitive in a global system dominated by capitalism and free trade.
> - Economic insecurity and associated social instability may be a strong contributing factor in the increase of militant violence in the region.

violent radicalism that spread through the region in the 1990s typically centered on poor urban areas.

Globalization may also be contributing to the growth of militant radicalism. Global communications, such as the internet and television, have made youth in poor countries deeply aware of the differences between their lives and those portrayed in Western television programs and films. There is a new and growing 'expectation gap' between what these youths can expect to have and what they desire. The internet has also greatly facilitated the spread of militant ideas across national borders, and as recent events in the region attest, spread democratic ideals as well. In this war for popular support, the widespread call for political reform in the region and the success of populist movements in overthrowing autocratic regimes has weakened the influence of militancy.

QUESTIONS FOR DISCUSSION

1. In what way does the demographic profile of the Middle East and North Africa differ from that of the US or UK? Are there any possible advantages to the MENA's demographic profile?
2. What policies could be implemented to lower fertility rates in the MENA?
3. What challenges do rural migrants face when they reach the city?
4. In what way does the US endorsement of the Arab Human Development Report hinder acceptance of its conclusions?
5. Globalization produces both 'winners' and 'losers', what is the likelihood that the MENA will be able to compete effectively in a global economy characterized by free trade and capitalism?
6. What are the links between globalization and the spread of ideas?
7. How can the countries of the region address their economic and social problems?

REFERENCES

Amnesty International (2005) 'Spain/Morocco: Migrant rights between two fires', October 3, http://www.amnesty.org/en/library/info/EUR41/011/2005/en [Accessed July 18, 2011].

Beinin, J. (1999) 'The working class and peasantry in the Middle East: from economic nationalism to neoliberalism'. *Middle East Report,* Spring 1999.

British Petroleum (2010) *Statistical Review of World Energy,* June 2010, http://www.bp.com/productlanding.do?categoryId=6929&contentId=7044622 oil [Accessed February 6, 2011].

Central Bureau of Statistics (2010) "Poverty and Well-Being of the Population in Israel and the European Union," State of Israel, http://www.cbs.gov.il/hodaot2010n/23_10_249e.pdf [Accessed July 18. 2011].

CIA World Factbook, https://www.cia.gov/library/publications/the-world-factbook/rankorder/2178rank.html [Accessed February 6, 2011].

Coury, T. and Dave, C. (2009) 'Oil, labor markets and economic diversification in the GCC: an empirical assessment' (Working Paper), November, Cambridge, US: Belfer Center for Science and International Affairs (Harvard).

de Haas, H. (2006) 'Trans-Saharan migration to North Africa and the EU: Historical roots and current trends', *Migration Information Source,* November 1, 2006. http://www.migrationinformation.org/Feature/print.cfm?ID=484 [Accessed July 18, 2011].

Di Meglio, F. (2007) 'A Fresh Take on Islamic Finance', *Business Week Online,* March 27.

International Crisis Group (2004) 'Can Saudi Arabia Reform Itself?' July 14.

Liangxiang, J. (2005) 'Energy First: China and the Middle East', *Middle East Quarterly,* Spring.

Looney, R. (2005) 'US Middle East Economic Policy: The Use of Free Trade Areas in the War on Terrorism', *Mediterranean Affairs,* 16: 102–117.

Madslien, J. (2006) 'Economic Boom Belies Israeli Poverty' BBC News, March 27, http://news.bbc.co.uk/2/hi/business/4833602.stm [Accessed 25 July 2007].

Moore, B. (2006) 'Iraq's Oil and the Saudi Welfare State, *Energy Bulletin,* March 23.

National Insurance Institute (Israel) (2004) *Annual Survey 2002–2003,* April.

Pamuk, S. (2006) 'Estimating Economic Growth in the Middle East since 1820', *The Journal of Economic History,* 66: 809–828.

Population Division of the Department of Economic and Social Affairs of the United Nations Secretariat, *World Population Prospects: The 2007 Revision* and *World Urbanization Prospects,* http://esa.un.org/unup [Accessed January 30, 2011].

Population Reference Bureau (2007) Challenges and opportunities: the population of the Middle East and North Africa', *Population Bulletin.* 62: 2.

Richards, A. (2002) 'Socioeconomic roots of Middle East radicalism', *Naval War College Review,* 55: 22–39.

Rubin, B. (1999) 'China's Middle East Strategy', *Middle East Review of international Affairs Journal,* March.

The Economist (2002) 'Self-doomed to failure' July 4.

The Irish Times (2011) 'Saudi king pledges $37bn in bid to avert protests', *The Irish Times,* February 24, 2011. http://www.irishtimes.com/newspaper/world/2011/0224/1224290733324.html

The World Bank, *World Development Indicators* (2010) economic data from ERS annual growth rate data US Department of Agriculture, Economic Research

Service (ERS), http://www.ers.usda.gov/data/mac-roeconomics/Data/HistoricalRealGDPValues.xls [Accessed July 18, 2011].

The World Bank, *World Development Indicators and Global Development Finance*, retrieved from World Bank Data Bank, http://databank.worldbank.org/ddp/home.do [Accessed January 30, 2011].

United Nations Development Program (2002) *Arab Human Development Report: Creating Opportunities for future Generations*, New York, US: UNDP Regional Bureau for Arab States

United Nations Development Program (2009) *Arab Human Development Report: Challenges to Human Security in the Arab Countries*, New York, US: Regional Bureau for Arab States.

United Nations Relief and World Agency (2009) 'Poverty in the occupied Palestinian Territory 2007'. http://www.unrwa.org/userfiles/20100118142147.pdf [Accessed July 18, 2011].

SUGGESTIONS FOR FURTHER READING

Beinin, J. (1999) 'The working class and peasantry in the Middle East: from economic nationalism to neoliberalism', *Middle East Report*, Spring 1999.

   Details the transition in Middle Eastern economies from state-led socialism to market capitalism.

The Economist (2002) "Self-doomed to failure", July 4.

   Offers a brief summary of the Arab Human Development Report.

Looney, R. (2005) 'US Middle East Economic Policy: The Use of Free Trade Areas in the War on Terrorism, *Mediterranean Affairs*, 16: 102-117.

   Assesses attempts by the Bush administration to link free trade agreements with security cooperation in countries in the Middle East and North Africa.

Martin, J. (2006) 'After the Oil...', *The Middle East*, February.

   A brief examination of attempts to diversify' the region's economies.

Noland, M. and Pack, H. (2004) Islam, globalization and economic performance in the Middle East', *Institute for International Economic Policy Brief*, PB04-4, June.

   Assesses the role of Islam in the region's economic performance, attitudes towards globalization and the region's demographic challenges.

Pamuk, S. (2006) 'Estimating Economic Growth in the Middle East since 1820', *The Journal of Economic History,* 66: 809–828.

   A highly detailed academic analysis of the Middle East's economic growth prior to and after independence.

Population Reference Bureau (2007) Challenges and opportunities: the population of the Middle East and North Africa', *Population Bulletin*, 62: 2.

   This short report lays out the region's demographic challenges, includes numerous easy-to-comprehend charts and tables.

Richards, A. (2002) 'Socioeconomic roots of Middle East radicalism', *Naval War College Review*, 55: 22–39.

   Explores the connection between the tremendous economic challenges facing the region and the rise of radical Islam.

Richards, A. and Waterbury, J. (1996) *A Political Economy of the Middle East,* Boulder, US: Westview Press.

   A comprehensive history of the region's economic development both during the colonial period and after independence.

United Nations Development Program (2002) *Arab Human Development Report: Creating Opportunities for future Generations*, New York, US: UNDP Regional Bureau for Arab States.

   A groundbreaking report that investigated the region's failure to thrive economically and the social and political aspects of relative underdevelopment.

United Nations Development Program (2009) *Arab Human Development Report: Challenges to Human Security in the Arab Countries*, New York, US: UNDP Regional Bureau for Arab States.

   This edition of the report offers an examination of human development through a human security lens, illustrating the relationship between development, security, good governance and human rights.

United Nations Economic and Social Commission for Western Asia (2001) *Economic Diversification in the Oil-Producing Countries: The Case of the Gulf Cooperation Council*, January 10, http://www.escwa.org.lb/information/publications/edit/upload/ed-01-l-e.pdf

   Detailed statistical assessment of the GCC countries' attempts to reduce their economic dependence on oil in the latter half of the twentieth century.

174

16

Africa's Freshwater Systems and Their Future

By Michele Thieme, Robin Abell, and Nell Burgess

A vision without action is just a dream; an action without vision just passes time; a vision with an action changes the world.

BARKER ET AL. (1990)

WHO'S WATCHING THE WATER?

Whereas terrestrial ecosystems and their inhabitants are clearly visible, freshwater biodiversity is largely hidden from view and therefore often neglected. Large-scale projects with a focus on conservation of terrestrial biodiversity are numerous in Africa (see Burgess et al. 2004 for a comprehensive review), especially compared with freshwater biodiversity—focused initiatives. Nevertheless, there are several ongoing large-scale freshwater projects in the Afro-Malagasy region, some of which have components that address biodiversity conservation. These include basin-wide initiatives for several of the Rift Valley lakes and for the Niger River and Lake Chad Basin (table 16.1).

We face the challenge of turning the set of large-scale continental priorities presented in this assessment into conservation achievements at finer geographic scales. This process involves developing spatially explicit and measurable plans defining what is needed to sustain biodiversity over the long term. For WWF, these plans are developed in the form of a biodiversity vision (Dinerstein et al. 2000;

Abell et al. 2002). Biodiversity visions are based on a fundamental but rarely asked question: from the perspective of conservation biologists, what would successful conservation for an ecoregion look like 30–50 years hence? Answering this question requires an understanding of what biological features must be saved now and what diminished features must be restored over the coming decades. The biodiversity vision also asks, if we cannot conserve everything everywhere, then what should we conserve? For African and Madagascan ecoregions, the biodiversity vision must also balance conservation with the needs of a growing human population and its reliance on natural resources. Meeting the needs of people and those of aquatic species will remain a major concern and challenge into the future.

Typically, a biodiversity vision identifies a set of priority sites or larger landscapes in an ecoregion that, if effectively conserved, would maintain the key biological values of the larger ecoregion. The vision may also identify parallel sets of actions in the policy and legal arenas that are needed to mitigate or remove threats to critical landscapes and ensure their long-term viability. In most freshwater ecoregions, many of the most important interventions are policy related; for example, maintaining water flow into a wetland may entail policies related to upstream dams and water withdrawals.

This chapter outlines the WWF approach to developing freshwater biodiversity visions. We conclude

176

with what we perceive as the greatest challenges to freshwater conservation in the Afro-Malagasy region.

CONSERVATION PLANNING IN ECOREGIONS AND RIVER BASINS

It is essential to plan and implement conservation actions at scales appropriate to the physical and biological processes that shape biodiversity features. Historically, inappropriate planning units or inattention to biological targets and biophysical processes have hampered freshwater conservation efforts (Abell et al. 2002; Groves 2003). Trying to conserve a floodplain system and its species without considering the source of the floodwaters has obvious limitations, yet this has been the dominant paradigm in many river conservation and restoration schemes (Wissmar and Beschta 1998; Frissell and Ralph 1998). Similarly, efforts that have focused on a single management site have done little to protect species that use a range of habitats over their life cycles (Saunders et al. 2002; Robinson et al. 2002). For freshwater systems, river and lake

basins provide the obvious organizing unit for conservation planning, and basin-scale planning promises to provide a significant advance over traditional single-site approaches. Yet basins are scale-independent and in themselves may not be the best representations of aquatic biogeographic patterns.

Current distributions of aquatic species are the result of multiple factors, including historical evolutionary processes that may have occurred in different hydrographic basins than those that exist today (Poff 1997). As a result of past connections, two river basins or portions of river basins may share many or most species assemblages, and biologists developing a plan to conserve those assemblages might group the two areas into a single unit. Alternatively, barriers to dispersal within a basin can facilitate the evolution of multiple distinct biotas; examples include a high waterfall isolating upstream species or a large river preventing dispersal between tributaries. From a biogeographic perspective, it is clear that a given river or lake basin may fail to capture the biogeographic patterns that should underpin biodiversity conservation planning. The freshwater

Table 16.1 Examples of Basin Projects with an Ecosystem Focus.

Basin Projects*	Funding and Implementing Organizations	Sources
Large-scale basin projects in the Nile, Niger, Okavango, Senegal, Lake Chad, Lake Tanganyika, Lake Victoria, and Volta	Global Environmental Facility, International Waters	Overview at http://www.iwlearn.net/region/ africa.php Specific sites: http://www.nilebasin.org, http://www.ltbp.org, http://www.lvemp.org
Various projects in the Niger, Lake Chad, Zambezi (especially River Kafue and Lake Malawi/Niassa/Nyasa), Great Ruaha River, River Mara and Lake Victoria, and Lake Bogoria	WWF	http://www.panda.org/about_wwf/what_we_do/ freshwater/index.cfm
Cape Action for People and the Environment	CAPE	http://www.capeaction.org.za/ and van Nieuwenhuizen and Day (2000a, 2000b)
Various projects in the Senegal, Niger, Volta, Kamadugu Yobe, Tanganyika, Victoria, Naivasha, Zambezi, Rufiji, Pangani, and Limpopo basins	IUCN Water and Nature Initiative and IUCN African Regional Offices	http://www.waterandnature.org/projects.html and http://www.iucn.org/themes/wetlands/ project.html

*Not a comprehensive list.

ecoregions that we offer in this assessment, which take into account both aquatic species distributions and drainage basin divides, are designed to serve as these biogeographic conservation planning units.

The fact that a biogeographically derived planning unit may not correspond to a single basin requires us to ask how to best reconcile the differences between these two planning units. The answer lies in the distinct uses of ecoregions and drainage basins in conservation. A freshwater ecoregion provides the template for a biological assessment. Through that assessment, we can identify the river reaches, floodplains, lakes, swamps, or other freshwater systems that support particularly

important biodiversity features. The biogeographic unit therefore defines the geographic universe of that assessment, allowing evaluation of key features across the entire area where they occur.

However, identifying important biological features is not equivalent to identifying management strategies for conserving them. Developing strategies entails assessing threats, and a threat assessment immediately takes us from the aquatic realm into the terrestrial, forcing consideration of the entire area of influence, upstream and even downstream. Even if a biogeographic unit consists of a portion of a basin, we inevitably must enlarge the scope of the analysis to include the

---

Box 16.1. Examples of Biodiversity Visions in Three African Freshwater Ecoregions.

Niger Basin Initiative. The Niger River flows through five ecoregions in West Africa, and its basin lies in eleven countries. Among these ecoregions are the globally outstanding Niger Delta [58], with one endemic freshwater fish family; the continentally outstanding Inner Niger Delta [7], with congregations of more than 1 million waterbirds; and the continentally outstanding Lower Niger-Benue [65], with high fish, mollusk, and herpetofaunal richness. The river is considered the cultural, economic, and ecological backbone of West Africa because human populations have depended on its vital freshwater supply in this essentially xeric region for thousands of years. Unfortunately, with burgeoning human populations and ever-increasing sources of pollution and degradation, the river is under severe threat.

The Niger Basin Initiative (NBI) is an environmental partnership between WWF, Wetlands International (WI), and the Nigerian Conservation Foundation created in May 2001 to address biodiversity conservation of the Niger River on a basin-wide scale. A cooperation agreement was then signed in October 2003 between the international organizations working on nature conservation in the basin (WWF, WI, BirdLife, and IUCN) and the Niger Basin Authority. The partner organizations are working together to ensure that biodiversity conservation and the sustainable use of natural wetland and forest resources are built into development plans for the basin.

In April 2002, the NBI hosted a workshop at which participants identified and mapped the most important areas in the basin for biodiversity, identified the most pressing socioeconomic issues, planned developments in the basin, and overlaid this information to prioritize conservation actions. Areas of biological importance were selected based on biodiversity data for fish, birds, and other vertebrates. Additionally, subbasins within the basin were evaluated for their ability to contribute to maintaining ecological and hydrological processes. About forty biologists, ecologists, and hydrologists from seven countries in the Niger River basin selected nineteen priority areas for the long-term conservation of freshwater biodiversity (figure 16.1).

—*Aboubacar Awaiss*

Guinean-Congolian Forest and Freshwater Region. The Guinean-Congolian Region, including twenty-two freshwater ecoregions, harbors some of the world's greatest tropical forests and rivers. Its enormous surface area and its high diversity of habitats, as well as climatic and environmental stability over a long period, have facilitated the evolution of a highly diverse freshwater fauna.

Although biological data and knowledge are incomplete for these forests and rivers, the rapidly changing political situation and emerging conservation opportunities demand the development of strategies based on the best available data. In March 2000, WWF convened a workshop to determine biological priorities in the Guinean-Congolian Forest and Freshwater Region (Kamdem Toham et al. 2003). The freshwater group focused on the hydrographic Congo Basin (excluding Lake Tanganyika [55] but including the Bangweulu-Mweru [6] ecoregion) and included the freshwater ecoregions of the West Coastal Equatorial bioregion [ecoregions 19, 26, and 29] and the Western Equatorial Crater Lakes [5] and Niger Delta [58] freshwater ecoregions.

The experts at the workshop produced the following vision statement for the freshwater systems of the region:

> Our vision for the Guinean-Congolian Freshwater Region is to conserve, to the fullest possible extent, its globally outstanding richness, diversity, and uniqueness in terms of the habitats, fishes, and other aquatic taxa. There must be clear and achievable conservation goals and programs must be properly planned, knowledge-based, and incorporate sound science—including fundamental data on species identity, distributions, and life cycles. Specially designed aquatic reserves, the protection of headwaters, and the minimization of the impacts of commercial aquaculture and damming are required. These aquatic conservation goals should be fully integrated into terrestrial conservation programs and vice versa. Conservation planning must be sensitive to the sustainable requirements of various stakeholders, such as fishing peoples and the agricultural community. Sound education, awareness, and training programs, and a regional network for the study and interpretation of aquatic biodiversity, will be crucial in securing the vision. The essentially unspoiled nature and vast scale of this aquatic ecosystem make it a singularly compelling conservation challenge. (Kamdem Toham et al. 2003: 42)

Freshwater experts first identified regions for which insufficient data were available to evaluate biodiversity importance and then identified areas of biodiversity priority within known portions of the region of analysis (figure 16.2). Experts identified known priorities to be the Ivindo River, the Kouilou-Niari, the Cuvette Centrale, Maï Ndombe, the middle Congo River mainstem, rapids upstream from Kisangani, Thysville Caves, Upemba, Kalengwe Rapids, Lac Fwa, and several areas in the larger Cameroonian highlands and Niger Delta regions. The experts expect further studies to reveal other biological and conservation priorities. Because data gaps largely overlap with areas of insecurity and conflict, many of the priority research areas are located in regions where conservation action is unfeasible. In addition to the areas shown in figure 16.2, head-water regions were also considered of priority because of their role in sustaining the flow regime.

After the workshop, the biological vision for the Guinean-Congolian terrestrial systems was adopted by country signatories of the Yaoundé Declaration as the blueprint for conservation in the region. Other initiatives are also adopting the results of the vision as a foundation for large-scale conservation projects. The Brazzaville Priority Action Plan outlines targets for the period 2002–2005 and focuses implementation on transborder forest areas identified within the biodiversity vision. Gabon has recently established a network of thirteen national parks based on the vision and on IUCN critical sites. Cameroon has refined its network of protected areas based on the vision, and the Central African Republic, Republic of the Congo, and Democratic Republic of the Congo will undergo the same process in the coming years. Although these efforts are largely terrestrial in focus, some work has also begun in freshwater priority areas, especially in those that overlap with terrestrial priority areas.

(Continued)

180

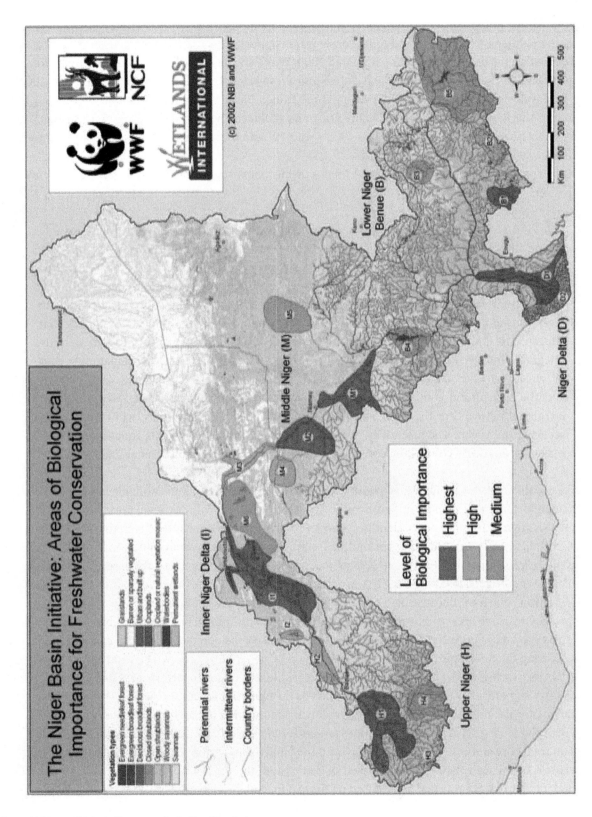

Figure 16.1 Areas of biological importance in the Niger River Basin.

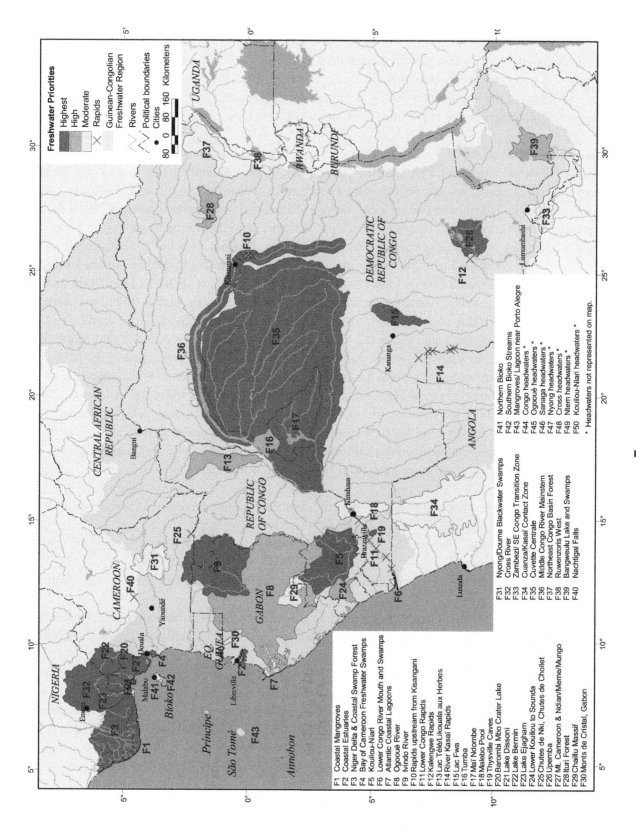

Figure 16.2 Freshwater priority areas in the Guinean-Congolian freshwater region.

Freshwater Priorities
- Highest
- High
- Moderate
- ✕ Rapids
- Guinean-Congolian Freshwater Region
- Rivers
- Political boundaries
- • Cities

80 0   80 160 Kilometers

F1 Coastal Mangroves
F2 Coastal Estuaries
F3 Niger Delta & Coastal Swamp Forest
F4 Bay of Cameroon Freshwater Swamps
F5 Kouilou-Niari
F6 Lower Congo River Mouth and Swamps
F7 Atlantic Coastal Lagoons
F8 Ogooué River
F9 Ivindo River
F10 Rapids upstream from Kisangani
F11 Lower Congo Rapids
F12 Kalengwe Rapids
F13 Lac Télé/Likouala aux Herbes
F14 River Kasai Rapids
F15 Lac Fwa
F16 Tumba
F17 Maï Ndombe
F18 Malebo Pool
F19 Thysville Caves
F20 Barombi Mbo Crater Lake
F21 Lake Dissoni
F22 Lake Bermin
F23 Lake Ejagham
F24 Lower Kouilou to Sounda
F25 Chutes de Nki, Chutes de Chollet
F26 Upemba
F27 Mt. Cameroon & Ndian/Meme/Mungo
F28 Ituri Forest
F29 Chaillu Massif
F30 Monts de Cristal, Gabon

F31 Nyong/Doume Blackwater Swamps
F32 Cross River
F33 Cuanza/SE Congo Transition Zone
F34 Cuvette Centrale
F35 Middle Congo River Mainstem
F36 Northeast Congo Basin Forest
F37 Ruwenzoris West
F38 Bangweulu Lake and Swamps
F39 Nachtigal Falls
F40

F41 Northern Bioko
F42 Southern Bioko Streams
F43 Mangroves/ Lagoon near Porto Alegre
F44 Congo headwaters *
F45 Ogooué headwaters *
F46 Sanaga headwaters *
F47 Nyong headwaters *
F48 Cross headwaters *
F49 Ntem headwaters *
F50 Kouilou-Niari headwaters *

* Headwaters not represented on map.

181

Box 16.1. (continued)

To our knowledge, the endorsement by governments of the biological vision and the multinational effort to establish and implement a region-wide conservation plan provides the first operational model in tropical Africa of the benefits of working to implement conservation at the ecoregional scale, and we encourage the further integration of the freshwater vision into these plans.

—Andre Kamdem Toham

Lake Malawi. Lake Malawi boasts one of the richest lake fish faunas in the world, hosting several species flocks of endemic cichlids and an endemic clariid flock (Lowe-McConnell 1987). The Lake Malawi/ Niassa/Nyasa ecoregion encompasses the lake basin and Lake Malombe to the south. The lake and its basin cover about 130,000 km^2 and include much of Malawi, the southwestern corner of Tanzania, and the northwestern corner of Mozambique. Each of the three riparian states manages its own portion of the lake according to national policies and strategies. At a workshop in October 2001, experts from the three bordering countries identified twenty priority conservation areas (figure 16.3) in the lake basin using overlays of geospatial data on biodiversity and threats (Chafota et al. 2002). In addition to areas in the lake itself, the experts identified seven river catchments (the Songwe, Lufirio, Ruhuhu, Dwangwa, Bua, Kaombe, and Linthipe basins) as priority areas for conservation activities, in recognition of the need to lessen impacts from land use in the basin. Workshop participants concluded that runoff from agricultural practices in southern Malawi and parts of Tanzania is the largest threat to the freshwater biodiversity of the ecoregion. In terms of fisheries, the most exploited section of the lake is at the southern and shallower end, where a combination of fishing pressure, eutrophication, and fish translocations is causing concern about the status of fish populations. Workshop participants identified conservation opportunities along the shores of Mozambique and Tanzania where human population levels are low and where large areas of undisturbed coastal habitats and less exploited aquatic habitats still occur.

The most important conservation targets for the lake were identified as follows:

- Reduce eutrophication of the lake's waters to levels that will not decrease biodiversity and fishery productivity.
- Maintain stocks of river-breeding fish species above levels that could decrease biodiversity and fishery productivity.
- Maintain populations of cichlid fish species above levels that could decrease biodiversity and fishery productivity.
- Establish and maintain institutional mechanisms that facilitate collaboration and cooperation between stakeholders who affect the use and management of lake-based resources and habitats.

Experts from the region suggested the establishment of a trilateral mechanism for coordinating basin management activities. Since the workshop, Malawi, Mozambique, and Tan-zania have announced a partnership with WWF, the Ramsar Secretariat, and the Swiss Agency for the Environment to work on joint conservation of the lake on a transboundary basis. The three countries will be supported in designating their respective parts of the lake as Ramsar sites. With assistance from the Danish Development and Aid Agency, Tan-zania has already begun designation of its portion of the lake as a Ramsar site.

A significant investment of time and resources will be needed to achieve the recommendations outlined here. This vision is larger than what any one organization could achieve alone. Therefore, partnerships with relevant government, nonprofit, and business organizations will be crucial.

—Jonas Chafota

182

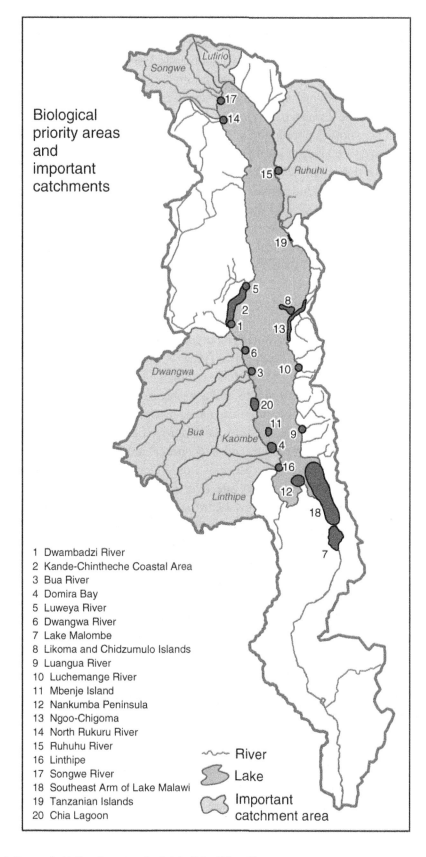

Biological
priority areas
and
important
catchments

1 Dwambadzi River
2 Kande-Chintheche Coastal Area
3 Bua River
4 Domira Bay
5 Luweya River
6 Dwangwa River
7 Lake Malombe
8 Likoma and Chidzumulo Islands
9 Luangua River
10 Luchemange River
11 Mbenje Island
12 Nankumba Peninsula
13 Ngoo-Chigoma
14 North Rukuru River
15 Ruhuhu River
16 Linthipe
17 Songwe River
18 Southeast Arm of Lake Malawi
19 Tanzanian Islands
20 Chia Lagoon

~~~ River

Lake

Important
catchment area

Figure 16.3 Final priority areas for biodiversity conservation in Lake Malawi/Niassa/Nyasa.

183

Box 16.2. Big Water: The Challenge of Conserving Biodiversity in Africa's Large Rivers and Lakes.

The complexities of conserving biodiversity in the ever-moving environment of freshwater are detailed elsewhere in this volume. Those complexities are compounded by the huge size of some African river and lake basins and the challenges of managing large freshwater systems within a patchwork of jurisdictions and interests. Consider the Zambezi. This junior partner in the fraternity of great African rivers drains eight countries and supports a population of 65 million people (Zambezi River Authority 2003). Within each country is a dizzying array of local governments and pastoral, agricultural, urban, and industrial interests that vie for their share of the freshwater resource, and their activities, such as logging, irrigation, and diversion, have profound impacts. This situation exists on almost all of Africa's great rivers and lakes. The solution lies in sewing the patchwork together into an integrated management framework within which governments can work together, stakeholders can be adequately represented, and decisions can be made at a basin-wide scale. Concerns about biodiversity and ecological integrity should underpin such a framework. This is the central tenet of integrated river basin management (IRBM).

IRBM is defined as a "process of coordinating conservation, management, and development of water, land, and related resources across sectors within a given river [or lake] basin, in order to maximize the economic and social benefits derived from water resources in an equitable manner while preserving and, where necessary, restoring freshwater ecosystems" (Jones et al. 2003: 2). Recognizing a central challenge of managing the freshwater resource—the fact that it moves—IRBM provides a tool for developing management solutions from headwaters to mouth and a strategic framework for action at basin-wide or smaller scales. Within an IRBM planning initiative, managers can bring the whole array of conservation tools to bear: protected areas, ecological restoration, improved forestry and agricultural practices, innovations in dam operations and ship design, and new energy and sanitation technologies. On the scale of a large African river, none of these interventions would be effective in isolation, but as parts of an integrated strategy, they could be tremendously effective.

This is easier said than done. In fact, very few IRBM schemes are in place and in full operation around the world. IRBM is a new idea, and it is an immensely complicated undertaking. The basins that are closest to full implementation—the Danube, the Everglades, and the Murray Darling—still have a long way to go before they are functioning optimally. However, planning and implementation are ongoing in dozens of river and lake basins, and governments are building the international frameworks necessary for IRBM on transboundary rivers and lakes (Gilman et al. 2004).

In Africa, this approach is being pursued on the largest scale imaginable: the River Nile. The Nile Basin Initiative (NBI) is a joint effort by ten of the eleven Nile basin countries to facilitate the common pursuit of sustainable development and management of Nile waters. The NBI, supported in large part by the World Bank, United Nations Development Programme, and Canadian International Development Agency, is developing a basin-wide strategic action program with projects to address energy, agriculture, water resource planning, stakeholder involvement, and the environment. All these projects are intended to be mutually supporting, creating basin-wide engagement, capacity, common strategic and analytical frameworks, and demonstration projects. The Nile Transboundary Environmental Action Project will support basin-wide action to address transboundary environmental issues including pollution, forest management, wetland conservation, and protected area establishment and management. Projects at the community level that fit within the overall strategy are also an important piece of the program (Nile Basin Initiative 2003).

Transboundary programs such as these are at some stage of development on many of Africa's rivers and lakes, through groups such as the Niger Basin Authority, the Organization for the Development of the Senegal River, the Lake Chad Basin Commission, and the Zambezi River Authority (Jones et al. 2003). Many such authorities are more talk and paper than action at present, but that is changing rapidly as planning advances and international donors take greater interest. Results are starting to appear.

A good example can be found in Zambia on the Kafue River, a major tributary and subbasin of the Zambezi where WWF has been working with local conservation partners since 1998. The floodplain of the river, known as the Kafue Flats, is home to zebra, buffalo, cheetah, wild dog, and an endemic ungulate, the Kafue lechwe or marsh antelope (*Kobus leche kafuensis*). The floodplain and wetlands are an important stopover point for migratory birds. More than 450 species of birds occur there, including the vulnerable wattled crane (*Bugeranus carunculatus*).

The construction of two large dams at either end of the Kafue Flats disrupted the natural hydrology of the floodplain, resulting in serious habitat loss and precipitous declines of many plant and animal species. For example, the Kafue lechwe population has fallen more than 50 percent in recent years. In addition, local communities blame the decline in fish yields and forage in riparian grazing areas on flow alterations produced by the dams.

The dams have important beneficiaries, however, including the sugar industry on the flats, which produces most of Zambia's crop for domestic consumption and export, and the private companies and government ministries concerned with energy production. The power station at the Kafue Gorge dam produces more than half of Zambia's electricity and a large amount that is sold to neighboring Zimbabwe and South Africa.

An integrated river basin management approach in the subbasin, bringing the key stakeholders of the flats together, has yielded a plan that addresses the needs of all major stakeholders and could restore the declining biodiversity of the flats. The sugar industry, the Zambian Electrical Supply Company, and the Ministry of Energy and Water Development have agreed to a set of protocols to change the operations of the dams to more closely mimic natural flows through the flats and plan to begin testing them in 2004. In addition, the sugar growers are exploring the use of biofilters such as wetlands and reedbeds to pretreat effluent from their farms. Local communities are participating in awareness-raising activities and exploring ecotourism opportunities. To date, through a partnership approach, WWF has also formally established the Mwanachingwala Conservation Area, through a combination of donations of private (mainly from the sugar growers) and traditional lands. The reintroduction of a select number of species into the conservation area is due to commence soon, and 500 km^2 of the flats are to be restored in the newly created conservation area (Jones et al. 2003). In terms of ecotourism, the Blue Lagoon National Park has reopened for visitation after receiving support for development of its infrastructure.

The benefits to freshwater biodiversity from such integrated management approaches could be enormous. Successfully implemented plans that address the hydrology, water quality, and connectivity of river systems from headwaters to estuary would be a boon for freshwater ecosystems, even if biodiversity conservation were not the stated goal of such an effort. Indeed, integrated strategies that benefit both human populations and biodiversity are the gold standard of conservation action and are entirely possible in the context of freshwater. This is particularly true in Africa and other parts of the developing world, where many freshwater ecosystems remain intact compared with those in much of the developed world (Richter et al. 2003).

(Continued)

Box 16.2. (continued)

The definition of IRBM mentioned earlier is not universally accepted, and the term often is used interchangeably with others such as "integrated water resource management," "watershed management," and "catchment management." Whatever the label, it is unfortunate that many such planning efforts lack emphasis on functioning ecosystems as the source of freshwater and a prerequisite to successful basin management. The challenge for scientists and conservationists is to ensure that these strategies are informed by sound conservation biology and that stakeholders, governments, and river basin managers are committed to preserving the ecological integrity of the freshwater resources on which we all depend. Only then can the potential of IRBM as a tool for biodiversity conservation be fully realized and the animals and plants of Africa's big water conserved.

—Christopher E. Williams

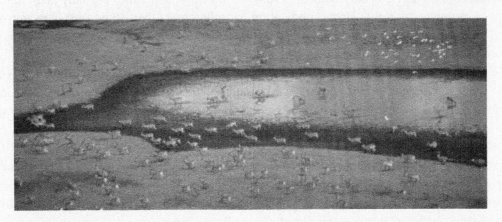

Kafue lechwe (*Kobus leche kafuensis*) with cattle egrets (*Bubulcus ibis*), Kafue Flats, Southern Province, Zambia. Photo credit: ©WWF-Cannon/Sarah Black.

entire basin. It is at this point that basin-wide and biogeographic conservation planning approaches merge.

VISIONARY WORK IN FRESHWATER ECOREGIONS AND RIVER BASINS

Ecoregion planning and the creation of a biodiversity vision provide an overview of the actions necessary at local, national, and international scales for biodiversity conservation in an ecoregion or river basin. Looking first at an ecoregion or river basin in its entirety allows us to understand what tradeoffs are associated with different land use

and development decisions and how projects can and should relate to each other. Actions that may be ongoing or nascent gain a new importance and synergy as they are implemented within a more coherent framework (Abell et al. 2002).

When undertaking ecoregion planning, we ask ourselves whether our vision for the future is ambitious enough to conserve an ecoregion's distinct biodiversity features over the long term. Creating and acting on a vision for the conservation of an ecoregion's biodiversity can be a powerful exercise. Within a year of completion, the freshwater visions outlined in box 16.1 assisted in catalyzing the formation of a transboundary management commission, the creation of new protected areas, and agreements for implementing international conventions and management recommendations. Numerous types of mechanisms, at the landscape or site scale and above, exist for implementing biodiversity visions, including community-based fishery or wetland management, Ramsar site designation and management, and the activities of river basin authorities (see essays 16.1, 16.2, and 16.3). Policies related to landscape development are critical components of freshwater conservation because of the highly interconnected nature of freshwater systems with upstream, upland, downstream, and groundwater areas. Effective implementation of a vision will incorporate many of these mechanisms, among others (box 16.2).

Working at a large scale has its challenges, including the need for long-term commitments and sustained financial resources. The realities of financial support, governance, poverty, political stability, peace, and human capacity are critical factors that can prevent or foster successful implementation. Recent priority-setting exercises have attempted to integrate socioeconomic factors into determining where conservation success might best be achieved (Balmford et al. 2002; O'Connor et al. 2003; Smith et al. 2003). Rivers and lakes also often cross national boundaries, necessitating international agreements and cooperation for their management; political obstacles to transboundary work can often seem insurmountable (van der Linde et al. 2001). Yet the conservation achievements produced by first planning at a large scale and then implementing at finer scales have the potential to be far more substantial than those produced by small projects conceived separately from one another (Abell et al. 2002; Groves 2003).

CHALLENGES TO FRESHWATER CONSERVATION AND SUSTAINABLE DEVELOPMENT IN AFRICA AND MADAGASCAR

In box 16.1 we provide examples of visioning exercises undertaken in several of the freshwater ecoregions of the Afro-Malagasy region. In this section we outline what we see as the greatest challenges to achieving sustainable use and conservation of the region's freshwater systems.

Political Instability and Civil Unrest

Across parts of Africa, civil unrest is a daily reality, affecting the lives of millions of Africans. Shambaugh et al. (2001) recommend that basic support for conservation continue through times of war and civil unrest because past experience has shown that this provides a solid foundation for postconflict conservation efforts. However, environmental degradation often occurs during times of civil unrest and war (Hart and Mwinyihali 2001; Blom and Yamindou 2001). In terms of freshwater systems, pollution of lakes and rivers, hunting of aquatic mammals, and exploitation of fish stocks are wartime activities that appear to have the most severe impact (e.g., see ecoregion descriptions for Northern Upper Guinea [25], Upper Nile [15], Cuvette Centrale [18], and Kasai [21]). Human populations rely more heavily on bush-meat and fisheries as protein sources are limited by decreased agricultural production and the suspension of trade. For example, in the Democratic Republic of the Congo (DRC) and Sudan, populations of large terrestrial and aquatic vertebrates have been affected by bushmeat hunting during the long years of civil conflict (Bakarr et al. 2001; Morjan et al. 2001). Movements and large settlements of refugees also cause land degradation, which in turn degrades freshwater systems. The relative effect of conflict on freshwater and terrestrial biodiversity in the region should be evaluated as studies resume in areas that have suffered from long-term unrest (e.g., Sudan, Angola, DRC).

Environmental Governance

In nations at war or at peace, environmental governance is critically important. Mugabe and Tumushabe (1999: 15) define *environmental governance* as "a body of values and norms that guide or regulate state-civil society relationships in the use, control, and management of the natural environment ... providing a conceptual framework within which public and private behavior is regulated in support of sound ecological stewardship." The need for effective policies, laws, and regulations that support conservation and sustainable use of freshwater systems is critical (essay 16.4). In many parts of Africa, laws are weak or mechanisms for enforcing them are not operational. Junk (2002) identifies policy deficiencies, deficient planning concepts, limited information and awareness, and institutional weakness as the main administrative limitations for sustainable wetland management in the tropics.

In the last several decades many tropical countries have experienced a resurgence of community-based management of natural resources that often integrates new governance structures with traditional management practices (see essays 16.2 and 16.5). These community-based initiatives are particularly relevant to the successful management of wetlands in Africa because of the high dependence of local communities on wetland resources for livelihoods and food security. An extensive review of these projects is beyond the scope of this book; we refer readers to a few texts with examples (e.g., IUCN 1995–2003; Acreman and Hollis 1996; Palfreman 2001; Gawler 2002).

188

Resource Extraction in Natural Resource-Based Economies (Logging, Mining, Agriculture, Oil)

In addition to pollution from municipal and industrial sewage, many freshwater systems receive sediments and associated chemicals from agricultural, mining, or forestry operations. About 85 percent of Africa's total water withdrawals are estimated to be directed toward agriculture (FAO 1995), and as of the year 2000, about one-third of its surface area was estimated to be under agricultural land use (FAO 2001a). Although the total land area of Africa under irrigation is small and rarely exceeds 1 percent of an individual basin's total area, it can represent a large proportion of the cultivated land in basins in the semi-arid and arid regions of Africa. As a percentage of total internal renewable water resources, water withdrawals vary widely from one region to another. For example, agricultural irrigation consumes only about 0.01 percent of runoff in the Congo Basin, but 20 percent of runoff in the Limpopo and 70 percent in the Nile are used in irrigation (FAO

2001a). In North Africa, about 95 percent of renewable water resources are withdrawn (Shiklomanov 1999 in Junk 2002). Some of the wetlands that have been degraded by large-scale irrigation schemes include the Nile Delta and floodplains along the lower Nile River, the Logone floodplain and the floodplain of the Benue River, the Hadejia-Nguru wetlands, the Phongolo floodplain, and the Senegal Delta (Junk 2002). By 2025, total water abstraction in Africa is expected to rise by 54 percent to 337 km^3/year, with agricultural use accounting for 53 percent of this amount (IUCN 2000).

Forestry operations can cause erosion and contribute sediments to freshwater systems, sometimes causing significant disturbance. Mining is similar to forestry in that it often causes pulses of sediment input, with the addition of heavy metals. Local populations may contribute significantly to loss of tree cover through cutting for building materials, firewood, or charcoal. Loss of forest cover can significantly affect the hydrology of an area, leading to changes in annual, dry season, and peak flows and significantly altering bio-geochemical processes and in-stream habitat.

Land Use Change and Habitat Loss

Africa still contains large areas of natural or near-natural vegetation and stream flow. Current economic patterns indicate that most of the next generation of Africans will continue to live subsistence lifestyles, farming for food and deriving their fuel-wood, protein, medicines, and building materials from natural resources. Given that future estimates show the population of Africa tripling between 1995 and 2050 (increasing from 0.7 billion people in 1995 to 2.0 billion in 2050) (United Nations Population Division 2001), Africa is predicted to undergo tremendous agricultural expansion. At a global level, an additional 30 percent of the remaining forests and natural woodlands are set to disappear in the next 50 years (Tilman et al. 2001), and much of this will occur in Africa. Rising water demand, a growing risk of pollution and physical destruction of habitats, and general changes in land use practices and traditions, eventually culminating in large-scale vegetation loss or desertification, are likely consequences. These changes obviously have enormous implications for the integrity of freshwater systems and their biotas.

Invasive Species

About fifty fish species have been introduced into or translo-cated within the inland waters of Africa, twenty-three of which are from outside Africa (Welcomme 1988). The well-known case of the introductions of Nile perch (*Lates niloticus*), four tilapiines, and water hyacinth (*Eichhornia crassipes*) into Lake Victoria and the subsequent decline and loss of populations of many fish taxa is a stark example of how species introductions, in tandem with other environmental changes, can negatively affect a system's ecology (Ogutu-Ohwayo 1990; Seehausen et al. 1997a). We suggest that many well-intentioned aquaculture projects may also be introducing invasive species into continental African waters. For example, the widespread translocation and introduction of tilapias (*Oreochromis* and *Tilapia* spp.) throughout the continent and into Madagascar have been associated with the decline of native species in several systems (e.g., lakes Victoria, Itasy, and Alaotra) (Reinthal and Stiassny 1991; Lévêque 1997). Although these projects may be productive in the short term, they may lead to longer-term ecological problems that will affect native freshwater species and human communities that rely on functioning systems.

Introduced aquatic plants, such as water hyacinth (*Eichhornia crassipes*) and giant salvinia (*Salvinia molesta*), are problems in many river and lake systems, resulting in mounting economic, social, and ecological costs (see essay 4.1). For example, in South Africa, about 150 species of more than 8,000 introduced plants are considered invasive (Department of Water Affairs and Forestry 2003). In the dry south, alien species generally consume more water than indigenous vegetation, in addition to threatening biodiversity and constituting a significant fire hazard (Davies and Day 1998; Dye et al. 2001; Binns et al. 2001). The Working for Water Programme provides an innovative approach to combating these problems. The program aims to increase water supply in select catchments by removal of invasive plants, with the work undertaken by trained people from the most marginalized sectors of South African society (Binns et al. 2001; Department of Water Affairs and Forestry 2003).

Water Management: Dams and Interbasin Water Transfers

The many and varied water management schemes that exist across the Afro-Malagasy region have a wide range of effects on freshwater ecosystems. The World Commission on Dams outlines many of the negative effects that large dams (more than 15m high) have had on aquatic systems and biodiversity, floodplain ecosystems, and fisheries in Africa. Recent studies also indicate that reservoirs may make a significant contribution to global greenhouse gas emissions (St. Louis et al. 2000). According to FAO data, current dams are concentrated in South Africa, Zimbabwe, Burkina Faso, and Nigeria (see figure 4.2). Three of the four largest rivers, the Nile, Niger, and the Zambezi, have all been significantly affected by the construction of large dams along their course. The two dams with the largest capacities, Aswan High Dam (about 180 billion m^3) and Kariba Dam (about 160 billion m^3), are sited along the Nile and Zambezi Rivers, respectively. Both of these dams have changed downstream ecology, largely through loss of seasonal high and low flows and sediments trapped behind the dam wall. In the delta flood plain of the Zambezi River, lowered shrimp catches, declines in the productivity of artisanal fisheries, floodplains invaded by upland vegetation, dying mangroves, and decreased wildlife populations are some of the results of the altered hydrology (Soils Incorporated [Pty] Ltd. and Chalo Environmental and Sustainable Development Consultants 2000). The Nile Delta is subsiding and eroding because of the lack of sediment input, and seawater intrusion threatens to increase salinity of the coastal lakes and rivers (Stanley and Warne 1998; Baha El Din 1999). Additionally, diminished nutrient levels in the flow of the Nile to the Mediterranean are considered

189

largely responsible for the declines in sardine (*Sardinella aurita* and *Sardinella maderensis*) landings (96 percent and 36 percent, respectively) since the closure of Aswan Dam (Lévêque 1997). The biggest river in Africa, the Congo, is largely undammed; however, the government of the DRC recently announced plans to move forward quickly with development of the Grand Inga plant, which, unlike the current Inga Dam, would extend across the entire river (Société Nationale d'Electricité (SNEL), République Démocratique de Congo 2003).

Davies et al. (2000b) outline the implications of inter-basin water transfers for river conservation. In addition to changing flows within basins, water transfers break down biogeographic barriers and introduce species across basins. For example, as a result of the Orange–Sundays–Great Fish River water transfer, several fish species have been introduced to the Great Fish River, despite devices installed to prevent their transfer (Skelton 1980; Laurenson and Hocutt 1984; Davies et al. 2000b). Large-scale interbasin transfers that are currently under negotiation or construction include the Lesotho Highlands Water Project (LHWP) and the Eastern National Water Carrier project in Namibia.

The Lesotho Highlands Water Project is the largest interbasin transfer in Africa and will transfer 2.2 billion m3 of water per year from the headwaters of the Orange River to the tributaries of the Vaal River in South Africa (Snaddon et al. 1998; Lesotho Highlands Water Project 2002). Many questions remain about the long-term environmental effects of this controversial project, despite numerous environmental studies and mitigation projects; altered flow regimes, water quality changes, introductions of alien species to both donor and recipient rivers, and declines in the critically endangered Maloti minnow (*Pseudobarbus quathlambae*) are among the many expected impacts (Davies and Day 1998).

Namibia is negotiating the extraction of an estimated 20 million m³ of water annually from the Okavango River via the Eastern National Water Carrier. Although this is less than 10 percent of the river's annual flow, it would be a significant amount during the dry season and could deleteriously affect functioning of the delta ecosystem, transfer species from the Okavango to more southerly drainages, and affect groundwater levels in the region (Davies and Day 1998).

Among several proposed future projects, there have been recent discussions of transferring water from the Oubangui Basin to the Lake Chad Basin. Such an action could introduce Congolian freshwater species into the Nilo-Sudanian bioregion and vice versa, with likely negative consequences for one or both native faunas.

Inland Fisheries and Overexploitation

According to a recent FAO study, the single most important issue for the future of inland fisheries is not increasing fishing pressure but the degradation of the environment and subsequent loss of freshwater habitats (FAO Inland Water Resources and Aquaculture Service, Fishery Resources Division 1999). Indeed, habitat loss is of highest concern. However, overexploitation of certain fisheries has been documented in select waterbodies of Africa and Madagascar, and sustainable fishery management will be increasingly important for the long-term viability of freshwater fish populations. Inland fish capture in Africa increased by an average of about 37,000 tons per year, or 2 percent, between 1984 and 1997, making Africa second only to the Asia-Pacific region in total catch of inland fisheries (FAO Inland Water Resources and Aquaculture Service, Fishery Resources Division 1999). Four of the top ten countries (Uganda, Tanzania, Egypt, and Kenya) for inland capture fishery production occur in Africa (FAO Fisheries Department 2002). Lévêque (1997) distinguishes between impacts on individual species, primarily large-bodied species of low reproductive capacity, and impacts on fish communities from heavy exploitation (Durand 1980; Daget et al. 1988; Coulter 1991; Witte et al. 1992; Kolding 1992; Turner 1994). Both types of effects have been documented in the Afro-Malagasy region, and Welcomme (see essay 4.2) considers many of the region's fisheries to have been fished at levels where damage to the assemblages has already occurred.

The region's fisheries are also of vital importance to human communities, providing livelihoods and a source of protein (see essay 1.1 and essay 6.4). On average, Africans get more than 20 percent of their animal protein from fish, and populations in several countries in the region get more than 50 percent of their animal protein from fish (FAO 2003). For example, in Ghana the fishery sector supports the livelihoods of 1.5 million people, and fish is the most important source of animal protein, supplying 60 percent of the daily intake of the average Ghanaian (Aggrey-Fynn 2001; Directorate of Fisheries–Ghana 2003).

Climate Change

Future climate changes are expected to severely affect the hydrological cycle of freshwater systems in many parts of Africa (see essay 4.3). Despite the inherent uncertainties in model calculations, some general trends indicate decreases in the available water resources for the Mediterranean coast of North Africa and particularly for large parts of southwestern Africa. Increasing tendencies are projected for West Africa south of the Sahara (including the Niger basin) and for parts of southeastern Africa and western Madagascar. Many other areas, such as the Congo Basin, show different trends depending on the applied climate change models and scenario assumptions. In addition to expected changes in long-term trends, increases in the seasonal variability of regional climate patterns are projected. These climatic changes may cause significant shifts in the magnitude, timing, and duration of river flows. As a consequence, not only alterations in long-term average flows or reductions in water resources are expected but also increasing intensities and frequencies of extreme events such as floods and droughts (IPCC 2001; Hulme et al. 2001; Desanker 2002). Although climate change is a global problem, the particular vulnerability of Africa has been highlighted by various authors and is largely attributed to the limited adaptive capacities of African countries to cope with the effects of climate change (IPCC 2001).

Data Gaps and Research Needs

Significant gaps in our knowledge of the Afro-Malagasy region's freshwater ecosystems remain, including a lack of basic species inventories for many areas, accurate taxonomic classifications and naming of many organisms, and a fundamental knowledge of ecosystem functioning in many parts of the Afrotropics. Also of critical importance to the sustainable management of freshwater systems are hydro-logic data. Unfortunately, the collection of this essential information is declining in the region. The number of monitoring stations for water flow and water quality in Africa declined by 90 percent between 1990 and 2000 (Vörösmarty et al. 2001). Obviously, these knowledge gaps are a significant hindrance to freshwater conservation activities across the region. Denny (2001) outlines a two-pronged approach to address some of the outstanding questions. He suggests that inventories, assessment, and monitoring of freshwater systems are of immediate urgency, and research into processes, structure, and functioning of the systems will be important in the long term. The generation and application of both biological and hydrological data ultimately will depend on the availability of an active network of freshwater scientists across the Afro-Malagasy region. The Environment Plan of the New Partnership for Africa's Development provides a recent opportunity for addressing many of the gaps and research needs. Under "Programme Area 2: Conserving Africa's Wetlands," it includes plans for the development of national wetland policies, the development of subregional networks of wetland scientists, long-term inventory and monitoring of Africa's wetlands, wetland restoration, and capacity building, along with subregional targets for meeting each of the goals (NEPAD 2003). One example of a recent regional initiative to build research capacity is the creation of the Centre for African Wetlands in West Africa (CAW 2003). As many others have suggested previously, the continued expansion and strengthening of a wetland network to achieve these goals in the global south should receive significant financial and technical investment from the north and information and experience exchange with other

191

parts of the global south (Wishart and Davies 1998; Denny 2001; Tiéga 2001; Junk 2002; NEPAD 2003).

Despite the many challenges outlined in this chapter, there are several points of hope for the future of the freshwater systems in Africa and Madagascar. Compared with wetlands in much of the north and in some other parts of the tropics, the wet tropics of Central Africa and other areas with low population densities retain areas with functioning freshwater systems. In these areas, there is an opportunity to limit or prevent the widespread degradation that has occurred in much of the north. The action plan of the Environment Initiative of NEPAD, recently endorsed by the African Ministerial Conference on the Environment, provides a new framework for wetland conservation in Africa with its detailed goals and targets (AMCEN 2002). The continued and active expansion of the Ramsar network in Africa is also a positive development, with thirty-eight countries now contracting parties to the Ramsar Convention and 130 sites designated as of March 2004 (Wetlands International 2004). The recently revised and enacted progressive

water law in South Africa also warrants mention; this piece of legislation is based on the principles of sustainability of use and equity of distribution. By explicitly recognizing the intrinsic value of freshwater systems, this new law marks a shift in public consciousness, recognizing the need to maintain healthy ecosystems to sustainably provide freshwater to human and aquatic communities over the long term (essay 16.6; Palmer 1999; Palmer et al. 2002). The value of the ecosystem services that freshwater systems provide is remarkable, and sustainable use is essential to maintaining the healthy systems that will continue to provide these services (Postel and Carpenter 1997; Costanza et al. 1997; essay 1.2). As nations across the region continue to grow and develop, it is our hope that they will follow a path that maintains these natural values, in the best of Afro-Malagasy traditions. The world will be greatly diminished if we fail to recognize the importance of the Afro-Malagasy region's freshwater habitats, species, and biological processes before it is too late.

Essay 16.1

The Convention on Wetlands (Ramsar): An International Treaty Sparks Freshwater Conservation

Aboubacar Awaiss and Denis Landenbergue

Freshwater ecosystems have increasingly become a focus of conservation attention in recent years, and this has been greatly assisted by the Ramsar Convention. Also known as the Convention on Wetlands (Ramsar, Iran, 1971), this intergovernment treaty had a total of 138 contracting parties as of December 31, 2003, of which 38 were from Africa (out of a total of 53 countries). Several additional African countries have been progressing toward becoming parties to the convention, some of them with support from WWF's Living Waters Programme.

The vision of the convention, as adopted by the Conference of Contracting Parties during its seventh session (May 1999), is "to develop and maintain a network of wetlands that are of international importance due to their ecological and hydrological functions, for the conservation of worldwide biological diversity and the endurance of human life" (Ramsar 1999).

In Africa, the seemingly inherent conflict between human livelihoods and wetland conservation presents a challenge to the successful implementation of the Convention on Wetlands mission. It is imperative to devise incentives for wetland conservation that maintain the standard of living of human populations in addition to the ecological functioning of the wetland (Tiéga 1998). Often, this mission is hampered by a lack of government guidelines and country policies and programs that acknowledge the importance of wetland biodiversity conservation.

Local fisher with fish traps in the flooded savanna on the northern side of Lake Chad on the edge of the Sahara Desert, Chad.
Photo credit: ©WWF-Canon/Jens-Uwe Heins

One of the pillars of the convention is the "List of Wetlands of International Importance." As of December 31, 2003, a total of 1,328 Wetlands of International Importance (or Ramsar sites) had been registered by contracting parties, covering 111,900,000 ha worldwide. Out of this, Africa had designated 29,300,000 ha in 131 Ramsar sites.

Although the total area of wetlands designated in the Africa-Madagascar region represents a valuable contribution, there is still much more to achieve, especially in terms of conservation of existing sites and representation of wetland types in new sites. WWF's Living Waters Programme has set an objective of designating at least 250 million ha of new freshwater protected areas worldwide by 2010. This objective was endorsed as a Ramsar Convention target by the 8th Conference of the Parties held in November 2002 in Valencia, Spain.

Freshwater Ecosystems in Africa: Conserving Their Biological Diversity and Maintaining Their Crucial Role in Livelihoods

An increasing number of Ramsar contracting parties have adopted policies to limit wetland degradation and loss and to foster sustainable management. As of the Ramsar Convention in November 2002, ten African countries had established national wetlands policies, and another eight had taken initial steps toward doing so.

In Africa, wetlands also are crucial contributors to economic and sociocultural activities, and Africans generally have an acute awareness of the importance of access to fresh water (Awaiss and Saadou 1998). This is well illustrated in the framework of the "Strategy and Action Plan for the Integrated Management of Africa's Wetlands," a component of the Environment Initiative of the New Partnership for Africa's Development (NEPAD 2002).

Indeed, for many African communities residing near wetlands of local, regional, or international importance, ensured access to a diversity of biological resources is an essential condition for survival. The

(Continued)

huge dependence of Africa's populations on these resources makes the continent particularly vulnerable to ecological deterioration (Awaiss and Seyni 1998).

In the event of reduced productivity caused by ecological deterioration, there are few available alternatives for development, and the financial resources needed to restore the environment are limited. This is why it is imperative to highlight the important link between sustainable development and preservation of biological diversity and to foster this understanding within society as a whole as well as within the political arena. Mechanisms by which sustainable development and conservation can jointly be achieved, such as the implementation of Ramsar site management plans to maintain the ecological character of each site, must be more widely adopted. Unfortunately, too few of the African sites registered on the list currently have a management plan for the aquatic resources of designated wetlands as stipulated in Article 3.1 of the convention.

The Ramsar List: A Critical Component of Integrated River or Lake Basin Management in Africa

Ramsar sites in Africa and Madagascar can limit the rate of regional biodiversity loss if innovative combinations of traditional and modern conservation methods are implemented both inside and outside sites. In this regard, WWF and Ramsar have promoted integrated river or lake basin management in Africa since 2000, with the goal of conserving and sustainably managing freshwater ecosystems and their natural resources while also contributing to livelihoods and poverty reduction.

Emphasizing Ramsar sites as crucial tools for the implementation of integrated river or lake basin management, this approach was first developed in pilot basins or ecoregions such as the Lake Chad Basin (jointly with the Lake Chad Basin Commission, its five member states, and the Global Environment Facility [GEF]), the Niger River Basin (with the Niger Basin Authority, its nine member states, and the GEF), and the Lake Malawi/Niassa/Nyasa Basin (with its three riparian countries and cooperation agencies such as the Swiss Development Cooperation). A key aspect of river or lake basin management in Africa has been the promotion of basin-wide networks of Ramsar sites and the development of networks of wetland managers based on the successful MedWet model. The MedWet Initiative, developed in 1991 for the Mediterranean Basin, is a long-term collaborative effort toward the conservation and wise use of Mediterranean wetlands. MedWet brings together all the governments

Peuhl woman washing up at sunset, Youwarou, Lake Walado-Débo, Inner Niger Delta, Mali. Photo credit: ©WWF-Canon/Meg Gawler

194

of the region, several international agencies and conventions, nongovernment organizations, and wetland centers to work for wetland conservation (MedWet 2004). It is Ram-sar's first regional initiative and considered to be a model for future regional initiatives elsewhere.

Whatever approach is adopted, the conservation of African Ramsar sites can succeed only with the cooperation of local populations. The convention has always emphasized that use by people, under sustainable conditions, is compatible with registration on the Ramsar List and with the preservation of wetlands in general (Ramsar 1999).

Conclusions

Registration of a wetland on the Ramsar List can help to maintain biological diversity in Africa if the issues of African values, priorities, and practices are taken into account in conservation plans. Until the recent past, international values, rather than national or local values, tended to dominate biological diversity conservation programs. For economic and cultural reasons, Africa's dependence on biological resources has not always received the attention it deserves, but there are signs that this is changing quickly. For example, in November 2005, the 9th Ramsar Conference of the Parties will for the first time ever take place in Africa (Kampala, Uganda) and will focus on wetlands and poverty reduction.

Essay 16.2

Lake Naivasha, Kenya: Community Management of a Ramsar Site

IUCN Eastern Africa Regional Programme, Nairobi, Kenya

Lake Naivasha is a rare example of a Ramsar site where the mandate to manage the site resides with the local community. Community members led the effort to develop a management plan and seek designation for the site. A voluntary association of concerned residents and commercial, agricultural, administrative, and municipal interests continues to meet regularly to discuss progress and matters arising in the implementation of the management plan. Lake Naivasha is a successful case of community-based natural resource management, and it may serve as a model for community participation in the management of other wetlands of international importance.

Lake Naivasha covers about 145 km^2 and lies on the floor of the eastern branch of the Rift Valley in East Africa, at 0°45'S and 36°21'E. At 1,887 m a.s.l., it is the highest of Kenya's Rift Valley lakes. Its freshwater is unusual among the Eastern Rift Valley lakes, most of which are sodic.

Lake Naivasha drains a basin of some 3,400 km^2, and it has two main influent rivers: the Gilgil and the Malewa. Together, these account for around 90 percent of the surface water entering the lake. Rainfall at Naivasha is around 650 mm a year, but evapotranspiration is an estimated 2,141 mm a year, and evaporation from the lake is 1,529 mm (Abiya 1996). The contribution of the lake's subsurface influents to the reduction of this deficit is significant. Intriguingly, Naivasha has no surface outlet, so its ability to flush out excess salts probably results from substantial water seepage into surrounding sediments.

Over the past 10,000 years, Lake Naivasha's water level has fluctuated widely, from drying out completely on several occasions to reaching 100 m higher than its current level. Water level fluctuations

(continued)

Pelicans (*Pelecanus onocrotalus*) along the shores of Lake Naivasha. Photo credit: Sarah Higgins, Lake Naivasha Riparian Association

196

continue to affect the lake, although fluctuations of more than 5 m rarely occur. The lake is shallow, with a maximum depth of around 8 m.

Biodiversity

Lake Naivasha has a noteworthy avian fauna. An estimated 495 bird species either reside in or pass through the Naivasha area; this estimate represents one of the highest counts in Kenya. Some of Kenya's largest congregations of waterfowl also occur at the lake: between 1991 and 1997, an average of 22,000 waterbirds gathered there (Bennun and Njoroge 1999). Addi tionally, the lake has held 1 percent or more of three bird species' biogeographic populations: red-knobbed coot (*Fulica cristata*), African spoonbill (*Platalea alba*), and little grebe (*Tachybaptus ruficollis capensis*).

The lake's aquatic fauna is spartan. Its fishery is dominated by introduced species, including three fish species (*Oreochromis leucostictus, Tilapia zillii,* and *Micropterus salmoides*) and a crayfish (*Procambarus clarkii*). The lake is home to large numbers of hippopotamus (*Hippopotamus amphibious*) and an esti mated fifty-five different mammal species occur in the Lake Naivasha area.

Forests and Other Vegetation

There are four main forest blocks in the lake's basin, all of which play a vital role in the basin's hydrology. Riparian vegetation includes *Acacia* woodland (*Acacia xanthophea*) and open grassland. Historically, most of the lakeshore was fringed with papyrus (*Cyperus papyrus*); currently, however, only about 12 km² of papyrus fringes the lake (Lopez 2002). Like its aquatic fauna, Lake Naivasha's vegetation became increasingly dominated by exotic species, particularly the free-floating aquatic fern (*Salvinia molesta*) and the notorious water hyacinth (*Eichhornia crassipes*). These formed dense and extensive floating mats on the lake. Efforts to control these weeds with introduced, host-specific weevils have been largely successful, and the plants are no longer the problem that they used to be.

Lake Naivasha's Economy

Most of the lake's riparian land is under private stewardship, in many cases by large-scale horticultural and floricultural farms. Farms cover an estimated 50 km^2 of land and yield net returns of some $63 million a year. These farms employ an estimated 30,000 people, who are attracted to the area from all over Kenya (Sayeed 2001).

Almost all of these farms are irrigated from the lake. An estimated 63.7 million m^3 of water is abstracted annually for human use. Irrigated agriculture continues to increase in the larger Naivasha Basin, as do water transfers out of the basin. Nakuru, a major town lying outside the basin to Naivasha's northwest, extracts 17,500 m^3 of water daily from the Turasha, a major tributary of the Malewa River.

An additional and important economic activity in the basin is geothermal power generation. The first plant at Ol Karia, close to Lake Naivasha, is Africa's first geothermal power station, producing 45 megawatts of electricity. The second plant at Ol Karia, completed recently, has a capacity of 70 megawatts, for a total capacity of 155 megawatts, or about 12.5 percent of the power flowing through Kenya's national grid.

Finally, tourism plays an important role in Naivasha, attracting day-trippers from Nairobi and foreign tourists keen to enjoy the lake's spectacular setting, visit the parks in the basin, or birdwatch around the lakeshores.

Key Threats

Almost all of the problems that threaten Lake Naivasha relate to unplanned development in the basin and the introduction of exotic species. These threats may be summarized as follows:

- *Water abstractions.* Abstractions from Lake Naivasha's tributaries and the lake itself are cause for concern, given the continued high rate of development in the irrigated agricultural sector. Also of concern are abstractions to supply the needs of growing numbers of migrant workers around the lake, of general population growth in the basin, and of an expanding industry.
- *Pollution.* The main sources of pollution are agricultural runoff and organic waste from growing migrant worker settlements. Pollution is a serious threat, given the loss of much of the lake's papyrus, which has been cleared to make room for agriculture and settlement. Previously, papyrus played a key role in filtering water entering the lake.
- *Catchment degradation.* Most catchment degradation originates from poor farming practices, including intensive land use and farming on riverbanks and steep slopes. Additional degradation arises from mining riverbanks for sand and from forest clearance for agriculture, timber, and charcoal manufacture.
- *Ecological changes caused by species introductions and overfishing.* The ecology of the lake continues to change as a result of species introductions and intense fishing pressure. For example, intense fishing of exotic black bass (*Micropterus salmoides*) has caused populations of exotic crayfish, a prey item of bass, to explode. Crayfish foraging, in turn, has decimated submerged macrophyte vegetation beds, the main food of the red-knobbed coot (*Fulica cristata*), such that this species now rarely occurs in large congregations. The red-knobbed coot features highly in the diet of Naivasha's fish eagles (*Halia-eetus vocifer*), which used to occur here in some of the highest densities on the

(*continued*)

African continent. With declining coot and fish populations, the undernourished fish eagles have failed to breed successfully on the lake for several years.

The Management of Lake Naivasha

Since 1929, the Lake Naivasha Riparian Association (LNRA) has managed the riparian land lying between Lake Naivasha's low and high water marks. The lake's management has traditionally fallen within the jurisdiction of multiple government agencies, with no clear leader among them and no clear management strategy for the lake.

Aware of the increasingly acute environmental problems facing Lake Naivasha, the LNRA has sought to address them via a two-pronged approach. First, the LNRA designed a management plan for the lake and its basin. Completed in 1996, the plan is being implemented by the Lake Naivasha Management Implementation Committee (LNMIC). On October 1, 2004, the Lake Naivasha Management Committee was officially gazetted by the Kenyan Minister for Environment and Natural Resources and charged with implementing the Lake Naivasha Management Plan. The committee includes representatives from the LNRA, government ministries and departments, the Naivasha Municipality, the local district authority, the geothermal power generation industry, the lake's fishers, and IUCN. There are also ten subcommittees, each representing a sector of managerial concern. Among the largest of these is the Lake Naivasha Growers' Group, which represents the lake's horticultural and other farming interests. The other subcommittees are composed of those representing the livestock industry, biodiversity conservation, the Naivasha Municipality, power production, fisheries, and tourism, among others.

The Lake Naivasha Management Plan provides an initial framework describing the lake's main threats and management objectives, and outlining the broad parameters within which management will operate. The plan's main operational guidelines are contained in a series of codes of conduct, developed by each of the LNMIC's subcommittees, which are responsible for implementing them and for dealing with any violators. In the event that a subcommittee faces challenges too large or complex for it to solve alone, the difficulty can be referred to the LNMIC for action.

The LNMIC encourages each subcommittee to solve its problems independently and to exercise as much autonomy as possible. The LNMIC has no legal policing powers, and much of the success of the management plan has been obtained through voluntary compliance.

Community members' sign showing their support for the Lake Naivasha Ramsar site. Photo credit: Sarah Higgins, Lake Naivasha Riparian Association

The second part of the LNRA's strategy has involved gaining alternative political support for implementing its eventual management plan and counterbalancing possible resistance from the state to community-based natural resource management. In 1993, as the Kenyan government sought to increase the number of Kenyan Ramsar sites, it occurred to the LNRA that some of the political strength it needed might be obtained via Ramsar. With technical help from IUCN and other agencies, the LNRA persuaded the Kenyan government to nominate Lake Naivasha as Kenya's second Ramsar site in 1995. Doing so placed Lake Naivasha's problems and the efforts made to deal with them on an international stage, so that any local resistance to the LNRA's activities would be scrutinized globally. In this way, Ramsar helped to overcome local administrative and bureaucratic objections to the LNRA's activities. At the same time, the Ramsar designation could yield important commercial dividends: flowers and other horticultural produce from the area could be advertised as having been grown on a Ramsar site, augmenting the environmental friendliness of the product. Finally, the designation was a source of pride to many of the lakeshore's inhabitants and helped them to maintain their energy and momentum in managing the lake.

The Ramsar designation has not solved all problems facing the lake's management. However, recent changes in Kenyan legislation should improve LNMIC's ability to deal with problems that still persist. Section 42 of the new Environmental Management and Co-ordination Act deals with lakes and rivers and provides the Minister for the Environment with a series of sweeping powers that include enacting any measure deemed necessary for the adequate management of lake and river resources. Through this act, the LNRA hopes to be recognized as a management authority for Lake Naivasha.

To date, much of the success of the LNRA and LNMIC is derived from a series of key components in the management process:

- *Consensus and dialogue.* These lie at the heart of the management process and provide stakeholders with ample opportunities to vent their concerns, contribute to the process, and together find solutions to the challenges they face.
- *High transaction costs.* The costs related to arriving at decisions are high, particularly in terms of time, discussion, and commitment. However, the dividends are significant. Once unanimous agreement has been reached, cohesion among stakeholders is maintained and conflict minimized.
- *Adequate management forums.* The LNMIC meets every 6 weeks and can call special general meetings to discuss matters of importance if necessary. Consensus and dialogue cannot occur in the absence of adequate forums designed for these purposes.
- *Adaptive or dynamic management.* The Lake Naivasha management plan is dynamic in that it is periodically reviewed and updated to meet challenges as they arise. This is particularly the case with the plan's sectoral codes of conduct.
- *Representation and equity.* The management process seeks to ensure that all stakeholders are represented and are given the opportunity to contribute meaningfully. Each member of the LNRA has one vote, regardless of size or wealth of the member's organization or company.
- In addition, subscriptions are kept as low as possible to ensure that impoverished stakeholders are not excluded from the process.
- *Awareness and wealth.* The generally high standards of living of riparian residents and their awareness of environmental issues have contributed substantially to the success of the LNRA and the LNMIC.
- *Leadership and commitment.* The management process benefits from strong and inspired leadership and a very high degree of commitment and initiative among committee members and a majority of riparian residents.

Among the most serious problems that the LNMIC has faced are the deep-rooted suspicions held by commercial horticultural interests of efforts designed to conserve the environment and promote its wise use. When the LNRA was seeking Ram-sar designation for the lake in 1994, many growers erroneously thought that the designation would pave the way for the government to declare the lake

(continued)

Essay 16.2 (Continued)

a protected area and prevent all water abstraction from it. Others thought it would mean that the Ramsar Bureau, based in Switzerland, would dictate what stakeholders were allowed to do in the basin. Although the majority of voters were in favor of Ramsar designation, consensus was necessary. Detractors were given 3 months to investigate Ramsar to their satisfaction. In the meantime, a radio report alleging extensive environmental damage to Lake Naivasha by the flower industry caused several flower export orders to be canceled. Seen in this light, the Ramsar designation suddenly seemed attractive because it implied that agricultural production in the basin could be environmentally friendly. Consensus was subsequently obtained. Similarly acute suspicions have plagued the development of the management plan. In every case, through a process of extraordinary patience, tact, and persuasion, consensus has been achieved and the management process carried forward.

An additional problem faced by the LNMIC is limited funding. Most funding comes from the judicious investment of contributions made by LNRA membership and small grants from nongovernment organizations and other international organizations. In 2002, for example, one of Naivasha's most important British flower purchasers, a major supermarket chain, partially funded an aerial survey of the lake and its riparian areas.

The outcome of the LNMIC's style of management has been impressive. Many of the lake's large-scale farmers have introduced more efficient irrigation systems, installed water meters so that abstractions can be monitored, submitted themselves to environmental audits, and implemented pesticide and fer-tilizer application practices that exceed international standards. The LNMIC's subcommittees actively seek to protect basin forests and the lake's fishery, provide environmental education and awareness, reduce the amount of sewage entering the lake, monitor all new developments on the lake's shores, and ensure that they are subjected to an environmental impact assessment. These achievements have all been the result of voluntary actions. In recognition of its successes, the LNRA was awarded the Ramsar Wetland Conservation Award in the nongovernment organization category in 1999 at the 7th Conference of Parties in Costa Rica. The LNRA chair gave a keynote address on the Lake Naivasha experience to this international audience.

The challenges facing the LNMIC remain substantial, particularly as it seeks to expand its activities into the Naivasha Basin. However, Lake Naivasha today is an outstanding wetland, rich in biodiversity and lying in the heart of intense economic activity. It is part of one of Africa's most successful community-based natural resource management systems.

Essay 16.3

African Wildlife Foundation Experience in the Management of Fishery Resources in Two Southern African Landscapes

Henry Mwima and Jimmiel Mandima

The African Wildlife Foundation (AWF) is the leading international conservation organization focused solely on the African continent. For more than 40 years, AWF has concentrated its efforts on building the capacity of Africa's people and institutions to manage natural resources and to protect the unique and rich biodiversity of the African continent. From the day AWF was founded in 1961, it has recognized that Africa's wildlife resources and ecosystems are key to the future prosperity of Africa and its people. Over the past 5 years AWF has established and built the African Heartlands Program, an integrated approach to conservation and development in selected large, wildlife-rich landscapes, or Heartlands, that offer both ecological and economic viability for the long term.

Heartlands are cohesive conservation landscapes that are biologically important and cover areas large enough to maintain healthy populations of wild species and natural processes well into the future. AWF currently works in eight Heartlands covering parts of eleven countries in central, eastern, and southern Africa (Botswana, Democratic Republic of the Congo, Kenya, Mozambique, Namibia, Rwanda, South Africa, Tanzania, Uganda, Zambia, and Zimbabwe; figure 16.4). Each Heartland forms a sizable economic unit in which tourism and other natural resource–based activities can contribute significantly to local livelihoods. Most Heartlands include a combination of government lands (such as national parks), community-owned lands, and private property. In these vast conservation landscapes, which often cross national boundaries, AWF works with a broad range of local partners to improve natural resource management and conservation practices and to mitigate threats to valuable resources. The number of Heartlands is expected to increase with time and resources to encompass other geopolitical areas and ecosystems of Africa (Muruthi 2004).

As the Heartland Program has developed, aquatic resources—rivers and wetlands and the species that depend on them (primarily fish)—have taken center stage as priority conservation targets[1] in several of our Heartlands. The Four Corners Transboundary Natural Resource Management (TBNRM) area[2] and the Zambezi Heartland are particularly rich in water-related conservation targets as they span large sections of the Zambezi River Basin. Waters of the Zambezi, Chobe, Kwando-Linyati system, Kafue, Okavango Delta, and Luangwa support a thriving tourism industry; commercial, subsistence, and recreational fisheries; and irrigation of commercial crops. All these activities have direct and indirect effects on the health of aquatic resources in the area. On the basis of extensive consultations with stakeholders, AWF and partners are working to identify and mitigate threats to water resources in the Zambezi Basin and to develop best practices that will enable local people to sustainably use and benefit from these resources.

This essay describes how AWF has applied its Heartland Conservation Process (HCP)[3] in identifying conservation targets and related threats in these two landscapes and discusses experience gained in the management of fishery resources. A brief description of the two landscapes follows.

Four Corners

The Four Corners TBNRM area covers approximately 220,000 km², including the eastern Caprivi Strip in Namibia, Ngamiland in Botswana, Hwange District in Zimbabwe, and parts of Southern and Western Provinces in Zambia (figure 16.5). The Zam-bezi River is the major drainage system and forms the core of the Four Corners TBNRM area ecosystem. The area extends along the Zambezi River from about 50 km below Victoria Falls upstream to the Chobe-Linyanti floodplains and parts of tributaries such as the Kwando and Machili. National parks and wildlife reserves in the area include Chobe and Moremi in Botswana; Mamili, Mudumo, and Bwabwata in Namibia; Mosi-Oa-Tunya and Sioma Ngwezi in Zambia; and Hwange and Zam-bezi in Zimbabwe. National parks and other protected areas (safari areas, game management areas, forest reserves, conservancies, and Moremi Wildlife Reserve) constitute about 50 percent of the total area. The Four Corners TBNRM area is a prime wildlife and tourism area and contains some of the most important terrestrial and freshwater ecosystems in Africa (such as Okavango Delta and the Victoria Falls; see figure 16.5).

(continued)

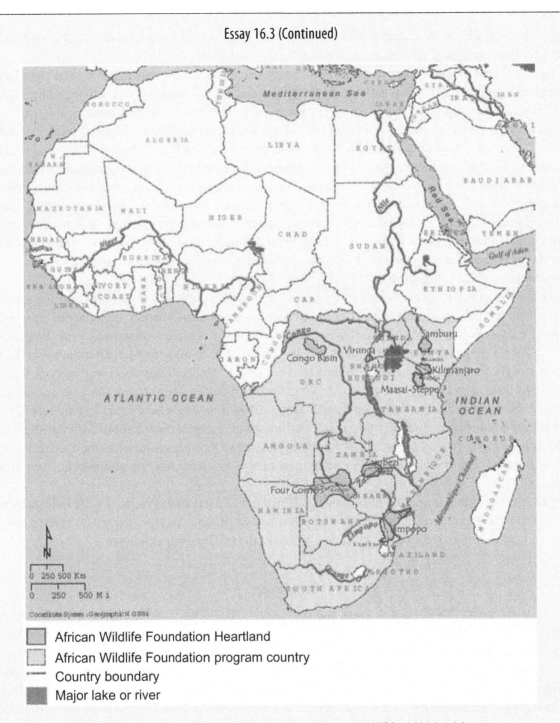

African Wildlife Foundation Heartland
African Wildlife Foundation program country
Country boundary
Major lake or river

Figure 16.4 African Wildlife Foundation Heartlands (as of January 2004). Map produced by AWF Spatial Analysis Laboratory.

Zambezi Heartland

The Zambezi Heartland extends from Lake Kariba to Cahora Bassa Reservoir and covers an area of approximately 39,000 km², consisting of 6,500 km² of national parkland, 4,900 km² in game management areas, 11,000 km² in safari areas, and the remainder in open communal areas (figure 16.6). In addition to the high diversity of terrestrial wildlife and plants in this Heartland, the Zambezi River

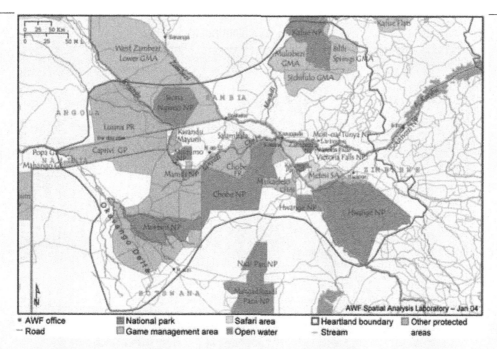

Figure 16.5 The Four Corners Transboundary Natural Resource Management Area.

and its tributaries also provide habitat for freshwater fish, including many species important for commercial and subsistence fisheries such as the tigerfish (*Hydrocynus vittatus*) and a wide variety of cichlid (tilapias) and cyprinid species.

Heartland Conservation Planning

In April 2000 and June 2001, AWF held planning meetings for the Zambezi Heartland and Four Corners TBNRM area, respectively. These meetings brought together local people, wildlife agencies, representatives of the private sector, and non-government organizations who identified conservation targets, threats to these targets, and related threat abatement strategies. AWF considers this a crucial step for successful conservation work in every Heartland (AWF 2003a, 2003b).

Conservation Targets

AWF and partners identified the following conservation targets for both the Four Corners TBNRM area and the Zambezi Heartland: river systems, wetlands, wildlife corridors, habitat complexes, native fishes, endangered and threatened species, and species assemblages. The aquatic conservation targets are described in this section.

River Systems

The key conservation target is the Zambezi River and its tributaries. The Zambezi is one of Africa's great rivers, with a catchment area of 1.42 million km^2 (Griffin et al. 1999). Along its entire stretch, the river is naturally divided into three sections: the Upper Zambezi [16, 76] from the source to Victoria Falls,

(continued)

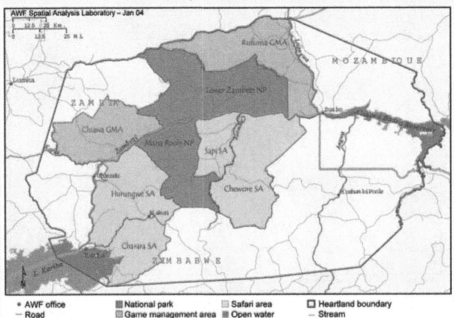

Figure 16.6. The Zambezi Heartland.

204

the Middle Zambezi downstream from Victoria Falls to Cahora Bassa in Mozambique [69], and the Lower Zambezi from Ca-hora Bassa to the Delta at the Indian Ocean in Mozambique [66]. The Zambezi River's natural flood regime is the driving ecological process supporting pervasive wetland and riparian habitats throughout the Four Corners TBNRM area.

The Upper Zambezi is separated from the lower sections by a natural barrier, Victoria Falls, so fish species composition is different from that in the lower sections of the river. The Middle Zambezi has been largely modified by the creation of artificial reservoirs at Kariba, Kafue, and Cahora Bassa gorges. The dams created permanent artificial barriers, and the resultant river fragmentation prohibits migration of fishes along the river channel (World Resources Institute 2003). These dams also alter the flood regime downstream in the Lower Zambezi, thereby influencing the viability of aquatic fauna and flora that use the fresh-brackish-seawater habitat continuum. AWF and partners identified the following threats for river systems: altered flow regime, habitat loss, siltation, eutrophication, and point source pollution.

Wetlands

Chobe/Kwando/Linyanti/Liambezi, Zambezi Floodplain (East Caprivi), Okavango Delta, Kazungula floodplains, Kazuma depressions, and dambos and pans constitute important habitats for aquatic and terrestrial biodiversity. These systems are critical for aquatic biodiversity, providing specialized fish breeding and feeding grounds, and as watering points for wildlife in the entire landscape. Some of these vleis, pans, and swamps are the only habitats for aquatic species such as the lungfish (*Protopterus annectens brieni*) that have limited distributions in southern Africa and are remnants of an ancient lineage of fishes related to the coelacanths (Skelton 2001).

AWF and partners identified a falling water table and habitat degradation and destruction as threats for wetlands. These threats are caused by a combination of factors such as dam operations, incompatible human settlements, deforestation, uneven elephant populations, incompatible tourism developments, and incompatible grazing practices.

Native Fishes

Fish are important in the region both for their contribution to biological diversity and for their role in commercial, sport, and subsistence fishing. A large portion of the freshwater fish catch for the basin's riparian countries comes from the Zambezi River and its tributaries, and fish provide a significant percentage of protein to the Zambezi Basin states. Zambezi fisheries also contribute substantially to the national economies of Botswana, Malawi, Mozambique, Zambia, and Zimbabwe. For example, the Barotse Floodplain fisheries in the Upper Zambezi support about 300,000 people (Chenje 2000). The commercial offshore pelagic fishery for the freshwater sardine (*Limnothrissa miodon,* locally called *kapenta*) on Lake Kariba yielded 30,000 tons of fish worth US$55 million in 1993 (Chenje 2000). Demand for fish has continued to rise as a result of human population growth, contributing to declines in some fish populations and altered species composition and structure.

There is subsistence fishing along the entire Zambezi River, from the Upper Zambezi to the Delta. Most fishers are from riverbank communities that undertake fishing as a livelihood in addition to traditional subsistence agriculture. In the Middle Zambezi, subsistence fishing is prevalent along the Kafue, Lu-angwa, and Zambezi rivers on the Zambian and Mozambican sides and to a lesser degree on the Zimbabwean side. Recreational fishing is increasing along the river, with a concurrent increase in tourist lodges and related facilities.

The Zambezi River system is endowed with a rich fish fauna, although the fauna is incompletely known. A basin-wide inventory of fishes of the Zambezi River and its tributaries (excluding Lake Malawi) totals 239 species (Skelton 2001). Recent surveys conducted by AWF and partners (the Aquatic Resources Working Group [ARWG] and the South African Institute of Aquatic Biodiversity [SAIAB]) suggest that there are about twenty additional species to be described, mainly from the headwater streams in northwestern Zambia. Research on these species is ongoing (D. Tweddle, pers. comm., 2004).

Threats to native fishes include river regulation and water withdrawals, poor land management, and water pollution. Globally, 20 percent of all freshwater fish species are threatened or endangered because of dams and water withdrawals that have destroyed or degraded free-flowing river ecosystems (Ricciardi and Rasmussen 1999). The mighty Zambezi River is no exception, with two of southern Africa's largest hydrological schemes: Kariba and Cahora Bassa (figure 16.6). Further threats to fishery resources include poor land management that causes erosion and deposition of silt in rivers and streams and can destroy breeding grounds. Water pollution from agricultural activities and urban settlements causes eutrophication, which often leads to the proliferation of invasive weeds and deoxygenation.

Intervention Strategies

Based on the conservation targets and threats identified in this essay, AWF and partners decided to focus its first intervention strategies on improving the management and condition of the native fisheries in the Four Corners and Zambezi Heartland (AWF 2000, 2001). Two intervention strategies have proven beneficial to collaborative management of fishery resources: establishment of the ARWG in the Four

(continued)

205

Corners TBNRM area and the creation of multi-institutional partnerships in both Heartlands. These interventions are discussed in this section.

Aquatic Resources Working Group

As part of the Four Corners TBNRM Initiative, AWF undertook a consultative process through which we identified partners and mechanisms for supporting projects aimed at joint and improved management of fisheries and strengthened collaboration between freshwater fish scientists, government officials, and conservation organizations. This culminated in the establishment of the ARWG. Subsequently, the Southern African Development Community (SADC) formally recognized the ARWG as the working group to address management of shared fishery resources in the Four Corners TBNRM area.

ARWG membership consists of representatives of fishery authorities from Botswana, Namibia, Zambia, and Zimbabwe and a representative of the SADC Inland Fisheries Sector Technical Coordinating Unit and the SAIAB. The group members also sit on the SADC Inland Fisheries Technical Committee, which plans and implements strategies for regional cooperation in the management of shared aquatic resources. The ARWG is composed of seasoned and experienced fishery biologists and ecologists, who have more than 150 years of combined experience in fishery biology and ecological monitoring.

ARWG's primary goal is to promote collaboration in the management of shared fishery resources and information exchange in the region. To this effect, AWF and its partners are working toward standardization of monitoring systems, surveys of fish biodiversity and related socioeconomic conditions, and establishment of a geographic information system database. When fully under way the ARWG will contribute significantly to a more efficient planning of conservation interventions in the Four Corners Heartland (see essay 3.3).

Multi-Institutional Partnerships

In recognition of the pool of expertise available in the subre-gion, AWF sought to work with institutions that would extend and complement its conservation activities. AWF has established multi-institutional technical teams to implement its work on monitoring water resources in the Zambezi Heartland. Key partners include the following:

- Lake Kariba Research Station (ULKRS), University of Zimbabwe
- Lake Kariba Fisheries Research Institute (LKFRI), Zimbabwe Parks and Wildlife Management Authority
- Zambia Department of Fisheries (DOF)
- Environmental Council of Zambia (ECZ)
- Zambezi River Authority (ZRA)
- Tchuma Tchato Community-Based Natural Resource Management (CBNRM) Program Staff in Mozambique

AWF has been coordinating the field activities of these institutions to enhance transboundary management of aquatic resources in the Zambezi Heartland. This strategy facilitated collaboration between institutions whose previous management activities were driven by national agendas. Because the impacts of many management decisions in the Zambezi basin transcend national boundaries, the multi-institutional management of these shared waters offers the best opportunity to improve the viability of its resources for the benefit of wildlife and the people of the region. This strategy has proven to be useful in bringing people with diverse expertise from different countries together to conserve shared fishery resources. Furthermore, smaller groups have emerged and are interacting in generating information necessary for formulating joint freshwater resource management plans. For example, fishery ecologists from ULKRS and DOF teamed up with AWF in August 2003, to do the following:

- Assess the diversity and relative abundance of fish species in different habitats in the vicinity of the confluence of the Zambezi and Luangwa rivers
- Measure key water quality parameters to assess the nutrient status of the aquatic systems in the vicinity of the confluence of the Zambezi and Luangwa rivers

These surveys improve the understanding of the distribution and abundance of species in the Zambezi ecosystem and contribute to more targeted management plans, as will water quality results when they become available. The pooled resources and expertise provided by the international collaboration extended the scope of the surveys, and the sharing of results will extend their impact across borders. Such international collaboration represents a vital step toward transboundary conservation management.

Acknowledgments

The U.S. Agency for International Development Regional Center for Southern Africa, the Netherlands, Directorate-General for International Cooperation, and the Ford Foundation are acknowledged for their financial support to the activities addressed in this essay. The work described in this essay would not have been possible without the efforts of our partners from ARWG, SAIAB, ULKRS, LKFRI, DOF, ECZ, ZRA, and Tchuma Tchato CBNRM Program. We would also like to thank our AWF colleagues, Joanna Elliot, Helen Gichohi, Harry van der Linde, Philip Muruthi, Elodie Sampéré, and David Williams, for their insights and invaluable remarks in the preparation of this essay.

Notes

1. Conservation targets are elements of biodiversity at a site and the natural processes that maintain them. These are the focus of Heartland planning around which strategies are developed. The intent of target identification is to develop a short, effective list of species, communities, or large-scale ecological systems whose protection will capture all the biodiversity at the site (AWF 2003b).
2. The area is called Four Corners TBNRM area because AWF is currently implementing a regional transboundary program defined largely by USAID. Revision of the Heartland boundary is anticipated considering ecological (including key species) and administrative factors.
3. HCP is a customized science-driven participatory conservation planning, implementation, and monitoring process developed by AWF with help from The Nature Conservancy

(continued)

Essay 16.4

Fish out of Water? Competing for Water for Africa's Freshwater Ecosystems

Patrick Dugan

The present volume highlights the multiple values of Africa's aquatic ecosystems and the benefits they bring at local, national, and international levels. Béné (essay 1.1), in particular, has highlighted the central role of inland fisheries in supporting livelihoods, ranging from those who catch the fish to fish processors and traders. Given their contribution to African livelihoods and their dependence on the quality of the continent's aquatic ecosystems, Africa's inland fisheries provide an impor tant barometer of the state of these ecosystems and the lives of the people who depend on them.

Other essays in this volume also highlight the threats facing Africa's aquatic ecosystems, including physical encroachment and loss, pollution, and overharvesting of resources (e.g., essays 4.1 and 4.2). However, by far the largest threat comes from the changes in land and water management that alter the hydrological dynamics that have driven the seasonal productivity of these ecosystems for millennia. As we look to the future and consider what is needed to sustain Africa's aquatic ecosystems, the single greatest challenge is to ensure that the quality and quantity of water needed to sustain this productivity are maintained. This essay considers some of the policy and management issues that must be addressed if we are to meet this challenge successfully and the importance of science as a basis for informed debate.

Sustaining Fisheries and Ecosystems in the Face of Growing Demand for Water

A first step toward providing water for aquatic ecosystems and the people who depend on them lies in recognizing the scale of the growing competition for water. Although there are already many examples of African rivers, such as the Senegal, Niger, and Zambezi, where the flow regime has been altered significantly by dams and irrigation schemes and the associated riverine floodplains and other wetlands have been degraded, the coming decade is likely to see a substantially increased investment to harness the continent's water resources for agricultural, industrial, and urban purposes. For example, Rosegrant et al. (2002) report that even under an optimistic scenario of "sustainable" water use, total mean water withdrawal in sub-Saharan Africa will rise from 128 km^3 in 1995 to 173 km^3 in 2025. Under a crisis scenario withdrawal is projected to be 247 km^3. In addition, there is continuing demand from national governments and the private sector for greater investment in the hydropower potential of Africa's rivers. How much of this potential will be realized, and how much will remain untapped, will be an issue of intense debate in coming years.

In the face of this growing demand for greater investment to harness the multiple benefits of Africa's freshwater, there is an urgent and growing need for the conservation movement to embrace a much more ambitious engagement in water management issues. This engagement should be rooted in recognition of Africa's development needs and in a willingness to join the growing policy debate over how best to use the continent's water resources for the long-term benefit of national and local economies. In this section I review the three major issues that will be central to a constructive debate: governance, valuation of goods and services, and water needs of aquatic ecosystems.

Governance and Institutions

A central premise of the conservation case for aquatic ecosystems is that many hundreds of thousands of people will benefit from investments in water management that sustain ecosystems and the livelihoods that depend on them. However, to translate this premise into policies and management practices that sustain water flow, effective systems of governance at the local and basin level are essential. These systems of governance should foster more effective engagement of all stakeholders and equitable sharing of the benefits from the water resources and the aquatic ecosystems under their jurisdiction. In simple terms this means that the people who are most closely dependent on these resources need to be better engaged in land and water use decisions at all scales.

At present, however, effective governance over aquatic resources is the exception rather than the norm in most developing countries, and all too often the majority of society is excluded from any involvement in policy-making. As a result, policy decisions often favor certain powerful sectors rather than the wider society and, in particular, the poor. This is especially true when the poor are located far from urban centers, as is the case for many of Africa's rural communities dependent on aquatic resources. If access by the poor to aquatic resources is to be improved and management of these resources is to be sustainable, then major reform of aquatic resource governance, policies, and institutions is needed. Such efforts to improve policies and systems of governance and to strengthen institutions must be grounded in a better understanding of how these policy-making processes function, how responsibilities for managing aquatic resources can be shared between government and community organizations, how different stakeholder groups in society affect policy-making and implementation, and how improved information can result in decisions that benefit the poor (Béné and Neiland 2004).

In conjunction with these changes in governance, institutions, and policies, information systems that support effective governance of aquatic ecosystems (and other natural resources) must be developed. The conventional view of policy-making and implementation assumes that policymakers will use new information and better understanding to improve policies for the benefit of society. In this situation, researchers provide information for policymakers, who make policy decisions and then hand these decisions down to administrators (managers) for implementation through various management arrangements. However, in many developing countries, policy-making and implementation systems do not function in this way. Instead, many decisions are made to favor certain powerful sectors of society rather than society as a whole. This problem is compounded by the fact that much current information about poor people's livelihoods and natural resource management issues tends to be disseminated within limited networks. At present, technical information gathering and dissemination is mainly in print, often in English, and usually packaged for presentation to a fairly well defined audience. In contrast, most poor people tend to share knowledge through local language text and oral and visual communication systems. As a result, natural resource users often are prevented from participating in technical information networks. More flexible, de-centralized systems of information exchange are needed (Dugan et al. 2002).

Valuation of Ecosystem Goods and Services

The major investments needed to develop and implement improved policies, institutions, and governance systems for aquatic ecosystems and fisheries will occur only when stakeholders are better aware of the value of aquatic ecosystems and their resources. However, only rarely is the information needed to build such awareness available and used to influence policy change. Rather, across much of Africa existing data are fragmentary, dispersed, and dated. Even for fisheries, which are generally the best-documented

(continued)

aquatic resource, there is widespread skepticism about the accuracy and relevance of current statistics. Most of these statistics are collected from a small number of monitored landing sites, an approach of limited value in assessing the importance of river fisheries in the tropics (Van Zalinge et al. 2000). Actual catches of many freshwater fisheries are believed to be at least twice the reported figures (FAO 1999; Welcomme 2001). Therefore, there is an urgent need to improve the quality of information available on aquatic resource use by various communities and social groups, the economic and social values of these resources, and their contribution to sustaining or enhancing livelihoods, reducing poverty, and improving food security, in addition to the potential cost to society of the loss or degradation of these systems.

The value of aquatic ecosystems varies widely between ecosystem types, depending on the biological characteristics of individual sites and the ways people use them (Neiland et al 2004). Although it can often be helpful to draw on information from several different river systems when trying to illustrate the importance of Africa's aquatic ecosystems and their resources, the information needed to improve policy and management in individual rivers must be drawn from the river system under consideration. Therefore, there is an urgent need for much greater investment in efforts to assess the value of Africa's aquatic ecosystems, wherever such information will assist in improving governance and the quality of decision-making about aquatic ecosystems and water use. At the same time, greater capacity to complete such analyses must be developed.

Managing Water for Aquatic Ecosystems

210

Although much effort is needed to build awareness of the value of Africa's aquatic ecosystems, these efforts can build on the growing international profile that aquatic ecosystems and their resources have received over the past few years. In particular, processes such as the World Water Vision, the Global Water Dialogue, and the World Commission on Dams (WCD) have increased awareness of the need for new approaches to managing water at the basin level so that benefits from natural ecosystems can be sustained. For example, Guidelines 15 and 16 of the WCD call for "Environmental Flow Assessments" and "Maintaining Productive Fisheries" and specify the need to assess water needs for fish populations. However, if the international awareness and policy frameworks generated by these and other initiatives are to bring sustained benefits to poor communities dependent on Africa's aquatic ecosystems, then they must lead to water management decisions at local, national, and regional levels that take account of the needs of aquatic ecosystems. This effort will include detailed information on the value of specific ecosystems and on the volumes and distribution of water needed to sustain these ecosystems and different levels of ecosystem benefits.

In practice, few aquatic ecosystems exist under natural hydrological conditions, and many are subject to highly modified flow regimes. Many systems continue to provide a range of goods and services to society, whereas the character of others has been so altered that previous uses are no longer sustained and serious health and other effects have been incurred. Thus, in the face of increasing competition for water, there is a critical need to be able to assess how ecosystems respond to changes in quantity, distribution, and quality of water and the relationship between changes in the flow regime and the level of benefits that they yield. Once the relationships between river flow and benefits of an aquatic ecosystem are established, the impacts of various management strategies can be assessed. Such information can then be used at a local or national level to inform decisions on the allocation of water from an ecosystem in such a manner as to optimize the overall benefit to society (Dugan et al. 2002).

As argued earlier, inland fisheries with their central role in sustaining food security and the livelihoods of millions of poor people across the developing world are one of the most important and visible benefits of natural aquatic ecosystems. Yet for most rivers little information is available on the water management regime needed to sustain the fishery and its benefits in the face of increasing demand and competition for water. Therefore, there is a particularly urgent need to develop methods to assess the impact of changes in flow regime on fish populations, fishery productivity, and fishing communities; to use these methods to provide such information for selected rivers; and to strengthen the capacity of local, national, and regional institutions to use these tools in making water allocation and river basin management decisions that improve food security and livelihoods of fishing-dependent communities.

To help address this need, a recent study (Arthington et al. 2004) reviewed existing environmental flow assessment methods and recent advances in modeling fish production in river fisheries. The results highlight the advantages of the Downstream Response to Imposed Flow Transformations method (Brown and King 2000; Tharme 2000), which relates the flow ecosystem response with the economic and social values of the aquatic resources provided. However, this method has been applied only in small river systems with limited fisheries in southern Africa and Australia. It remains to be tested and expanded for use in larger and more complex floodplain river systems and adjusted to incorporate recent advances in modeling of fish population dynamics and their responses to changes in river flow (Arthington et al. 2004). Channels for delivering the results of flow assessments to poor stakeholders through decentralized institutional arrangements also must be identified and developed. The relevance of the information to stakeholders, and the efficacy with which it is transferred from the research arena to local communities and authorities, will dictate its ultimate influence on and value to the development agenda.

211

Building Partnerships

A major investment is needed if the institutions responsible for sustaining Africa's aquatic ecosystems are to emerge and be supported with the information needed for effective decision-making. In addressing this challenge it is important to build effective partnerships with other stakeholders concerned with the management of Africa's water resources. Although historically there has been little effective dialogue between the conservation community and those concerned with water management for agricultural, industrial, and urban uses, the scale of the growing water crisis provides a climate in which new approaches and partnerships are emerging. As a recent study by the International Food Policy Research Institute has emphasized, "business as usual" will lead to steady growth in environmental degradation, food insecurity, and a long-term water crisis (Rosegrant et al. 2002). New approaches to water and land management that can resolve these problems must be developed.

In this context, those concerned with the conservation and use of aquatic ecosystems have much in common with many other water users. For example, more equitable and effective use of irrigation water for agriculture entails a reassessment of water rights and devolution of water management roles, responsibilities, and resources to the local level. The debate over where and how to achieve this reassessment of water rights in agriculture has much in common with that concerning the development of governance structures for rivers and aquatic ecosystems. Conservationists will gain much by engaging in partnerships with those who are seeking a policy environment in which the water rights of poor farmers, poor fishers, and others who use aquatic ecosystems can be upheld.

(continued)

Similarly, there is growing recognition that agriculture and water productivity can be improved by greater investment in rain-fed agriculture rather than the conventional approach of expanding or intensifying irrigation. The potential benefits of rain-fed agriculture include increased on-farm productivity, reduced encroachment on marginal lands, reduced erosion, and greater sustainability of hydrological flows.

At present, many of these benefits remain theoretical, and achieving them will necessitate a sustained investment. However, it is clear that there is much to be gained from investing in dialogue between the agricultural and environmental communities in the field of water management. The Dialogue in Water, Food, and Environment provides an international forum for fostering such partnerships, but this type of dialogue must be replicated and implemented at the local level. The conservation community and the agriculture sector need to seize this opportunity.

Conclusions

Among the challenges being faced by Africa's aquatic ecosystems, competition for the water that sustains them is the most critical. As argued here, a major investment is needed to address this challenge, focusing on the development of governance systems that take into account the needs of people whose livelihoods depend on these ecosystems. These governance systems must be informed by high-quality, locally relevant information on the value and water needs of aquatic ecosystems.

In addressing these challenges there is much room for partnerships with other interest groups concerned with water management, particularly those engaged in water management for agriculture. The case for conservation should be based on the best possible data on aquatic ecosystems, particularly on their values, uses, and flow needs. As demand for water grows and the need for hard decisions increases, the case for conservation of Africa's aquatic ecosystems must be rooted in the best possible science.

Essay 16.5

Freshwater Ornamental Fishes: A Rural Livelihood Option for Africa?

Randall E. Brummett

The impressive aquatic biodiversity of Africa documented in this volume is at risk of extirpation, if not extinction, in large parts of its current distribution. Unlike in the marine realm, where overfishing poses a dominant threat, the largest threats to freshwater fishes in most parts of Africa are competition for water, habitat loss, and attendant changes in hydrographic regimes. Freshwater habitats continue to be degraded as forests are cleared, swamps drained, and streams and lakes silted by unsustainable agriculture or polluted by rapid urbanization and unregulated industry. Focal areas of concern are those where fish biodiversity is the highest: the rainforest rivers of Central and West Africa (Upper and Lower Guinean Ichthyological Provinces and the Congo Basin) and the East African lakes Al-bert, Edward, Kivu, Malawi, Rukwa, Tanganyika, Turkana, and Victoria (including a number of small satellites). Without substantial changes to local strategies for natural resource management, these biodiversity assets will continue to be lost.

It is hypothesized that the fish fauna of West and Central African rivers is derived from an older and more widely distributed fauna that inhabited the continent at least since the Miocene (25 m.y.a.) and possibly much earlier (Reid 1996). In these rivers live an estimated 1,000 species, between 50 and 80 percent of which are thought to be endemic (Roberts 1975; Lowe-McConnell 1987). Major families are the Mormyridae, Cyprinidae, Alestiidae/Citharinidae (old Characidae), Aplocheil-idae (old Cyprinodontidae), and the Siluridae and Mochokidae (Lowe-McConnell 1987; Lévêque and Paugy 1999). The lakes of East Africa are young, the oldest being Lake Tanganyika at 6–10 million years (Lévêque 1997). In these lakes live at least 1,500 fish species, of which the Cichlidae represent some 90 percent, often in the form of endemic, sympatric species flocks of closely related forms (Goldschmidt 1996).

Overexploitation, particularly with the use of chemical poisons, has been increasing in recent years, but West and Central African freshwater ecosystems are most threatened by deforestation. Deforestation results in sedimentation and serious water quality changes (Kamdem Toham and Teugels 1998) and disrupts important trophic relationships between the forest and the rivers that sustain it (Reid 1996; Chapman and Chapman 2003). Estimates of deforestation in Central Africa are in the range of 11,000 km^2/year (Revenga et al. 1998; Somé et al. 2001).

Overfishing is a much more serious problem in the lakes of East Africa than in the rivers to the west. Beach seining with very fine mesh nets, even in protected areas, has had significant impacts on fish populations in Lake Malawi (pers. obs.). Introduction of alien species has seriously eroded the biodiversity of Lake Victoria. In addition, watersheds in much drier eastern and southern Africa have been deforested by 40 to 80 percent through a combination of firewood harvesting and slash-and-burn agriculture, resulting in the transfer from croplands of an average of some 20 tons/ha/year of silt onto fish feeding and spawning grounds (Revenga et al. 1998; Lévêque and Paugy 1999; Jamu et al. 2003).

In Africa, as elsewhere, conflict between commerce and conservation generally results in loss of biodiversity. However, it is not only the wildlife that suffers; local human communities also suffer the consequences of environmental degradation. Communities that have relied for generations on forest and aquatic resources for their livelihoods may find themselves dispossessed of their natural inheritance, often by vested commercial interests based outside of the area (Jansen 1997; Godoy et al. 2000; Somé et al. 2001).

Community-Based Natural Resource Management

To justify conservation of aquatic biodiversity from the point of view of local communities, the value of resources must be substantial and accrue locally. There must also be a system of governance that empowers local communities and authorities to set and enforce exploitation methods and quotas. Adaptive co-management, in which communities undertake to sustainably manage their own resources, is an emerging concept that has been used in a number of places. By transferring management and enforcement to local communities, this structure aims to increase control over natural resources while reducing central government expenditures. Adaptive co-management of freshwater capture fisheries is being tested in a number of African countries (Khan et al. 2004). To date, the track record of community management and conservation interventions is mixed, but new knowledge about how such efforts might be improved and what time frames to expect is encouraging (Hulme and Murphree 2001).

A key aspect of adaptive co-management is the valuation of resources from the point of view of indigenous people (Sheil and Wunder 2002). For example, in the case of forests, timber may not be the largest potential source of income (Peters et al. 1989), but because timber companies have already made substantial investments in equipment, infrastructure, and market development, there is a comparative advantage of large-scale tree exploitation in terms of short-term realizable profits. Also, profits accrue at a level and in such a way as to be more accessible to policymakers. A similar logic applies

(*continued*)

213

to large- versus small-scale capture fisheries, hence the continued presence of foreign fishing fleets off the coast of Africa at a time when local fishing communities are suffering extreme poverty and declining catches. In contrast to these large-scale operations, the value of most nontimber forest products and artisanal fisheries accrues locally and in a dispersed manner that makes accounting and taxation impossible.

However, it has been shown that such small businesses can produce wider economic growth. Delgado et al. (1998: 4) reviewed results from Burkina Faso, Niger, Senegal, and Zambia and found that "even small increments to rural incomes that are widely distributed can make large net additions to growth and improve food security." Winkelmann (1998: 10) identified interventions that lead to improved incomes at the level of the rural resource manager as "having a larger impact on countrywide income than increases in any other sector."

From the point of view of rural communities, directly confronting the timber and large fishing companies over ownership of resources is an uphill task. For artisanal fishers who are being required to increase mesh sizes and respect closed seasons, watching even small trawlers take several tons of fish in a single haul seriously undermines the credibility of regulatory bodies, whether local or national, whether or not the fish stocks are related. In fact, rather than struggling to protect remaining

Children play a major role in the ornamental fish industry in many less developed tropical countries. Here, a young fisher from the Ntem River valley in southern Cameroon shows his catch of killifish (*Epiplatys* spp.) and freshwater prawns (*Macrobrachium vollenhovenii*) destined for aquaria in Yaoundé. Photo credit: R. E. Brummett, WorldFish, Cameroon

resources, local fishing communities confronted with expropriation have often joined in the ravaging of their own resources to capture whatever profit they can before the big companies arrive (pers. obs.).

Rather than competing with large companies, small operators might be able to create value for heretofore underexploited resources that offer a competitive advantage. By targeting new species, new products, or new (local or international) marketing channels or using culture-based and satellite exploitation systems, smaller investors could have an advantage over larger companies that lack the same economies of scale.

The Ornamental Fish Trade

Exploitation or culture of ornamental fishes for the aquarium trade is one such small-scale operation that could potentially accrue large benefits for both local communities and ecosystems. Ornamental fishes generally are not amenable to mass capture techniques and are seldom available in such large quantities that wholesale extrapolation is economically feasible for investors with high overheads. Typical ornamental fishes tend to be small, prefer habitats with large amounts of submerged structure, and are most often found singly or in small groups. Ornamentals are most commonly exploited by individual fishers, often children, who wade in the water with hand nets or set small basket traps.

Sustainable exploitation of this aquatic resource for local markets and export to the international ornamental fish trade may offer lucrative livelihood alternatives to local communities. A successful example of a locally managed ornamental fishery occurs in the Brazilian state of Amazonas, where some sixty to seventy small businesspeople manage the activities of hundreds of fish collectors in the communities of Barcelos and Santa Is-abel do Rio Negro. On trade of 30–50 million ornamental fishes (of which more than 80 percent are cardinal tetras, *Paracheiro-don axelrodi*), local communities earn some $250,000 per year, approximately 60 percent of total income for the region. Ornamental exports from the state of Amazonas as a whole generate some $3 million/year (Chao and Prang 2002).

Capture and sale of ornamental fishes are widespread in tropical countries. FAO estimates the export value of ornamental fishes at $200 million/year, of which more than 60 percent accrues to developing countries (FAO Forest Resource Assessment Programme 1999). Major importers of ornamental fishes are the United States, Japan, Germany, France, the United Kingdom, the Netherlands, Belgium, Italy, Singapore, and Spain, each purchasing at least $6 million worth of fish per year. Overall, ninety-eight countries imported ornamental fishes in 1998 (Yap 2002). Only 5–10 percent of total trade in ornamental fishes is of captured specimens; most are cultured under controlled conditions. The dominant exporting countries include Singapore, Haiti, the United States, the Czech Republic, Hong Kong, Malaysia, Sri Lanka, Japan, Israel, and the Philippines, each with more than $4.5 million in overseas sales. Impressive as they are, these figures represent only a fraction of the total market because some of the major producers are also major consumers (United States, Singapore, Japan). Overall trade, domestic and international, in ornamentals in 1998 was $4.5 billion (Yap 2002).

More than 1,500 ornamental fish species are regularly traded, and 95 percent of these are destined for home aquaria managed by nonspecialists (Chapman et al. 1997; Olivier 2001). A fish suitable as an ornamental is fairly hardy, takes artificial food, is not aggressive, is brightly colored, does not eat aquatic plants, and is not afraid of light. The major groups traded are as follows:

- Minnows (Cyprinidae): *Barbus* from Asia and Africa; *Capoeta* from West Asia; *Puntius, Brachyda-nio, Danio, Rasbora, Epalzeorhynchus,* and *Labeo* from South and Southeast Asia; and *Tanichthys, Carassius* (goldfish), and *Cyprinus* (koi) originally from China but now produced widely
- Tetras (Alestiidae): *Astyanax, Colossoma, Gymnocorymbus, Hemigrammus, Hyphessobrycon,* and *Paracheirodon,* primarily from South America
- Catfishes (Callichthyidae and Loricariidae): *Corydoras, Callichthys, Hoplosternum, Ancistrus, Hypostomus,* and *Pterygoplichthys* from South America
- Rainbow fishes (Melanotaeniidae, Pseudomugilidae, Telmatherinidae): *Bedotia* from Madagascar; *Glossolepis* and *Melanotaenia* from Australia and New Guinea; and *Telmatherina* from Indonesia
- Livebearers (Poeciliidae): *Molienesia, Poecilia,* and *Xipho-phorus* from Latin America but now widely bred and introduced
- Cichlids (Cichlidae): *Pterophyllum, Symphysodon, Geopha-gus, Apistogramma, Gymnogeopha-gus, Astronotus, Cichla,* and *Cichlasoma* from Latin America; and *Haplochromis, Hemichromis, Pelvicachromis, Melanochromis, Pseudotropheus, Tropheus, Julidochromis,* and *Neolamprologus* from Africa
- Killifish (Aplocheilidae): *Aphyosemion, Nothobranchius,* and *Epiplatys* from Africa; and *Rivulus* from South America
- Anabantoids (Belontiidae, Helostomatidae): *Betta, Colisa, Trichogaster, Macropodus, Pseudosphro-menus,* and *Helo-stoma* from South and Southeast Asia

(continued)

Typically, the chain of distribution from the wild to market for ornamental fishes is as follows: fish breeders or exporters sell to wholesalers, wholesalers then sell to retailers, and finally the retailers sell to aquariophiles. With each transfer, substantial losses of fish are incurred due to stress, and aquarium shops try to recoup the lost revenue by increasing retail prices. There is some debate as to the exact magnitude of losses, with importers claiming much higher mortality rates than exporters. Nevertheless, whereas the retail prices of the major species start at $10 per fish, the wholesale price often is between 10 and 50 cents (Olivier 2001).

Lessons for Africa

Although several of the most valuable and widely traded genera are African, none of the major ornamental fish importing or exporting countries are in Africa. However, a number of exporters based in Malawi, Nigeria, Tanzania, and Democratic Republic of the Congo make regular shipments to Europe and Asia of mostly wild-caught fish. From the rivers of West and Central Africa come representatives of the Mormyridae (*Campylo-mormyrus, Gnathonemus*), Mochochidae (*Synodontis, Auchenoglanis*), and Cichlidae (*Pelvicachromis, Nanochromis, Teleo-gramma,* known in the aquarium trade as dwarf cichlids). From the rift lakes of eastern Africa come the popular small cichlids known as *mbuna.*

Unfortunately for local exporters, the bulk of the profit on sales of these easy-to-spawn fish accrues to the large wholesale breeders in Asia and the United States (S. Grant, pers. comm., 1995). South Africa has a number of breeders, but they focus primarily on the more common alien species such as *Molienesia, Poecilia, Xiphophorus, Pterophyllum, Trichogaster, Apistogramma,* and *Tanichthys* (Hoffman et al. 2000). Reports from Europe indicate that a large percentage of the indigenous (wild capture) fishes exported from Africa arrive in very poor condition, eroding confidence and harming the standing of reputable traders (C. Eon, pers. comm., 2003).

There are four major markets for ornamental fishes that African producers might access. The largest (95 percent of total trade) and most regular is that for home aquaria and includes the species and countries mentioned earlier. There is also a spe-cialty market, dominated by Germany, for wild-caught fish, particularly the dwarf cichlids and *mbuna.* A third market is for new broodstock for commercial breeders in Florida and Singapore. Finally, museums and public aquaria pay high prices for rare species or particularly large individuals.

Like any global business, the international ornamental fish trade is highly competitive. To make a successful venture based on the culture or capture of ornamentals, African traders would do well to consider some of the lessons learned by trial and error in other parts of the world:

- Fishers should focus on a few species for which capture, handling, feeding, and markets can be standardized.
- Exporters need to maintain a wider range of species to overcome problems of seasonal supply and increase market opportunities. For example, wholesalers in Europe prefer minimum shipments of forty to fifty boxes with about 100 fish per box, depending on individual size.
- To maximize profits at the local level, the number of intermediaries should be kept to a minimum. Cooperative management has been successful in some parts of the world, and such a management structure might be helpful in cases of limited capital for investment (Bérubé 1992).

- Local markets may offer opportunities to sell excess stock or species of less interest to importers and can help improve overall cash flow in times of low overseas demand.
- Fish should be handled carefully and kept in good condition. Bad handling leads to the majority of losses and a bad reputation with clients.
- Use of antibiotics and other quarantine treatments can increase survival, but regulations on use of these substances are becoming increasingly strict.
- Fish should not be colored or otherwise altered. Importers and animal rights groups are watching the fish trade closely for abuses.
- Fishers should work with local communities and government to obtain exclusive access to fishing grounds. Too many operators in an area depresses prices (Brichard 1980).
- The fishery should be well managed and wisely used. Overexploitation is the fastest route out of business.
- Producers should concentrate on species that cannot be reproduced easily outside their native habitat because of their large adult size or peculiar reproductive ecology. Monopoly, even if short-lived, provides important market protection for new investors.
- Investors should consider branching out into aquatic crustaceans and plants to diversify marketing options and spread risk.
- Rather than relying on capture, producers interested in export markets should attempt to reproduce and culture as many species as possible. Reliance on seasonal capture complicates marketing, and tank-reared individuals handle and ship with fewer mortalities.

These conditions for success are not specific to Africa. However, Africa is by far the continent with the least development of its capacity to capture or culture ornamental fishes for profitable exportation. Consequently, new investors on the continent will come into the international market at a great disadvantage in terms of production technology and market knowledge. To be profitable in the long term, careful management of the natural fish populations on which the exploitation is based is essential.

On the other hand, Africa has a strong comparative advantage in having a large number of species that are unknown to the majority of aquariophiles, and many of them are difficult or impossible to reproduce outside their native habitat. Whereas Asian, American, and European producers rely predominantly on alien species and often have difficulty obtaining new broodstock when existing fish become either inbred or contaminated by antibiotic-resistant diseases (Olivier 2001), African breeders working with naturally spawning species can obtain new broodstock easily and thus maintain the high quality that will be increasingly demanded by the international ornamental fish industry.

Some, for All, Forever: A New South African Water Law

Carolyn (Tally) G. Palmer

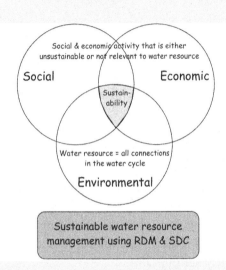

Figure 16.7. In the interaction among social, economic, and environmental issues the goal is to increase the intersecting domain of sustainability. RDM (resource-directed measures) and SDC (source-directed controls) are National Water Act approaches to sustainable water resource management.

Water for people and people for water. Palmer et al. (2002: 1)

Everyone depends on water for life, well-being, and economic prosperity. In homes water is used for drinking, cooking, and washing. In workplaces water is used for agriculture and industry. Water also provides for recreation and meets aesthetic and spiritual needs. Water is so important and is used in so many ways that if it is overused, we risk damaging our very life source. Potentially damaging overuse of water comes mainly from taking too much water out of aquatic ecosystems and putting in too much waste.

South Africa is a dry country. We share an average rainfall of 500 mm/year with Australia and Canada, but in Canada 67 percent of rainfall becomes runoff, whereas in Australia the percentage is 9.8 and in South Africa only 8.6 because of high levels of evapotranspiration. Additionally, uneven rainfall distribution makes it difficult to distribute water to all users. In the past decade, some of the most advanced water law and policy in the world has come from South Africa. The originality of the approach lies in clearly setting two primary objectives—equity and sustainability—while accepting the complexity of water resources.

The National Water Act (NWA) (No. 36 of 1998) recognizes that water resources are part of the integrated water cycle made up of freshwater ecosystems such as rivers, wetlands, lakes, estuaries, and groundwater and the processes of precipitation, transpiration, infiltration, and evaporation (South African Government 1998). Closely connected to the water cycle is human use of water resources. The NWA promotes protection of water resources precisely so that people can use water both now and into the future. Water is at the heart of a better life for all.

Water and Democracy

In 1994, after South Africa's first democratic elections, water law was recognized as an important area for legal reform. There were two main reasons for this. Before 1994 there was enough water for people, but previous governments had not provided the pipes, pumps, and purification works to allow access to safe, clean water for all of the population. The other reason for legal reform was more fundamental. The 1956 Water Act was based on a principle called riparianity. This meant that the right of people to use water was linked to land ownership. Land ownership was discriminatory, so a privileged few had much more access to water. The NWA abolished riparianity and requires the South African government to be the public trustee of water resources and therefore to be responsible for water resource protection in order to ensure long-term, sustainable water resource use.

The main aims of the NWA are encapsulated in a Department of Water Affairs and Forestry slogan: "Some, for all, forever." *Some* acknowledges that water is a limited resource, *for all* emphasizes fairness (all people must be able to use the resource), and *forever* reminds us to use water and water-linked ecosystems wisely to protect them for the future.

The NWA provides for only two rights to water: water for basic human needs (washing, cooking, and drinking) and water to sustain aquatic ecosystems, called the Reserve. These rights ensure adequacy of supply, not delivery. The Water Services Act ensures that water is equitably distributed to people. The Reserve has priority before water is allocated to users in the broader domestic, industrial, and agricultural sectors (where water use includes both abstraction and waste disposal). Given that water is a scarce, essential resource, the NWA recognizes that aquatic ecosystems need protection so that they can continue to provide goods and services. A flexible approach to resource protection is needed, which promotes simultaneous social and economic benefits. South African corporate governance requires management and auditing against a triple bottom line: economic, social, and environmental (figure 16.7).

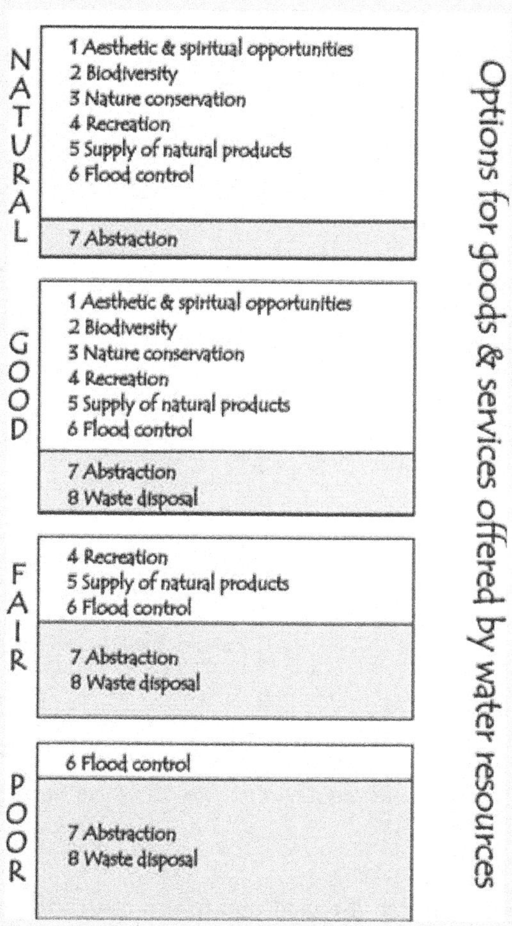

Resource Protection and Use

Integrated water resource management is a balance between water resource protection and water resource use. It is in the interest of all to protect water resources and use them efficiently. Both overprotection and underprotection are inefficient and expensive. The NWA provides two mechanisms to ensure water resource protection at an appropriate

Options for goods & services offered by water resources

NATURAL
1 Aesthetic & spiritual opportunities
2 Biodiversity
3 Nature conservation
4 Recreation
5 Supply of natural products
6 Flood control
7 Abstraction

GOOD
1 Aesthetic & spiritual opportunities
2 Biodiversity
3 Nature conservation
4 Recreation
5 Supply of natural products
6 Flood control
7 Abstraction
8 Waste disposal

FAIR
4 Recreation
5 Supply of natural products
6 Flood control
7 Abstraction
8 Waste disposal

POOR
6 Flood control
7 Abstraction
8 Waste disposal

Figure 16.8. Decisions about selecting a class for a water resource are informed by an understanding of the different goods and services offered by each ecosystem health class. Of the goods and services listed, water abstraction and waste disposal offer the greatest economic benefits of water use, whereas the others offer mainly social and environmental benefits. Resources in the Poor class offer few benefits because of increasing uncertainty of supply, degraded water quality, and high costs of purification. In South Africa, systems may be classified as Natural, Good, Fair, or Poor but may be managed only for Natural, Good or Fair condition. Poor systems must be rehabilitated.

219

(continued)

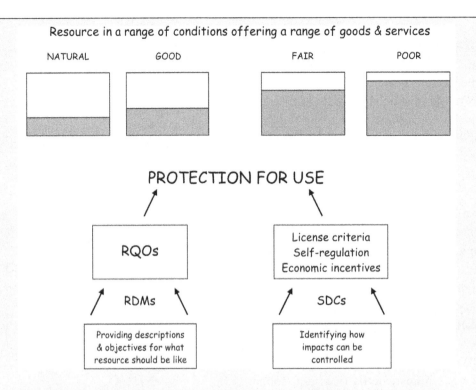

Figure 16.9. Summary diagram of flexible water resource protection and use. Monitoring is needed to document progress toward the achievement of resource quality objectives (RQOs) and to meet license criteria. RDMs, resource-directed measures; SDCs, source directed controls.

level: resource-directed measures and source-directed controls. Resource-directed measures provide descriptive and quantitative goals for the state of the resource, and source-directed controls specify the criteria for controlling impacts in authorizations such as waste discharge and abstraction licenses.

The national strategy for implementing the NWA recognizes two sources of ecosystem goals: "ecospecs" are quantitative and descriptive objectives specifying ecosystem conditions, and "userspecs" describe user requirements. Ecospecs ensure the maintenance of ecosystem processes at a designated level of ecosystem health; userspecs allow water users with more sensitive needs than provided for by ecospecs to promote a stricter objective. Userspecs that will not impair ecosystem function are combined with ecospecs into the formal resource quality objectives that will guide water resource management. (A decision support system for providing quantitative and qualitative objectives for different water levels of ecosystem health may be found at http://www.ru.ac.za/iwr; click on link to "Hydrological Models & Software").

Different levels of ecosystem health are described by a classification system ranging from "Natural" (unaffected), to "Good" (slightly to moderately degraded), to "Fair" (heavily degraded), to "Poor" (unacceptably heavily degraded) (figure 16.8).

This classification is a key step in resource protection. Each resource class has its own specific ecospecs and therefore can be protected and used to a different degree. Specialists, stakeholders, and resource managers identify the appropriate class for a particular water resource, and the government, as the public trustee, decides on the class and the particular range of resource quality objectives that will guide management decisions. Managers then define the appropriate license criteria to control water use. This flexible approach provides for both resource protection and resource use (figure 16.9)

Sustainability and Governance

It is difficult to evaluate the relative values of all the goods and services offered by aquatic ecosystems, although environmental economists have attempted to quantify the value of natural systems and social impacts. The equity and sustainability aims of the NWA will be met only if social, economic, and environmental outcomes are taken into consideration in both the short term and the long term. Government and institutions need an integrated approach so that their actions reflect real environmental and social values as well as economic values. It is a huge challenge to actually achieve the lofty aims of protecting water resources for long-term benefits.

Nevertheless, South Africa has taken significant steps in this direction. The first step has been to recognize that a catchment or river basin is the natural unit for water resource management and to put into place the necessary management structures. The NWA provides for catchment management agencies to manage groups of catchments in large water management areas. The decisions of these catchment management agencies will affect the quality of life for both this generation and generations to come.

An integrated approach to water policy, law, and implementation means recognizing links and understanding how abi-otic ecosystem components (e.g., water quality, flow, and physical shape) influence the responses of living organisms and ecosystem processes. The combined biophysical processes link to social and economic processes through the human use of water resources.

Traditionally, understanding natural systems and their biophysical characteristics has been separated from social science approaches to understanding the needs and aspirations of people and from economic approaches to financial and governance issues. Sustainable resource management demands that these three areas be integrated. The key linking concept is that only functioning ecosystems can provide people with valuable goods and services.

221

17

Social Impact Assessment and the Anthropology of the Future in Canada's Tar Sands

By Clinton N. Westman

INTRODUCTION

This article asserts that one implicit goal of policy processes assessing the future impacts of tar sands development on indigenous people is to present potential futures, thereby both showing, and more subtly, influencing how development will impact future generations of indigenous people in northern Alberta. In so doing, impact assessment documents rhetorically work to preclude certain futures; they, thus, can be read as texts with power to inscribe, rather than just describe, the future. Rather than *assessing* cultural impacts then, such documents and processes may work to *entail* such future impacts. Alas, in the tar sands sector, documents produced through such legally mandated social impact assessment (SIA) studies are ethnographically thin. They, thus, tend to present future scenarios with little empirical basis, partly because they show little understanding of present conditions. Furthermore, consultants authoring such documents systematically avoid discussion of topics that are not easily rendered technical, thus largely dismissing, for example, spiritual, cosmological, or ontological issues at the heart of indigenous cultural traditions (Westman n.d.2). In studying the "traditional land use" (TLU) components of such environmental

impact assessment (EIA) reports from the tar sands region (Westman 2006, n.d.1, n.d.3), I have concluded that impact assessment on tar sands projects is not being carried out in a manner consistent with either sound anthropological practices, with federal legislation, or with the constitutionally protected rights to a subsistence livelihood explicitly enshrined in Treaty Number Eight (signed c. 1899 by representatives of Cree and Dene First Nations and of the British Crown). According to a well-known oral tradition, the treaty's promises were to last long into the future: "for as long as the sun shines, the grass grows, and the rivers flow." Protection of foraging rights and lands was a principal goal of First Nations people in negotiating the treaty. Nevertheless, in this article, I argue that SIA documents have contributed to the breach of this solemn promise about the future, while remaining implicated in the discursive construction of another sort of future, one in which the extraction of energy is more highly valorized. The goal of this article is to show how SIA documents work to create such a future.

Documents assessing the potential impacts of energy development are interesting for a discussion of Anthropology of the Future, both in the insight they provide on people's ideas about their own present and future and as discursive texts about state and corporate intentions. Through such documents, the imagined future becomes a way of projecting power into the present (Espeland 1993). These future scenarios are both a matter of professional and personal interest for me. Since 1996, I have conducted over 16 months of ethnographic fieldwork in northern Alberta: in Cree/Métis communities impacted by tar sands development, as well as by conventional energy and forestry. While this article is informed by this ethnographic perspective, it draws mainly on data from SIA documents, filed since 1995 as part of the approval process for various tar sands projects, and touching on indigenous interests in TLU. The article considers the nature and credibility of future predictions made in impact assessment documents, in part by exploring the rather different concerns and predictions expressed by indigenous research subjects whom the consultant authors of these reports encountered in their work.

SIA is an important component of EIA more broadly, with governments in Canada and elsewhere requiring assessment of social impacts prior to approving major projects. Since 1995, Canada's federal impact assessment legislation (the *Canadian Environmental Assessment Act* or CEAA) specifically requires the evaluation of impacts that a major project could have on TLU of indigenous people. While, as a matter of policy, SIA preceded the passage of CEAA, Canada's SIA provisions were greatly strengthened by the CEAA, particularly in the case of evaluating impacts on TLU of indigenous people. While recently the federal government has made steps in CEAA 2012, a new piece of legislation, to streamline and speed up environmental assessment, the requirement for assessing the impact of large projects on TLU remains. (All of the case studies I am analyzing were conducted under the previous CEAA.) It is important to note that, to date, no tar sands project has been rejected or significantly modified through this process, in spite of objections of indigenous communities, municipal officials, health authorities, and other representatives of civil society. In making their recommendations, EIA panels and regulators generally declare that projects pose no likely significant impact. I contend that the construction of energy futures within SIA documents—read by lawyers, activists, bureaucrats, and EIA panelists, and the subject of deliberations at public hearings—plays a significant role in inducing such conclusions.

The bitumen (tar sands) deposits underlying northern Alberta (and, to a lesser extent, Saskatchewan) constitute one of the world's major proven energy reserves, with billions of barrels of oil and hundreds of billions in capital investments at stake. After largely experimental, publically subsidized beginnings, the exploitation of tar sands deposits has increased rapidly since the mid-1990s, with continuing public subsidies in the form of royalty and tax treatment. Currently dozens of approved and proposed megaprojects involving nearly all of the world's major energy companies are forthcoming. While the majority of tar sands deposits are not accessible by mining, to date over 650 km^2 of land have been disturbed by mining, while over 1,350 km^2 of land are approved for future mining development (with the most high profile developments centering around the Athabasca River valley, north of the city of Fort McMurray). Although the paradigmatic image of the tar sands is a pit mine, in fact a large majority of the 100 or so projects currently operating are not mines but *in situ* projects (drilling, heating, and pumping networks installed over a large area), which are extensive rather than intensive in their impact on the land. Both extractive modes are relatively intensive consumers of energy, water, capital, and labor. Tar sands production is set to triple between 2005 and 2015 to over three million barrels of oil per day. Given their large scale, the tar sands—a principal source of fuel for both Canada and the USA—are more prominent and controversial than ever, thanks in part to a series of high profile public interest studies (Dowdeswell et al. 2010; Gosselin et al. 2010), which have shown considerable problems in assessment and monitoring of environmental and social risks. One of these reports, authored by physical scientists and an economist, established that tar sands SIAs typically do not provide data to support their predictions of social and economic benefits from the projects (Gosselin et al. 2010).

Northern Alberta's boreal forest landscape is populated by Cree, Dene, and Métis indigenous peoples, most of whom lived a semi-nomadic foraging lifestyle well into the post-war period and who today constitute the most visible minority group in the region. Many of these people continue to hunt and fish for a significant portion of their food. Gathering plants is an important source of nourishment, medicine, and cultural continuity, while trapping and snaring fur-bearing animals remains an important source of income (and food) for some individuals and families. Many people continue to spend weeks or months each year on the land in networks of cabins and camps. The protection of the landscape and their constitutionally protected Treaty and Aboriginal rights to subsistence are key concerns expressed by indigenous representatives through the EIA process, as well as through litigation and political action. Such efforts are oriented to maintaining the viability of foraging pursuits and indigenous identity into the future.

IMPACT ASSESSMENT AND FUTURE SCENARIOS: THE VIEW FROM ANTHROPOLOGY

At the most basic level, impact assessment studies are exercises in envisioning, inscribing, and engineering the future. The production of impact assessment documents as scenarios of the future is a creative undertaking, drawing on existing knowledge, hopes, and fears. The practice of impact assessment is, in turn, related to planning and to the concept of opportunity costs. At the root of these discussions lie differentials in power: power to tell the story of the future and then to enact it. Recent writing on the Anthropology of the Future provides a promising avenue for theorizing SIA documents, even if many of those writing on Anthropology of the Future do not refer to SIA as such. Focusing this theoretical literature clearly on the problem of SIA is one of the main scholarly contributions of this article.

As Alfred Gell writes, "opportunity costs"—the hypothetical loss of actions not taken—do not exist in the real world, since the world is incapable of being in an alternative relationship with itself. Cognitively and culturally, however, they are very real and, moreover, are socially constructed:

> The value of an event, the advantages and disadvantages which accrue from having that event come about, are a function of the feasible substitutes for that event in alternative possible worlds … . The definitions of what constitutes a "feasible" alternative world to the actual one are hermeneutic, depending on socially determined ideas not objective facts. (Gell 1992: 217)

Gell's insight implies the importance of interpretive processes in impact assessment and the socially constructed nature of the knowledge produced in such processes. This brings to mind Richard Howitt's (1995) insights that EIA draws largely on the power of narratives to enact or repress given visions of the future.

Despite the fact that the alternative worlds of the opportunity cost and the hypothetical future do not exist, they have an impact in the real world that goes beyond the hermeneutic: "Our evaluations of both objects and events in the actual world depend crucially on our notion of what constitute the alternatives to these objects and events, in the penumbra of non-actual worlds surrounding this one" (Gell 1992: 217). In other words, the futures "produced" in these reports may be constructed, but they have tangible effects in the world. With this in mind, we can see the difficulty of indigenous hunters and Euro-Canadian bureaucrats sitting down together to share knowledge (Nadasdy 2003), since they may not share common assumptions about the nature of reality or expertise, let alone the question of what sort of future is more desirable or feasible (Nader 2010a, 2010b).

In using Gell's (1992: 255) terms, but extending their application to EIA, impact assessment documents resemble "time maps"—a "linear enchainment of possible worlds," arising from discrete choices based on opportunity costs:

When we contemplate future courses of action, we compare particular (time maps), and we make our decision by singling out a particular sequence as optimal, i.e., the one with the lowest opportunity cost.... Our considerations are determined by the fact that, although our maps show us many possible futures, there is, in fact, only going to be *one* future, and we had better make sure that that future is the one we want it to be.

Rhetorically, the importance of impact assessment as a quasi-profession lies in its claims of expertise, particularly in preventing disastrous futures.

Sandra Wallman (1992: 1) also acknowledges the importance of future-oriented discussions in domains such as the environment, but notes that anthropologists have typically not been among those claiming expert knowledge of the future, being "nervous" of prediction:

Thus, the effects of demographic, medical, ecological, and cultural change are expertly predicted and confidently assumed, but on the whole the discussion proceeds without direct input from anthropology, and the projected impact of present "trends" on ordinary future life is nowhere anything but guessing.

Samuel Gerald Collins (2008) similarly notes that, in many futuristic models, culture is taken out, with any social change assumed to be predicated on technological change in a manner that many anthropologists might consider naively materialistic.

Wallman (1992) underlines key lines of inquiry for an Anthropology of the Future. She suggests studying scenarios of the future to examine how they function to illuminate the present. Furthermore, she notes that belief in the future both functions as a social charter and "underpins the sense of self and its survival" in such a way that "changes in those beliefs, however generated, can work radically to alter the way individuals and groups relate to each other, to the natural environment, and to culture

itself' (Ibid.: 16). As Wallman (Ibid.: 17) notes, images of the future "govern what we expect of and allocate to other peoples and the ways in which we interpret what they do." Indeed, assumptions about the future are embedded in political processes as well as in public policy. Specifically, she (Ibid.: 3) writes, such assumptions "govern the management of resources at every level—domestic, national, and global." In turn, ideas about the future are what give notions of progress and development their meaning (Ibid.: 8).

Michael M. J. Fischer (2009: 50) calls for an anthropology of "public futures," which would examine the knowledge generation practices that underlie major attempts to engineer the future, such as EIA. These processes are sites where the knowledge of some is empowered while the knowledge of others is disempowered, calling for "engagement across cultural difference" (Ibid.). For Fischer (Ibid.: 51), processes of risk assessment "are responses to decision making requirements when unprecedented ethical dilemmas arise ... in environmental.. .arenas." The inequitable access to expert knowledge on the part of subject communities in impact assessment and risk management further politicizes discussions of public futures.

Public futures themselves are "at stake where multiple technologies interact to create complex terrains or 'ethical plateaus' for decision making" (Ibid.: 51). Fischer (Ibid.: 77) further focuses on the differences between "normal science, working within stabilized paradigms, consultancy science, working with well-defined questions and given information, and regulatory or post-normal science, in which consequential health and environmental decisions must be made in the absence of good data or well-formed questions." I assert that EIA in the tar sands sector embodies the third type of science, masquerading as the second or first types.

In the same way that impact assessment is explicitly future-oriented, "resource imagination" (Ferry and Limbert 2008: 4) more broadly (of which EIA is an integral visioning component) is inherently associated with given assumptions about the future. Elizabeth Ferry and Mandana Limbert

(Ibid.) ask, "What kinds of temporal experiences, concepts, or narratives does thinking of things as resources entail?" "Resource imaginations," they point out, " frame the past, present, and future in certain ways … they inscribe teleologies" (Ibid.). In some cases, as the next section will show in detail, resource imaginations are "imbued with affects of time" (Ibid.), such as hope or dread.

One result of SIA and EIA processes is that consultants and their writings on the future assume an authority which takes discussion of the future out of the political arena and places it solidly in the technical arena, rendering debates open to technical interventions, but not to political, legal, or popular challenge. In this technical sphere, knowledge and concerns of indigenous people may be written off as community "perspectives" (Ferguson and Lohmann 2006; cf. Li 2007). This is accomplished in part by privileging scientific knowledge and in part by making development seem inevitable.

"WE NEED TO STAND UP NOW FOR THE KIDS AND THE FUTURE": SIA AND FUTURE PROJECTION

Tar sands EIA studies typically characterize future development impacts on foraging people by using terms such as "moderate" and "short-term." Future scenarios seen in the TLU components of three EIAs provide case studies for evaluating such predictions through document analysis. In each study, one chapter relates primarily or partially to TLU concerns. Three particular EIA chapters were selected as case studies because of their rich discourse of future prediction. I examine these consulting reports as future scenarios, which value differentially subsistence pursuits and industrial development.

These future scenarios have the potential to illuminate the value system and the social charter of our energy dependent society as well as the aspirations and concerns of indigenous research subjects. As such, I will analyze both the hermeneutic aspect of these documents (what is taken for granted in the interpretations and formulations of consultants) and

also their practical applications (how do such documents function to make the future and how reliable are their predictions of it). As Wallman suggests, the energy futures envisioned in these documents have potential to radically alter the sense of self of indigenous inhabitants of northern Alberta, particularly in respect to the ways in which indigenous people relate to the natural environment, each other, and to their culture. Correspondingly, the future scenarios embedded in EIAs provide blueprints for how political and natural resources will be allocated to minority populations, by means of a technical discourse that leaves politics and rights aside—treaty rights are typically not mentioned. In spite of such attempts to put things in a technical frame, it is notable that none of the reports I discuss here seem to be written by consultants with advanced training in social sciences. Thus, it appears that the predictions are largely fatuous guesses, as Wallman points out in another context.

Each of these case studies refers to an EIA document submitted since 1995, after the coming into force of the CEAA, which explicitly called for consideration of any impacts on TLU of indigenous people. None of the three case studies reviewed here are successful in this regard, owing to shortcomings in methodology, data analysis, literature reviews, and other problems. While each claims that no long-term significant impact on foragers is likely to result from the proposed development, in fact the reports do not make this case. Rather, what is interesting is to see how these future scenarios function to make inevitable certain views of the future.

Syncrude Aurora Mine: EIA filed 1995; approved barrels/day (bpd)

Located approximately 40 km north of Ft. McMurray, Syncrude's Aurora mine was one of the first "new generation" tar sands projects approved following federal and provincial tax and royalty inducements of the mid-1990s. The expansion confirmed the status of Syncrude, a joint venture, as a major tar sands player. Syncrude bills itself as Canada's largest employer of indigenous people (representing the future) and has funded a major museum gallery on indigenous cultures (representing the past) at the Royal Alberta Museum in Edmonton. The company, thus, represents itself as in tune with indigenous trends and issues. Conversely, this EIA study, prepared by Bovar Environmental, offers little mention of indigenous concerns. The EIA was filed and approved following the coming into force of the CEAA, which called explicitly for consideration and analysis of cumulative impacts and of potential impacts on TLU of indigenous people. Nevertheless, it can be seen that the study does not conform particularly well to these standards. The proposed development was approved notwithstanding these problems.

This study is unique among my case studies in that there is not a chapter specifically devoted to indigenous issues. Rather, the most relevant section, Section Five (Resource Use), of the EIA study considers hunting and trapping alongside pastimes such as photography. The authors use a technical discourse of "links" and "pathways" to assess likely impacts on a variety of "resource uses" during both the construction/operations and reclamation phases. The means of prediction is hubristic, as the assumptions and methods that predictions were based on are not disclosed. Generally, the goal of social impact assessment is an analysis of risks and alternatives (not discussed in any of my case studies), not a prediction that no risk will occur (Carley 1983).

For each of the activities of hunting, fishing, and plant gathering, it is argued that, while there may be some impact during construction and operations phase, in the long run, access to the activity will be *improved* following tar sands development and reclamation. For instance, although the authors themselves raise the possibility of future fish tainting, they subsequently reject it out of hand with little apparent support in doing so. With no tainting predicted and the creation of new habitat predicted through the proposed creation (following reclamation) of end-use "pit lakes," the mine is actually a boon to future fishing, according to Bovar. This prediction proved to be wildly optimistic: numerous photos of ill fish have surfaced from

many sources, and serious water pollution has been conclusively established in the tar sands region (Kelly et al. 2010).

Similarly, with respect to cumulative impacts, it is acknowledged that previous projects had already had impacts on foraging; however, these impacts are characterized as having positive as well as negative aspects. Interestingly, the only "positive" impact mentioned as being associated with the mine, for hunters specifically, is increased access to formerly remote hunting areas. This may be a positive for sport hunters and tourists; however, the problem of increased access is briefly mentioned elsewhere by Bovar (1995) as being a negative impact on indigenous people. Thus, it is curious that it is mentioned as a positive cumulative impact in the next paragraph and throughout the rest of the report.

Reclamation of mine site lands following the project is understood as the key to resolving any impacts, few of which are recognized as permanent. Full reclamation on this scale is not only unproven but is acknowledged in the report itself to be most unlikely. Although it is stated that reclamation will expand the proportion of upland and dry terrain in the study area, since it is more difficult to restore wetlands and since northern Alberta is generally a rather wet landscape, elsewhere the return of aquatic animals (an important fur and food source) is predicted in large numbers following reclamation. Similarly, it is acknowledged that moose habitat and moose populations in the study area will decline markedly during the operation phase and not fully return following "reclamation" of an altered environment. Yet, one might ask, how can hunting opportunities be predicted to improve when this key food and cultural species is forecast to decline permanently?

The sections on plant gathering and aesthetics are particularly disappointing in terms of their treatment of indigenous interests. Forecasts that aesthetics will actually improve following reclamation, with the addition of more hills and lakes, are ethnocentric and do not square with the spectrum of indigenous landscape practices, based on the use of environments such as wetlands. Also, forecasts by Bovar that medicinal and spiritual plant gathering opportunities will improve following reclamation are weakened by admissions in the report that monitoring will not be conducted on key plant species. Furthermore, such forecasts do not acknowledge the feeling held by many active foragers that one cannot effectively gather efficacious medicinal plants on land that has been used as a mine, given the damage that has been done to the spirit of the place.

For all these fantastic predictions—derived through an impersonal and inevitable narrative discourse of pathways and linkages—that the physical prerequisites of fishing, hunting, trapping, and gathering will be restored or even improved, questions remain. Who will be the cultured and socialized individuals who will return to practice these pursuits? Where will they have learned the skills and values to practice TLU effectively? Which elders will have taught them, and which spirits of the reclaimed place will watch over them? Which language will they be speaking, and where will they have learned the terms to display their full knowledge in and of this language with respect to TLU? Such questions are in the social domain and fall within the purview of the CEAA and of good SIA practice. Acceptable answers to these questions must go well beyond the assurances of technological fixes such as restoration that are proffered in this report. Overall, then, the report treats the future as an event to be conjured up, not a process which is always in the process of becoming. Moreover, we see that evidence and monitoring are apparently not required to support such predictions. Thus, this study is notable for its hubristic predictions, as well as its insistence on commensurability, implying that the reclaimed environment will be comparable to—better than, even—the existing environment in a deep sense. Such assertions simply do not take the complexity of indigenous lifeworlds, nor the cultural vitality that they imply, into account.

Husky Sunrise Project: EIA filed 2004; approved 2005, 270,000 bpd

Husky Energy's Sunrise Energy Project represents this major Canadian company's biggest play in the tar sands. Located 60 km northeast of Ft. McMurray, this project is not a mine but an *in-situ* development using steam-assisted gravity drainage to heat and pump bitumen through a network of pipes. The central facility consists of water heating, wastewater treatment, and bitumen handling facilities. However, unlike Syncrude, which processes bitumen on-site, Husky will conduct final processing in Ohio. Oil production will begin in 2014.

Particularly revealing in this EIA is the use of computer modeling and simulation for a discussion of the future of TLU. Tar sands proponents have found future modeling and simulation useful, as they are less expensive than conducting ongoing large-scale studies, while appearing to satisfy regulators through claims of expertise. Like many other tar sands TLU documents, this one relies to a great extent on modeling assumptions in a 2002 work by Jennifer A. McKillop (cited in Husky Energy 2004), a Master in Environmental Design project from the University of Calgary. McKillop's project is based on predictive computer modeling of sensitive ecosystems used in TLU by the Fort McKay First Nation (FMFN), one of several indigenous communities in the tar sands region. This modeling study purports to set out a means of conducting action research in partnership with FMFN and has become a TLU bible of sorts to tar sands EIA consultants. Various EIA reports now cite McKillop as an expert on regional history, ethnology, and cultural change: quite a load for a Master's project, based on computer modeling, to carry! Many of these characterizations in the EIA reports were made on the basis of earlier, incomplete versions of McKillop's work.

Several points are relevant here: one is the degree to which all EIA studies emphasize the TLU of FMFN above any other group (although FMFN is closest to the epicenter of tar sands mining in the Athabasca region, there are at least five directly impacted First Nations, as well as Métis communities, with TLU interests in the area); second is the assumption that computer modeling can provide a predictive platform that will allow consultants to fill holes created by the short duration and questionable quality of their field data collection. Moreover, the results of this FMFN-based model are explicitly said to be relevant to the TLU of other groups, based on the universality of the model. The result is that the model serves to break down consultation beyond the FMFN, rendering it less important, rather than enhancing and broadening the scope of public consultation. Minimally, this model's rapid uptake among EIA consultants shows the narrow range of literature upon which the field is drawing.

In Husky's study, the proposed development is referred to in the present tense. The outcome of the process is not questioned. Rhetorically, the assessment document, thus, becomes part of a discursive power play, suggesting this development is inevitable and had best be accommodated (Howitt 1995).

As with Bovar, the framework of the report makes predictions based on a series of arbitrarily determined "indicators." Again, the general assertion is that reclamation will solve any problems. Yet, one wonders, do the authors of this study, and the proponents of the project, continue to stand by assertions made in 2005? These assumptions include the following: no contamination of traditional plants, negligible changes in water quality/quantity, minimal impact on air quality, minimal impacts on human health from cumulative tar sands developments, low likelihood of cumulative impacts to fish, effective pollution monitoring, and between one and 10 individual moose directly impacted by a large project. Many such claims or predictions are now the subject of hot public debate, at minimum, or have been discredited in subsequent scientific studies (Candler et al. 2010; Kelly et al. 2010; Schindler 2010; Timoney and Lee 2009). Yet, such anonymous predictions of a hassle-free future were allowed to pass muster by regulators.

On the positive side, this study includes an environmental emergency scenario. Other studies typically do not consider social or TLU aspects of such an emergency, even though it is required by CEAA (cf. Gosselin et al. 2010). Without support, Husky assesses the likely impact on TLU of an environmental emergency (the nature of which is not clearly specified) as short-term and reversible.

While assessing the overall project impact in terms such as low, moderate, and medium-term, the consultants provide little discussion at how these assessments were arrived or what their impact on the lived experience of indigenous people would be. Indeed, the authors state that their own confidence in the accuracy of their own future projections is merely "moderate." Are the authors asserting that the domain of study is only moderately amenable to expert prediction? Such a conclusion will reflect, then, on the reliability of the entire enterprise being undertaken in this and other reports under analysis here.

Relevant in this case study is the reliance on modeling to enhance the predictive capacity, bringing to the fore the methods of prediction that Bovar kept backstage. Regrettably, given that the level of reliability in the model is only moderate, this suggests problems with the SIA as a whole. Future research could benefit from the attention to models in SIA, including the reliance in future prediction on assumptions of certain models, such as McKillop's, by an entire class of EIA.

Imperial Kearl Mine: EIA filed 2005; approved 2007, 300,000 bpd

Imperial Oil is Canada's second largest energy company, owns 25 percent of Syncrude, and is controlled by ExxonMobil. The Kearl mine, 70 km north of Ft. McMurray, is a joint venture between Imperial and ExxonMobil. The project will not process bitumen on-site but consists of a very large mine with an estimated 40-year lifespan. Noting the project lifespan, it is important to consider cumulative impacts, particularly when recalling that the Kearl project, like the other case studies, is or will be largely surrounded by contiguous large-scale tar sands developments.

This study backgrounds, and thus diminishes, the remarks of impacted indigenous trappers by presenting them as data in grids, point form, or tables: an assertion of the authorial expert voice

229

which threatens to reduce the potential effect of the given data. Given that the trappers' interview summaries are frequently the most effective, least managed parts of these studies, their removal provides decision makers with even less information from an indigenous perspective. Nevertheless, the author sometimes allows the voices of other indigenous people—those who participated in public meetings—to come through. These voices express a rather different view of the future than that seen in the study as a whole.

It is acknowledged in the study that tar sands development has caused considerable impacts on indigenous communities. Nevertheless, a number of passages indicate that the author's interpretation and elaboration are weak when discussing culturally informed remarks of elders regarding future impacts and, therefore, do not provide the required information to regulators. One elder stated:

> They're going to plant trees and everything else the same. Sure, trees are easy to plant. Anyone can plant trees anywhere. What about all the herbs that they destroy or the *muskeg* (wetlands) and all over the place that us Indians, we use those herbs for medicines. If they destroy all those things, how are they going to plant those herbs? They don't know what's underground, under the muskeg. They'll never plant those herbs again in this world, never .... You don't know the herbs you destroy (quoted in Imperial 2005: 6-40).

The author's interpretation of these remarks is that one can't replace the whole if a small part has been damaged. This discussion fails to recognize that the elder's remarks regarding medicinal plants actually concern the nature of traditional knowledge and spiritual power in relation to the structure of the natural world. Moreover, the elder refers to a future in which certain ecosystem characteristics are relatively easily replaced, while others, including spiritual aspects, will be impossible to replace due to lack of proper knowledge and respect in the present. This questions the assumptions of commensurability seen in all three case studies' claims about landscape reclamation.

In paraphrasing the remarks of other indigenous people, the author states:

> Participants note that there is a spiritual essence to the land that is an integral part of the environment. One participant stated that, "... when you dig a hole (e.g., a mine pit), the spirit of the land is gone." *This was interpreted to mean that when the fabric of the environment has been altered, it can never be fully replaced* (Imperial 2005: 6-41, emphasis added).

Again, this paraphrase seems an attempt to take the given remarks of participants out of a religious frame and put them in a technical frame more amenable to expert management. Yet, TLU is a spiritual activity not merely a technical one. It is a duty of the consultants to convey the meaning of these remarks, which manifestly deal with "the spirit of the land" rather than "the fabric of the environment." This contrast between the technical and spiritual suggests major problems for the current framing and representation of impact assessments on indigenous lands. No substantial ethnographic or historical information on Cree, Dene, or Métis religious practices is provided in this report or in the others I analyzed.

Kearl Lake, now heavily impacted by contiguous tar sands projects, emerges in this study as a focal site within the seasonal round, formerly featuring especially good moose hunting. Nevertheless, the author acknowledges, "Imperial Oil has advised elders that it is impossible to reclaim the landscape back to the way it was" (Imperil 2005: 6-35). This frank statement certainly seems to belie the regular commitments made for full and favorable reclamation of other mine sites in the reports discussed above.

It is relevant that regional indigenous communities are in the process of restoring and reasserting traditional cultural practices and governance structures after a period of internal colonialism, perhaps exemplified best by decades of forcible residential schooling for most minors. Such renewal processes are especially vulnerable in a neo-colonial context to being disrupted, and maintaining space for continued cultural renewal is a key aspiration of indigenous people. As members of Mikisew Cree First Nation (MCFN) stated at a public meeting, "We need to speak up for the sake of our grandchildren … . We need to stand up now for the kids and the future." MCFN members put their objections in tangibly future-oriented terms, tying their fears to children, grandchildren, and the spirit of the land, as well as practical matters such as landscape values and health of wildlife populations.

Proponents and consultant authors attempt to distance themselves from the remarks of youth and children and from suggestions that young people should be involved in the EIA. In spite of this, elders and other participants continue to view the voices of children and youth as critical to the process (Imperial Oil 2005). Youth are the voices of the future, but emphasizing youth concerns would conflict with the largely past-oriented, salvage approach to tar sands TLU research, which focuses on the knowledge and practice of elders, implying an end point for foraging modes of production. This suggests problems in the way that EIA is conceptualized and carried out in indigenous communities.

General Comments

In examining TLU studies from three EIA documents filed for use in public review processes under the CEAA for major tar sands developments, I have focused on the ways these documents discuss the future. I have shown the deep gap between cultural assumptions of consultants and indigenous people about the futures being projected—their likelihood as well as their desirability and meaning. Moreover, I have emphasized that such documents use hubristic means of prediction, often without disclosing the empirical basis of the projection. In more recent cases, the SIAs are dominated by citations of a small number of studies purporting to use computer modeling to describe and map impacts on a complex social, cultural, and ecological terrain (apart from

the consideration of accidents, which are more difficult to model). Finally, we see the lack of attention to cumulative future impacts, in breach of the law but also in breach of lived experience of temporality as complex and multi-faceted. Moreover, we have seen that not only consultants but also indigenous people seem drawn to discussing impacts in terms of the future, focusing on their own children and grandchildren as cultural and knowledgeable actors whose interests should be paramount. The point is not to reify these case studies but to understand in general the ways that consultants writing each of them strive to inscribe the future of the energy imaginary, at the same time as indigenous participants are striving to be heard over the authorial voice, arguing for their own preferred future.

CONCLUSIONS: SOCIAL IMPACT ASSESSMENT, REGULATORY SCIENCE, AND THE ANTHROPOLOGY OF THE FUTURE

Literature from the Anthropology of the Future has provided a theoretical vantage point for understanding how SIA documents function as future design blueprints. Vestiges of Wallman's future-oriented emotions (hope and dread) can be inferred from among those participating in tar sands impact assessments. Specifically, a sense of dread is implied among those more oriented to a hunting lifestyle, while the consultants writing the EIA documents portray things in a more hopeful manner.

The consultants' reports range from predicting few longterm impacts for TLU harvesters to implicitly acknowledging the impending ecological crisis in the area. The ways in which TLU is positioned in the EIAs rhetorically functions to make these documents "narratives" (Howitt 1995) about the future and about the "inevitability" (Asch 1990) of the assimilation and acculturation of indigenous people. This is contrasted with many indications in the reports (and the regional ethnographic literature: e.g., Asch 1990) that local indigenous people are still using the bush in important ways: many extended families regularly eat a varied diet of wild foods, while most children consulted report ongoing experience with TLU. The aspiration to continue practicing TLU is consistent with Treaty promises to First Nations people and with the slowly developing, but constitutionally protected, foraging rights of Métis people. The desire to continue living in a traditional manner, and the fear of change, come through in the voices of indigenous consultation participants, in spite of the techno-scientific discourse of the authors. Author-consultants construct the EIA documents as narratives or time maps, which seem to lead inexorably to certain futures, while precluding others. Yet, these narrativizing time maps and their cause-effect relationships are not always convincing. Are they really leading to a desirable future? What are the stakes of a wrong move or cartographical error in this spatiotemporal field?

Plants, animals, lands, minerals, air, and waters—natural resources, in western terms—are always political and always temporal. "Resource imaginations," as Ferry and Limbert state (2008: 4), "inscribe teleologies" and, accordingly, inspire both hope and dread. Such teleologies are socially constructed in the same way that opportunity costs are, so that some possible futures are unquestioned while others are simply unimaginable. The power of future-oriented or teleological assumptions such as progress, development, and technological fixes is such that we fail to see that the methodology used to induce such predictions is weak; it often amounts to little more than fatuously citing generic and aggregated trends or quoting other trendy but non-authoritative grey literature to bolster one's case.

As future scenarios, SIA documents show images of the future that "govern what we expect of and allocate to other peoples and the ways in which we interpret what they do" (Wallman 1992: 17). Specifically, the contested importance of energy development and a foraging future for indigenous people calls for "engagement across cultural difference" (Fischer 2009: 50). Yet, it is not clear that such cultural and aspirational differences are being taken into account in planning tar sands extraction, as the SIA documents typically equate foraging with the past rather than the future. Moreover, the rapid expansion of tar sands developments and

the unproven technologies of solutions such as reclaimed wetlands, end-pit lakes, and pollution monitoring systems constitute "unprecedented ethical dilemmas" (Ibid.: 51). Rather than being addressed through an open consultation process that takes indigenous views into account in setting political goals for the sector as a whole, including alternatives to tar sands development, such concerns are sidetracked into technical processes that do not seem to take such unprecedented dilemmas into account theoretically, methodologically, or ethically. Thinking of things as "resources"—rather than considering a known, nurturing, landscape full of sentient beings—implies a rather different set of temporal experiences and narratives behind the resource imagination of consultants and proponents than those behind the environmental knowledge of foragers (Ferry and Limbert 2008). Given its different temporal moorings, such local knowledge is instead represented as community "perspectives" (Ferguson and Lohmann 2006), which don't fit into technical frame and which are, thus, devalued.

The power of such future scenarios makes it difficult to act for the type of consultative, reflexive, public futures research, in Anthropology and beyond, for which Fischer is calling. The ethical dilemmas posed by unequal access to knowledge and the unknown consequences of current developments suggest that anthropologists and other social scientists might play a bigger role, or at least more carefully attend to EIA and SIA research as futures research. Current tar sands SIA/EIA research manifestly occurs within Fischer's (2009: 77) paradigm of "regulatory or post-normal science, in which consequential health and environmental decisions must be made in the absence of good data or wellformed questions." This is particularly the case respecting new technologies, which are identified as future fixes, and respecting cumulative impact assessment of many existing and approved tar sands projects, which is inadequate. Thus, there is a pressing need to open up the tar sands EIA process to broader scholarly and public oversight and debate.

In this article, I have pinpointed the ways that SIA is speaking of futures. In this, I depart from other SIA literature, which tends to address more normatively the quality of information and predictions in SIA documents. I have focused on how these technical documents (fail to) predict and constitute sustainable futures. While SIA studies may only be read by a few people, they are powerful in the sense that they legitimize deeply assimilationist arguments about indigenous people, while under-writing the inevitability of continuing megaproject development with a technical aura. Addressing power differentials in the political arena is part of a bigger conversation, one that also should focus on the future. Yet, while I am not naïve about the potential of EIA to change political currents on its own, I assert that SIA is worth fighting over precisely because it offers scope for a legal and public opportunity for speaking truth to and about power. I believe there is potential for EIA and SIA—in concert with other legal and political processes—to give people tools to see projects cancelled or altered and, thus, to seize control of the future. Admittedly, this is problematic in the tar sands given the sheer number of projects being assessed simultaneously with little regard for cumulative impacts.

It is apparent that Canada as a "new energy superpower" (to quote Prime Minister Stephen Harper) likely is not a future compatible with northern Alberta Métis researcher Elmer Ghostkeeper's (1996) vision of living with the land as a form of "spirit gifting" through ceremony, story, and practice. It is this spiritual component, as well the power differential, that consultants fail to represent in their scenarios of the future, based on the resource imaginations of the present, which are represented in these consultants' reports. Yet, even the blithe, blasé style of the consultant authors cannot render some of the statements from First Nations participants into a technically thin discourse of indicators and pathways. Local people's predictions of a future with no moose to hunt, no medicinal plants to harvest, no muskeg to trap in, no untainted fisheries, and no voice for the children remain powerful, in spite of the editorial constraints of the authors and their proponent paymasters, deadening the effect of such remarks. A critical analysis of impact assessment as a future design process, in which some

visions of the future are soft-pedaled, while others may become unthinkable and impracticable, potentially provides a powerful tool for understanding, critiquing, and improving SIA, in keeping with ethnographic insights about indigenous peoples and about the future itself.

REFERENCES

Asch, Michael
  1990 The Future of Hunting and Trapping and Economic Development in Alberta's North: Some Myths and Facts About Inevitability. *In* Proceedings of the Fort Chipewyan and Fort Vermillion Bicentennial Conference. Patricia A. McCormack and R. Geoffrey Ironsides, eds. Pp. 25–29. Edmonton, Canada: Boreal Institute for Northern Studies.
Bovar Environmental
  1995 Syncrude Aurora Environmental Impact Assessment Study. North York, Canada: Bovar Environmental.
Candler, Craig, Rachel Olson, Steven DeRoy, and the Firelight Group Research Cooperative, with the Athabasca Chipewyan First Nation and the Mikisew Cree First Nation
  2010 As Long as the Rivers Flow: Athabasca River Knowledge, Use, and Change. Edmonton, Canada: Parkland Institute.
Carley, Michael J.
  1983 A Review of Selected Methods. *In* Social Impact Assessment Methods. Kurt Finsterbusch, Lynn G. Llewelllyn, and Charles P. Wolf, eds. Pp. 35–54. Beverly Hills, Calif.: Sage Publications.
Collins, Samuel Gerald
  2008 All Tomorrow's Cultures: Anthropological Engagements With the Future. New York: Berghahn Books.
Dowdeswell, Liz, Peter Dillon, Subhasis Goshal, Andrew Miall, Joseph Rasmussen, and John P. Smol
  2010 A Foundation for the Future: Building an Environmental Monitoring System for the

Oil Sands. Ottawa, Canada: Department of Environment.

Espeland, Wendy

1993 Power, Policy, and Paperwork: The Bureaucratic Representation of Interests. Qualitative Sociology 16(3):297–317.

Ferguson, James, with Larry Lohmann

2006 The Anti-Politics Machine: "Development" and Bureaucratic Power in Lesotho. *In* The Environment in Anthropology: A Reader in Ecology, Culture, and Sustainable Living. Nora Haenn and Richard R. Wilk, eds. Pp. 163-172. New York: New York University Press.

Ferry, Elizabeth Emma, and Mandana E. Limbert

2008 Introduction. *In* Timely Assets: The Politics of Resources and Their Temporalities. Elizabeth Emma Ferry and Mandana E. Limbert, eds. Pp. 3–24. Santa Fe, N.Mex.: School For Advanced Research Press.

Fischer, Michael M.J.

2009 Anthropological Futures. Durham, N.C.: Duke University Press.

Gell, Alfred

1992 The Anthropology of Time: Cultural Constructions of Temporal Maps and Images. Oxford, United Kingdom: Berg.

Ghostkeeper, Elmer

1996 Spirit Gifting: The Concept of Spiritual Exchange. Calgary, Canada: Arctic Institute of North America.

Gosselin, Pierre, Steve E. Hrudey, M. Anne Naeth, André Plourde, René Therrien, Glen Van Der Kraak, and Zhenghe Xu

2010 Environmental and Health Impacts of Canada's Oil Sands Industry. Ottawa: The Royal Society of Canada.

Howitt, Richard

1995 Social Impact Assessment, Sustainability, and Developmentalist Narratives of Resource Regions. Impact Assessment 13(4):387–402.

Husky Energy

2004 Husky Sunrise Environmental Impact Assessment Study. Calgary, Canada: Husky Energy.

Imperial Oil

2005 Kearl Oil Sands Project Environmental Impact Assessment Study. Calgary, Canada: Imperial Oil.

Kelly, Erin N„ Jeffrey W. Short, David W. Schindler, Peter V. Hodson, Mingsheng Ma, Alvin K. Kwan, and Barbra L. Fortin

2010 Oil Sands Development Contributes Polycyclic Aromatic Compounds to the Athabasca River and Its Tributaries. Proceedings of the National Academy of Sciences 106(52):22346–22351.

Li, Tania Murray

2007 The Will to Improve: Govemmentality, Development, and the Practice of Politics. Durham, N.C.: Duke University Press.

Nadasdy, Paul

2003 Hunters and Bureaucrats: Power, Knowledge, and Aboriginal-State Relations in the Southwest Yukon. Vancouver, Canada: University of British Columbia Press.

Nader, Laura

2010a Barriers to New Thinking About Energy. *In* The Energy Reader. Laura Nader, ed. Pp. 198–204. Malden, Mass.: Wiley-Blackwell.

2010b Who Shall Decide? *In* The Energy Reader. Laura Nader, ed. Pp. 538–540. Malden, Mass.: Wiley-Blackwell.

Schindler, David W.

2010 Tar Sands Need Solid Science. Nature 468(4723):499–501.

Timoney, Kevin P., and Peter Lee

2009 Does the Alberta Tar Sands Industry Pollute? The Scientific Evidence. Open Conservation Biology Journal 2009 (3):65–81.

Wallman, Sandra

1992 Introduction: Contemporary Futures. *In* Contemporary Futures: Perspectives From Social Anthropology. Sandra Wallman, ed. Pp. 1–22. London, United Kingdom: Routledge.

Westman, Clinton N.

2006 Assessing the Impacts of Oilsands Development on Indigenous Peoples in Alberta, Canada. Indigenous Affairs 2006 (2–3): 30–39.

n.d.l A Critical Review of Traditional Land Use Components for Environmental Impact Assessment Studies in the Oilsands Region. Unpublished report prepared for Mikisew Cree First Nation.

234

n.d.2 Cautionary Tales: Making and Breaking Community in the Oil Sands Region. Canadian Journal of Sociology. In press.

n.d.3 Exploitation des sables bitumieux et Peuples autochtones d'Alberta, Canada: Impacts, processus et réponses. *In* Terres (dés)humanisées: Ressources et climat. Charlotte Breda, Mélanie Chaplier, Julie Hermesse, and Emmanuelle Picolli, eds. Louvain- la-Neuve, Belgium: Academia- L'Harmattan. In press.

18

Toxic Cities: Globalizing the Problem of Waste

By Rob White

INTRODUCTION

This article provides a detailed case study of a toxic event that occurred in Abidjan, Ivory Coast, in August 2006. This is a continuing event, in the sense that people are still suffering the full effects and consequences of the toxic waste that was dumped in their city. Meanwhile, the event itself has sparked ongoing legal and political fallout within the West African nation, as well as in Europe, the United Kingdom, and Jamaica.

The significance of this event resides in the fact that it highlights both the larger problem of how to deal with toxic waste and the global character of some forms of "resolving" this problem. As the case study reveals, there are multiple players, diverse interests, and conflicting purposes that underpin toxic waste disposal. The internationalization of the issue, and the globalization of the problem, are integral elements to understanding how events such as the toxic waste dumping in Abidjan occurred.

This article begins by describing what occurred in August 2006, as well as the response of "responsible" parties to the event. A discussion of what happened in the aftermath of the dumping follows. The article concludes with an interpretation of current trends and issues, and the challenges relating to toxic waste disposal now and into the future.

A key message here is that the dumping of toxic and other waste in Third World countries in not exceptional, but rather is part of the normal "contracted out" disposal process common to global capitalism. A worldwide scandal, of sorts, occurred in this instance because of the scale of the disaster. In a similar vein, the high costs of remediation, which involved transferring the waste back to Europe for final disposal, were directly linked to focusing the world spotlight on what happened in Abidjan. Even so, the sheer scale of the disaster was not enough to generate much interest in other parts of the world. This, too, deserves comment.

A BRIEF NOTE ON METHODOLOGY

The impetus for this article comes from the circumstances surrounding my first hearing of the original incident. In the middle of the night in Hobart, Tasmania, in August 2006, I happened to be listening to ABC-News Radio, a news service that broadcasts overseas news services (such as the BBC and Deutsche Welle), as well as Australian-provided news. There was a brief report from the BBC about a toxic disaster in the Ivory Coast. The next morning I turned on ABC radio, then the TV morning news, and there was no mention of the story. I checked the local newspaper. Nothing.

By sheer chance, that day at work I discovered a facility on my computer called "Google Alert." I typed in "Ivory Coast Toxic Waste" and over the next 12 months (and indeed to this day) received periodic reports about the event and its aftermath

Rob White, "Toxic Cities: The Globalizing Problem of Waste," *Social Justice*, vol. 35, no. 3, pp. 107-119. Copyright © 2009 by Social Justice. Reprinted with permission. Provided by ProQuest LLC. All rights reserved.

from news services worldwide. What struck me then, and still does today, was the relative lack of reporting in the Australian media, much less the North American media. In this light, I share the sentiments expressed on-line by one journalist:

> While the toxic-waste scandal has garnered headlines around the world, in the United States the story has been largely relegated to tiny squibs in the "World Briefs" sections of newspapers—if it has been covered at all. None of the country's leading newspapers—the *Wall Street Journal, New York Times, Washington Post, Los Angeles Times,* or *USA Today*—has run staff-written stories from the scene of the disaster. The story has not been covered by any of the major TV networks. CNN's Anderson Cooper has not rushed off to Abidjan to feel the victims' pain and demand justice on their behalf, as he has with other recent disasters. His cable-news competitors have also missed the story (Kahn, 2006).

In my collection of materials on the Ivory Coast, I noticed that most newspaper reports in the United States did mainly rely upon Reuters or Associated Press feeds. Sporadic stories appeared in media outlets in Holland, the U.K., Germany, Turkey, Vietnam, Angola, South Africa, Jamaica, and the Ivory Coast itself. Stories also appeared in "alternative" news sources such as Inner City Press in the United States and in web-based information sites such as Environment News. As others have observed, there are often media silences when it comes to certain types of environmental crimes, due in no small part to the intersections between the large polluting corporations and the media (see, for example, Simon, 2000).

In this specific instance, there was little consistent coverage. Yet, detail by detail, a picture of what occurred in the Ivory Coast did emerge. Information from many different media sources and from a variety of national contexts provides a fascinating composite portrait of toxic waste in its global context. I read hundreds of pages of media reports, and after a long culling out process, deleted repetition and stories of no consequence. What remained formed the basis for the presentation below.

The bulk of the article is devoted to a detailed portrayal of what happened that fateful August night, and what has happened since. The article thus provides selected but comprehensive "information," rather than a more sophisticated conceptual analysis. This is because I felt it was useful to concentrate on what some social scientists refer to as "thick description" to best elucidate the processes and complexities of the people, behaviors, and consequences of the toxic event. The final section of the article nevertheless provides a series of analytical observations that suggest ways in which we might interpret what happened in this specific case, and more generally what is occurring vis-à-vis toxic waste production and disposal generally.

THE EVENT

In August 2006, some 600 tons of caustic soda and petroleum residues were dumped at 18 open-air public waste sites in Abidjan, the main city of the western African nation of Ivory Coast. Early news reports stated that fumes from the waste had caused nosebleeds, nausea, and vomiting. A terrible stench, smelling of rotten eggs, permeated the city of around five million inhabitants. Most of the waste was dumped in the poorer parts of the city. Among the dumpsites were the city's lagoon-side main garbage dump, a roadside field beside a prison, and a sewage canal.

To date, 16 people are acknowledged to have died due to this event. Over 100,000 people sought medical attention, with around 75 people hospitalized. The source of the complaint was "slops," a general term for cargo and tank-washing residues. In this case, they contained substantial quantities of hydrogen sulfide, sodium hydroxide (caustic soda), and chemicals called mercaptans that smell like garlic or rotting cabbage.

The dumping of these toxic slops involved various international bodies. A Dutch company, Trafigura Beheer BV, chartered the boat to carry its toxic cargo. Trafigura is a global oil and metals trading company. With offices in London and its headquarters in Lucerne, Switzerland, its chief executives include French nationals. The *Probo Koala*, a Korean-built tanker, is Greek-owned and Panamanian registered; it has a Russian crew. The final disposal of the waste was devolved to a local Ivorian company, Tommy. To remove the waste, the Ivorian government brought in a French cleanup company, Tredi International, because it could only be destroyed using European technologies. Upon returning to Europe, the ship was impounded in Estonia, where a criminal investigation found that samples taken from the ship showed traces of environmentally dangerous poisonous chemicals (*Turkish Weekly*, in BBC, 2006). The section below provides a chronological account of the disaster in Abidjan, from events leading up to it through to the immediate aftermath.

A CHRONOLOGY OF EVENTS

According to media and United Nations reports, the path to the Ivory Coast involved a series of choices and decisions (Associated Press, February 14, 2007; BBC News, 2007b; UNDAC, 2006; Bridgland, 2006; Reuters, 2006b; Dutch News, 2007; *International Herald Tribune*, 2007b).

- Amsterdam Port Services (APS) initially agreed to dispose of the waste for $15,000;
- However, when a subcontractor pumped the waste to an unloading ship, it was evident the washings were more concentrated than expected;
- APS took a sample from the "waste water" and it proved to be a highly lethal cocktail of petroleum, caustic soda, and other agents;
- People around the docking area complained about feeling ill and about the smell, and the waste was pumped back into the *Probo Koala*;

- The port authorities reclassified the tank contents as toxic waste and then instructed the ship's captain to take the waste to a special facility and dispose of it, at a cost of $650,000;
- Trafigura refused to pay and, mindful of "significant financial time penalties" if it waited to resolve the issue in Amsterdam, the *Probo Koala* left;
- An independent Dutch committee ordered by the city of Amsterdam to investigate the handling of the *Probo Koala* ship was to subsequently find that the ship could have been detained at the port of Amsterdam;
- A later study of events by independent lawyers for Dutch members of parliament said that transport ministry officials had not dared to prevent the ship from leaving Dutch waters because the ship's owners, Trafigura, had threatened to sue for damages if the ban proved to be groundless;
- The ship then traveled on to Estonia, where it turned down an offer to dispose of the waste for $260,000;
- The next port of call was Nigeria, where no agreement for disposal of the waste was possible after negotiations with two local waste disposal firms;
- Both Estonia and Nigeria have ratified an international ban on the shipping of hazardous waste from rich to poor countries, but Ivory Coast had not;
- In Ivory Coast, Trafigura "found" a local company called Tommy, which agreed to dispose of the waste for roughly the original price;
- Tommy was an off-the-shelf company that had been quickly formed between two French commodity traders and executives of a waste disposal company in Ivory Coast;
- From the beginning, however, no company in Ivory Coast had the facilities to deal with this kind of waste;
- More than a dozen trucks contracted by Tommy simply poured the tons of waste out at multiple sites across the city, after midnight of August 19;

- On the night of September 14–15, further dumpings were reported to have taken place.

In February 2007, two employees of APS, the Amsterdam waste disposal company, were detained for questioning in a criminal investigation related to the dumping of the toxic waste in Ivory Coast. An arrest warrant was also issued for the captain of the *Probo Koala*. Many agreed *post facto* that permission should not have been granted for pumping back the waste, yet the rules at the time were unclear and the situation was unprecedented. Various court cases in the Netherlands, England, and the Ivory Coast have been initiated and/or continued to run their course well into 2008. Most have not been resolved at the time of writing. They involve local and transnational company directors, victims' groups, and the ship's captain and others involved in the waste disposal industry.

THE ROLE OF TRAFIGURA

Trafigura claimed it had not violated international conventions on the disposal of toxic waste. It maintained that the slops were handed over to a certified local Abidjan slops disposal company, Compagnie Tommy, following Trafigura's communication to the authorities concerning the nature of the slops and a written request seeking safe disposal of the material.

Local press reports linked Ivorian First Lady, Simone Ehivet Gbagbo, with the company that disposed toxic waste. She denied ownership of Tommy, insisting that "apart from the document signed by former Transports Minister authorizing Tommy to remove the waste, there is no other document establishing Tommy as a company" (Angola Press, 2006). Tommy's headquarters is a two-story building in a poor residential neighborhood of Abidjan (*International Herald Tribune*, 2006a).

An Ivorian government commission investigating the dumping of the toxic waste released its findings in November 2006. The commission found that Compagnie Tommy showed all the signs of being a front company set up specifically to handle the Trafigura waste. According to the report, the company was established in a period between Trafigura's decision not to pay for expensive waste disposal in Amsterdam and its ship's arrival in Abidjan. The panel notes that Tommy charged 16 times less than estimates Trafigura received at the port of Amsterdam (VOA News, 2006a). Tommy was set up specifically for the waste dumping operation and singled out Nigerian owner and manager, Salomon Ugborugbo, to facilitate the tragedy. A day before the toxic shipment was secretly unloaded, the report continued, Ugborugbo wrote a letter to Trafigura "clearly stating that he had found a place outside the city called ' Akwedo' (*sic*), where he would dump the products." Akouedo is Abidjan's main garbage landfill. The report said Trafigura was aware that Tommy was dumping the waste, rather than neutralizing it (*International Herald Tribune*, 2006b).

Trafigura said it could not explain why the waste contained poisonous, highly toxic components such as hydrogen sulfide. In February 2007, Trafigura's director of operations, Graham Sharp, stated that "Trafigura did not 'dump' any waste product in Abidjan where the Company has traded for 10 years and has employees, facilities, and long-term investments. The 'slops' from the *Probo Koala*'s waste tanks were offloaded into road tankers operated by an accredited local contractor under the normal supervision of port, customs, and environmental authorities" (BBC News, February 13, 2007). The company continued to maintain that its gasoline tanker contained nontoxic "chemical slops" consisting of spent caustic soda, gasoline residues, and water.

The Estonian prosecutor's office said its tests found the chemicals in *Probo Koala* to be toxic. Trafigura countered that its own tests showed that the chemicals had little or no toxicity (VOA News, 2006b). It has also argued that the waste on the *Probo Koala* in Estonia was not the same as was discharged in Ivory Coast.

Dutch lawyer Bob van der Goen lodged a compensation claim against Trafigura, demanding millions of euros in damages for the victims of toxic waste dumped in Abidjan. In February 2007,

239

van der Goen also began legal action against the Amsterdam city council for its role in the *Probo Koala* affair (*Dutch News,* 2007).

British lawyer Martyn Day also started legal proceedings against Trafigura. Asserting that the firm was negligent and flouted international rules on toxic cargoes, he is seeking millions of pounds in damages for the victims' families. In response, Trafigura said it was suing the lawyer: "Trafigura has today issued proceedings for libel against solicitors Leigh Day and Co. in respect of a press release and website publication in which Trafigura is wrongly accused of causing death and injury" (Reuters, 2006a).

The Ivorian government jailed Claude Dauphin, Jean-Pierre Valentini, and Nzi Kablan on September 18. Dauphin is the director of Trafigura and Valentini is its West Africa regional director; Kablan is from a subsidiary called Puma Energy. They were released on February 14, 2007, after Trafigura agreed to pay U.S.$198 million to the Ivorian government. The deal absolves the Ivorian government and the firm Trafigura of any liability in the scandal and forbids future prosecutions or claims by the Ivory Coast on the company. In justification, the statement released said: "Trafigura and the government of Ivory Coast dismiss any responsibility for the happenings in August emphatically. Of course, Trafigura takes its social role as a player in the world market very seriously and therefore wants to support the government financially in order to offer its citizens a better health situation" (*International Herald Tribune,* 2007b). Trafigura denies any connection between the release of its executives and the payment. Upon his release, Dauphin said:

> My colleagues and I are relieved and overjoyed to be in the arms of our families again after five months in jail as innocent men. We went to the Ivory Coast on a mission to help the people of Abidjan, and to find ourselves arrested and in jail as a result has been a terrible ordeal for ourselves and our families. If any good can come of this, myself and colleagues

now look forward to Trafigura and the Ivorian government working together for a better future for the people of Abidjan (*Environmental News,* 2007).

Innocence, being Good Samaritans, and beneficial collaboration are supposedly the hallmarks of Trafigura and its executives. Is this so?

THE CORPORATE TRACK RECORD OF TRAFIGURA

Founded in 1993 by a group of eight independent oil traders, Trafigura Beheer BV is a subsidiary of the Trafigura Group, which specializes in energy and base metals, and is represented in 36 countries worldwide. Some of Trafigura's major international units (Wikipedia, 2007) include:

- Trafigura Beheer BV, based in the Netherlands;
- Trafigura AG, is the main office, based in Lucerne, Switzerland;
- Trafigura Ptd. Ltd. runs the Group's petroleum trading in the Far East;
- Puma Group of Companies operate the group's worldwide oil storage and distribution assets and investments; and
- Galena Asset Management, which is based in London. In 2005, the group made U.S.$28.4 billion (*Jamaica Observer,* 2006).

In May 2006, Trafigura was prosecuted in the United States and fined $20 million for illegal oil exports out of Iraq (*Deutsche Welle,* 2006). It was convicted of lying to two American energy companies when it said that 500,000 barrels of imported Iraqi oil sold to them in 2001 were sourced in compliance with the United Nations Oil-for-Food Program. Begun in 1995, the Oil-for-Food Program was intended to allow Iraq to sell oil, despite heavy sanctions, to buy food and medicine for ordinary citizens (*Jamaica Observer,* 2006). The statement Trafigura issued regarding its compliance with U.N. regulations proved to be false. It has also been accused of evading taxes on oil imports into Thailand

and is suspected of involvement in the Sudanese oil industry (Inner City Press, 2006).

Trafigura held the Jamaican oil contract for over a decade. It contracted with the state-owned Petroleum Corporation of Jamaica to handle its shipment and sale of crude oil on world markets. After originally winning the contract in 2000, the company's contract was automatically renewed annually thereafter, without competitive tender. More than two months after the Petroleum Corporation of Jamaica announced that it would be putting the contract to lift oil from Nigeria to public tender, nothing had been done (as of January 11, 2007; RJR 94 FM, Jamaica, 2007). Finally, on June 28, 2007, it was announced that Trafigura had lost out on the new contract, which went to a Switzerland-based firm, Glencore (RadioJamaica, 2007). Trafigura was one of four bidders for the contract.

Jamaican Information Minister Colin Campbell resigned in October 2006 after reports of a donation made by Trafigura to the ruling People's National Party (PNP). Trafigura is reported to have paid 31 million Jamaican dollars ($467,000 U.S.) into an account in the name of CCOC—Colin Campbell Our Candidate. The PNP has said the donations were above board, while Trafigura said in a statement that it regretted "any misunderstanding that may have been caused" by its contribution (BBC News, 2006).

Meanwhile, the Dutch media reported in May 2007 that the editors of Wikipedia were forced to repeatedly restore the entry for *Probo Koala,* after it was discovered that someone from Trafigura kept changing the Dutch-language entry to say that they had done nothing wrong. The entry was changed to non-editable (*Dutch News,* May 18, 2007). This type of practice is apparently known as "sock-puppeting," and it is not unusual for company executives to sneak changes onto their own entries on Wikipedia (*New York Times,* 2007).

The following information also sheds light on the company's track record. Both Trafigura and Glencore (the company that picked up the Jamaican oil contract in place of Trafigura) were started with funds provided by Marc Rich, one of the most wanted white-collar criminals in U.S. history until his controversial pardon on President Bill Clinton's last day of office in 2001 (*Jamaica Observer,* 2006; Australian Broadcasting Corporation, 2005). Each company has been accused of giving illegal kickbacks to Saddam Hussein's regime to obtain oil in violation of U.N. sanctions. The people and the processes in each company are closely linked. Indeed, Trafigura was set up by Claude Dauphin and Eric de Turkheim, who had worked as oil traders at Glencore (Wikipedia, 2007).

REFLECTIONS ON WASTE AS A SOCIAL PHENOMENON

So far, this article has provided a brief case study of toxic waste dumping in Abidjan, Ivory Coast. This final section highlights several issues that warrant closer analysis and action regarding waste issues (see also White, 2008).

Inequality, Not Legality, as the Central Problem

As indicated, the poor and minorities worldwide bear the brunt of waste disposal practices, whether legal or illegal. Ample evidence shows that the transfer of dirty industries and dirty waste to the Third World is a feature of globalization (Schmidt, 2004; Harvey, 1996). Characteristically, the biggest polluters and generators of waste—such as the United States and the European Union—are also the most likely to export their waste to other less-developed counties.

There is also strong evidence within particular national contexts, such as the United States, as well as internationally, that those who are forced to live close to polluting industries and waste disposal sites are the poor, who are frequently people of color and indigenous people (Brook, 2000; Bullard, 1994; Simon, 2000). This is known as "environmental racism" (Pellow, 2004; Julian, 2004).

Regardless of whether it comes to them legally or illegally, the same people must put up with the worst and most hazardous kinds of waste. In short, from the point of view of equality, equity, and fairness, waste is basically a problem for the poor, with the rich generally avoiding it. As in the Ivory Coast, the most disadvantaged sections of the community live in closest proximity to legal landfill sites and garbage dumps. They are also the most susceptible to illegal dumping, whether in Abidjan or Chicago (see Pellow, 2004).

Production of Waste Is a Social Process

Changes in the nature of production, and therefore of waste, are in turn linked to a rising-costs model of waste disposal. The costs of recycling waste must be absorbed by business insofar as human activity must assume the recycling functions no longer assumed by nature (Deleage, 1994). Pouring waste directly into the air, water, or land is now increasingly regulated. Hence, waste management is more expensive in the advanced capitalist countries. Legal provisions guaranteeing clean air and clean water have basically transformed waste into a problem of land pollution (Field, 1998).

The substantive nature of the waste has changed as well. In the post-World War II period, reliance upon and growth in chemical and synthetic products have increased. New problems and complexities in waste disposal followed, especially in relation to its toxicity and extent *(Ibid.)*. The emergence of e-waste (computers, mobile phones, etc.) has compounded existing waste management problems (White, 2008).

According to the principle of proximity, which is partly reflected in the Basel Convention on the transfer of hazardous waste, hazardous materials should be disposed of where they are produced. Implementation of this principle is bound to be fiercely contested, since waste has been transformed from a particular to a universal in the recent history of waste disposal.

In the regulation of waste and waste disposal methods, waste has been transformed into a "commodity," something to be bought and sold on the market. Its economic manifestation as "exchange-value" means that waste becomes an abstract, tradable commodity. As such, it transcends its place of production to take its place in global marketplaces as a commodity. Large corporations have been built upon the back of waste disposal. These companies derive profit from the fact that waste must be treated, transported, neutralized, and disposed of, as set out in legislation.

> Commodified waste is disassociated from the particular plant or region which produced it and placed in commerce for handling by the now huge waste disposal industry. This directly impacts the spatial distribution of pollution. Since there is no tie between a given industry and the companies which handle waste, the treatment and disposal of waste can occur anywhere. Prior to the rise of the waste industry, a company would generally arrange for disposal at or near its plant. To this extent, the beneficiaries of the plant who generally lived nearest to it were also those who bore the problem (Field, 1998: 87).

The reconstitution of waste as a commodity thus transforms the specific nature of waste into an "unrecognizable" universal quality. Its origins no longer matter.

Control Rather Than Prevention Increases the Value of Waste

Present concerns about waste regulation and control, as evident in the European Union's moves to tighten monitoring and adherence to rules, substantially reinforce the notion of a "waste crisis" and that waste ought to continue to be treated as a "commodity." The problem in this framework is not the waste itself, but the ways in which it is treated and disposed. Remaining "hidden" is the source of waste, such as a particular plant. Private companies are thus absolved of having to deal with the "waste crisis." Instead, the state (specific nation-states or supranational bodies such as the European Union) takes responsibility for waste issues. Thus, "waste disposal becomes a locational problem for the state rather than a production problem for capital" *(Ibid.: 88)*.

Disasters such as Abidjan tend to call forth even greater regulation and the tightening up of formal controls over waste disposal. This feeds into the spiral of rising waste management costs. The net result is profit for those who trade in this commodity. Rarely, if ever, is prevention on the agenda, because prevention goes to the heart of the production process itself. As such, it challenges the right of capital to produce what it wants, how it wants, how much it wants, and under what conditions it wants. In other words, the issue of prevention opens up a Pandora's box of the foul nature of the mode of production itself (Harvey, 1996; Field, 1998).

Nexus Between Corporations, States, and Organized Crime

The lucrative trade in waste means that people in positions of power and influence are more likely to want to receive their cut as waste is transferred around the globe. Corporations such as Trafigura shop around to get the best deal in waste disposal. Corrupt and/or inept government officials take the money and turn a blind eye. Criminal organizations move in to take advantage of new markets for clandestine illegal dumping (Schmidt, 2004; Simon, 2000; Block, 2002).

Ever stricter European environmental laws have meant increasing costs of cleaning up and disposing of waste. Therefore, criminal middlemen step in and offer low-cost solutions in Africa. Similar developments have been documented regarding organized crime and waste disposal in the United States (Simon, 2000). Bridgland (2006) has described how the seas off Gibraltar are believed to be a gathering point for "garbage cowboys," where ships with unwanted poisonous cargoes transfer them to other vessels specializing in the illegal dispersal of waste in Third World countries.

The costs of doing business are further reduced in "failed states," such as Somalia, or nations at civil war, such as the Ivory Coast. Lack of adequate legislation, regulatory measures, law enforcement, technical training and skill development, or a culture of compliance contribute to loose borders and the greater possibility of illegal dumping. Poor

countries are also susceptible to legal and illegal bribes from powerful corporations, and many of the poorest of the poor are willing through circumstance to trade health for cash-producing activities, including recycling hazardous waste (Schmidt, 2004). Environmental racism does not mean that interracial divisions are not possible. Corrupt officials can and do collude with outsiders to dump toxic waste in the backyards of their own people (see also Pellow, 2004). This is not just a problem of "color" per se, but of class and corruption. And it is ongoing: "British lawyers for 31,000 Africans allegedly injured by toxic waste dumped by an oil company [Trafigura] yesterday accused the oil company involved of trying to 'nobble' the African witnesses with lavish inducements" (*Times*, 2009).

CONCLUSION

This article describes events in Abidjan, Ivory Coast, that cost many lives and the good health of thousands of people. The Abidjan disaster is a story of the transfer of environmental harm across continents, cultures, and peoples. No single person is to blame for the event. Yet, there is adequate evidence to suggest that powerful interests ought to shoulder the liability and responsibility for the disaster. There are disturbing indications that this event was neither unique nor likely to be that last. Trade in toxic waste, whether legal or illegal, is going to get worse in the future. In part this is due to the prevalence of Western regulatory mechanisms for waste disposal.

Beyond tracking waste and documenting events, we must expose the culprits (see Pearce and Tombs, 1998; Lynch and Stretesky, 2006). Specific companies, such as Trafigura, need to be scrutinized, with careful surveillance of their activities in many parts of the world. So, too, must specific political parties and leaders, such as those in the Ivory Coast and Jamaica, whose financial dealings and policymaking demand utmost public accountability. Most important, we need to discover who is creating the waste, and where and how they are doing so. This is essential if we are to mobilize resistance at the point of production to the "waste crisis," one that is generated by and within the capitalist mode of production on a global scale.

REFERENCES

Angola Press
2006   "Gbagbo's Wife Denies Involvement in Toxic Waste Scandal." September 22.

Australian Broadcasting Corporation
2005   "AM—Swiss Link Undermines Xstrata's Bid for WMC." February 11.

BBC News
2007a   "UK Action over 'Toxic Waste' Case." February 2.
2007b   "Poisoned Ivorians Reject Payout" June 23.
2006   "'Toxic Ship' Firm in Jamaica Row." October 13.

Block, A.
2002   "Environmental Crime and Pollution: Wasteful Reflections." *Social Justice* 29,1-2: 61–81.

Bridgland, F.
2006   "Europe's New Dumping Ground: Fred Bridgland Reports on How the West's Toxic Waste Is Poisoning Africa." *Sunday Herald* (October 1).

Brook, D.
2000   "Environmental Genocide: Native Americans and Toxic Waste." *American Journal of Economics and Sociology* 57,1: 105–113.

Bullard, R.
1994   *Unequal Protection: Environmental Justice and Communities of Color.* San Francisco: Sierra Club Books.

Deleage, J.P.
1994   "Eco-Marxist Critique of Political Economy." M. O'Connor (ed.). *Is Capitalism Sustainable? Political Economy and the Politics of Ecology.* New York: The Guildford Press.

Deutsche Welle
2006   "European Hazardous Waste to Africa and Back." October 18.

DutchNews.nl
2007   "Transport Ministry Failed over *Probo Koala*" March 9.

Environment News
2007   "Ivory Coast Toxic Dumping Case Settled for US$198 Million." February 15.

Field, R.
1998   "Risk and Justice: Capitalist Production and the Environment" D. Faber (ed.), *The Struggle for Ecological Democracy: Environmental Justice Movements in the U.S.* New York: Guilford Press.

Harvey, D.
1996   *Justice, Nature and the Geography of Difference.* Oxford: Blackwell.

IC Publications
2007a   "I Coast Pollution Victims Reject Proposed Allocation of Pay-Out" June 25.
2007b   "One Third of Ivory Coast Toxic Waste Victims Get Payout" August 18.

Inner City Press
2006   "As UN Checks Toxins in Abidjan, the Dumper Trafigura Figured in Food Scandal, Funded by RBS and BNP Paribas." September 10.

International Herald Tribune
2007a   "Dutch Firm Pays Ivory Coast $197 Million to Settle Toxic Waste Case." February 14.
2007b   "Two Employees of Dutch Company Detained in Netherlands in Ivory Coast Toxic Waste Case." February 16.
2006a   "U.N. Says Waste Dumped in Ivory Coast Clearly Violated International Agreements." September 19.
2006b   "Ivory Coast Report Blames Corrupt, Negligent Officials for Toxic Waste Scandal." November 27.

Jamaica Observer
2006   "Trafigura No Stranger to Controversy." October 5.

Julian, R.
2004   "Inequality, Social Differences and Environmental Resources." R. White (ed.), *Controversies in Environmental Sociology.* Melbourne: Cambridge University Press.

Kahn, J.
2006   "How First-World Garbage Makes Africans Sick: And What Washington Can Do to Clean up Its Act" *Slate.com On-Line Magazine,* posted September 22.

Living on Earth—U.K.

2007   "Toxic Delivery." February 23.

Lynch, M. and P. Stretesky

2006   *Toxic Crimes: Examining Corporate Victimization of the General Public Employing Medical and Epidemiological Evidence.* N. South and P. Beime (eds.), *Green Criminology.* The International Library of Criminology, Criminal Justice and Penology, Second Series. Aldershot: Ashgate.

Monsters and Critics.com

2007   "'Dirty Deal' for Victims of Ivory Coast Waste Scandal." February 14.

New York Times

2007   "Anonymity on the Web Lures Some Executives." Reproduced in 'Times Digest.' July 16.

Pearce, F. and S. Tombs

1998   *Toxic Capitalism: Corporate Crime and the Chemical Industry.* Aldershot: Dartmouth Publishing Company.

Pellow, D.

2004   "The Politics of Illegal Dumping: An Environmental Justice Framework." *Qualitative Sociology* 27,4: 511–525.

RadioJamaica.com

2007   "PCJ Dumps Trafigura Beheer as Oil Lifting Contractor." June 28.

Reuters

2007   "Ivorian Toxic Waste Victims Reject Payout Offer." June 23.

2006a   "Ivorian Prisoners Target French Toxic Waste Suspects." November 14.

2006b   "Dutch Could Have Stopped Toxic Ship—Report." December 6.

RJR 94 FM—Jamaica

2007   "News." January 11.

San Diego Union-Tribune

2006   "Dutch Trafigura Settles with Ivory Coast over Toxic Waste for $197 Million." February 14.

Schmidt, C.

2004   "Environmental Crimes: Profiting at the Earth's Expense." *Environmental Health Perspectives* 112,2: A96–A103.

Simon, D.

2000   "Corporate Environmental Crimes and Social Inequality: New Directions for Environmental Justice Research." *American Behavioral Scientist* 43,4: 633–645.

Times

2009   "Oil Company Accused of 'Nobbling' Witnesses in African Toxic Waste Case." March 24, online version.

Turkish Weekly

2006   "Ivory Coast 'Toxic Ship' Inquiry." September 27.

United Nations Disaster Assessment and Coordination (UNDAC)

2006   *Report on Cote D'Ivoire Urban Hazardous Waste Dumping.* September. 11–19. Abidjan: UNDAC.

VOA News.com

2007   "Ivorians Seek Justice for Illegal Toxic Waste Dumping." January 11.

2006a   "Ivory Coast Government Panel Releases Toxic Waste Findings." November 23.

2006b   "Ivory Coast Toxic Waste Health Risk Lessens, Criminal Inquiry Continues." September 27.

White, R.

2008   *Crimes Against Nature: Environmental Criminology and Ecological Justice.* Devon: Willan Press.

Wikipedia

2007   'Trafigura.'

245

19

The Use and Abuse of Aquifers

Can the Hopi Indians Survive Multinational Mining?

By Peter Whiteley and Vernon Masayesva

A very long time ago there was nothing but water. In the east Hurúing Wuhti, the deity of all hard substances, lived in the ocean.... The Sun also existed at that time.... By and by these two deities caused some dry land to appear in the midst of the water, the waters receding eastward and westward.

("Origin Myth" recorded by
H. R. Voth [1905b])

This is ... one of the most arid countries in the world, and we need that water. That is why we do Kachina dances in the summer, just to get a drop of rain. And to us, this water is worth more than gold, or the money. Maybe we cannot stop the mining of the coal, but we sure would like to stop the use of water.

(Dennis Tewa, Munqapi village)[1]

HOPI SOCIETY AND ENVIRONMENTAL ADAPTATION

The Hopi Indians of northeastern Arizona are an epitome of human endurance: they are farmers without water. According to their genesis narrative, the Hopi emerged from a layer under the earth into this, the fourth, world by climbing up inside a reed. On their arrival, they met a deity, Maasaw, who presented them with a philosophy of life based on three elements: maize seeds, a planting stick, and a gourd full of water. Qa'ö, maize, was the soul of the Hopi

people, representing their very identity. *Sooya*, the planting stick, represented the simple technology they should depend on: there was an explicit warning against over-dependency on technology, which had taken on a life of its own in the third world below, producing destruction through materialism, greed, and egotism. *Wikoro*, the gourd filled with water, represented the environment—the land and all its life-forms—as well as the sign of the Creator's blessing, if the Hopis would uphold Maasaw's covenant and live right. Maasaw told them that life in this place would be arduous and daunting, but through resolute perseverance and industry, they would live long and be spiritually rich.[2]

The twelve Hopi villages lie on a generally southeast-northwest axis stretching roughly one hundred kilometers (sixty-two miles) as the crow flies (see figure 19.1).[3] The villages cluster in groups around the tips of three fingerlike promontories, known as the Hopi mesas, that form the southwesternmost extensions of Black Mesa, an upthrust plate of the Colorado Plateau (see figure 19.2 on page 20). Black Mesa is bisected by four principal southwest-trending washes, Moenkopi, Dinnebito, Oraibi, and Polacca; all but Moenkopi are ephemeral and flow only after significant precipitation. Smaller washes, Jeddito and Wepo, near First Mesa, are also locally important. The Wepo and Oraibi Washes separate the Hopi mesas from one another, cutting arroyo channels in valleys some 90 to 120 meters (300 to 400 feet) below the mesa tops, on which the villages perch. The washes and their tributary fans are main areas of Hopi floodwater farming. Only the

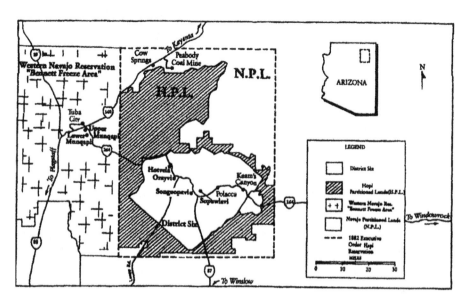

Figure 19.1 Navajo and Hopi reservations relative to the pabody western coal company mine

The 1882 Executive Order Hopi Reservation emcompassed District Six, originally a grazing district, which included most of the Hopi village sites; the Hopi Partitioned Lands (HPL); and the Navajo Partitioned Lands (NPL), which were created as a result of the Navajo-Hopi Indian Land Settlement Act of 1974. The Black Mesa mine straddles the north-central border of the HPL and the NPL. The villages of Upper and Lower Munqapi fall within the Western Navajo Reservation "Bennett Freeze Area," which currently is also in process of partition between the Hopi Tribe and the Navajo Nation. Courtesy of the University of Arizona Press (modified from Whiteley 1988b).

Moenkopi Wash (far removed from the central area of Hopi villages) supports irrigation, in farmlands below the villages of Upper and Lower Munqapi, which remain the most productive areas for Hopi crops (the name *Munqapi*, anglicized to *Moenkopi*, means "continuously flowing water place"—an index of its social importance). The Moenkopi Wash is fed by tributary stream flows and springs but also is fed directly by an aquifer in a layer of sandstone called "Navajo" that sits below the surface of Black Mesa within the hydrological province known as the Black Mesa Basin.[4]

The Hopi's principal supply of drinking water is traditionally found in springs—indeed, Hopi history, which focuses on centripetal migrations by independent clans from all points of the compass, specifically remarks on the abundance and reliability of the springs that stud the walls of First, Second, and Third Mesas.[5] The springs have determined Hopi settlement patterns and uses of natural resources. As geologist Herbert Gregory, an early

visitor to the Navajo and Hopi Indian Reservations, pointed out:

> One of the surprises ... is the large number of springs widely distributed over the reservation. Tucked away in alcoves in the high mesa walls or issuing from crevices in the canyon sides or bubbling up through the sands in the long wash floors, these tiny supplies of water appear to be distributed in haphazard fashion .... The ancient cliff dweller was well aware of the desirability of these small permanent supplies as centers for settlement, and many of the present-day Indian trails owe their position to the location of springs rather than to topography or to length of route.
>
> (Gregory 1916 132)

Insofar as the archaeological record confirms traditional history, the period between 1300 and

1500 c.e. saw a concentric contraction of more widespread villages—from Mesa Verde, Navajo Mountain, Tsegi Canyon, the Little Colorado River, and the Hopi Buttes—into such centers as are still populated by the Hopi today.[6]

Hopi presence in the region and engagement with its particular environmental exigencies is thus ancient. The Hopi are a Puebloan people, direct descendants of the Anasazi (an archaeologist's term from the Navajo word meaning "ancestors of the enemy"; the Hopi, not surprisingly, prefer *Hisatsinom*, meaning simply "ancestors"), who between 800 and 1300 c.e. built some of the most impressive architectural structures in prehistoric North America. Chaco Canyon to the east figures in some Hopi migration legends, as do Mesa Verde to the northeast, Betatakin and Keet Seel to the north, Homol'ovi to the south, Wupatki to the southwest, and numerous other ruins throughout the greater Southwest.[7] The common refrain of southwestern archaeologists, "What happened to the Anasazi?," is unequivocally answered by the Hopi and other modern Pueblos: "Nothing; we are still here." In Hopi country itself, there is evidence of continuous occupation by sedentary agriculturalists for a good 1,500 years, and the Third Mesa town of Orayvi—the oldest continuously inhabited village in North America—has been dated to at least 1150 c.e. In sum, the Hopi have learned to live by farming in this semiarid environment over the course of a long presence.

The persistent occupation of the Hopi mesas for more than a millennium is both remarkable and paradoxical. Unlike the other Pueblos, the Hopi, with no streams or rivers to support their subsistence economy's dependence on maize, beans, and squash, must seek their water elsewhere. The ways in which the Hopi get and use water are a major part of identity, religious beliefs, ritual practices, and daily engagements and concerns. Much of the complex Hopi religious system is devoted, in one way or another, to securing necessary blessings of water—in the form of rainfall, snow, spring replenishment, and so forth—to sustain living beings, whether humans, animals, or plants.

A calendar of elaborate ritual performances is divided into the ka-china season—roughly from December to July—and, from August to December, a season of more esoteric practices by higher-order religious sodalities—the Snake, Flute, *Wuwtsim* (Manhood), and *Maraw* (Womanhood) societies and the great *Soyalangw* society festival at the winter solstice. All these concentrate in some measure on ensuring beneficial environmental conditions, on keeping the world in balance. The Hopi regard ritual, if performed properly—the cardinal values being pure intentions and good hearts in harmony with one another, sentiments that translate into the philosophical concept of *namit-nangwu*—as instrumentally efficacious ipso facto, not as mere symbolic embroidery on a techno-rationalist means of production.

The phrase *Hopi environmentalism* is practically a redundancy.[8] So much of Hopi culture and thought, both religious and secular, revolves around an attention to balance and harmony in the forces of nature that environmental ethics are in many ways critical to the very meaning of the word *Hopi*.[9] Hopi society is organized into clans, the majority of which are named after, and have specific associations with, natural species and elements—Bear, Sun, Spider, Parrot, Badger, Corn, Butterfly, Greasewood, Tobacco, Cloud—indicating the utter centrality of environmental forms and ecological relationships in Hopi thought. Myriad usages of natural species and agents in Hopi religious ritual express the depth and detail of this ecological awareness and concern. A kachina, for example, in appearance, song, and performance, typically embodies and encapsulates key vital principles of the natural world. Even a casual observation of a *Hemis* kachina at *Niman* (the Home Dance, in July), to just take one case, discloses a being festooned with spruce branches, wild wheat, clouds, butterflies, tadpoles, sea-shells, and so on. The bringing together of these natural symbols is in many instances designed to both evoke and celebrate the life-giving force of water in the world.

SPRINGS, WATER, AND RAIN IN HOPI SECULAR AND RELIGIOUS PHILOSOPHY

Paahu, "natural water" or "spring," is absolutely central in Hopi social and environmental thought. Indeed, the identity of the term points to the significance springs hold: they are the prototypical water sources. Supplemented by wells dug by the Bureau of Indian Affairs Agency over the past century, springs supply drinking water and water for livestock. They also feed a series of irrigated terraced gardens on the slopes below the mesa tops, which form another basic site of crop production; the gardens include chilis, beans, a little corn, onions, radishes, and fruit trees (see photo 19.1). The areas around the larger springs are also the only significant wetlands in much of the region. For this reason, they, too, are objects of religious veneration.

Even with the introduction of piped water (for the most part, only within the past thirty years), springs remain critical in Hopi philosophy and practice. Springs and their immediate pond life environs serve as the ideal model of life and growth. Such places attract denser presences of life-forms than are found elsewhere in the semiarid landscape. Doves, dragonflies, ducks, cranes, frogs, sand-grass, cattails, reeds, cottonwoods, willows, and numerous other species concentrate at these locations—simultaneously the index and the manifestation of abundant, water-charged life. Such species serve as key symbols of the life-giving force of water in Hopi secular and religious philosophy.

Photo 19.1 Hopi gardens

These terraced gardens below the Third Mesa village of Hotvela are irrigated with water brought by surface pipes and carried by hand from the Hotvela Spring, on the slope below the mesa's edge. Courtesy of the Arizona State Museum, Tuscon.

It is hard to imagine anything more sacred—as substance or as symbol—than water in Hopi religious thought and practice. To be sure, some elements may appear more prominent: corn, the staff of life, which is ubiquitous in Hopi religious imagery; rattlesnakes in the spectacular Snake Dance; or performances by masked kachina spirits. But intrinsic to these, and underlying much other symbolism in the panoply of Hopi ritual, is the concern with water. Springs, water, and rain are focal themes in ritual costumes, kiva iconography, mythological narratives, personal names, and many, many songs that call the cloud chiefs from the varicolored directions to bear their fructifying essence back into the cycle of human, animal, and vegetal life. That essence—as clouds, rain, and other water forms—manifests the spirits of the dead. When people die, in part they become clouds; songs call to the clouds as ascendant relatives. Arriving clouds are returning ancestors, their rain both communion with and blessing of the living. The waters of the earth (where kachina spirits live) are, then, transubstantiated human life.

In general, springs and groundwater serve as homes for the deity Paalölöqangw, Plumed Water-Snake, who is a powerful patron of the water sources of the earth and the heavens. Paalölöqangw is appealed to in the Snake and Flute ceremonies, and is religiously portrayed during winter night dances. Springs and their immediate surroundings are places of particular religious worship in some instances, as in the Flute ceremony or during *Powamuy* (the Bean Dance) and *Niman* (the Home Dance). The Flute ceremony is specifically devoted to the consecration and regeneration of major springs; during this ceremony, in an archetypal gesture, the *Lenmongwi,* head of the Flute society, dives to the bottom of a particularly sacred spring to plant prayer sticks for Paalölöqangw.

Resources from spring areas such as water, clay, reeds, and spruce branches are gathered for use in village ceremonies, in which they are deemed to draw in the life-giving power of the springs themselves. Springs as distant as 160 kilometers (100 miles) are visited on a regular basis in order to bring back their sacred water for ceremonies, especially by

clan descendants from former settlements adjacent to the springs. Early ethnographers Jesse Walter Fewkes and Walter Hough both remarked on Hopi veneration of springs:

> In a general way every spring is supposed to be sacred and therefore a place for the deposit of prayer sticks and other offerings .... Every spring is a place of worship and hence a shrine.
>
> (Fewkes 1906, 370–371)

> No spring in the region is without evidence of many offerings to the deities of water .... Sacred Springs may ... be regarded as altars, and the offerings as sacrifices, whose essence may be carried by the water.
>
> (Hough 1906, 165)

Since time immemorial, the Hopi have offered blessings of cornmeal and prayers at springs, during specific visits for the purpose or simply while passing through the landscape (say, during herding, hunting, or treks to distant cornfields). When blessing a spring, typically a man also scoops up a handful of water and splashes it back toward his village or fields as a way to encourage the water to transfer some of its power to where humans most need it. Springs attract the rain and snow to themselves and thus serve as powerful foci of value in Hopi thought. Indeed, this is why they are sacred places: if much of Hopi religious thought celebrates life, then springs are self-evident indexes of the dynamic process that produces and sustains life. At the winter solstice ceremonies, feathered prayer sticks are placed over major springs around every Hopi village as both protection and supplication.

Among sources of water, there is a quasi-magnetic relationship: the Pacific Ocean, the Colorado River, rain, underground aquifers, springs, and living plants are mutually attractive—"contagious" in the anthropological sense: "The land is a living organ, it breathes ... the Hopis say that it is the underground water that sucks in, that breathes the rain" (Vernon Masayesva).[10] *Paatuwaqatsi,* literally "the ocean," is simultaneously a central philosophical principle denoting the universally sustaining water of life. To attract the world's powers of moisture, spring names are used frequently in ritual narrative and song: for example, Talakwavi, Dawn Coming-Up Spring; Tsorspa, Bluebird Spring; Kwaava, Eagle Spring; Paatuwi, Spring on the Rock Shelf; Höwiipa, Dove Spring; Hoonawpa, Bear Spring; Konva, Chipmunk Spring; Kookyangwva, Spider Spring; Tsinngava, Water Droplets Splashing Spring; Söhöpva, Cottonwood Spring. Springwater properly placed in one's field, mud from spring bottoms used as body plaster in kachina costumes, and images of tadpoles or dragonflies decorating kachina spirits—all sympathetically entice the rain.

Springs themselves, like maize in fields, were originally "planted" in the earth by deities or gifted individuals. There was even a special instrument, a *paa'u'uypi* ("spring planter"), known to the elect and used for this purpose. (A spring near Munqapi, for example, is said to have been planted in this way by a man named Kwaavaho—for whom the spring is named—in the late nineteenth century.) Pilgrimages to reconsecrate and draw in regenerative power from especially significant springs at distant points are common in the Hopi religious calendar. Villages may be named for springs, as in the mother village, Songoopavi, "Sand-Grass Spring Place." Some clans have exceptional responsibilities to springs, as does *Patkingyam,* the Water clan, and some springs are sacred to specific clans or religious societies at the different villages. Clan migration routes from former villages are often retraced—both literally in pilgrimages and figuratively in narratives and songs—at certain times of the year. In many instances, clan associations with springs at their ruins or along the route are mentioned as locations of important historical events. Thus, the Water clan has a series of historic points along its migration route from the south that are frequently marked by springs, such as Isva, Coyote Springs, north of Winslow. Similarly, Kiisiwu, Shady Springs, for the Badger and Butterfly clan; Sa'lako, Shalako (a kachina spirit) Spring, for the Bow clan; and Lengyanovi Spring, for the Flute

clan, are all memorialized in clan tradition and visited in pilgrimage. In this sense, then, the living springs embody Hopi history: they are cultural landmarks, inscribed with significance, and commemorative reminders of the continuing legitimacy of clan rights and interests in specific areas.

Springs and the life-forms associated with them thus appear in many Hopi stories and sacred traditions, in literary forms such as personal names, and in artistic forms such as basketry, pottery, weaving, and painting. In these intellectual and aesthetic contexts, the substance and forms of springs and wetland life are both described objectively and celebrated with pleasurable appreciation and spiritual gratitude. Personal names, a prime form of Hopi poetic images, often reference springs and water: Paahongva, Water Standing Up (after the tiny columns of water that leap up from raindrops splashing on a pond or puddle); Paanömtiwa, Water Covering Up (perhaps covering a cornfield after a rain); Paatala, Water Light, referring to reflected light on water's surface, particularly in the dark.[11] Many of the species that are totemic emblems of Hopi clans are associated with springs—*paawiki,* the duck; *atoko,* the crane; *paakwa,* the frog; *paaqavi,* reeds; and so on. The celebration of water, its origins or results, forms a major proportion—perhaps half—of all Hopi names. References to flowers—an explicit mark of the Creator's rain blessings—celebrate water as well, such as *Siitala,* "flower light," the reflected sunlight from flowers newly blossomed after a rain, and *Sikyakuku,* literally "yellow foot," which refers to walking along through blossoming flowers while the pollen clings to one's moccasined feet. There are also references to rain, such as Yooyoki "raining," and Yoyvwölö, "rainwater" (there is a priest in one of the ritual orders referred to as the Yoymongwi, "rain chief") as well as lightning, such as Talwiipi, "a single lightning flash," or Talwipta, "lightning in the ongoing process of flashing." Even species that are not so directly associated with water sources are frequently subjects of interest in relation to their behavior toward water. One name, Sharp Hearer, given by a Spider clan member, refers to the fact that when rain begins to fall, certain spiders secreted inside houses

251

hear the rain and emerge from their cover, running out to drink from the freshly emerging puddles (Voth 1905a). Even here, then, when the species in question has no explicit conceptual link with water, the Hopi denote its significance by its habitual practices in relation to water. The concern with natural water depicted in this name details a precise knowledge of the behavior of the species as well as an aesthetic and creatural delight in the pleasure and happiness that the presence of water affords all beings of the world.

In short, springs are key in Hopi social life, cultural values, and conceptualization of the landscape, all of which form the ground of deeper religious thought and action. The Hopi smoke for rain, dance for it, sing for it, and offer many other forms of prayer for it. In the cycle of life, rainwater and snowmelt nourish the plants, which feed animals and human beings. Thus, prayers for rain are not abstract; they call the clouds to replenish the waters of the earth so that all life-forms will benefit and "be happy." Here, then, is an environment populated not by Western science's instinct-driven organisms without spirit or consciousness but by intentional, spiritual entities that are part and parcel of the same moral system that encompasses human beings. The Hopi have, so to speak, both a moral ecology and an ecological morality. As one Hopi man put it, "We pray for rain so that all the animals, birds, insects, and other life-forms will have enough to drink too." The prolific complexity of Hopi ritual attends to springs specifically and as sources of blessing and vehicles of prayer in general.

OF COAL MINES AND SLURRIES

The springs, however, are drying up, and with them the essential force of Hopi religious life and culture itself. Flows have been progressively declining over the past three decades. Numerous springs and seeps have ceased to produce enough water to sustain crops planted below them. The Moenkopi Wash no longer "continuously flows," and the only major Hopi farming area that depends on irrigation water is in serious jeopardy. In recent years, the Moenkopi Wash has been down

to a trickle by late May; not long ago, Munqapi children plunged into swimming holes long into the summer. Even the trickle that does come is supplied by only two upstream tributaries; much of the water from the mainstream itself is channeled into impoundment ponds by the Peabody Western Coal Company.

Peabody, which operates twenty-seven mines in the United States, is the largest private producer of coal in the world. Until recently, the company was part of the British multinational Hanson Industries, which demerged in February 1997. Peabody then became part of a newly formed Hanson spinoff, The Energy Group PLC, but top management remains virtually identical. In 1996, Peabody's total operating profit (including all its mining interests worldwide) was $240 million, and its profit on coal sales was in excess of $2 billion; Hanson's total sales, including its chemical and tobacco interests, exceeded $19 billion, and its total after-tax profit was $2.3 billion (*Hanson Annual Report* 1996). This is no small enterprise.

Peabody's Black Mesa-Kayenta Mine is the only mine in the United States that transports its coal by slurry (see figure 19.2). The strip-mined coal is crushed, mixed with drinking-quality water, and flushed by pipeline to the Mohave Generating Station in Laughlin, Nevada. The cities of Las Vegas and Phoenix—electric oases in the desert—buy some of the power, but most of it goes to the electric toothbrushes, garage door openers, outsize television sets, and other necessities of life in southern California. Most of the slurry water comes directly from the "Navajo" or N-aquifer, 300 to 900 meters (1,000 to 3,000 feet) within the geologic formation of Black Mesa (see figure 19.3).

The pumping, Peabody has claimed, has no effect on the Hopi springs. Those springs, it maintains, are fed not by the N-aquifer but by the overlying "Dakota" or D-aquifer and by snowmelt. The Hopi do not believe Peabody's assertion. But an escalating series of letters from Hopi individuals and officials, both traditional leaders and Tribal Council chairs; petitions signed by several hundred Hopi; protests in public hearings; dissenting interpretations by independent geologists;[12] and repeated refusals by

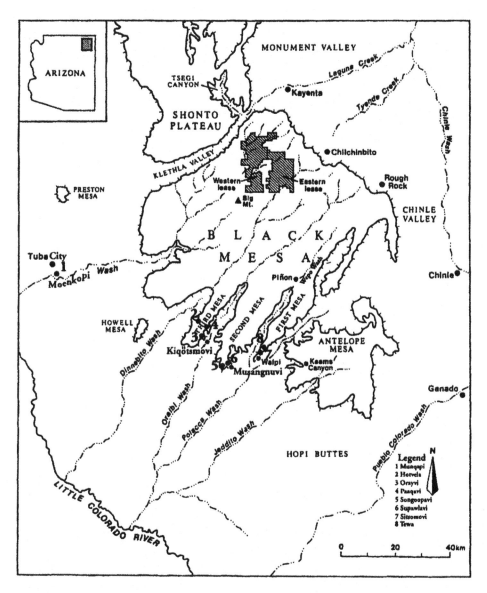

Figure 19.2 Black Mesa and the Peabody Coal Company's lease Areas

The geological formation of Black Mesa, with the Hopi mesas and principal washes. The Peabody Western Coal company's two lease areas are marked by hatched lines. Black Mesa tilts downward from north to south. The mining lease areas lie on top of its northern, higher end. The Hopi villages are at the lowest, southern extremity, where the aquifers are significantly closer to the surfaces. Courtesy of the Center for Archaeological Investigations, Southern Illinois University.

the Tribal Council to sanction the Department of the Interior's renewal of the mining lease have all fallen on deaf ears. Flat rebuttals to Hopi protests continue to be retailed by Peabody and Hanson representatives, and a personal invitation to engage in direct dialogue issued to Lord Hanson, chairman of Hanson PLC, by Tribal Chairman Ferrell Secakuku in June 1994

went ignored. On 30 April 1994, W. Howard Carson, president of Peabody Western Coal Company, voiced the company's party line in a letter to the editor published in the *Los Angeles Times:* "Changes in the flows from their springs may be the result of drought conditions in the region, and perhaps from the increased pumpage from Hopi community wells

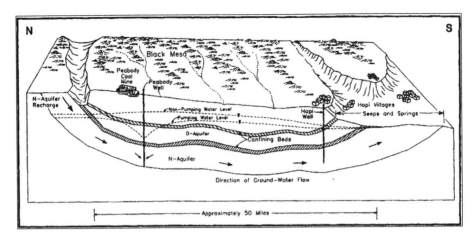

Figure 19.3 Groundwater flow in the N-aquifer

The N- or Navajo Aquifer is composed of three layers: from top to bottom, Navajo Sandstone, the Kayenta Formation, and Wingate Sandstone. The N-Aquaifer is separated from the overlying D- or Dakota aquifer by the Carmel Formation (indicated by the Confining Beds in the diagram). The D-aquifer also is composed of three layers: from top to bottom, Dakota Sandstone, the Morrison Formation, and Entrada Sandstone. For more on the geologic and hydrological stratigraphy of the aquifers, see Cooley et al. 1969. Courtesy of the Hopi Tribe, Water Resources Office.

located near these springs.... Peabody Western's pumping from wells that are 2,500–3,000 feet deep does not affect these springs."

Yet Peabody's characterizations of hydrological effects are eminently untrustworthy. Comments and hearings on the U.S. Office of Surface Mining and Reclamation Enforcement's draft environmental impact statement (DEIS) (U.S. Department of the Interior 1990)[13] produced a welter of objections, both to the sociocultural and environmental effects of the mine and to the shoddy research that produced general ratings of minor or minimal environmental impacts. For example, the Environmental Protection Agency's official response noted:

We have classified the DEIS as Category EO-2: Environmental Objections— Insufficient Information.[14] ... We believe the project may result in significant adverse environmental impacts to water resources and air quality that should be avoided. We have also found that the lack of sufficient information on water, air, and biotic resource conditions severely impedes evaluation of impacts, alternatives,

and appropriate mitigation measures. We are particularly concerned that the DEIS lacks an alternatives analysis which would enable the Federal agencies and the public to consider less environmentally damaging actions than the preferred alternative [i.e., the slurry].

(U.S. Department of the
Interior 1990, 263)

The EPA's more detailed comments on the mine's hydrological compliance with the National Environmental Policy Act noted:

Conclusions based on N-aquifer modelling. While EPA accepts the approach taken in modelling hydrologic baseline conditions and impacts, the conclusiveness of this effort is undermined by lack of data. This limitation, compounded by use of material damage criteria based on thresholds much less sensitive than "significance" under NEPA, leads us to reject the evaluation of hydrologic impacts. EPA believes that the available data do not support statements in the

DEIS that the cumulative effects of current and foreseeable mining and related operations (principally the coal transport slurry) are expected to result in only minor hydrological impacts.

(U.S. Department of the Interior 1990, 267)

Six months prior to W. Howard Carson's 1994 statement in the *Los Angeles Times,* top hydrologists with the U.S. Geological Survey (USGS) concluded that Peabody's ongoing analysis of water impacts was based on a wholly inadequate model. Among other shortcomings, "The model is not sufficient to answer the concerns of the Hopi regarding adverse local, short-term impacts on wetlands, riparian wildlife habitat, and spring flow at individual springs" (Nichols 1993). Recent figures (U.S. Geological Survey 1995) suggest that as much as two-thirds of the decline in water level of area wells (ranging from 9.1 to 29.6 meters, or 30 to 97 feet, from 1965 to 1993) is caused by the mine's pumping. Peabody's claim that throughout its thirty-five-year life, the mine would use only one-tenth of 1 percent of N-aquifer water, which would naturally recharge itself, is seriously questioned by a USGS recharge study in 1995 that charted a recharge rate 85 percent less than Peabody's estimate.[15] (It has been suggested that Peabody tried to suppress public release of these discrepant figures because if the figures were verified, the company would be obligated by the terms of the lease to post a bond for aquifer restoration.)

It also seems evident that depletion of the N-aquifer has had serious impacts on the D-aquifer and on the springs themselves; the Moenkopi Wash is directly affected, since it is supplied by N-aquifer seepage and since Peabody impounds surface water at a rate surpassing 2.2 million cubic meters (1,800 acre-feet) per year—water that would otherwise directly supply this wash (U.S. Department of the Interior 1960, 268). Computer simulations by the USGS predict total drying of some major Hopi wells beginning in the year 2011. Upstream Navajo communities are also significantly affected by the drying and by deteriorating

water quality; Forest Lake has been particularly hard hit. In recent documents, Peabody has finally acknowledged that it takes water not only from the N-aquifer but also from other aquifers, including the D-aquifer. This has come as no surprise to the Hopi. But as Nat Nutongla, head of the Hopi Tribe's Water Resources Office, puts it, "The elders regard all water as sacred. It doesn't matter whether the springs are supplied directly by the D-aquifer or the N-aquifer or whatever; they represent *all* sources of water."

Peabody's position that declines in Hopi springs derive from increased domestic and municipal consumption, reflecting population growth (principally Navajo) and water development by the Navajo Nation and the Hopi Tribe, is not entirely untrue. Tuba City wells and a significant increase in local population since the 1960s directly impinge on Munqapi area springs. Hopi domestic water use has definitely expanded as newer villages have adopted indoor plumbing over the past thirty years. But these changes, the Hopi argue, are all the more reason not to waste the reserves of N-aquifer water. As co-author and former Tribal Chairman Vernon Masayesva has put it elsewhere:

I believe there is a water crisis. Peabody Mining Company says that if there is a lowering of the water in the wells, it's because of domestic uses and not as a result of their pumping. And to that, I simply said, "All the more reason why you should not be pumping that water, because the domestic users are already having a significant impact on that N-aquifer water." So why throw away the savings? I see aquifers as money in the bank, in a savings account. So why are we dipping into it?

(BBC Television 1995)

A serious, compromising quandary is that 80 percent of the Hopi Tribe's annual operating revenue is supplied by coal royalties and water lease fees from Peabody. The Hopi Tribal Council (or "Tribe"), a creation of the Indian Reorganization Act of 1934, is formally supported by about half the villages, though even traditionalists opposed to the

255

council rely on numerous benefits it administers. Many people believe they were duped by the council's attorneys when the original leases were signed in the 1960s[16] and that some tribal leaders were coopted by Peabody. But this is scarcely a factional issue. The Hopi directly involved with the council, including the two most recent chairmen, Ferrell Secakuku and Vernon Masayesva, have strongly opposed renewal of the coal leases in lieu of an alternative means of transporting the coal.

Hopi of all factions, from traditionalist *Kikmongwis* (village chiefs) to modernist technocrats, have been unanimous and clear in their opposition to the use of pristine groundwater to transport coal and in their disbelief of Peabody's denials that the pumping affects the springs. Two examples will suffice. The first is more traditionally inclined. At a public hearing on the environmental impact of the mine held in Munqapi on 8 August 1989, William Garcia recounted a childhood discussion he and his brothers had engaged in with their grandfather, Kyarsyawma, while out herding sheep. Kyarsyawma had first asked for his grandsons' impressions of the land:

> Our response was, "Well, it is just there. It is just there, you know, and we use it now and then, maybe to farm on and to herd our sheep. There is really nothing to it."
>
> He said, "Look at yourself. Look at your body, what do you have? You got some parts there, it looks pretty simple on the outside, but on the inside, inside of you as a person you have a soul, you have a heart. You have some blood running through your body to keep your vital organs going," and he said, "It is the same thing with the land. The land has a soul, the land that we are on has a soul, it has a heart. It also has its own blood. The blood running through it are the streams to keep it alive, to keep us alive."
>
> I always remember that, so to me, after I kind of learned that concept, it wasn't just there anymore. There was a purpose behind it just like there is a purpose here

for each and every one of us. We are not just here ....

> I guarantee you that if we continue to draw this lifeline from mother Earth, then we will no longer exist, just as if someone stuck a needle in your arm and sucked out all the blood, you would be nothing, you would be dead.
>
> (U.S. Department of the Interior 1990, 374–375)

The second example is a petition presented by Mishongnovi village that same year:

> Be advised that we the undersigned members of the village of Mishongnovi are deeply concerned about the effects the mining of coal, by Peabody Coal Company, has had on our water resources. This is most evident in our springs drying up, our farms not producing crops, and our range wells drying up.
>
> Our village leaders have been and are still opposed to use of our water for mining operations. Our water is our life and we stand firm with our leaders in opposition to future use of our water for this purpose.
>
> (U.S. Department of the Interior 1990, 296)

The Tribal Council favors economic development and does not oppose the mine as such (although some traditionalists do): part of the allure of the mine in the first place was the promise of Hopi employment. But the Hopi say Peabody has aligned itself with the Navajo Nation and ignores Hopi interests, a position borne out in employment figures. Of as many as 900 "Native American"—a useful elision in Peabody's public pronouncements—employees, fewer than 20 are Hopi; the great majority are Navajo, represented by the United Mine Workers Union, which enjoys a special relationship with the Navajo Labor Relations Board.[17] The original leases guaranteed 50 percent of local employment to the Hopi. And Peabody's overall attitude seems to be flagrant disdain for Hopi concerns. In W. Howard

Carson's words, "We wouldn't [stop pumping] just to get the Hopi off our backs, because it could create another nightmare. These things snowball" (*Gallup (NewMexico) Independent* 1993).

Several alternatives to the slurrying of aquifer water have been proposed, and progress has been made on one: the construction of another pipeline from Lake Powell, which would provide domestic water for the Hopi and the Navajo and water for industrial use by Peabody. But Peabody, ever mindful of the bottom line, is evidently using delaying tactics, suspending negotiations and playing the tribes against each other despite support for the project by Secretary of the Interior Bruce Babbitt. Like most negotiations involving the Hopi and the Navajo, the pipeline proposal is subject to the cumulative politics of major land disputes between the tribes, and the Navajo Nation has sought concessions from the Hopi Tribe that it has been unable to gain otherwise. Such disputes affect Hopi interests in other ways, including the Hopi's freedom to conduct religious pilgrimages to some springs. A major sacred spring, Kiisiwu, is on land that was partitioned to the Navajo Nation by Congress in 1974. This spring, associated with principal kachina ceremonies, is visited by ritual-society pilgrims, especially during *Powamuy* (the Bean Dance) and *Niman* (the Home Dance). Formerly, local Navajo maintained a respectful distance, but younger generations are impressed less by the ceremonies' religious purpose and more by secular conflict. Recently, there have been physical assaults. If Kiisiwu dries up, this may solve some temporal problems between the Hopi and the Navajo, but at what spiritual cost?

Meanwhile, the Hopi are deeply anxious about all spring declines, for both obvious reasons and deeper metaphysical ones. The Hopi moral philosophy, following a covenant entered into with the deity Maasaw on their emergence into the present world, charges them with the responsibility of taking care of the earth and all its resources; indeed, such behavior is a significant measure of whether one is worthy of the name *Hopi* (see note 9). If the Hopi break the covenant, a cataclysm of cosmic proportions threatens. During the early 1980s, when co-author Whiteley began ethnographic research

at Third Mesa, Tsakwani'yma, an older Spider clan man, would sometimes tell me of prophecies he had heard from his uncle, Lomayestiwa (an early twentieth-century leader in the so-called "Hostile" faction at Orayvi). He returned to one such prophecy repeatedly: a time would come when Paaloloqangw, the Water Serpent deity, would turn over and lash his tail deep within the waters of the earth and all land life would tumble back down to the bottom of the ocean. "Can you interpret it?" he would challenge. "It means earthquake. But it's also symbolic of the life we are leading today: *koyaanisqatsi*, a life of chaos." In 1987 and 1988, shortly after Tsakwani'yma passed on, there were two earthquakes on Black Mesa (a rarity), which the Arizona Earthquake Information Center connected to the removal of massive quantities of coal and water. The perception of some elders that this is the result of their souls having been sold out from under them—literally, in the link between groundwater and spirits of the dead—causes profound sadness and a sense of intractable religious desecration.

In addition to long-term Hopi interests, regional economic and demographic patterns make the continued pumping of 4 million cubic meters, or more than a billion gallons of potable water every year for a coal slurry incredibly shortsighted. The twenty-first century will undoubtedly see ever more serious problems of water supply for the rapidly growing conurbations in the West. In this light, Hopi religious concerns with springs become metaphorical of larger issues of global development and natural resource management. But although the Hopi are typically attuned to such universal implications, in the immediate term they are concerned with basic physical, cultural, and spiritual survival. If the springs are to be saved, and with them continued Hopi cultural and religious existence, Peabody's relentless drive toward short-term profits, at the expense of stakeholder concerns, needs a dramatic makeover in line with trends toward local-global balance pursued by more progressive multinationals.[18] In the meantime, the pumps siphon the essence of life from the water roots of Black Mesa and the Hopi springs are withering on the vine.

FOOD FOR THOUGHT: STAKEHOLDERS, SHAREHOLDERS, AND REGULATORS

At the heart of this conflict over resource use is the confrontation between market capitalism and small-scale subsistence economies, or, in other terms, the opposing interests of shareholder and stakeholder. Much talk of sustainable development practices has been grounded in the inexorable logic of rationalist economics, with scant attention paid to different cultural and religious conceptions of the environment and how these might affect practical engagement with the transformation of nature for production.

Regarding stakeholder and shareholder interests, the powers of government to protect the former and regulate resource use are seriously called into question here. The government has a series of trust responsibilities to Indian tribes that surpass its obligations to most other sectors of American society. Specific provisions, such as the Winters Doctrine, could be invoked to protect Hopi and Navajo water resources and life chances. Vernon Masayesva places some of the blame squarely on the government agencies charged with protecting Hopi interests:

> It's a *tragic* chapter in United States-Hopi relations. *Very tragic.* They put our culture at risk, is the way I put it. The reason why Navajo aquifer water is so important is not only because, according to the Hopis, it's what sucks in the rain, but it also feeds the springs where ceremonies are occurring. It also sits in a bowl: *it's the only source of potable water available to the Hopi people* [his emphasis].
> (BBC Television 1995)

As a concatenation of powers, the multiplicity of government branches seems to militate against effective stakeholder representation: what the left hand gives, the right will take away. For example, the EPA has been clear in its opposition to the mine's hydrological practices, but it is overridden by the Office of Surface Mining Reclamation and Enforcement (OSMRE), which, not to put too fine

a point on it, has seemed to be largely a regulatory surrogate for Peabody's corporate interests. Throughout the public hearings on the DEIS at the Hopi Tribal Headquarters in Kiqotsmovi in August 1989, for example, OSMRE's representative, Peter Rutledge, seemed interested in speaking only on behalf of Peabody; to the Hopi who were present, the difference between the two entities was not clear. I (Whiteley) was sitting next to Stanley Bahnimptewa, then the *Kikmongwi* of Orayvi, who shortly into the hearings grew disgusted, turned to me and said, "Looks like we're going to be here all day," got up, and left.

Recently, the OSMRE renewed Peabody's Black Mesa-Kayenta mine permit. The Kayenta mine itself transports coal by railroad, but the two mines (Black Mesa and Kayenta) are linked administratively and are geographically close, so the renewal demonstrates tacit support (or, at least, benign neglect) of the Black Mesa mine operation, despite widespread public knowledge of the information contained in this chapter.[19] At the annual meeting of Hanson Industries in February 1996, Hopi and Navajo protestors, along with supporters from various environmental groups, succeeded in shutting down the meeting (*Private Eye* 1996). That OSMRE would override the many Hopi protests and renew the mine permit suggests that the rules of the market and the market's control by multinational capital are so entrenched in the thinking of government and industry that even in such a flagrant case, local constructions of environmental interest will not be heard and possible government uses of legal tools to protect stakeholders will go by the board.

If the imbrication of government and corporate interests in water uses seems Orwellian, the bureaucratic labyrinth overseeing regulation is positively Kafkaesque. A series of government agencies have made appearances in this chapter as involved at one level or another with the issues in question, and additional agencies are also involved. All told, the following are included: The Hopi Tribal Council (and various departmental agencies); the Navajo Nation (and various departmental agencies); the U.S. Secretary of the Interior; the U.S. Geological Survey, Water Resources Division; the U.S. Environmental

Protection Agency; the U.S. Office of Surface Mining Reclamation and Enforcement; the U.S. Army Corps of Engineers; the U.S. Fish and Wildlife Service; the U.S. Bureau of Land Management; the U.S. Bureau of Indian Affairs; the U.S. Department of Health and Human Services (Indian Health Service); the U.S. Department of Justice; the State of Arizona; the Arizona Department of Health and Human Services; the Arizona Game and Fish Department; and the Arizona Department of Mines and Mineral Resources. This list does not include the municipal interests party to Little Colorado basin water rights adjudications. Multilateral negotiations over the water rights in question—involving the Hopi, the Navajo, Peabody, and municipalities in northern Arizona, and overseen by the U.S. Department of Justice—are ongoing as of this writing. The possibility, say, that the Hopi Tribe could sue Peabody over environmental damage is held in abeyance by these negotiations (in which Peabody is the major player, with most of the wealth) and their attachment to a web of bureaucratic strings. From this governmental quagmire, some Hopi have recently turned to the environmental group the National Resources Defense Council, which is supplying a hydrologist to conduct independent tests of the aquifer.

The key question for the future—how local communities can ensure basic resource needs vis-à-vis the demands of the metropolitan economy—will be played out in many contexts in the American West and in other regions where conflict over resource rights is exacerbated by demographic shifts, increasing urbanization, and absorption of small communities by ever more encompassing forces of market production. Global climate change will be another major factor in the capacity of small-scale indigenous societies to retain control of their environments and resources. It is quite likely that dislocations from climatically marginal areas will produce a significant tide of environmental refugees (see, e.g., Intergovernmental Report on Global Climate Change 1995). In locales like the Hopi Indian Reservation, where water supply is so limited, the threat posed by industrial exploitation of the present sort may well tip the balance prior to changes produced by longer-term impacts.

If we are genuinely committed to sustainability, it is time to expand our understanding of it by listening to members of communities—for example, some Native American communities—that have practiced it for a very long time. If, to be realistic, we do not see an end to global markets as the mainspring of future economic frameworks, the key issue will be how to balance short-term profitability with long-term sustainability. The crux of that, surely, is empowering local stakeholders in the decision-making processes of companies themselves—but that will require corporate willingness to be inclusive, which may be anathema to the current ethos and praxis of the market. Without that will, the only hope for stakeholders is the intervention of government regulatory agencies, but if the actions of the OSMRE and the bureaucratic labyrinth in which decision making is currently trapped in the case presented here are anything to go by, that glimmer of hope offers precious little comfort. During his first campaign for the U.S. presidency, Bill Clinton announced that he would be the "environment president." Perhaps, in the apparent failure of the secretary of the interior to step in here, what is needed to cut through the bureaucracy is an "environment czar" who could respond to stakeholder situations like the Hopi water crisis more effectively. One Hopi commentator, Rebekah Masayesva, summed up the situation with admirable conciseness: "The pumping of pure underground water for slurrying of coal is unconscionable and must stop" (U.S. Department of the Interior 1990: 416). Yet eight years after the public hearings, the slurrying persists, and there is still no indication that it will stop soon, no matter how environmentally damaging, socioculturally destructive, economically shortsighted, or, indeed, unconscionable it may be. If we can summon the courage to recognize that in the long term we are all stakeholders, the question for both industry and government is "Why not?"

RESOURCES

The following bibliographic references and internet sites are useful for further study of Hopi and Native American water rights issues.

Lloyd Burton. 1991. *American Indian Water Rights and the Limits of the Law.* Lawrence: University Press of Kansas.

Richard O. Clemmer. 1978. "Black Mesa and the Hopi," in *Native Americans and Energy Development,* edited by Joseph Jorgenson. Boston: Anthropology Resource Center. (Very useful for earlier phases of Hopi resistance to mine.)

Richard O. Clemmer. 1984. "The Effects of the Energy Economy on Pueblo Peoples," in *Native Americans and Energy Development,* Vol. 2, edited by Joseph Jorgenson. Boston: Anthropology Resource Center and the Seventh Generation Fund.

Gallup Independent, 12-20-1993, "Coal Mining May Threaten Hopi Water, Culture." Gallup, NM.

Al Gedicks. 1993. *The New Resource Wars: Native and Environmental Struggles against Multinational Corporations.* Boston: South End Press.

Marianna Guerrero. 1992. "American Indian Water Rights: The Blood of Life in Native North America," in *The State of Native America: Genocide, Colonization, and Resistance,* edited by M. Annette Jaimes. Boston: South End Press. (Includes useful bibliographic references to Native American water issues and conflicts more generally.)

Los Angeles Times, 4-30-1994, "Coal Mining and Hopi Water." Letter to the editor by W. Howard Carson, president, Peabody Western Coal Company.

William D. Nichols (Western Region Groundwater Specialist, U.S.G.S.), 10-28-1993, letter to William M. Alley, chief, Office of Groundwater, Water Resources Division, U.S.G.S.

U.S. Dept, of the Interior, 1990, Proposed Permit Application, "Black Mesa-Kayenta Mine, Navajo and Hopi Indian Reservations, Arizona, 2 vols. Final Environmental Impact Statement OSM-EIS-25. Denver: Office of Surface Mining Reclamation and Enforcement. (Vol. 2, Comments and Responses, includes the full text of numerous Hopi letters, petitions, and oral testimony.)

U.S. Geological Survey. 1995. Results of Groundwater, Surfacewater, and Water-Quality Monitoring, Black Mesa Area, Northeastern Arizona 1992–93. *Water Resources Investigations Report* 95-4156. No. 95-4156. Tucson. U.S.G.S.

Charles F. Wilkinson. 1996. "Home Dance, the Hopi, and Black Mesa Coal: Conquest and Endurance in the American Southwest." *Brigham Young University Law Review,* 1996, no. 2. (A detailed account of the original lease negotiation for the mine, in which Hopi tribal attorney, John Boyden, is clearly shown to have also been working on behalf of the energy companies.)

Hopi Information Network:
http : //www. inf omagic. com/~aby te/hopi .html

Native Americans and the Environment: http:// conbio.rice.edu/nae/

ACKNOWLEDGMENTS

Nat Nutongla and Phillip Tuwaletstiwa of the Water Resources Office, Department of Natural Resources, Hopi Tribe, gave indispensable help and comments and were most generous with sources.

We wish to thank *Cultural Survival Quarterly* (1996) for permission to use material that first appeared in "Paavahu and Paanaqawu: The Wellsprings of Life and the Slurry of Death."

NOTES

1. Comments at public hearing on the environmental impact of the Black Mesa–Kayenta Mine, Kykotsmovi, Hopi Indian Reservation, Arizona, 9 August 1989, reprinted in U.S. Department of the Interior 1990, 418

2. See, for example, the accounts of Hopi emergence narratives in H. R. Voth's *Traditions of the Hopi* (1905b) or Armin Geertz's "A Reed Pierced the Sky" (1984). Edmund Nequatewa's *Truth of a Hopi* (1936) contains additional Hopi traditional

narratives. Frank Waters's *Book of the Hopi* (1963), the most popular work ever published on the Hopi, is best avoided, however, for its confabulation of the imaginary with the ethnographically accurate.

3. From east to west, the mesa-top villages are arranged as follows:
First Mesa: Walpi, Sitsomovi, Tewa
Second Mesa: Songoopavi, Supawlavi, Musangnuvi
Third Mesa: Orayvi, Kiqotsmovi, Paaqavi, Hotvela
Seventy-two kilometers (forty-five miles) by highway to the west of Third Mesa lie the two villages of Upper and Lower Munqapi, which trace their principal heritage to their mother village, Orayvi. These spellings of village names follow current orthographic conventions established for the Hopi language, which are, as yet, not much used locally—hence the variations between, for example, Munqapi and Moenkopi, Songoopavi and Shungopavi, Hotvela and Hotevilla. Good general accounts of Hopi society, economy, and religion appear in Ortiz 1979.

4. For a description of the area's hydrogeology, see Cooley et al. 1969; Gregory 1916 and Hack 1942 provide more detailed local observations of the Hopi environment.

5. The most comprehensive accounts of these migrations, contested by later generations of archaeologists but still systematically articulated by Hopi clan historians, are found in Mindeleff 1891 and Fewkes 1900.

6. See, for example, Brew 1979, Upham 1982, and Cordell 1989; for more general accounts of Puebloan prehistory, in addition to Ortiz 1979, see Cordell 1984 and Cordell and Gumerman 1989.

7. The other Pueblos—Zuni, Laguna, Acoma, and the Rio Grande Tewa, Tiwa, Towa, and Keres villages—also chart their migrations from some of these ancestral stone and adobe ruins.

8. Hopi attitudes toward the environment accord well with J. Baird Callicott's general meditations on Native American environmental ethics (e.g., 1982, 1996), as contrasted with European conceptions of environment. Amid often uncritical projections of the "ecologically noble savage" by some Western environmentalists, more careful statements on Native American attitudes toward the landscape include Momaday 1974, Vecsey 1980, Brody 1981, White 1984, Brightman 1993, Nelson 1993, and Basso 1996. Although the countervailing position—that Native Americans often despoiled their environments and modified them in major ways (Calvin Martin's well-known *Keepers of the Game* [1978] is an example; see also Redford 1991, Denevan 1992, Alvard 1993, andBuege 1996)—has some validity in specific instances, it must be dismissed in general as motivated by the same tendency toward oppositive projection, but of ecologically ignoble savagery. Any careful ethnographic description of Native American environmental praxis typically discloses fine-grained attention to ecological concerns. For comprehensive discussions of anthropological approaches to environmentalism, see Milton 1993 and Orlove et al. 1996.

9. *Hopi* is more than simply an ethnic identity descriptor; in use, it carries specific implications of ethical engagement—in social action, moral thought, and religious practice. The oft-heard opposite, *qahopi* ("un-Hopi," "badly behaved"), used to chastise transgression of behavioral rules, highlights the ethical dimension of the concept of Hopi-ness.

10. Comments at public hearing on the environmental impact of the Black Mesa–Kayenta Mine, Kykotsmovi, Hopi Indian Reservation, Arizona, 9 August 1989, reprinted in U.S. Department of the Interior 1990, 417. Masayesva, sometime chairman of the Hopi Tribe, elaborated on this perspective in the BBC film *The Hopi Way* (Under the Sun series, 1995), which focuses in part on the Hopi water crisis.

11. For more on the aesthetics, poetics, and natural history aspects of Hopi names, see Whiteley 1992.

12. Examples of all these are found in U.S. Department of the Interior 1990. One petition,

for example, circulated among several villages in August 1989:

> We the members of the Hopi Tribe hereby strongly protest Peabody Coal Company's use of a valuable natural resource, water, to transport coal. We demand that Peabody Coal Company immediately cease the use of water to deliver coal to the generating plant(s) and further demand that the Hopi Tribal Council, the Office of Surface Mining and the Bureau of Indian Affairs put pressure on Peabody to immediately seek alternative means to transport coal.
>
> Water is among our most precious resources and we feel that the millions of gallons pumped to feed the slurry lines are affecting our springs and thus impacting our cultural way of life.
>
> (U.S. Department of the Interior 1990, 261)

13. The permitting procedure for the mine is complex (see Wilkinson 1996 for the original lease history). The lessors are the Navajo Nation and the Hopi Tribe, but mining permits must be approved by a series of regulatory agencies (U.S. Department of the Interior 1990):

    1. The Bureau of Land Management, for a life-of-mining plan (until the year 2023)
    2. The U.S. Army Corps of Engineers, for a Clean Water Act Section 404 permit
    3. The Office of Surface Mining Reclamation and Enforcement, for a permit package that allows renewal of the mining lease, with five-yearly reviews until 2011

14. A source close to the process of EPA review indicated that the DEIS received the EO-2 rating only by the skin of its teeth, and even then with some backstage arm-twisting: the EPA, the source indicated, wanted to rate the DEIS as EO-3 (Environmental Objections—Inadequate), which would have indicated formal failure of the DEIS to satisfy provisions of the National Environmental Policy Act and

may well have led to rejection of the permit application without further study.

15. Peabody modeled the recharge rate at 16 million cubic meters (13,000 acre-feet) per year; the USGS study, conducted by an Arizona office, recorded a recharge rate of 2.5 million cubic meters (2,000 acre-feet) per year (figures provided by the Water Resources Office, Department of Natural Resources, Hopi Tribe).

16. Working with Hopi tribal attorney John Boyden's legal files, which were recently made public at the University of Utah, Charles Wilkinson (1996) describes in impressive detail how Boyden was simultaneously working for both the Tribe and the Peabody Western Coal Company regarding water and mineral rights on Black Mesa.

17. Robbie Honani of Supawlavi, then chairman of the Hopi Tribal Council's Resources Committee, noted at the public hearings on the DEIS:

> There's less than ten Hopi people working at the Peabody mine and over 800 Navajos. Peabody has built the town of Kayenta for the Navajo and for other employees. They have erected a trailer court for its non-Indian employees and flies their top management people every day from Flagstaff, and then flies them back again. Yet there is no trailer court for the Hopi people. And there is no major road system going up to Peabody.
>
> All taxes in the form of education monies go to the … Kayenta Public School District. Does the Hopi get any of these monies? No … . The State of Arizona receives twice as much money in taxes than the Hopi Tribe does in actual revenues. The tribe receives approximately $8 million in coal royalty, yet the State of Arizona receives between $18 to $20 million in taxes a year. Only a mere drop of that comes back to the Hopi.
>
> (U.S. Department of the Interior 1990, 409)

18. See, for example, *The Economist's* focus on stakeholders and multinationals, June 24, 1995. In a veritable tide of discussion on stakeholder questions, see, for example, Altman 1994 and Collins 1995. For excellent discussions of indigenous stakeholder interests in relation to local and multinational economic development in different parts of the world, see any issue of *Cultural Survival Quarterly.*

19. W. Howard Carson marked this event with a two-page letter to the Hopi tribal newspaper, *Hopi Tutuveni,* published on 30 December 1996, detailing the benefits the mine had brought to the community, implying that opposition to the mine was the work of cranks and extremists, and completely ignoring the widespread Hopi opposition to the slurry.

CPSIA information can be obtained
at www.ICGtesting.com
Printed in the USA
LVOW03s0731240817
546121LV00016B/156/P